AF838915

Texas Supreme Court Justice Bob Gammage

Texas Supreme Court Justice Bob Gammage

A Jurisprudence of Rights and Liberties

John C. Domino

LEXINGTON BOOKS
Lanham • Boulder • New York • London

Published by Lexington Books
An imprint of The Rowman & Littlefield Publishing Group, Inc.
4501 Forbes Boulevard, Suite 200, Lanham, Maryland 20706
www.rowman.com

6 Tinworth Street, London SE11 5AL, United Kingdom

Copyright © 2020 by The Rowman & Littlefield Publishing Group, Inc.

All rights reserved. No part of this book may be reproduced in any form or by any electronic or mechanical means, including information storage and retrieval systems, without written permission from the publisher, except by a reviewer who may quote passages in a review.

British Library Cataloguing in Publication Information Available

Library of Congress Cataloging-in-Publication Data Available

ISBN 978-1-4985-7858-5 (cloth)
ISBN 978-1-4985-7859-2 (electronic)

In memory of my parents, John and Angela Domino

Contents

Acknowledgments

This book would not have been possible without the support of the faculty, administration, staff, and students at Sam Houston State University (SHSU). I began the book during a sabbatical in 2013, following Bob Gammage's death a year earlier. The leave made it possible for me to conduct research in Austin at the Texas State Archives and at Dolph Briscoe Center for American History at the University of Texas at Austin, as well as present my research at various professional conferences, including the annual meeting of the Western Political Science Association. The staff in Special Collections at the Newton Gresham Library at SHSU are owed thanks for organizing and curating Gammage's personal papers, photographs, and campaign memorabilia that were donated by his wife, Lynda Hallmark Gammage. Over the years, several of my constitutional law and judicial systems students provided research assistance during the early phase of this project. I would also thank those who reviewed the book prospectus and manuscript. The Texas Supreme Court Historical Society provided me with opportunities to learn from many people who know far more than I about the justices who have served on the Texas Supreme Court. Tiffany Gillman, archivist at the Court, provided research guidance and helped secure photographs and other material. Finally, I would like to express my gratitude to Lynda Hallmark Gammage, and to the Gammage family, who donated the late justice's papers, campaign materials, photographs, and memorabilia to SHSU.

Chapter 1

Justice Bob Gammage

> Baseless and irrational discrimination in all of its forms, at whomever directed and whatever its source or motivation, is still baseless and irrational discrimination. In a free society we may not always be able to prevent its private exercise, but in Texas our fundamental law does not permit it in our public schools and other governmental institutions. They should not teach it, condone it, or engage in it, and our courts and other legal institutions should not—even passively and benignly—enforce it.
>
> —Justice Gammage dissenting in *Barber v. Colorado ISD*.[1]

INTRODUCTION

This passage is one of Justice Bob Gammage's strongest affirmations of civil rights. It was penned as a dissent in *Barber v. Colorado Independent School District*, a class-action suit that challenged the legality of hair-length restrictions for male students imposed by the school district.[2] Hair-length and dress-code cases constitute a substantial body of case law, and the *Barber* ruling was one of the most influential of these cases in Texas. The Texas Supreme Court rejected Barber's claims as not substantial enough to "merit . . . intervention in this case."[3] Dissenting, Gammage argued that the majority's dismissal of Barber's claim without the benefit of providing a full legal analysis was more a matter of judicial abdication, rather than "nonintervention."[4] Gammage recognized the validity of Barber's privacy and free-speech claims under the Texas constitution but chose to analyze the Colorado Independent School District (CISD) policy under the Texas Equal Rights Amendment.[5]

As a judge and justice, Gammage argued for a more expansive interpretation of the legal doctrines and constitutional provisions that protect individual rights and equality. To borrow a phrase from Professor Ronald Dworkin, Gammage took rights seriously[6] by embracing an expansive interpretation of the legal doctrines and constitutional provisions that protect individual rights and equality. His written opinions show that he challenged the hesitancy of many conservative Texas judges to apply judicial review to laws or policies that were constitutionally suspect. Gammage had a strong record as a civil libertarian in the areas of the right to privacy, freedom of expression, and due process; and articulated a traditionally liberal position on discrimination on the basis of gender, race, and sexual orientation. He was a strong advocate for individual rights and liberties, while at the same time maintaining a commitment to the principle of stare decisis and the express provisions of the Texas constitution. With a legal scholar's attention to detail, his opinions were based on solid reasoning, precedent, and the rule of law. But in the end, his fundamental sense of fairness and justice emerged.

Many students of Texas legal history may remember him best for his role in the politically charged *Edgewood* saga but for reasons that may not be obvious to most. His dissent in *Kirby v. Edgewood*[7] in 1988 while on the Texas Third Court of Appeals (Austin) is one the most cogent and comprehensive arguments for equal rights and fundamental freedoms made by a Texas judge. His interpretation of the education clauses of the Texas constitution helped build the argument that ultimately persuaded a majority of judges and legislators to recognize that the state's system of education funding discriminated against students living in poorer school districts. Prior to the *Edgewood* litigation, many of the state's courts were divided and unable to overcome the barrier of *San Antonio Independent School District v. Rodriguez*,[8] the US Supreme Court precedent that refused to recognize education as a fundamental right. But Gammage pointed out that in deciding *Rodriguez*, the US Supreme Court relied on the US Constitution, which does not include a specific provision for education. The claim in *Edgewood*, he argued, must rely on the Texas constitution, which expressly recognizes education as indispensable to the exercise of fundamental rights and liberties.

Robert Alton "Bob" Gammage was a lawyer, state legislator, assistant state attorney general, US congressman, military judge, state court of appeals judge, and Texas Supreme Court justice. As a state legislator, Gammage served in the Texas House of Representatives from 1971 to 1973 and in the Texas Senate from 1973 to 1976, sponsoring or supporting numerous pieces of progressive reform legislation. Gammage was also a member of the legendary "Dirty-Thirty," a bipartisan group of state legislators in the 1970s that fought widespread corruption in state government.[9]

Before becoming a justice, Gammage's terms in the state legislature included the sixty-third Texas legislature, which is regarded as one of the most important and impactful legislatures in Texas history.[10] A progressive reform legislature in a conservative state, it enacted bills requiring open records and open meetings for government bodies and state agencies; it also adopted campaign finance reform, the mandatory registration of lobbyists, and ethics laws that criminalized bribery of public officials. The sixty-third legislature passed the state's first bilingual education laws and enacted a host of pro-consumer measures, including tort law modifications and the Deceptive Trade Practices Act.[11]

On January 8, 1974, the sixty-third legislature also convened as a constitutional convention in the Texas House of Representatives chamber, meeting as a unitary body. It was a momentous opportunity to replace the state's archaic, long, and ineffectual 1876 constitution with a document suited to a modern urbanized state. "Con-con," as it would become known, was "limited" in that it could not alter the Bill of Rights, which is the first article of the Texas charter. Among the proposed changes was a requirement that the legislature meet annually—instead of biennially in odd-numbered years as it does currently.[12] The delegates also debated whether the governor's veto should be overridden by the legislature, which would also be able to reconsider vetoed bills. Gammage's General Provisions committee was tasked with seventy-seven proposals by April 1974, including everything from banking, gambling, liquor, and the public's right to free access to beaches.[13]

The convention, which was originally intended to last for ninety days, dragged on for seven long months, eventually falling short of the two-thirds majority in both houses required to present a draft of the new constitution to the voters. After the convention's 1974 collapse, Gammage proposed to the senate a compromise "package" of amendments. Hoping to salvage something from their hard work, the legislature approved the proposed amendments through the normal legislative process during the sixty-fourth legislative session. If approved by the voters, "Gammage's constitutional revision package" would have: (1) created a full-time legislature (including strengthening of the separation of powers, so that members of one branch could not exercise any power attached to either of the other branches); (2) modernized the structure of the judicial branch and changed the method of judicial selection from partisan election to gubernatorial appointment; (3) revised the education provision of the constitution, for the purpose of equalizing school funding; (4) revised voter qualifications and election law; and (5) changed the manner in which the constitution is amended.[14] By June 1975, the legislature seemed to support Gammage's plan, now backed by Attorney General John Hill.[15] The Gammage amendments were placed on the ballot in the form of propositions in a November 4, 1975, special election, but all eight were rejected by voters. Only 23 percent of the state's eligible voters cast ballots. After over four and a half years work by hundreds of people and over 3 million dollars spent, the 1876 constitution—with its myriad of flaws and anachronisms—was not revised.

In November 1976, Gammage was elected to the ninety-fifth US Congress, unseating freshman Republican congressman Ron Paul from Lake Jackson in a closely contested election.[16] Paul demanded a recount, unsuccessfully pursuing legal action in a state district court, the Texas Supreme Court, and the US Supreme Court.[17] On January 4, 1977, Gammage was sworn in as a member of Congress but served only one term, however, before fortunes were reversed and Paul won back his old congressional seat. After he left Congress, Gammage served a short stint as an assistant attorney general of Texas from 1979 to 1980.[18]

Gammage embarked on his judicial career when he was elected to the Third Court of Appeals in Austin in 1982 and then to the Texas Supreme Court in 1990. He wrote a career total of more than 250 opinions in major cases in the areas of constitutional law, civil rights and liberties, tort law, criminal due process, and school finance (areas of law that are the focus of this book). This number does not include cases in areas of law such as family, insurance, property, and administrative law, and in cases in which he did not write opinions. All total, Gammage participated in approximately 2,000 cases. While his judicial record was well-known by members of the Texas bench and bar, as well as by reporters who covered the judicial beat in Austin, Gammage garnered national attention when he resigned from the Texas Supreme Court in 1995 to draw attention to the increasing amount of influence that big campaign contributors and political action committees had on judicial elections.

By the late-1980s in Texas, the sudden rise of million-dollar judicial campaigns, coupled with nonexistent campaign limits, had formed a perfect storm that undermined the capacity of judges to protect the rights and liberties of persons against unwarranted intrusions by the government and exploitation by powerful corporations. For most of Texas legal history, conservative Democrats controlled statewide judicial offices. Then, for a brief period —from the early 1970s to the mid-1990s—a majority of justices on the court consistently voted to support civil rights and liberties.[19] The court as a whole during this period also had the reputation of being pro-plaintiff, willing to uphold million dollar jury awards in medical malpractice and tort claims lawsuits.

Beginning in the 1980s, however, the medical profession, the business community, and fiscal and social conservatives began to make inroads in judicial races to elect judges who would advance their interests. In 1988, the Texas Medical Association (TMA) spearheaded a political campaign by the business community to "take back" the courts and bring about "tort reform." The notion of "taking back" the court caught on like a prairie fire in Texas. Slick videos and infomercials were produced with the intent of mobilizing physicians and business leaders to dig deep into their pockets and support anti-trial lawyer judges. "Clean Slate '88" was a successful grassroots campaign to mobilize physicians and other members of the healthcare profession using stories of massive medical malpractice settlements against innocent physicians brought by greedy personal injury attorneys. Millions of dollars in campaign contributions were poured into judicial races to not only wrest control of the court from trial lawyers (the plaintiff bar) but also to target judges whose qualifications and impartiality were called into question (we will discuss this period in greater detail in chapter 4) in high-profile scandals and investigations. "Clean Slate '90" was a continuation of the TMA's campaign to elect a bipartisan slate of impartial and respected jurists. Ironically, Gammage, a liberal Democrat, benefited from both Clean Slate campaigns; but the campaign contribution arms race that began in 1988, with the intent to change the ideological composition of the court, would ultimately lead to complete Republican domination of the Supreme Court and Gammage's relegation to the minority. Texas Supreme Court elections became a battleground for competing political and economic interests that were determined to influence the court's direction on issues ranging from tort reform, environmental regulations, education funding, and civil rights.

At the end of 1995, Justice Bob Gammage unexpectedly announced that he would not seek another term on the Texas Supreme Court. Resigning from one of the most influential and coveted elected offices in the state was not only a difficult personal decision but one that had broader ramifications for the direction of the court's jurisprudence and for the diminishing influence of civil libertarians and progressives on appellate courts in Texas. Highly respected jurists—many receiving bipartisan support from voters—called for reform and adopted voluntary limits on campaign contributions, but they were trapped by the system. By 1988, many candidates for seats on the high court were spending upward of $2 million on their campaigns and running negative attack ads in order to maintain their seats on the bench. Justices with moderate and centrist judicial philosophies were soon an endangered species. Prominent members of the bench, bar, and legislature called for reforming the system amid declining public confidence, but no change occurred because of vested interests and political gridlock.

Gammage's colleague, Chief Justice Thomas R. Phillips, once said that Gammage took up the issue of judicial election reform "before it became a popular topic in the Texas Legislature and editorial boards around the state" and that "Judge Gammage believed that a judiciary could only be truly independent if it was appointed rather than elected." Phillips, one of the state's most consistent and efficacious advocates of judicial election reform for thirty years, also called Gammage "a dedicated jurist who discharged his duties without fear or favor."[20] Upon Gammage's resignation from the Texas Supreme Court in 1995 Phillips wrote:

> Although Justice Gammage frequently held strong views about the proper application of the law to particular facts, he never advocated hose views in a contentious or partisan manner. He has been a fearless public servant whose decisions were never influenced in the least by partisan or personal considerations.[21]

Gammage loved his life on the court, but he was a pragmatic politician who saw the proverbial writing on the wall. In 1995, with one year remaining in his six-year term, he faced an uphill battle of fending off challenges for his seat on the court. An aggressive fundraising campaign would need to commence immediately, as millions would be spent by conservative groups to unseat Gammage, one of the few liberal Democrats remaining on the court. Gammage had the benefit of incumbency, as well as his reputation for integrity and independence, so a second term on the high court was within reach. However, had he won reelection in 1996, as one of the few remaining progressive justices he would be permanently relegated to the minority, forced to write strong dissents, especially civil rights and liberties cases and in disputes pitting individuals against powerful interests. Gammage understood politics, and was not naïve to the role it could play in judicial decisions, but he felt that the court had turned the corner where ideology and partisanship trumped objectivity.

His announcement of his resignation was documented on August 24, 1995, by Ken Herman of the *Austin American Statesman*, calling Gammage as a jurist who often found himself in the minority in high-profile cases, and quoted Gammage for his reason for leaving the court was to make a statement on the way Texans pick judges. Gammage was quoted: "It seems to me that rather than expose whoever my successor is to the bloodbath of a political primary of either party, I'd give the governor [Bush] some time to deliberate and try to put someone with appropriate credential and temperament on the court." At that time, the court consisted of five Republicans and four Democrats. Since Democrat Jack Hightower had announced in June 1995 that he too planned to retire, Governor George W. Bush had the opportunity to fill two seats. The high court from which Gammage retired was much different than the one to which he was elected in 1990. When Gammage took the oath of office in January 1991, the court now had a 5-4 Democratic majority, down from a 6-3 majority in 1990. When Republican justices gained a majority for the first time on the court after the 1994 elections, Gammage increasingly became a dissenter, a role that played to his strengths at pointing out not just substantive legal differences but attempts by some justices to advance a conservative agenda that put ideology over law.

Gammage was also a fierce advocate for the integrity and independence of the Texas judiciary. Long before US Supreme Court's 2009 groundbreaking ruling in *Caperton v. Massey Coal Co*,[22] that the refusal of a West Virginia state supreme court justice to recuse himself from a case violated the constitution's due process guarantee of a fair tribunal, Gammage argued for the adoption of a progressive judicial recusal policy in the oft-cited case of *Rogers v. Bradley.*[23] Judicial disqualification and recusal involve a body of law and rules that to most people would seem painfully dull, until they learn that judges often preside over high-profile cases involving parties and lawyers who have contributed money to their campaign the media take notice. Foreshadowing *Caperton*, Gammage argued that the norms and canons of recusal should focus not only on the behavior of the individual judge but also on the actions of organizations that have a disproportionate influence on the outcome on judicial elections. His opinion would not change Texas recusal law in the short term, but his progressive (and often criticized) views on recusal were later reflected by the justices in *Caperton.*

Gammage's opinions, majority and dissenting, were forward-thinking and continue to have an impact on Texas jurisprudence. For instance, seven years prior to the US Supreme Court's historic and celebrated ruling in *Lawrence v. Texas*,[24] which struck down homosexual sodomy laws nationwide, and in doing so expanded the privacy rights of all Americans, Gammage took part in a Texas Supreme Court case that had the opportunity to invalidate Texas's sodomy law.[25] In *State v. Morales*, three lesbian women and two gay men challenged the law on the grounds that it violated the Texas constitution.[26] The State of Texas argued that since the sodomy law was rarely if ever enforced it should be left standing, but Gammage recognized that, in fact, the law was used to stigmatize and discriminate against gays and lesbians in housing, family law, education, and employment. A conservative majority of the justices on the Texas Supreme Court refused to strike down the law on the grounds that the court lacked jurisdiction. However, in a forceful dissent, Gammage argued that even if the sodomy law is rarely enforced for individual sex acts—as the state argued—the law still caused gays and lesbians to face discrimination and were made to "suffer psychological harm to their relationships because they are labeled criminals by the very existence of the statute."[27]

As will become evident in this book, Gammage followed a discernible set of principles, which included the position that the state judiciary must remain a coequal branch of government. Deference should never be given to the political branches when fundamental rights are at stake. For example, in applying this position, he fought against the established judicial doctrine that held—and still holds—that school districts are autonomous entities that should be largely unfettered by judicial intrusion. He challenged the position that schools should be free from being held to too high of a standard when constitutional rights are violated.

As a Texas Supreme Court justice, Gammage had the discretion to analyze and resolve disputes from either the standpoint of the Texas constitution, the US Constitution, or some combination of the two. Indeed, the US Supreme Court has ruled that when a state supreme court decides a case on "an adequate and independent state ground" alone, the court will not subject the ruling of the state court to judicial review.[28] This approach to judicial interpretation—where a state court looks primarily at the state constitution to resolve disputes—has been referred to as the primacy model of state judicial decision-making.[29] In cases where constitutional claims were raised, Justice Gammage's opinions relied on the Texas constitution or state law whenever possible.[30] Of course, he was not unique in this approach, but his judicial philosophy looked first to the state's constitution to resolve a dispute, and then to the federal constitution. Gammage also made certain that the ruling did not fall short of the "minimal rule for a diverse nation," established by US Supreme Court precedent.[31] His judicial philosophy reflected Justice William J. Brennan's view that "state courts no less than federal are and ought to be the guardians of our liberties," by extending protections and by going beyond those required by the US Supreme Court's interpretation of federal law.[32]

Gammage came down on the side of rights and liberties neither reflexively nor ideologically but because those who sought to restrict those rights often did so by employing baseless or non-compelling justifications. His written opinions and participation in oral arguments before the court demonstrate that he respected the unique perspectives that each of his colleagues brought to the bench, but his profound respect for the American legal tradition and its antecedents would not allow him to leave unchallenged the abdication of the independent judicial role—the insulation of the state from judicial scrutiny of laws affecting civil or personal rights.

Those who worked alongside Bob Gammage observed that he never took education for granted, and was one of the most well-read people they knew. Drawn to the life of the mind, Gammage was a voracious reader, having collected and read hundreds of works on the common law of England, tomes on jurisprudence—or the philosophy of law—missives on political theory, and volumes of American history, all of them in neat rows on the bookshelves that lined his private library in his Llano home. Bagehot's *The English Constitution*, Oliver Wendell Holmes's *The Common Law*, Hogues's *Origins of the Common Law*, Bodenheimer's *Jurisprudence*, Hobbes's *Leviathan*, Locke's *Second Treatise of Government*, and Jefferson's collected writings were among his favorites. However, aside from his legal opinions, sponsored legislation, and a smattering of white papers, Gammage never seemed to sit still long enough to publish a scholarly article or book during and after his long career of public service.

His formal degrees were not from Ivy League institutions but from public state institutions comprised of students who were mostly first-generation college students often from working-class backgrounds, many of whom were veterans benefiting from the G.I. Bill.[33] His undergraduate degrees were from Del Mar College (1958) and the University of Corpus Christi (1963). He earned a master's degree from Sam Houston State University (1965) and is a graduate of the University of Texas School of Law (1969). While serving on the Third Court of Appeals in Austin he completed an LLM—an advanced degree in the law—from the University of Virginia School of Law (1986). He regularly attended and taught at judicial education programs at New York University School of Law and Harvard Law School. He had even pursued a PhD in American Civilization at the University of Texas in the 1990s. He taught courses in history, political science, and law as a visiting professor at Texas A&M—Corpus Christi, Sam Houston State University, South Texas College of Law, Texas State University, and St. Edwards University.

Gammage cut a rather imposing figure, with a deep booming voice that served him well in politics. Chief Justice Thomas Phillips once recounted how reporters described Gammage, stating that he had a "Roman nose, jutting jaw, gray-streaked hair with dark sideburns, dark foreboding eyebrows and the stocky muscular frame of an ex-football lineman. He looks like one of Julius Caesar's legionnaires, A Cherokee chieftain, a riverboat card shark or maybe a handsome young Mafia don on the late movie."[34] However, he also had a sardonic wit that involved him wearing hoop earrings to a conference, following oral arguments in a case involving what he believed to be arbitrary dress-code restrictions on high school students; or bringing a tray of poppy seed muffins and pastries to his colleagues after they heard oral argument in a *Seinfeld*-esque case that involved a false positive drug test resulting from a breakfast muffin.

PURPOSE AND ORGANIZATION OF THE BOOK

The purpose of this book is to profile Gammage's jurisprudence of rights and liberties that are set out in cases involving the rights of minors, privacy, freedom of speech and press, equal protection, consumer protection, and others that were decided during his tenure on the Texas Supreme Court and the Texas Court of Appeals. It is a profile of Gammage's jurisprudence, but because any appellate court consists of individual justices with unique backgrounds and distinct philosophies, the book is also an examination of the views of other jurists with whom he served,[35] and the social and political conflict during an era of Texas history from which these cases arose. This book transcends the career of one man by documenting a tumultuous transitionary period in Texas judicial history of which Gammage was a part—a period that witnessed not only a shift in the way judicial elections were conducted but saw the last of the liberal/progressive justices on the Texas Supreme Court.

A book-length study of a judge's jurisprudence evokes an image of a massive tome that examines a body of opinions produced by a justice of the US Supreme Court. G. Edward White's work on Oliver Wendell Holmes, Phillipa Strum's books on Louis D. Brandeis, Bernard Schwartz's biography of Earl Warren, and Richard A. Brisbin's analysis of Antonin Scalia's jurisprudence come to mind.[36] In the realm of the lower federal courts is Gerald Gunther's definitive work on Learned Hand, who is regarded as the greatest American judge not to serve on the Supreme Court; and Frank R. Kemerer's book on William Wayne Justice, one of the most influential federal district court judges in American history.[37] There are few scholarly accounts of the jurisprudence or collected writings of judges and justices that have served on state courts, although Jacqueline A. McLeod's book on New York judge Jane Bolin is an excellent work on the nation's first African-American state trial judge.[38] Empirical studies of state supreme courts exist, as do law reviews and scholarly articles paying tribute to state judges after they have left the bench. Overwhelmingly, however, scholars have traditionally cast their gaze upward to the US Supreme Court. State judges deserve more scholarly attention, since they play an integral role in the legal tradition that dates back to the early republic and before, passing down to each new generation the principles of the common law and many ideas and doctrines that are later adopted by the federal courts.

This book is the first written on Justice Gammage, as well as on a period of Texas legal history that requires further study. Professor Anthony Champagne's decades of research on the impact of campaign contributions on Texas judicial races, during this period and beyond, is of immeasurable value and is referenced throughout this book. Furthermore, crucial to the understanding of this period are two excellent and definitive works: *Lone Star Law* by Michael Ariens and the *Texas Supreme Court: A Narrative History, 1836–1986* by James L. Haley.[39] News articles and obituaries exist, as do one or two television interviews, but there are no books, articles in social science, history or law journals about Gammage' judicial record, with the exception of my article "The Jurisprudence of Texas Supreme Court Justice Robert 'Bob' Gammage: A Legacy in Civil Rights & Liberties," which appeared in the *South Texas Law Review* in 2013. I hope that my book will fill a major gap that exists in the literature documenting the history of judicial politics in Texas.[40]

I met Gammage in August 1989, not long after I accepted a teaching position at Sam Houston State University. At that time, Gammage was serving in his penultimate year on the Third Court of Appeals and preparing for a run for a seat on the Texas Supreme Court. Many of my colleagues at the time worked on the campaigns of Democratic candidates, and a few knew Gammage from his days in the legislature. He introduced himself to me and slapped a blue "Bob Gammage for Supreme Court" campaign button in my hand. I still have the button in my office. Over the years, we had many conversations during his visits to Sam Houston State University, in his office at the Texas Supreme Court in Austin, at conferences, and at more than a few pubs and eateries.

Shortly after his untimely passing in 2012 at age 72, I began to research Gammage's judicial record and comb through his legal opinions. After spending time at the Dolph Briscoe Center at the University of Texas and the Texas State Archives in Austin, I was invited by his wife, Lynda Hallmark Gammage, to visit Judge Gammage's office in his home in Llano, Texas. Football memorabilia from Gammage's gridiron days were carefully preserved, as were campaign posters and photos of political elites. Bookshelf after bookshelf were packed with books on history, political science, and law. A large subset of his collection reflected his love of the English common law, which he often referenced in his legal opinions. Banker's boxes stuffed with correspondence and photographs from his political life were stacked in the corner. The walls surrounding his desk were cluttered with not only plaques and framed certificates accumulated throughout the years but newspaper clippings documenting the fact that real people, and not just legal abstractions, were at stake in the cases decided; persons suffering harm at the hands of vindictive boyfriends, arrogant corporations, protesting zealots, and arbitrary governmental actions. There were also yellowed articles pasted long ago in huge leather-bound scrapbooks, attesting to the elections won and lost, and the myriad efforts to reform the judicial branch through changes in judicial selection, campaign finance, and proposed changes in the code of judicial ethics. Surrounded by the records and mementos of pitched battles long passed, I began to understand Gammage's jurisprudence of rights and liberties; and a tradition of Texas judges and justices who held liberal or progressive views on civil rights and liberties in this conservative state.

The chapters that follow are based on Gammage's reasoning in majority, concurring, and dissenting opinions in a number of milestone cases. A milestone is a marker that represents a new way of thinking, often beginning a new decisional path that judges take when analyzing disputes involving rights and liberties. In these milestone cases, Gammage argued for a more expansive interpretation of the legal doctrines and constitutional provisions that protect individual rights and equality. The cases and opinions examined in this book by no means constitute an exhaustive list of cases in which Justice

Gammage participated; however, they are among the most important in shaping civil rights and liberties in Texas, and they are the most representative of his jurisprudence and legacy.

To understand Gammage's jurisprudence of rights and liberties, I have relied on sources including judicial opinions and court records, oral arguments, campaign records, media, and personal correspondence. There are major gaps in the record. Although most of Gammage's published opinions are preserved, not all oral arguments (recorded or written transcripts) are available, due to less than methodical record keeping by the state during that period. Other than written published opinions, very few documents remain from his tenure on the Third Court of Appeals. I have attempted to fill in the many existing gaps with newspaper accounts of the time, academic articles, a few interviews, and my own recollections of conversations with Gammage. The book is about Bob Gammage, who had a liberal/progressive record as a justice, and about a reform movement that sought, among many things, to adopt a method of judicial selection other than popular election. It is not my intention here to take the position that Gammage's ideas were correct or superior to those of other justices; nor is it my intent to argue for or against the popular election of judges.

Following this introductory chapter, chapter 2 documents his record on the Third Court of Appeals at Austin which spans the years of 1982–1990. It is in his first term that Gammage begins to develop a judicial philosophy and voting record in a wide range of civil and criminal cases. He makes the transition from his role as a legislator—where he is one of 150 members in the state house and of thirty-one members in the senate—to that of a judge, hearing appeals from trial courts, usually voting in panels of no more than three judges, and assigned with the solo task of writing legal opinions. It is also different from his role he will eventually fill on the Texas Supreme Court, where as a member of a collegial body of nine justices he must grapple with some of the most high-profile legal disputes in the state's history. Some of the cases in his first term deal with the due process rights of the accused, including a few high-profile murder cases and an unusual privacy case. Chapter 2 continues to examine his tenure on the court of appeals during his second term, focusing primarily on the beginning of the *Edgewood v. Kirby* school funding litigation saga, but also including additional privacy cases, tort claims, negligence doctrines, and his first encounter with the infamous sexual bondage case.

Chapter 3 focuses on his record on the Texas Supreme Court (1991–1995 term). After a tumultuous election to the high court, Gammage attempts to exercise influence on the direction of the court but finds himself increasingly dissenting from conservative rulings as Republicans make gains on the court and ultimately achieve majority. The chapter analyzes key cases dealing with civil rights and liberties and protecting ordinary Texans, including a return to the *Edgewood* school finance saga, balancing the first amendment rights of abortion protestors with the privacy of individuals, a challenge to the state's sodomy law, and the high-profile sex tape case.

Chapter 4—titled "Court Wars: Judicial Politics and Reform in Texas"—begins with Gammage's decision to leave the court at the end of the 1995 term because of increasing ideological polarization on the court, the rise of million-dollar judicial campaigns and failed attempts to reform the system. He begins his work along with other prominent judicial reformers to change the system. Texas judicial politics enters a new era of Republican domination of the judiciary in the twenty-first century. This chapter is an overview of a long and complex history of judicial politics and reform in the Lone Star State. The discussion here transcends Gammage's record on the bench and contribution to the reform movement to examine the judicial politics and proposed reforms of that period and beyond. Advocated reforms included the adoption of an appointive system or merit plan, nonpartisan elections, more representative election schemes, limits on campaign contributions, caps on spending by judicial candidates, public funding of campaigns and tougher judicial recusal and ethics rules, to name but a few. The chapter concludes with a discussion of current judicial politics at the state and national level.

Finally, chapter 5—"Jurisprudence and Judicial Politics"—concludes the book with, first, a final assessment of Gammage's jurisprudence and, second, a discussion of some of the trends in judicial politics as Texas and the nation move toward the second decade of the twenty-first century.

NOTES

1. *Barber v. Colo. Independent School District*, 901 S.W.2d 447, 455 (Tex. 1995) (Gammage, J., dissenting).
2. *Barber v. Colo. Independent School District*, 901 S.W.2d.
3. *Id.,* at 447, 450 (coming to a 7–2 decision).
4. *Ibid.,* at 451 (Gammage, J., dissenting).
5. *Id.*
6. *See generally* Ronald Dworkin, *Taking Rights Seriously* (Cambridge: Harvard University Press, 1977) (discussing and coining the phrase "taking rights seriously," in a judicial context).
7. *Kirby v. Edgewood Independent School District*, 761 S.W.2d 859 (Tex. App – Austin 1988).
8. *San Antonino Independent School District v. Rodriquez,* 411 U.S. 1 (1973).

9. See Charles Denton, *The Year They Threw the Rascals Out* (Austin: Shoal Creek, 1973).

10. See Michael Ariens, *Lone Star Law: A Legal History of Texas* (Lubbock: Texas Tech University Press, 2011), 148–149; and "Accomplishments of the 63rd Legislature," *Legislative Reference Library of Texas*, https://lrl.texas.gov/scanned/sessionoverviews/63_Accomplishments_1.pdf.

11. Id.

12. Dixie Shipp, "Annual state session passed," *Austin American-Statesman*, April 6, 1974.

13. "Constitutional convention committees," *Austin American-Statesman,* February 8, 1974.

14. Jon Ford, "Senators approve five articles," *Austin American-Statesman,* April 1, 1975.

15. "Technical work started," *Victoria Advocate*, June 23, 1975.

16. What was then the 22nd Congressional District of Texas.

17. See *Gammage v. Compton,* 548 S.W.2d 1 (1977); and *Paul v. Gammage*, On Petition for a Writ of Certiorari to the Supreme Court of Texas, No. 76-1408 (1977).

18. He was appointed by Attorney General Mark White. There are no written records available from Gammage's one year as assistant attorney general.

19. Justices such as Gammage, Oscar Mauzy, Lloyd Doggett, and, later, Rose Spector had the strongest voting records in support of rights and liberties. Two other Democratic justices with whom Gammage served, Raul Gonzales and Jack Hightower, were more moderate to conservative in their voting record. See the discussion of the court's composition in chapters 2 and 3, and the ideology of justices in chapter 5.

20. Press advisory from the Texas Supreme Court, http://www.supreme.court.state.tx.us/advisories/pdf/.

21. Press release from Chief Justice Thomas R. Phillips, August 24, 1995.

22. 129 S.Ct. 2252 (2009).

23. 909 S.W.2d 872 (1995). See chapters 3 and 4 for further discussion of *Rogers v. Bradley.*

24. *Lawrence v. Texas,* 539 U.S. 558 (2003).

25. *See State v. Morales,* 869 S.W.2d 941 (Tex. 1994).

26. *See Morales*, 869 S.W.2d at 942 n.4 (citing Tex. Const. art. I, §§ 3(a), 13, 19).

27. *Ibid.,* at 953–54 (Gammage, J., dissenting) (emphasis added) (footnote omitted).

28. *Michigan v. Long, 463 U.S. 1032, 1035 (1983).*

29. *See* Judith S. Kaye, "Dual constitutionalism in practice and principle," *St. John's Law Review* 61 (1987): 399, 417 n. 67; *see also* Julie F. Siegel, "The Supreme Court of Texas from 1989–1998: Independence determined by six-year terms," *Alabama Law Review,* 62 (1999): 1649 (providing a summary of the literature on state court decision-making).

30. *See generally* Robert F. Utter, "Swimming in the jaws of the crocodile: State Court comment of federal constitutional issues when disposing of cases on state constitutional grounds," *Texas Law Review,* 63 (1985): 1025 (discussing the modes of state constitutional analysis).

31. Judith S. Kaye, "Contributions of state constitutional law to the third century of American federalism," *Vermont Law Review* 13 (1988): 49 (noting that principles of federalism cannot be ignored).

32. William J. Brennan, Jr., "State constitutions and the protection of individual rights," *Harvard Law Review,* 90 (1977): 489.

33. Gammage served in the U.S. Army (1959–1964), and the U.S. Navy Reserve (1965–2000).

34. Chief Justice Phillips' presentation of Gammage's Portrait Unveiling at the Supreme Court Courtroom on June 7, 2002.

35. During his tenure in the Third Court of Appeals, Gammage's most cases were decided by three-judge panels that typically included Bob Gammage, Bob Shannon, and Marilyn Aboussie. On the Texas Supreme Court, Gammage served with Chief Justice Thomas R. Phillips, and Justices Raul Gonzales, Oscar Mauzy, Eugene Cook, Jack Hightower, Lloyd Doggett, Nathan Hecht, John Cornyn, Craig Enoch, and Rose Spector. See tables 5.1 and 5.2 in chapter 5 for the ideology of the justices.

36. G. Edward White, *Justice Oliver Wendell Homes: Law and the Inner Self* (Oxford: Oxford University Press, 1993); Phillipa Strum, *Louis D. Brandeis: Justice for the People* (Cambridge: Harvard University Press, 1984) and *Brandeis: Beyond Progressivism* (Lawrence: University of Kansas Press, 1993); and Bernard Schwartz, *Super Chief: Earl Warren and His Supreme Court – A Judicial Biography* (New York: New York University Press, 1983).

37. Gerald Gunther, *Learned Hand: The Man and the Judge* (Oxford: Oxford University Press, 1998); and Frank R. Kemerer, *William Wayne Justice: A Judicial Biography* (Austin: University of Texas Press, 1991)

38. Jacqueline A. McLeod, *The Life of Judge Jane Bolin: Daughter of the Empire State* (Champaign, IL: University of Illinois Press, 2011).

39. Ariens, *Lone Star Law*; and James L. Haley, *The Texas Supreme Court: A Narrative History, 1836–1986* (Austin: University of Texas Press, 2013).

40. This book grew from my article, "The jurisprudence of Texas Supreme Court Justice Robert 'Bob' Gammage: A legacy in civil rights & liberties," *South Texas Law Review,* 55, no. 1 (Fall 2013): 27–70.

Chapter 2

Texas Court of Appeals at Austin

The majority opinion implies, by its reasoning, that the Texas Constitution places no limit whatsoever on the power of the legislature to establish school district boundaries. Such reasoning dangerously erodes that most precious of political rights—the right to be treated with respect and equality by the government, the right to full and participating citizenship in the state.

—Justice Gammage dissenting
in *Kirby v. Edgewood*[1]

ELECTION TO THE THIRD COURT OF APPEALS AT AUSTIN

Gammage served for eight years on the Third Court of Appeals at Austin from 1982 to 1990. Initially appointed by Republican governor Bill Clements in October 1982, he ran unopposed in the November 1982 election, served a six-year term, and was then reelected for a second term in 1988. He then served two years of his second term before his election to the Texas Supreme Court in 1990.

Gammage did not have experience as a trial judge before serving as an appellate judge, as was the case for many appellate judges at that time in Texas, but he was known statewide as a respected, ethical, and hardworking legislator and assistant attorney general of Texas under one-term Democratic governor Mark White. In 1982, Gammage announced his intent to run for a seat on the Third Court of Appeals at Austin. His campaign flyers (see Figure 2.1) provided a photo of forty-four-year-old Gammage and bore his quote:

> Justice is best served when the law serves all the people. The people's best guarantee of justice is a record of dedication, experience, and proven service.[2]

The opposite side of the flyer touted his experience as an army veteran (Korea), assistant attorney general, legislator, law professor, and Austin lawyer.[3]

This chapter examines Gammage's major decisions while serving on the Third Court of Appeals that best represent his jurisprudence in the areas of civil rights, personal liberties, and criminal due process. The organization of the following analysis of his opinions while on the court of appeals does not proceed in a strictly chronological fashion. Since the court of appeals possesses both criminal and civil jurisdiction, the discussion is divided into separate sections, the first examining major opinions in the areas of criminal due process and the rights of the accused and then in the second, major civil cases that involved personal rights, liberties, and equal protection are discussed. Within each of the respective sections, cases are organized chronologically. Since he served only one-third of his second term on the court, his entire tenure on the Third Court of Appeals is covered in this one chapter.

Two years prior to his run for a seat on the court of appeals, the structure of the Texas court system underwent significant reforms. A constitutional amendment changed the name of the state's intermediate courts of appeal from the court of civil appeals to the court of appeals and, more importantly, expanded the jurisdiction of these courts to hear criminal as well as civil appeals.[4] This fundamental constitutional change in the role of the state's intermediate appellate courts was intended to relieve the Texas Court of Criminal Appeals of a major backlog of criminal appeals. Prior to this change, appeals in criminal cases proceeded directly from trial courts to the court of criminal appeals—which is the state's highest court of last resort with criminal jurisdiction.

Currently in Texas there are fourteen courts of appeal that possess jurisdiction to hear civil and criminal appeals from trial courts in each of their respective districts. Appeals from the decisions of the courts of appeals in civil cases are heard by the Texas Supreme Court, whereas criminal appeals are heard by the Texas Court of Criminal Appeals. Appeals in capital cases proceed directly, or automatically, to the court of criminal appeals from the sentencing trial court.[5] The 1981 constitutional amendment expanded the jurisdiction of the courts of civil appeals to hear criminal cases, except in capital cases which would proceed directly from the sentencing trial court to the court of criminal appeals.[6]

Long before the 1981 reforms, the state's intermediate courts of appeal were created by a constitutional amendment passed by the voters in 1891 and by a subsequent act of the legislature enacted in 1892. The act divided

Figure 2.1 Court of Appeals Campaign Card. *Source:* Robert A. Gammage Collection. SHSU Special Collections, Newton Gresham Library, Sam Houston State University, Huntsville, Texas.

the state into three judicial districts, within each district one court of appeals with civil jurisdiction would be seated: the First Court of Civil Appeals at Galveston, the Second Court of Civil Appeals at Fort Worth, and the Third Court of Civil Appeals at Austin.

The 1891 amendment also changed the court of appeals from a statewide intermediate appellate body, with mostly criminal but some civil jurisdiction, into the court of criminal appeals and vested it with jurisdiction to hear appeals solely in criminal cases. The Supreme Court of Texas, first established by the 1836 Constitution of the Republic of Texas, retained its appellate jurisdiction to hear appeals in civil cases but was stripped of its criminal jurisdiction. It was at that point in history that the basic bifurcated structure of the modern judiciary of Texas was born. The 1891 amendment also authorized the legislature to increase the number of courts of civil appeals as the population and caseload grew.[7]

The popular election of judges—with vacant seats filled through gubernatorial appointment—was established by the 1876 (current) constitution. The question of whether elections should be partisan or nonpartisan is not addressed by the constitution. However, under state election law judicial candidates run for office as a nominee of their party, thus effectively promoting partisan elections.[8]

The court on which Gammage was seeking a seat, the Third Court of Appeals at Austin—also referred to as the Court of Appeals at Austin—is so named for the third of fourteen districts that encompasses twenty-four counties in central Texas. Because it is located in the state capital, the court has jurisdiction over administrative law cases in addition to the range of typical civil and criminal cases heard by all fourteen intermediate courts of appeal. In Texas, administrative law is a body of state case law dealing with disputes arising from the state regulation of utilities, transportation, air quality, and oil and gas. Lawsuits filed against state government are usually filed in Travis County in this area of law, the Court of Appeals at Austin hears appeals from all state trial courts. Therefore, the impact of the Third's decisions can be greater than those of the other thirteen appeals courts. Each court of appeals in the state has from three to thirteen justices including a chief justice, deciding cases in three-judge panels, although the entire court may sit en banc to hear cases of high importance or to review a prior panel's decision in order to promote consistency in that court of appeal's jurisprudence. Justices serve for six-year renewable terms elected by the voters in that district.[9]

The May 1, 1982, Democratic primary election resulted in neither Gammage nor his major opponent, Austin attorney Dick Criss, receiving a majority of the vote, due to a third candidate named Austen Furse. A runoff was called for June 1. Both men campaigned furiously in and around Austin. Criss bought up media time, while Gammage ran a ground game making numerous appearances in and around Austin. Gammage was under some criticism by his opponents during the campaign for having no prior judicial experience, so he touted his legislative experience as a strength, citing his understanding of legislative intent and his leadership role in reforming the penal code. Prior judicial experience is not required under law to serve on a court of appeals; only that the candidate is thirty-five years old and has been a practicing lawyer, or a lawyer and judge, for at least ten years. Criss tried to frame Gammage's legislative experience as a negative, calling him a longtime politician rather than a judge. As of that May 1 primary, Criss spent $49,000 and Gammage spent $23,000, with Gammage's largest contributions including $2,500 from the political action committees of the Houston Builders Association and Texas Business Political Action Committee.[10]

In June 1982, Gammage narrowly won the runoff election in the Democratic primary election with 51.3 of the 59,257 votes cast.[11] Then, three months later, on August 11, 1982, Governor Clements announced the appointment of Gammage to the Third Court of Appeals, effective September 1. The governor's press release noted of Gammage that his appointee had previously served as assistant attorney general of Texas under Governor Mark White, member of the US House of Representatives, and member of the Texas Senate and Texas House of Representatives.[12] It further noted that Gammage was unopposed in the upcoming November 1982 general election. That year Clements also appointed Judge Earl Wesley Smith and James C. Brady to the Court of Appeals at Austin. A headline in the *Austin American- Statesman* in February 1982 read, "Republicans duck court races."[13] A November 1982 headline read "Democrats edging up in courts." An election day "a wave of support" was good for Democrats seeking high court seats. Democrat Ted Robertson defeated Republican John Bates, and Chuck Miller easily won a seat on the Texas Court of Criminal Appeals. Incumbent Bill Kilgarlin, a liberal Democrat, ran unopposed to keep his seat on the Texas Supreme Court. In the 1982 race for seats on the Court of Appeals at Austin it was reported that Bob Shannon was elected to Place 1, Gammage to Place 2, and Earl Smith to Place 3 and Jim Brady to Place 4.[14] (Gammage would become the first justice who had served on the Court of Appeals at Austin to be elected to the Texas Supreme Court).[15] Gammage served a full six-year term and then ran for his seat again unopposed in November 1988, serving on the court of appeals until his election to the Supreme Court in November 1990.

Other than news of the 1982 election, Gammage was featured in a Paris, Texas, newspaper that reported that his car hit a dog while driving from Corsicana to Austin. Local vets wouldn't treat the dog because it had no tags, so Gammage took the injured dog to an emergency veterinary clinic in Austin.

The dog needed the type of surgery the clinic could not perform so he took the dog to his personal veterinarian. The article concluded that he was looking for a home for the dog.[16]

During Gammage's tenure on the court of appeals, he served with Justices John C. Phillips (1963–1985), Bob E. Shannon (1971–1991), John E. Powers (1981–2004), Earl W. Smith (1982–1986), James C. Brady (1982–1988), James L. Carroll (1985–), Marilyn Aboussie (1986–), and J. Woodfin Jones (1989–2000),[17] although in most cases he heard cases in three-judge panels, primarily with Justices Powers, Phillips, and Aboussie. In the vast majority of cases, the three judges reached unanimous decisions, with Gammage dissenting in rare instances.

During his two terms on the Third Court of Appeals, the full court handed down 550 published opinions. Gammage authored opinions in 112 major cases, or 20 percent, from October 1982 to the end of his term in late 1990. Seventy-four of Gammage's opinions are classified broadly as "civil" and thirty-eight as "criminal."[18] Each of these decisions was important because they affected the liberty and property of real people, but only a handful of these cases are "high profile" or precedential (cited as authority in a number of subsequent cases), compared to his term on the Supreme Court.

However, while on the Third Court of Appeals he did write a highly influential dissenting opinion in *Kirby v. Edgewood* that was ultimately adopted by the Supreme Court in *Edgewood v. Kirby*. He also wrote the majority opinion in *Colquette v. Forbes*, an unusual but frequently cited privacy case, and in *Twyman v. Twyman*,[19] a highly publicized dispute involving the coerced sexual bondage of a wife by her husband. On the court of appeals, Gammage also had the opportunity to develop his thinking on criminal procedure and the due process rights of the accused in a large number of important appeals from criminal convictions. Aside from written opinions of the Third Court of Appeals, which tend to be in most instances rather brief compared to Supreme Court opinions, recorded oral argument from that period does not exist, and supporting documents such as briefs and conference notes were not methodically archived.

CRIMINAL DUE PROCESS RIGHTS

Circumstantial Evidence

During Gammage's tenure on the court of appeals, he heard appeals in a number of highly publicized murder cases. In 1983, in *Jones v. Texas*,[20] the court of appeals voted to reverse the murder conviction of Sandra Jones on the basis of a series of errors made by the trial court, including insufficient evidence, the use of testimony by the defendant during the punishment stage of trial to establish guilt, misuse of the "read-back rule," and the use of polygraph results. The case originated when a Chicago woman who was visiting her mother in Luling, Texas, a small town near San Marcos, allegedly murdered a man that she met in a local bar. The day before David Johnson was found murdered in a roadside ditch, Johnson, Sandra Jones, and her brother were seen about town drinking beer, shopping for groceries and attending a cattle auction. The next morning Johnson was found dead. His pockets were obviously emptied by someone, and rifle bullets were found strewn on the ground. A hunting rifle was leaning against a fence near where he lay. There were signs that he was dragged across the road. Two brands of cigarette butts were strewn about and dozens of little finger size holes punctuated the dry dirt road. Investigators determined that he was killed by a gunshot wound in his head caused by a slug fired at point-blank range. Johnson's pickup truck was discovered abandoned 200 yards from Sandra Jones's mother's home. Law enforcement determined that Jones was a suspect, but there was little evidence directly linking her to the crime.[21]

About the same time that Johnson's body was discovered, Jones returned to her mother's home very upset and wearing a blouse bearing a dark stain. Her mother testified that on that day, Jones and her brother were engaged in an intense discussion, after which she caught a flight back to Chicago. A ballistics expert could not positively state that the deceased was killed by the rifle discovered nearby, because the rifle slug shattered into small pieces upon striking Johnson's skull. However, Jones fingerprints were found throughout the interior of the truck. There were no witnesses to the incident or anyone who could testify that they either heard or saw Johnson and Jones arguing or Jones threatening Johnson.[22]

At the end of the trial, Jones's lawyer filed a motion seeking an instructed verdict from the trial judge, citing that during the guilt-innocence phase of the trial there was insufficient evidence to convict. The trial judge denied the motion and Jones was convicted of murder. During the punishment phase of her trial, Jones decided to become more forthcoming with information, testifying that Johnson attacked and raped her. After he threatened to assault her further, Jones explained, she ran from him down a dirt road but Johnson caught up to her in his pickup truck. He then apologized and convinced Jones to get back into the truck. According to Jones's testimony, Johnson once again threatened her with sexual assault, so Jones picked up Johnson's rifle and pointed it at Johnson, demanding that he take her home. She stated that when Johnson "grabbed the gun . . . it went off." She denied that she intentionally shot Johnson. Then, after Johnson was shot, Jones, still wearing her high heel shoes, dragged the deceased across the road into a ditch and drove to her mother's house in his pickup truck.[23]

The sheriff testified that Jones had initially told him that Johnson had been killed by two black men, but then changed her story several times. The sheriff had also questioned Jones using a polygraph, which indicated that she was lying about her role in Johnson's murder. In the end, her testimony that she "grabbed the gun" and it accidentally fired led to her conviction for murder.

On appeal in *Jones*, the Third Court of Appeals reversed her conviction but remanded the case for a new trial. The majority held that the trial court erred by admitting the results of the polygraph, even though the defendant did not raise objections. The trial court should not have allowed the jury to hear evidence regarding the polygraph test because the results of a polygraph are never admissible in court. Further, during the guilt-innocence phase there was insufficient evidence to support a verdict of guilty beyond a reasonable doubt; however, her admission during the punishment phase convinced the jury that she killed Johnson. Because of her testimony during the punishment phase, Jones was not permitted to appeal errors that occurred during the guilt-innocence phase. In sum, Jones can be retried.[24]

Concurring in part and dissenting in part, Gammage agreed that the court should reverse Jones conviction, but he disagreed with the majority's decision to remand her case for a new trial. At the "guilt-innocence" stage of the trial, the evidence presented to the jury was purely circumstantial and insufficient to support the conviction of Jones for murder or any other crime. The trial court erred in denying the defendant's motion for a directed verdict before the jury was allowed to render its verdict. A directed verdict is a challenge to the legal sufficiency of evidence presented by the state. The trial court judge should not have allowed her testimony during the punishment phase to be "read-back" and used to determine guilt or innocence because at no time did Jones make a "judicial confession"—that is, during the trial in front of a judge admitting firing the rifle or intentionally or knowingly causing the death of Johnson. She didn't take the stand and say, "I shot him and I ask forgiveness." She admitted only that Johnson grabbed the gun and it went off. Gammage wrote:

> While we have clearly insufficient evidence at the guilt innocence stage to sustain conviction for murder, we do *not* have a judicial confession at the punishment stage which may be read-back to overcome this deficiency. Furthermore, even were appellant's statement in this case sufficient to constitute a judicial confession, I believe the rationale for the read-back rule—to allow the statement's use in testing sufficiency of the evidence in order to avoid further trial—no longer has valid application.[25]

Unless the defendant confesses to the crime during the punishment phase, argued Gammage, he or she still has legal grounds to challenge the conviction when, during guilt-innocent phase, there was insufficient evidence to prove he or she committed murder.[26] Trying Jones again under these circumstances constitutes double jeopardy in violation of the Fifth Amendment. According to the US Supreme Court in *Greene v. Massey*, the double jeopardy clause prohibits a retrial if the first conviction is reversed solely on the basis of insufficient evidence to support a verdict.[27] Based on state and federal precedent, retrial is "no longer possible" in cases where verdicts are reversed for insufficient evidence. Furthermore, retrials should be avoided under the read-back rule because the incriminating testimony of the accused read back at the punishment phase of a murder trial would only be used to provide sufficient evidence for the jury to find the defendant guilty at a retrial.[28]

The position that Gammage embraced in the case raised the standard of proof for the prosecution, therefore bolstering the right of a defendant to an appeal when there is insufficient evidence at the guilt-innocence phase. His stance differs somewhat from precedent at the time, which held that objections based on insufficient evidence would be waived if the defendant made a partial judicial confession or incriminating statements or provided additional information about the crime. The confession must be unequivocal and must admit guilt to the specific crime with which she is charged in the indictment. However, the position that the courts maintained until recently was that a defendant who admits guilt at the punishment phase waives his or her right to appeal based on insufficient evidence during the guilt-innocence phase. A defendant who is convicted will often confess at the punishment phase so that the jury will go easy on her. So this is a hard call for the defendant. Under the 2013 ruling of *Jacobson v. Texas*, the court of criminal appeals ruled that a defendant who admits his or her guilt at the punishment stage does *not* forfeit the right to appeal on the grounds that errors occurred during the guilt-innocence stage of the trial.[29]

In another influential case, *England v. Texas*,[30] Gammage wrote the majority opinion addressing the question of the amount of circumstantial evidence that is sufficient to convict a person of a crime.[31] The case originated in February 1985, when Barbara Gamboa entered her apartment around noon and discovered that her stereo and some jewelry were missing. The next morning, Gamboa discovered that her clothing in the closet was covered in dust. The closet ceiling had a trap door that led to an attic that was shared by other residents in the apartment building. Once she realized that the burglar had entered her apartment through this door, she told her next-door neighbor, Asa England, of her suspicions and that the police were on their way to "check things out." Upon hearing this, England grew "nervous," Gamboa later testified.[32]

Back in her apartment, ten to fifteen minutes later, Gamboa heard a loud clatter coming from the attic. Just before the police arrived, England told Gamboa that he had found the stereo in the attic and that he was afraid the police might conclude he had stolen her property. The police found no signs of forcible entry through the windows or door, but they discovered a hole cut through the sheetrock wall separating the attic space of the two residents. They then found Gamboa's missing stereo in England's area of the attic. Her jewelry was not found. England denied taking her stereo or jewelry but openly conjectured that someone had entered his apartment through a broken window. Over the next several days England pleaded with Gamboa not to press charges and told her that he suspected his roommate may have stolen her property. She agreed not to press charges if the jewelry was returned. Later that day Gamboa found a crumpled piece of aluminum foil on the hood of her car. She discarded it as trash. England asked her if she found her jewelry. She said no and England left. When Gamboa returned to her car the foil with the jewelry appeared on her car. She carefully unwrapped it and found her jewelry.

England was ultimately tried and convicted in a district court and sentenced to six years in a correctional facility. The only problem was that there was no direct evidence linking England to the theft of the stereo and jewelry, so his conviction was based solely on inference—on circumstantial evidence.

The Third Court of Appeals reversed the trial court's conviction and acquitted England. Writing for the majority, Gammage argued that the evidence was insufficient to convict because the state failed to show that England was the only person who had sole access to the apartment attic where the stolen goods were found and that if others had access, then a conspiracy or joint venture involving England and others led to the burglary. The state also failed to prove that England made "a conscious assertion of right to the property," or in other words, that he never confessed that he was in actual possession of the stolen property. According to Gamboa, England did say that he found her property in the attic and then gave her the property shortly thereafter. Without any additional evidence England's conviction was based solely on Gamboa's skepticism of England's explanation and her observation of his "nervousness."

Gammage argued that while Gamboa's conclusions drawn from England's odd behavior may have been "[a] . . . reasonable inference from the sequence of events, it is just as reasonable to infer that England persuaded his roommate to return the jewelry." When is there sufficient circumstantial evidence to support a conviction? The answer is whether a rational finder of fact, viewing the "evidence in a light most favorable to the verdict of guilt," could have found the essential elements of the crime beyond a reasonable doubt.[33] Gammage wrote that

> Circumstantial evidence is sufficient to support a conviction only if the proven facts support a reasonable inference that the accused committed the crime and exclude to a moral certainty any inference consistent with his innocence.[34]

The state failed to produce evidence contradicting England's explanation that he had a roommate and that there were others that had access to the attic where the stolen property was found. In most criminal prosecutions, in determining the sufficiency of the evidence a court must view the evidence in a light that is most favorable to the prosecution. Gammage concluded, however, that in circumstantial evidence cases the evidence is insufficient if the circumstances do not exclude every other reasonable hypothesis except that of the guilt of the accused.[35] The case was not subject to further review.

The Lesser-included Offense Doctrine

In 1987 in *Drew v. State of Texas*[36] Gammage wrote the opinion in a case stemming from the attempted murder of a police officer. The case generated media attention statewide not only because of a vicious attack on a peace officer but because of the lurid and sensational circumstances of the crime.[37] The case raised a complex rule in criminal justice called the lesser-included offense doctrine. Rooted in both English and American common law, the concept has been subject to a great deal of analysis by both state and federal courts.[38] Many appellate courts in Texas have come to conflicting conclusions as to when the doctrine should be applied and in which instances the failure to do so violates the due process rights of the accused.[39] *Drew v. State* originated in April 1985 when Officer Mark Jackson was patrolling a dirt road in a dark corner of a rural area in Temple, Texas. On that dark and lonely road, he observed a suspicious car driving without lights. Carrying a flashlight he slowly exited his marked patrol car to investigate. The headlights of the police car were turned on but the overhead flashing lights were not, so it in the dark early morning hours in central Texas, a person observing Officer Jackson's car might not have known it was a police car. As he approached the suspect's car, Jackson was wearing a short sleeve dark blue uniform and badge, but he was not wearing a hat or cap. He shined his flashlight into the window of the now parked car and saw Julius Drew naked from the waist down. He also saw a woman was lying in the back seat with her clothing draped around her. When Officer Jackson knocked on the car window and asked for Drew's identification, Drew quickly dressed and the woman immediately asked the officer to be taken back to her car. With his flashlight switched on, Jackson opened the passenger side door and kneeled on the front seat to ask the woman what was wrong. At that point, Drew attempted to start the car but then decided to jump from his car and flee. After Jackson unsuccessfully pursued Drew on foot, he returned and escorted the woman to the backseat of his patrol car. While the officer was leaning inside the patrol car attending to the woman, Drew attacked Jackson, hitting him on the side of his face and attacking him with a pocket knife. Jackson warned Drew that if he did not stop he would shoot him. Drew did not stop his attack, so Officer Jackson shot Drew twice in the chest.[40]

The wound resulted in Officer Jackson requiring surgery for a severed nerve in his jaw and punctured lung. Drew was charged and convicted of knowingly and intentionally attempting to cause the death of a peace officer acting in an official capacity, which is a capital offense. During the trial Drew's doctor testified that Drew would be unable to walk without the use of a cane or crutches and would suffer from bladder, bowel, and sexual dysfunction as a result of the gunshot wound. Drew testified that because it was pitch dark, he did not know Jackson was a police officer; all he knew was that a large man had grabbed him from behind. Therefore, he had acted in self-defense out of fear for his life and that of his companion. Officer Jackson testified that he had not turned on his patrol car's overhead lights and was not he certain that he identified himself to Drew as a police officer.

The trial judge denied Drew the right under law to provide the jury with instruction on the lesser-included offense of attempted murder, which would apply if there was reasonable doubt that Drew knew that he was attacking a police office. So the question in this case was whether the trial court erred in not allowing the jury to consider the lesser-included offense. Did Drew's ignorance of the fact that Jackson was a police officer require the jury to be read the charge including the lesser-included offense (attempted murder) rather than attempted capital murder of a peace officer? Under precedent, a jury must have the opportunity to consider the lesser-included offense if there is some evidence in the record that if the defendant is guilty he is guilty of only the lesser offense.[41]

Reversing the trial court and ordering a new trial, the Third Court of Appeals ruled in *Drew v. State*[42] that based on the correct application of the controlling precedent,[43] if he is guilty on the lesser offense—because of his uncertainty of whether Jackson was a police officer— the jury needs to be instructed on the lesser offense as well as the more serious offense. Gammage reasoned:

> We must consider all of the evidence raised at trial. If evidence from any source raises the issue and a jury charge on the issue is properly requested, the issue must be submitted to the jury.[44]
>
> Drew's testimony together with all the circumstances presents a factual question as to a required elements of capital murder—knowledge by Drew that Jackson was a police officer. Because this element distinguishes attempted capital murder from the lesser offence of attempted murder, Drew was entitled to have the issue determined by the jury, and the trial court erred in denying Drew's requested instruction.[45]

Therefore, a criminal defendant has the right to have a jury and not a judge decide the issue of whether the jury should consider instruction on the lesser-included offense regardless of whether the defendant's testimony is strong, weak, impeached or contradictory. The state argued that Drew was not entitled to the requested jury instruction because the jury could not reasonably believe the conflicting versions of what happened that night on the dirt road, but Gammage concluded that once Drew provided evidence that he did not know if Jackson was a peace officer, it did not matter that this evidence was credible, controverted or conflicting. A criminal defendant has "the right to have the jury under proper instruction, and not the court, decide that issue."[46] Drew was denied the right to have the jury given the opportunity of finding him guilty of a lesser offense.

Gammage believed that due process requires the law to consider the element of a crime that is less serious, such as assault with a deadly weapon, which is committed during the perpetration of a more serious crime, murder. The assault with the deadly weapon is a necessary element of the crime of murder that is "included" in the more serious crime. The lesser crime contains some of the same elements of the greater crime. The prosecution cannot prove that the defendant committed the greater crime unless it is proven that all of the elements of the lesser crime were committed. The defendant, of course, would prefer to be found not guilty, but if she is to be found guilty, preferably it would be guilty of the lesser-included offense.[47]

Since 1987, when *Drew v. State* was decided, Texas courts have come to conflicting interpretations and application of this concept of lesser-included offense, and it has often been misunderstood or misapplied. The Texas Court of Criminal Appeals has recognized the confusion and has over the years revisited the doctrine with the intent to clarify how it should be applied.[48]

The Texas Oral Confession Rule

In 1987, the Third Court of Appeals was asked to address Texas' unique confession law that raises the issue of the admissibility of self-incriminating oral statements. *Port v. Texas*[49] received intense media coverage at the time of the trial in 1984[50] and again in 2014, when the man who brutally killed a twenty-three-year-old Houston woman walked out of prison after serving thirty years of a seventy-five-year sentence.[51] *Port v. Texas*, an unpopular and excoriated decision, was actually two rulings by the Third Court of Appeals: the initial appeal (*Port* I) and then a rehearing to reconsider its opinion (*Port* II).

The infamous case originated when Debra Sue Schatz, a young postal carrier, disappeared on June 7, 1984. On the morning of June 8, one of Port's neighbors called the police to report that a mail delivery truck had been parked overnight on her street in a subdivision in West Houston. The murder suspect's father also contacted the police to inform them that his son was missing and that he discovered bullet holes in the walls of their home. Port's father then turned over six guns to the police, one of which was a Ruger .22

that would later prove to be the murder weapon. Officers also found a bloody shoe, bloodstains, bullet holes in the stairwell, and Schatz's fingerprints.[52]

After a police chase, three Houston police officers apprehended Port. He was handcuffed and placed in the backseat of a vehicle where he was read his *Miranda* warning. Shortly afterward, Port began chatting with the officers, freely admitting that he had abducted Debra Schatz and then shot her when she tried to escape. He boasted that he disposed of her body in a bayou. At that point the officers drove Port to the bayou, but Schatz's body was not found. Her body was later found by a tow truck driver in an open field. Port subsequently admitted that some of the information he had volunteered to the police was fabricated.[53]

Port also provided information to the officers while on route from the bayou to the police station thirty minutes after his arrest. He volunteered more details about the shooting, such as "I started shooting at her," and "I know I missed her many times, but I know I hit her at least two times, maybe in the head, I don't know."[54] The police car then arrived at the station. As the officer was exiting her patrol car in front of the police station, Port noticed that she was carrying on a clipboard the gun that he used to kill Schatz. Upon seeing the gun, Port excitedly asked, "Is that my gun?" The officer responded, "Do you recognize it?" Port then admitted, "Yes, that is the one I used to kill her." Ballistics tests and an autopsy later corroborated Port's oral confession.

The legal question in the case was whether any of Port's statement could be admitted as evidence under the Texas "confession law." Under the oral confessions doctrine, which dates back to the 1850s, and is unique to the state of Texas, the trial court judge determined that Port's oral inaccurate statements made after his arrest and during the trip to out to the bayou were not admissible but that Port's statements during the ride from the bayou to the police station would be admitted as evidence, including Port's own admission to an officer that the gun she was carrying on her clipboard was the one he used to kill Schatz. Also admitted as evidence was physical evidence found in several places: at the murder scene, in the field where the body had been disposed, and from Port's car. Testimony from neighbors who had heard screaming the night Schatz was brutally murdered was also included as evidence. Because of the intense publicity surrounding the crime, the murder trial was moved from Houston to New Braunfels. The evidence used against Port proved sufficient for the jury to find beyond a reasonable doubt that he was guilty; he was sentenced to seventy-five years in prison. Port's lawyers then appealed on the grounds that Port's confession could not legally be admitted as evidence.

On appeal in *Port v. State (Port I)*,[55] two-and-a-half years later, the court of appeals unanimously[56] reversed Port's conviction,[57] concluding that oral statements made by Port about the gun following his arrest were inadmissible under both state criminal procedure rules governing confessions[58] and two previous rulings by the Texas Court of Criminal Appeals.[59]

Suspects in police custody often make oral statements about the crime even when they are not being interrogated. In some instances, the statements are true and in other instances a mere fabrication by the suspect. Often suspects change their story. Consequently, Texas courts have historically been reluctant to allow as evidence oral extrajudicial custodial statements or confessions because they are generally unreliable. The oral confession doctrine can be traced back to the mid-1850s when the legislature adopted the Code of Criminal Procedure. Under the Code, a confession could be used as evidence against a defendant if it was made freely without coercion. However, there were conditions attached, such as if the defendant was in jail or in custody of a law enforcement officer the confession was generally inadmissible at trial.[60] Simply put, the objectives of the law are to give an assurance of the accuracy of the defendant's statements, to prohibit coercive police conduct, and safeguard the suspect's decision to admit guilt without outside pressure.

Port's statements alone did not lead investigators to evidence not already known to the state, but since the statements made by the defendant during custodial interrogation were the only direct evidence of his guilt placed before the jury, these statements very likely contributed to his conviction and sentencing. Thus, the court of appeals ruled, the admission of his statements was not considered harmless error and the jury's verdict was reversed.[61]

The reversal of Port's conviction produced a loud and angry response from the public. In an interview appearing in the *Houston Chronicle* in 1987, Debra Schatz's mother stated that "I think justice stinks if they are giving him a new trial."[62] The Harris County district attorney, John Holmes, vowed to fight the reversal and stated that Texas' oral confession law was out of step with the rest of the United States.[63] The law was blasted as a "technicality" and a "loophole" created by a legislature dominated by liberal defense lawyers, although, in reality, the law goes back to 1856 and had already been subject to numerous reforms.[64] Following *Port* I, between 1985 and 1987, bills were introduced in the legislature to abolish Texas' confession law but no changes were adopted.[65]

Further developments occurred when, granting the state's motion for a rehearing in *Port* II,[66] the court of appeals reconsidered its previous opinion in *Port* I in light of an intervening Court of Criminal Appeals ruling in *Briddle v. State* a month earlier, which rejected the established rule that in order to be admissible an oral statement *must lead to the discovery of incriminating evidence.* In *Briddle* the accused described a shotgun and machete used in the killing and guided the police to where he had hidden them. Unknown to the confessing defendant was the fact that the police had already found the shotgun in the location described by the defendant but were unable to locate the machete. The victim's mother, completely unaware of the defendant's confession, corroborated the information independent of the confession. The Court of Criminal Appeals held that even though the defendant's oral statement did not lead to any new evidence, discovering the evidence under these circumstances established the reliability of the confessions and rendered it admissible.[67] Therefore, in light of the intervening *Briddle* decision, the court of appeals in *Port* II modified the language of its previous opinion, but the majority *refused* to reverse its ruling in *Port* I. David Port's conviction remained overturned. The court reasoned that before Port's incriminating confession about the gun, the police already believed that the gun was likely used in the killing. It had been taken from the defendant's bedroom by his father and given to officers. An odor emanating from the barrel revealed that it had been recently fired. The ballistics tests later performed confirmed what the police already knew. The confessions law, however, requires that the facts given by the defendant be unknown to the police and that the facts be incriminating. Then and only then is the oral confession admissible.[68] Writing for the majority, Justice Aboussie argued that:

> Logically, if a person knows intimate facts concerning a criminal transaction, whether or not those facts were previously known to the police, that knowledge is itself incriminating and tends to establish the reliability of the statement. However, the requirements for admission of an oral confession pursuant to section 3 (c) are much stricter than this. The statute and the cases decided thereunder clearly require that the facts assorted be *unknown to the police* and the *facts be incriminating* . . . Clearly, the legislature did not intend for every confession to be admissible.[69]

In one of Gammage's few dissenting opinions while on the Third Court of Appeals, he argued to affirm Port's conviction by the trial court. Port's admission that he shot his victim at least two times in the head and his assertion that the gun was the one he used to kill Schatz are admissible under Texas law. When Port made these statements the police could only suspect that he was telling the truth. However, when the medical examiner concluded that Schatz's died of two gunshot wounds to the head and a ballistics test established that the gun identified by Port while he exited the car in front of the police station was indeed the murder weapon, the truth and reliability of his confession were established. Gammage wrote:

> Nowhere does the statutory language require that the "facts or circumstances that are found to be true and which conduce to establish the guilt of the accused," do so independent of the accused's statement. Indeed, it is the corroboration of the accused own statement which damns him.[70]
>
> [O]nly when the fact or circumstance corroborated the accused's disclosure of guilty knowledge did the fact or circumstance conduce to establish the

> accused guilt. David Port made assertions of fact and circumstances which were not within the knowledge of the police and which only the killer of Debra Schatz could have known at the time. When these facts and circumstances were found to be true they conduced to establish Port's guilt and his assertions became admissible under [law].[71]

On appeal two-and-a-half years later in 1990, the Court of Criminal Appeals explicitly adopted Gammage's dissenting opinion in *Port* to reverse the court of appeals and order David Port to resume his seventy-five-year prison sentence. The district court subsequently granted a motion to reincarnate Port who was free on a $20,000 appeal bond for three years.[72]

Although it is difficult to classify his opinion as either conservative or liberal, Gammage's position was adopted by the Court of Criminal Appeals and was part of an existing trend in Texas to make it easier for the state to overcome the oral confessions law and introduce as admissible evidence defendant's oral statements or confessions given to police. After *Port*, the confessions law still maintained substantial restrictions on the admissibility of oral statements, but the final outcome in the *Port* decision held that the code does not require that the statement given to the police by the suspect lead to or result in the discovery of evidence that corroborates the statement.

Search and Seizure

In 1990, his last year on the Third Court of Appeals, Gammage wrote the opinion in an intriguing search and seizure case. Stemming from an appeal in a bizarre and tragic murder conviction, the case of *Bryant v. Texas*[73] originated a few days after Christmas in 1986 when a deputy sheriff pursued a speeding car down a state highway. The deputy was unable to catch the car until the driver stopped at Round Rock Hospital outside of Austin. The driver, Lori Chilek, rushed into the hospital carrying her three-year-old daughter who would soon perish from a gunshot wound in her head. Chilek told the officer that her daughter had been shot by Earl Bryant, her boyfriend.[74] The *Austin American-Statesman* covered the case closely, reporting that the young girl's death was linked to a "dope stash."[75]

On the evening of the murder, Chilek and her two young daughters were in Bryant's mobile home when he began firing his pistol because—as he later explained to police—he believed that men outside were sent to execute him. After the deputy spoke with Chilek at the hospital, he and back up officers proceeded immediately to Bryant's residence. Upon their arrival they heard Bryant forlornly calling from a distance, "Lori, where are you?" "Come back!" They found Bryant half-naked in the nearby woods, shaking from the cold, and scratched and bruised. Officers unsuccessfully searched nearby for the men that Bryant claimed were out to kill him. With Bryant handcuffed in the patrol car, officers made a decision to conduct a quick search of Bryant's trailer based on the possibility that someone, either a victim or a perpetrator, was inside. The officers found shell casings strewn on the floor and blood on the sofa and floor but no one inside. They exited the trailer several minutes later.[76]

As one of the officers handcuffed Bryant in the patrol car and read him his *Miranda* rights, other officers then entered the trailer without a warrant, taking photos and collecting evidence that was in plain view. They led Bryant into his residence and began to interrogate him. The police officers had found two small bags of marijuana during their initial search, so they asked Bryant if there was more in the house. Bryant directed the officers to a larger cache of marijuana hidden in the bathroom.[77]

At that point, the officers told Bryant the news that they had just been notified that Lori Chilek's three-year-old daughter had died. Shocked, upset, and emotional, Bryant said, "I might as well tell you the whole story." Bryant confessed that earlier that month he and an accomplice had stolen a 60 pound bale of marijuana and some cash from a drug dealer named Jesus. Bryant's share was 25 pounds from the bale, which he admitted was hidden inside of a lamp table in the living room. He further stated that on the night that the little girl was murdered, Bryant received a phone call from Jesus. Later, upon hearing someone outside of his trailer and his dogs barking, Bryant grew paranoid and began wildly firing his pistol at men outside of his trailer. He claimed that he was trying to protect Lori and her daughters, ultimately attempting to draw the men away from the residence into the woods. He repeated this story in a signed written statement eleven hours later in the sheriff's office.[78]

The trial court judge ruled that the officer's initial entry into Bryant's residence to determine whether anyone was inside was lawful and that Bryant's statements to the police were admissible. However, the judge ruled that the officer's second entry into the trailer was unlawful and all of the marijuana found was inadmissible as evidence. The following day, however, the trial court judge reversed himself on this motion and allowed the large bale of marijuana to be admitted as evidence because it was seized after Bryant made his statement and not after the search.[79]

Bryant's attorney argued that his client's confession, the photographs taken in the trailer, and the hidden bale of marijuana found after his statement to the police was not admissible as evidence because it was the product of warrantless and thus unconstitutional search under the Fourth Amendment of the US Constitution and Article I, section 9 of the Texas constitution.[80] Bryant was tried before a jury and convicted of felony murder. He was sentenced to ninety-nine years in prison. Bryant's lawyers appealed.

The Third Court of Appeals affirmed Bryant's conviction. Writing for the majority, Gammage argued that under state and federal precedent, the warrantless search of the trailer *was* unconstitutional, but that Bryant's confession to the police, after learning of the death of his girlfriend's daughter, was not tainted by the illegal search of the mobile home. Bryant's oral confession after the police told him about the girl's death, as well as his written confession eleven hours later at the sheriff's office, was admissible. Gammage stated that the written confession penned at the police station was indistinguishable from Bryant's oral confession. The admission of the photographs was constitutional as well because "qualitatively" they were no different from the deputy's description of what he found in the trailer during the initial search. Gammage wrote:

> A search conducted without a warrant issued upon probable cause is *per se* unreasonable under the fourth and fourteenth amendments of the United States Constitution, subject only to a few specifically established and well-delineated exceptions . . . . The five basic exceptions are (1) consent, (2) incident to a lawful arrest, (3) with probable cause to search with exigent circumstances, (4) in hot pursuit, and (5) stop and frisk.[81]

Since none of these exceptions applied to the search of Bryant's residence, the search was a violation of Bryant's rights. However, the admissibility of the bale of marijuana as evidence was based on the fact that Bryant made the confession while lawfully arrested, after he had been read his *Miranda* rights, stated that he understood his rights, and consented to telling the police what had transpired. One might ask whether the confession was tainted by the illegal search that simultaneously occurred during Bryant's *mea culpa*. Yes, that search was illegal, but Bryant's statement was not tainted by the police's "exploitation of that illegality"; it was tainted by Bryant's confession about the bale of marijuana. Gammage wrote that "having already concluded that the oral confession is not a fruit of the illegal search, we further conclude that no taint of that illegality extends to the written confession."[82]

Gammage stated that it is well established under Texas search and seizure law that Article I, section 9 of the Texas constitution is to be interpreted in harmony with the US Supreme Court's Fourth Amendment rulings, but he recognized the Texas constitution provides even provide broader protections. His thinking in this search and seizure case, and others, was compatible with precedent and can be characterized as moderate to conservative philosophically. For example, applying precedent, he affirmed the power of the police to make a warrantless arrest of persons found in suspicious places and acting in such a manner that would reasonably show that they are guilty of some criminal activity, felony or breach of the peace.[83] In *Bryant* he cited the 1983 precedent case of *Brown v. State* in which the Texas Court of Criminal Appeals held that Texas is free to accept or reject federal precedent in the area of search and seizures and establish its own standards as long as they do not "fall below the minimum standards provided by the federal constitutional protections.[84]

Although the majority in *Brown* recognized a "harmony" of interpretation of federal and state precedent, the Texas courts have been all over the Lone Star map expounding the relationship between federal and state search and seizure case law. Suffice it to say that the relationship between state and federal precedent is less "harmonious" and more contentious in many instances,[85] but the Texas courts have historically recognized "stricter, more protective [search and seizure] provisions, such as providing for a statutory exclusionary rule well in advance of the 1961 Supreme Court decision in *Mapp v. Ohio*."[86] As Judge Sam Houston Clinton, Jr., aptly wrote in *Brown v. State*:

> Merely to parrot opinions of the Supreme Court of the United States interpreting the Fourth Amendment is to denigrate the special importance our Texan forebearers attached to their rights to privacy and other guarantees vouchsafed by the Bill of Rights they first declared and then insisted on retaining in every successive constitution.[87]

It is worth noting that Judge Sam Houston Clinton, Jr., is a prominent figure in Texas legal history. Elected as a liberal Democrat, he served three consecutive six-year terms (1978–1996) as a judge on the Texas Court of Criminal Appeals, authoring over 1,000 opinions. Attacked by conservatives as a liberal judicial activist who coddled criminals, Judge Clinton was a civil libertarian who penned a host of opinions expounding on the rights of the accused in Texas. As an attorney, Clinton successfully defended a number of well-known and infamous clients, including Jack Ruby, the man who shot and killed Lee Harvey Oswald in Dallas. Ruby's shooting of Oswald was captured on film and was shown to a national television audience. Clinton managed to get Ruby's conviction in his first trial reversed on procedural grounds. Adding to the conspiracy surrounding President John F. Kennedy's assassination by Oswald, Ruby died of cancer in prison while awaiting a new trial. Clinton also won a lawsuit in federal district court to desegregate women's dormitories at the University of Texas in the early 1960s. Before the desegregation order, African American women were housed in two makeshift wooden buildings.[88]

Judge Clinton also represented Madalyn Murray O'Hair, the famous atheist leader who brought numerous lawsuits under the Establishment Clause of the First Amendment and defended Vietnam War protesters. In addition, Clinton served as the general counsel for the AFL-CIO and the Texas Civil Liberties Union. Many of his opponents grumbled that it was impossible to run against a man named "Sam Houston" Clinton. To do so would require a name change to Davy Crockett or Stephen F. Austin. Like Gammage, Clinton was one of the few progressives to serve on one of the state's highest courts.

CIVIL LAW: THE RIGHTS AND LIBERTIES OF TEXANS

The Right to Privacy

In 1984, Gammage wrote the majority opinion in a highly unusual privacy decision, *Colquette v. Forbes.*[89] The case raised the question of whether a consensual agreement made between two persons, free from governmental interference or action, can violate a person's right to privacy.[90] The case originated when Nancy Colquette claimed that the terms of the property settlement of her divorce decree violated her constitutional right to privacy.[91] As part of a divorce property settlement, Thomas Forbes agreed to convey his interest in the marital home to Nancy Colquette if she signed a promissory note that would come due in five years, "with immediate acceleration of maturity upon Colquette's remarriage or . . . cohabitation with an unrelated adult male" at the home.[92] Ms. Colquette was faced with a decision: if she married or entered into a relationship that involved any form of "cohabitation" with a man, the balance of the note would come due immediately, creating a financial hardship. If she didn't have the money to pay the note in full at that point, then the ownership of the house would automatically revert to her ex-husband.

Mr. Forbes brought suit to collect on the note, arguing that that the note had matured because Colquette had been cohabitating with an adult male for several weeks.[93] The trial court acknowledged that the note was due, agreed that Mr. Forbes could place a lien on the house, and ordered foreclosure if the note was not paid in full.[94] Ms. Colquette appealed and argued that the acceleration of the note and the placing of the lien, merely because of her personal decision to cohabitate with an adult male, violated her right to privacy as defined in the US Supreme Court ruling in *Griswold v. Connecticut.*[95] In that well-known landmark case the US Supreme Court invalidated a Connecticut law prohibiting the use of contraceptives. The Connecticut law made it a criminal offense to use or counsel the use of any drug or instrument for the purpose of preventing conception. The Court overturned the law, arguing that the law directly and adversely affected the intimacy of the marital relationship and represented an unwarranted governmental intrusion into the sphere of private matters. The contraceptives law placed severe limitations on a woman's personal autonomy, or freedom to enter into the most fundamental sort of personal and intimate relations.[96]

Colquette's lawyers argued before the Third Court of Appeals that any contract or policy supporting the terms of such a contract is void if it violates the right to privacy, which protects one's ability to autonomously enter into a relationship with another person.[97] In its landmark privacy decision, *Industrial Foundation of the South v. Texas Industrial Accident Board* in 1976, the Texas Supreme Court recognized that the right to privacy prohibits "unwarranted government interference or intrusion into those areas deemed to be within the protected zone of privacy.[98]

However, the court of appeals dismissed Colquette's application of *Griswold* to a private contractual agreement, and ruled for Forbes.[99] Writing for the majority, Gammage, argued that the mere judicial enforcement of the promissory note, according to the mutually agreed-upon terms, is not the kind of intrusion into Colquette's privacy that is recognized in *Griswold* or *Industrial Foundation.* It is somewhat surprising that Gammage, a lifelong advocate for a robust right to privacy, rejected Colquette's argument because she had willingly agreed to the terms of the contract so that she could keep her house.[100]

However, one might ask, wouldn't a contract be void if it violated a privacy interest to live with one's lover or partner? Can it be assumed that merely because Colquette was cohabitating with a boyfriend or new husband, that she now had the ability to pay the note in full? Were the terms of the note the means by which her ex-husband was controlling her life? The so-called acceleration clause appeared to be an intrusion upon Colquette's personal and intimate decisions. Gammage reasoned that the acceleration clause was a part of a mutual agreement between two individuals, it was *not* public policy promulgated by the government.[101] If it were, then Colquette could assert her privacy rights against the intrusion of the state; but the only involvement of the state in this case, was the "judicial enforcement of private contractual obligations."[102] Colquette consented to the intrusion into her privacy and relationship choices when she signed the promissory note.[103]

Another interesting question is: Doesn't "judicial enforcement" constitute state action? Gammage rejected Colquette's second contention, which was that the judicial enforcement of the cohabitation clause of the promissory note was contrary to public policy and in violation of *Shelley v. Kramer.*[104] In *Shelley*, the US Supreme Court struck down judicially enforced racially restrictive covenants used to maintain racially segregated neighborhoods.[105] If the state by law had *required* the cohabitation clause, then it might have been possible to challenge the law under *Shelley*—asserting that a state action had violated the constitution.[106] Gammage concluded:

> It is apparent to us that the justifications for the *Shelley* rule are not present in this case. Here, the affected parties consented to the intrusion—if acceleration of maturity of the debt and the particular conditions giving rise thereto can be construed as such—by their mutual acceptance of the terms of the note. . . . We

> hold that, under the facts of this case, judicial approval of the property settlement agreement and subsequent enforcement of the obligations created therein are, in nature and degree, not the type of government involvement restrained by a constitutional right of privacy.[107]

An agreement in the divorce decree is a contract. The contract's legal obligation and its meaning are governed by the law of contracts between private individuals, not by the law of judgments. Family and real estate law in Texas provides the legal language but in no way requires such a property settlement agreement between private parties. Forbes was no doubt anxious to receive payment for his interest in the house but agreed, per the promissory note, to wait a period of five years to be paid by Colquette.[108] Colquette agreed to these conditions to give her time to save money.[109] The likely presumption made was that if Colquette remarried or cohabitated with an unrelated adult male at the home, money would be available to help the ex-wife pay the note in full. Could Forbes have insisted on conditions that the note be accelerated if she merely dated a man who regularly spent the night? What if she had a female lover as opposed to male as stipulated in the agreement? Suppose further that a tenant agrees not to have premarital sex, as a mutually agreed-upon condition of a lease agreement. Can the tenant ultimately bring a cause of action for a tort invasion of privacy if the landlord has grounds for terminating the lease?[110] Such agreements seem very intrusive into a person's private intimate affairs, but it is all academic since, as Gammage pointed out, the obligations created by the note were consensual and not the type of government involvement that would infringe on a constitutional right to privacy.

In the history of privacy jurisprudence in Texas, the courts have ruled that although the Texas constitution does not contain an express guarantee of a right to privacy, it *does* contain provisions and protections that parallel those found in the US Constitution that taken together imply a right to privacy.[111] To fall within these "zones of privacy," an activity must be one in which an individual has a reasonable expectation of privacy against unwarranted government interference or intrusion,[112] or include matters that concern the most intimate aspects of human affairs.[113] No invasion of the right of privacy occurs however when one's activities are exposed to public view.[114]

The first Texas case to recognize the right to privacy as a distinct tort is *Billings v. Atkinson* in 1973.[115] In *Billings*, a jury awarded damages to a customer named Mrs. Lloyd Billings after several days of hearing "popping noises" it was learned that a telephone repairman for Southwestern Bell Telephone Company named Norman Atkinson, attached a wiretap device to Mrs. Billing's home phone line. The device transmitted her conversations over a standard FM radio. Atkinson was fired after Billings reported him to the telephone company, and a trial court jury found that Mr. Atkinson intentionally violated Mrs. Billings's right to privacy, which caused her to suffer mental anguish.[116] The Court of Civil Appeals (as the court of appeals was then called) reversed, holding that no common law right to privacy existed under Texas law.[117] At the time of *Billings*, the law of the state did not recognized a cause of action for breach of privacy, although a number of interests related to privacy were afforded protection under the doctrines of libel and slander, wrongful search and seizure, eavesdropping and other invasions into the private affairs of individuals.[118]

In *Billings*, the Texas Supreme Court reversed the appeals court and recognized that a right to privacy is distinctive in itself, and not incidental to some other right or tort that extends to wiretapping.[119] Writing for the majority, Justice Gray Denton[120] pointed out that prior to the 1890s the courts had not expressly granted relief for an injury resulting directly from the "invasion of privacy." A right to be let alone had been recognized as emanating from the tort of defamation, the invasion of a property right, or a person's breach of another's confidence.[121] The term "right of privacy," Justice Denton continued, was not even introduced into the legal lexicon until the 1890 publication of Samuel D. Warren and Louis D. Brandeis's famous *Harvard Law Review* article "The Right to Privacy."[122] It was there that the authors concluded that a distinct common law right to privacy, existing independently of the common law rights of property, contracts, protection of one's reputation and physical integrity.[123]

Returning to the telephone repairman's wiretapping of Mrs. Billings's telephone, Justice Denton further explained that eavesdropping was an offense at common law in the nineteenth century, defined as those persons who "listen under walls or windows or eaves of houses to harken after the disclosure and thereupon proclaim slanderous and mischievous tales."[124] So it is that for these and other historical and legal precedents outlined in *Billings* the court adopted the rule that "an unwarranted invasion of the right to privacy constitutes a legal injury for which a remedy will be granted."[125]

In 1976, in *Industrial Foundation of the South v. Texas Industrial Accident Board*, a dispute arising under the Texas Opens Record Act,[126] the Texas Supreme Court adopted a second type of privacy tort—the right to "freedom from public disclosure of embarrassing private facts."[127] The private-facts privacy case originated when a private nonprofit foundation requested the State of Texas' Industrial Accident Board to furnish personal information of all workers who filed claims for workmen's compensation.[128] The Board argued that such information is protected by the right to privacy.[129] Several claimants for employment compensation had arrest records and the Foundation sued to enjoin the release of these records.[130] However, the Texas Supreme Court ruled that the Board could not withhold information. Justice Ross E. Doughty[131] wrote:

> The State's right to make available for public inspection information pertaining to an individual does not conflict with the individual's constitutional right of privacy unless the State's action restricts his freedom in a sphere recognized to be within a zone of privacy protected by the Constitution.[132]

The Court found that no privacy interests were violated because the records dealt with public arrests and not personal information protected by the right to privacy, such as the nature of injuries or matters of marriage, procreation, or association. Nevertheless, in *Industrial Foundation*, the court did expressly recognize the right to be free from public disclosure of embarrassing private facts.[133] Doughty continued:

> We must decide. Therefore, whether any of the information requested by the Foundation is "private" within the meaning of the tort law, and whether the Board's action in making the information available to the public would constitute a wrongful "publicizing" of such information and thus an invasion of a claimant's right to privacy.[134]

According to *Industrial Foundation*, in order to recover under public disclosure right to privacy, a person must prove that the information contains intimate and embarrassing facts about a person's private affairs and that its publication to the public at large would be objectionable to a person or ordinary sensibilities. Invasion of privacy protected by public disclosure doctrine also requires the injured party to show that publicity be given to the individual's private affairs. The definition of publicity requires the communication of the private information to more than small group of persons—that is, to the public at large. Finally, the information that is publicized is not of legitimate concern to the public.

The most influential Texas privacy case is *Texas State Employees Union (TSEU) v. Texas Department of Mental Health & Mental Retardation*,[135] in which the Texas Supreme Court ruled in 1987 that the right to privacy contained in the Texas constitution offered broader protections than the right to privacy under the US Constitution. The Employee's Union challenged the Department's polygraph policy that required employees to submit to a polygraph test during any investigation of suspected patient abuse, theft, or other criminal activity that posed a threat to the health or safety of patients or employees.[136] The Texas Supreme Court held that although the Texas constitution does not contain an express guarantee of a right to privacy, the state's constitution *does* contain the following five provisions from which the right to privacy is derived:[137]

1. Section 19 of the Texas Bill of Rights protects against arbitrary deprivation of life and liberty.[138]
2. Section 8 provides the freedom to speak, write, or publish.[139]

3. Section 10 protects a person's privilege against self-incrimination.[140]
4. Sections 9 and 25 guarantee the right to be free from intrusions into the sanctity of the home and person against intrusion.[141]
5. Section 6 protects an individual's right to freedom of conscience and religion.[142]

Writing for the court, Chief Justice John Hill,[143] who had a solid record as a civil libertarian, argued that a right of individual privacy is implicit among those provisions—that also parallel those found in the US Constitution—and protects personal privacy from unreasonable intrusion. This right to privacy "should yield only when the government can demonstrate that an intrusion is reasonably warranted for the achievement of a compelling government objective that can be achieved by no less intrusive, more reasonable means."[144] Does the polygraph policy achieve a compelling governmental objective? Hill concluded that the Department is entitled to require employees to answer questions that are related to their job duties; however, the use of lie detectors constitutes an unnecessary intrusion that violates the employee's right to privacy. He wrote that "when the state acts as an employer, it may not without substantial justification condition employment on the relinquishment of constitutional rights."[145]

Tort Law: Negligence and Infliction of Mental Distress

While on the Third Court of Appeals Gammage wrote the majority opinions in two important negligence cases and in one infliction of mental distress case that are representative of his views on the legal rights of individuals to recover damages after being physically or emotionally harmed. While the importance of these legal doctrines may seem to pale in significance compared to the right to privacy and due process rights of those accused of crimes, decisions in this area of law are far more numerous than those in constitutional law, and are often the only means by which ordinary Texans have to assert their rights against negligent, careless or vindictive individuals and corporations.

In short, in a negligence case in Texas, the injured party must prove by a preponderance of evidence that the defendant, typically the person or persons responsible for the harm, had a duty to act or not act in a certain way and that the defendant was responsible for a breach of that duty. The plaintiff must further prove that the injury was in fact caused by the breach of duty and that a reasonable person would find it obvious that the behavior that constituted the breach of duty that their action or inaction might cause harm. Finally, the plaintiff must prove that he or she suffered damages—real physical, emotional, reputational harm. Texas is a state that uses a standard called "modified comparative fault," which apportions or distributes fault when making a determination of the amount of monetary damages awarded to the injured person. For example, suppose a person is injured while walking her dog next to a residential construction site near her home. She steps in a hole and breaks her leg. During the trial it is revealed that while crossing the construction site she was updating her music playlist on her smartphone or she was focused on her dog. A court might find that she was 30 percent at fault and the home builder was 70 percent at fault. In negligence cases the plaintiff must show a preponderance of the evidence in order to prevail. This is beyond a "mere scintilla" of evidence in order to conclude that the defendant is responsible for the harm. In Texas, negligence and proximate cause cannot be established by mere conjecture, guess, or speculation.[146]

In 1984 in *Figure World v. Farley*,[147] Lois Farley brought an action against a health club in San Antonio, alleging that one of the club staff caused her to fall off a treadmill and break her arm. Anyone who belongs to a gym or fitness club, may have read the fine print disclaimers that attempt to immunize the owners from liability in the event that a member is injured. If the machines or facilities are used improperly by the member, then it might be plausibly argued that the fault rests with the member. At what point does the action or inaction of the club lead to liability of the club?

In 1981, Ms. Farley was excited to become a member of Figure World, a chain of women's fitness clubs. She was given a thorough orientation on the use of the equipment and facilities. One day at the club while running on a treadmill she was shocked by a Figure World employee who shouted "suck in that stomach!" to Farley as she was running on the machine. Distracted by the insult, she fell off the machine and broke her arm. It was obvious to any reasonable person, but not to Figure World, that shouting at a customer would be unprofessional if not bizarre behavior. A jury found that there was sufficient evidence to establish that the club employee's shouting constituted negligence—a breach of duty to Farley—and was the proximate cause of the Farley's injuries. As it was explained to the jury, negligence is the failure to act with the level of care that someone of ordinary prudence would exercise under similar circumstances.

Did Figure World owe Farley a legal duty of care and if so did the company's conduct lack reasonable care and breach that duty? Could it have been reasonably foreseen that the employee's conduct would result in harm to Farley? Was there proof that the employee's action was a proximate cause of her injury? Of course, the employee did not push Farley off the treadmill as in a cause and effect scenario but proximately caused her to fall. This doctrine holds that the conduct proximately caused the injury when it can be shown that the conduct is more likely than not related to the injury. So, it is not cause and effect as is commonly thought in personal injury cases but proximate cause.

The jury found for Farley. Figure World appealed the judgment, arguing that they owed Farley no duty and it was questionable as to whether someone joking with her proximately caused her to fall. If an employee did shout at her, which they would not concede, then Farley did not lose her balance and fall because of the employee's shouting but because she "sucked in her stomach" while running. The Third Court of Appeals unanimously affirmed the trial court's judgment, with Gammage writing that Farley succeeded in establishing a breach of a duty owed her by Figure World. The important rule that Gammage promulgated in *Farley*, is that in ordinary negligence cases, the existence of a legal duty to the injured person is established by proof of the standard of care appropriate under the circumstances. Any reasonably prudent person would understand the possibility of harm occurring if you shouted an insult at someone who was running on a treadmill. The fact that the evidence showed that a Figure World employee did shout at Farley established a legal duty to Farley and a breach of that duty. Thus, the employee's shouting was a proximate cause of Farley's injury.[148]

Gammage concluded that there was also clear evidence to show the "foreseeability element of proximate cause" Proximate cause often is a highly subjective determination by the jury based on the circumstances surrounding the event that led to an injury. It is a fact that conservative judges tend to be highly skeptical of juries determining proximate cause, while liberal judges are more open to such jury verdicts. While the standards used in negligence cases seem straightforward, tort law is often just as affected by judicial philosophy or politics as any other area of law. Changes in the composition of the courts and legislature make it easier or more difficult for injured parties to seek relief. However, in *Farley*, even in light of the subjectivity of the determination, Gammage believed that the jury should be allowed broad discretion in weighing the evidence and testimony and determining whether proximate cause exists.

In some instances of negligence, the cause of harm is easier for the defendant to prove. Suppose that after an exhilarating run on the treadmill Ms. Farley decided to take a swim. On her way to the club pool she tripped over water hose used to fill the pool and broke her arm. There was no warning sign alerting club members that there was a hose near the pool, and club workers simply left the hose on the floor and walked away. In this instance it is much more clear that that the action of club employees was a proximate cause of her injury. Suppose further that the club was not privately owned by owned and operated by one of the state's universities. In this instance, not only would the plaintiff need to prove the elements of negligence, she would need to seek a waiver of sovereign immunity under the Texas Tort Claim Act (Act)[149] to bring a lawsuit against the state.

Sovereign immunity is the doctrine that all government entities are presumed to have immunity from lawsuits. In Texas, the only way to sue the government is to seek a waiver of sovereign immunity under the law. Under the Texas Tort Claims Act, immunity is waived in three situations: when a person is injured as a result of the use of government vehicles, when there are defects in premises used or owned by the government, and when "personal injury and death so caused by a condition or use of tangible personal or real property if the government unit would, were it a private person, be liable to the claimant according to Texas law.

Gammage addressed the issue of sovereign immunity in 1983 in *Rawlings v. Angelo State University.*[150] Patricia Rawlings, a student attending Angelo state tripped and fell over a water hose placed across a sidewalk on campus. She sustained serious injuries and sued the state arguing that the university's negligence was a proximate cause of the accident. The trial court dismissed the student's lawsuit and the Third Court of Appeals reversed and remanded the case for trial. Gammage argued that if the facts are true then the university would be liable for negligence under the Act just as a private person would be under Texas law. He argued that under Texas law in general, when a path across private property is used by the public, if a rope, wire or chain is placed across it, then the owner or other person has the duty of giving notice or warning to persons using the path. This rule extends both to private property owners, as well as those who operate the university. Also, under law the occupier of property owes a duty to maintain the premises in a reasonably safe condition. Therefore, there is an implied warranty to all who cross the property that reasonable care has been exercised for their safety. Gammage wrote:

> The unequivocal language of the [Tort Claims] Act makes it clear that the use of property in a negligent manner or method which causes injuries falls within the Act's waiver of immunity, if the facts show that such use of property by a "private person . . . would [make him] liable to the claimant in according with the law of this state."[151]

A tragic 1985 case involving a tort doctrine called the "bystander" negligence doctrine, coupled with the theory of sovereign immunity, is *City of Austin v. Davis.*[152] After his son Kenny Davis suffered severe brain damage from head injuries resulting from a motor vehicle accident, Richard Davis, visited Kenny every day during his long hospitalization at a city-owned hospital. During his hospitalization, Kenny was either medicated or restrained so that he would not injure himself or others. On the day that Kenny died, however, hospital staff did neither, and Kenny wandered away. He climbed to the top of an airshaft, entered the airshaft, and fell to his death. When his father appeared for his daily visit, neither he nor hospital staff could find Kenny. Ultimately, his father and a security guard discovered Kenny's body at the bottom of a ten-story air shaft at the hospital.

Several of Kenny's family members settled with the City of Austin for wrongful death, but his father brought legal action against the hospital for negligent infliction of mental distress and physical harm under the "bystander doctrine" of negligence.[153] According to this doctrine, a bystander who sees the result of a physical injury or shocking event caused by negligence, has the right to recover for emotional injuries that are proximately caused by the witnessing of the injury negligently inflicted on another person. Of course, there are limits on legal claims brought by bystanders. Typically, it is required that the bystander must be closely related to the injured person to recover damages. In 1978 the courts recognized the right of a bystander, who sees ("contemporaneously perceives") a shocking event, to recover damages.[154]

The trial court found for the father and city appealed. The city argued that under the bystander doctrine, in order to recover, Davis needed to be present at the very moment his son fell to his death. The hospital was not negligent because it could not have reasonably foreseen Kenny Davis climbing into the air shaft and falling to his death.

Lawyers for the city also attempted to cast doubt on whether a person could even recover under the negligent infliction of emotional distress doctrine. The Third Court of Appeals rejected the city's argument and affirmed the judgment of the trial court. According to the majority, in order to recover under the bystander doctrine, Davis need only prove that (1) he was in close proximity to the incident and (2) his injuries were proximately caused by his "contemporaneous perception" of the incident. Davis was not present at the very moment that his son fell; the father did not need to be at the foot of the airshaft at the moment Kenny plummeted to his death. He did not need to be told that his son's body was found there. He and a security guard found the body. This fact satisfied the bystander doctrine. Gammage wrote:

> The requirement of a contemporaneous perception of the incident giving rise to the injuries has been liberally construed. In *Landreth* it was held that actual observance of the incident was unnecessary, if there was some perception of the incident other than learning of it from others after it happened.[155]
>
> The City's argument essentially rests on the premise that Davis should be denied recovery because he was not at the foot of the airshaft at the moment his son fell. We decline to so hold . . . Davis was intensely involved in the search and subsequent discovery of his son. He did not learn of the incident from others, but found his son's body at the bottom of the airshaft.[156]

Lawyers for the city attempted to cast doubt on the existence of the tort of negligent infliction of emotional distress in Texas, but Gammage argued that the Texas courts have recognized the doctrine since the nineteenth century.[157] However, at the time of *City of Austin v. Davis* in 1985, the existence of this doctrine was not a settled matter of law in the state. Indeed, as discussed in this chapter, and in the next, in 1993, a majority of the Texas Supreme Court in *Boyles v. Kerr* refused to recognize the existence of this tort.

Tort Law and the Rights of Women: The Sexual Bondage Case

Twyman v. Twyman[158] was a highly publicized case involving a pattern of coerced sexual bondage and alleged "deviate sexual acts" in which a wife sought to recover damages against her estranged husband for negligent infliction of emotional distress. The case originated when Sheila Twyman alleged that her husband William introduced bondage activities soon after they were married and "intentionally and cruelly" attempted to engage her in "deviate sexual acts." She pleaded with him that she could not emotionally tolerate such activities because she had been forcibly raped at knife-point before their marriage. He persisted and even confessed that he was engaging in these activities with other women while out of town and that he visited sex parlors. At one point their ten-year-old son had discovered magazines depicting sexual bondage that William had hidden away in the house. William repeatedly told Shelia that there was something wrong with her for not engaging in bondage. She saw three different psychologists. Under pressure from her husband and at the advice of one of her therapists she attempted to resume bondage activities. Their last encounter was so rough that it caused her to bleed. She feared not only for her emotional health but physical safety. At that point, after sixteen years of marriage (and ten years of coerced sex acts by her husband), she sued for divorce and for negligent infliction of mental distress.[159] The legal arguments and doctrines at issue in *Twyman* pale in comparison to the pain and anguish that Sheila Twyman suffered but the final outcome would have a significant impact on the ability of women in abusive relationships and marriages to seek protection from the courts.

The trial court granted the divorce, gave Shelia custody of her children, ordered that William pay child support, and awarded her $15,000 plus interest for her claim of negligent infliction of emotional distress. Gammage heard the case in 1985, while it was on appeal to the Third Court of Appeals. William's lawyers stated that there was insufficient evidence to prove negligent infliction of mental distress—in fact, he argued, no such tort even existed in Texas—and that, furthermore, inter-spousal tort immunity prevented Sheila's recovery of damages.

The Third Court of Appeals upheld the trial court's judgment. Writing for the majority, Gammage argued, as he had in *City of Austin v. Davis* in 1985, that the doctrine of negligent infliction of emotional distress did exist in Texas. In order to recover under this tort, a complainant must show "*the tortfeasor acted knowingly or with conscious indifference*, causing a relatively high degree of mental pain and distress, such as a mental sensation of pain resulting from such painful emotions as grief, severe disappointment, indignation, wounded pride, shame, despair, or public humiliation."[160] What may seem like legal hair splitting, the recognition negligent infliction of emotional distress (versus intentional), made it easier for Sheila to prove that William's actions caused her harm. At that time of the *Twyman* case the answer to the question of whether a tort claim for either intentional or negligent infliction of emotional distress could be brought in a Texas court was uncertain. Another question was whether the doctrine of inter-spousal immunity precluded the wife from bringing a tort claim against the husband in a divorce proceeding. In 1977 the Texas Supreme Court had abolished the doctrine of inter-spousal immunity in intentional tort actions[161] and in 1987 abolished inter-spousal immunity in any lawsuit including negligence or even assault or battery occurring in a marriage.[162]

Gammage wrote that the husband's actions did not involve one act but a continuing course of conduct which over a period of years caused the wife's injury. So the cumulative effect of the conduct over time was actionable and gave rise to the injury. He pointed out that an injury that occurs as a result of conduct over time is referred to as the tolling concept of continuing tort.[163] Texas courts first recognized the tolling concept of continuing tort in the nineteenth century in cases involving repeated trespass on land and in sustained instances of nuisance.[164] Gammage wrote:

> Viewing the evidence as a whole, we cannot say the evidence is insufficient to support the trial court's finding or mental anguish . . . The record demonstrates that although William knew of Sheila's previous violent rape and her inability to emotionally 'handle' participation in sexual bondage activities, he repeatedly conditioned the continuance of their marriage upon such activities, participated in sexual bondage activities with extramarital partners, [and] cruelly described such partners and experiences to her . . . We conclude this evidence, if believed, is sufficient to sustain the trial court's finding of mental anguish.[165]

Sadly for Sheila Twyman, two years later the Texas Supreme Court reversed Gammage. A divided Court refused to recognize the tort of negligent infliction of emotional distress. The Court then remanded the case for a new trial under the tort of *intentional* infliction of mental distress as a possible remedy. Justice Gammage, now serving on the Texas Supreme Court, recused himself from the case because he had heard the case while on the court of appeals.[166] Writing the high court's majority opinion in *Twyman v. Twyman* in 1993,[167] Justice John Cornyn[168] pointed out that while the *Twyman* case was pending appeal from the lower court, the Supreme Court ruled in *Boyles v. Kerr*[169] (the infamous sex tape case) that the tort of negligent infliction of emotional distress is *not* recognized by law in Texas.[170] However, in *Twyman* the court decided to expressly recognize that the tort of *intentional* infliction of emotional distress *does* exist in Texas jurisprudence. Cornyn wrote:

> As distinguished from the tort of negligent infliction of emotional distress, we believe that the rigorous legal standards of the Restatement [of Torts] formulation of intentional infliction of emotional distress help to assure a meaningful delineation between inadvertence and intentionally or recklessly outrageous misconduct. The requirements of intent, extreme and outrageous conduct, and severe emotional distress before liability can be established will we think, strike a proper balance between diverse interests in a free society.[171]

Chief Justice Phillips[172] concurred with the majority's recognition of the tort of intentional infliction of emotional distress, pointing out that the tort is recognized in almost every other state but did not believe that the tort should extend to actions between spouses or former spouses for conduct occurring during their marriage.[173]

Justice Nathan Hecht dissented from the majority's decision to adopt the tort of intentional infliction. He believed that "intentional or reckless infliction of emotional distress is too broad a rubric to describe actionable conduct, as this case illustrates." He feared that this new tort would be asserted not only in divorce litigation but in disputes involving employers and employees, patients and physicians, clients and lawyers, and others.[174]

The Constitutionality of Literacy Tests for Teachers

In 1986 the Third Court of Appeals ruled on the constitutionality of a newly required mandatory skills and literacy exam for public school teachers.[175] The new law emerged from the professional accountability movement that was born in the 1980s and continues to impact nearly every profession today. A minor requirement by contemporary standards, it represents a trend whereby legislatures enacted policies extending or expanding regulations over many professions that were historically subject to minimal regulations or self-regulated by the professions themselves. Physicians, university and college professors, school teachers and others began to chafe at the idea that the government knew what was best for patients, clients, and students. Fiscally conservative lawmakers demanded greater accountability, especially in the professions that were funded by tax dollars, like teaching or government service. Of course, all professions were impacted by a growing number of federal regulations as well.

The new Texas law thrust the Third Court of Appeals into a noisy political skirmish between legislators and teachers' unions and organizations. House Bill 72[176] was a comprehensive education law raising teacher's salaries, adopting the "no pass, no play" for athletes, and mandating skills testing for all teachers in the public schools. At the time approximately forty states had similar teacher literacy laws. The intent was part of an effort to modernize Texas schools. The test, known as the Texas Examination of Current Administrators and Teachers required all teachers—regardless of years of service or degrees—who were already certified by the state to take an exam measuring basic literacy ("reading and writing") and subject matter skills.[177] The examination was formulated by the State Board of Education. Test takers had access to prep classes and remedial assistance and were permitted to take the test twice.[178] The law seems reasonable by today's standards but was then perceived to be a radical shift in policy that threatened traditional employment rights for public school teachers. One of the rally cries of groups opposed to the law was, "First they came for the teachers . . . "[179]

The Texas State Teachers Association (TSTA) sued the State of Texas arguing that the requirement was unnecessary, damaging to a teacher's reputation, and unconstitutional. Specifically, TSTA's major argument was that the testing requirement unconstitutionally violated to clauses in the Texas constitution that protect the obligation of contracts and prohibit retroactive laws. Article I, section 16 of the Texas constitution prohibits "retroactive laws" and laws that impair the obligation of contracts. A teacher's certification was considered a statutory contract and vested right that the legislature could not impair through the testing scheme. At the time a teaching certificate contained the language "valid for life, unless canceled by lawful authority." If a certification is not a contract *per se*, then it is a vested property right that cannot be retroactively infringed.[180] On the one hand, TSTA acknowledged that under certain important circumstances the legislature could restrict this right but no legitimate circumstances existed in this instance. On the other hand, the state argued that the certificate is not a contract or right but a professional license subject to the state's broad police powers to grant licenses and regulate professional or business activities.

A state district court declared the law constitutional. Argument before the court of appeals judges focused mainly on these constitutional questions but also on practical matters such as what would be the ramifications of teachers losing jobs before the beginning of the new school year. In *Texas State Teacher's Association v. State* in 1986, end, the Third Court of Appeals rejected the teacher's constitutional claims and upheld the policy. Gammage joined the unanimous opinion. The court argued that the constitutional rules against impairing contracts and retroactive laws are not absolute and must be balanced with the state's responsibility to safeguard public safety and welfare. Writing for the court, Chief Justice Shannon stated that teacher testing is a valid exercise of the police power, which "is broad and comprehensive. Police power is not static and unchanging. As the affairs of the people and government change and progress, so the police power changes and progresses to meet the needs."[181]

According to state and national news coverage of the case, the message that was sent by the court was that the state has the power to fire illiterate teachers even if those teachers are experienced, effective and well-respected.[182] Fears of massive teacher layoffs were unfounded. The failure rate on the first round of testing of 202,000 teachers and administrators was only slightly more than 3 percent, or 6,500 teachers.[183] Yet, teachers continued to rally and protest at the capitol while the appeal was pending before the Supreme Court. Finally in February 1987 the Texas Supreme Court unanimously ruled that the state can constitutionally require teacher literacy tests, stating that "competency testing bears a rational relation to the legitimate state objective of maintaining competent teachers in the public schools." The supreme court also ruled that a certification is not a contract but a license subject to renewal or restrictions. By 1987, it was reported that 99 percent of the state's teachers passed the reading and writing exam.[184]

Free Speech and Due Process Rights of Government Officials

A private citizen enjoys broad freedom of expression,[185] but when he or she is affiliated with a public institution—such as a government agency or public university—degrees of speech protection are lost.[186] Many employers promulgate policies that allow for disciplinary action or termination of employees who criticize supervisors. Similar policies are used to punish employees who, when speaking in their official capacity, make a highly controversial statement. While on the Third Court of Appeals, Gammage heard a case involving the issue of whether a government official holding office in one government body could be terminated for exercising his right to advocate his private interests before another governing entity.[187]

In August 1984, Patrick Price was removed from an appointed position on the city planning commission because on two occasions he represented himself before the city zoning board. Although he was representing himself before the board as a private homeowner, his actions were still considered to be a violation of city ethics rules. The city's code of ethics prohibits all city officials from appearing before any commission or board of the city even when representing themselves as private citizens. As a private citizen, Price sought two variances from city zoning ordinances, one so that he could build a carport at his home, second, so that he could expand parking at his wife's dress shop. These actions were considered conflict of interest ethics violations.

Because of the ethics violations, Price was removed from his seat on the city planning commission. He then sued the city of San Marcos, Texas, and several public officials alleging that his removal deprived of him of property and liberty without due process under the Fourteenth Amendment of the US Constitution, and Article 1, section 19 of the Texas constitution. He also alleged that the City's actions classified him in violation of the equal-protection clause of the Fourteenth Amendment by singling him out as a person who is not entitled to represent himself before the zoning board; this classification was not rationally related to a legitimate interest, he argued. The trial court dismissed the case and the Third Court of Appeals ruled for the city.

Writing for the majority in *Price v. City of San Marcos*,[188] Gammage argued that in Texas, an office holder's interest in his or her appointed position is not a property interest in the conventional sense of the term, but it is a recognizable interest for purposes of due process analysis.[189] Since the right to hold office is not a fundamental right, the loss of the position is not subject to heightened judicial scrutiny if it is violated. So the question that remained was whether the removal of Price from the commission due to his violation of the code of ethics was rationally related to a legitimate governmental interest. The city's interest of preventing the appearance of impropriety and corruption in local government justified the application of ethics ordinance to Price.[190] Price even admitted that he violated the ethics rules by appearing before the zoning board while he was a member of the planning commission. He was not denied procedural rights—he was informed that his removal would be discussed at a City Council meeting to which he could attend and that he would be given an opportunity to respond to allegations. He was, however, denied a trial-type hearing where the facts could be adjudicated since he had already admitted the ethical violations and because the decision to remove him from office was a legislative decision intended to advance public policy.[191]

Under law, "any party may appear in person" before a zoning board. Was Price removed from office merely for exercising his right as a citizen to appear before a representative body? Wouldn't the code of ethics conflict with that right? Gammage answered no. Price was not arbitrarily fired and deprived of liberty without due process of law. Nor did Price have a fundamental right to hold office. Gammage wrote:

> Price contends it was arbitrary and capricious to remove him for exercising . . . a statutory right. The effect of the City's decision, however, was not to deny Price his statutory right, but to prevent him from holding office at the same time he chose to exercise this particular right. The issue is whether the City may constitutionally burden Price's office with this restriction. We conclude it may. The City's action was not arbitrary and capricious and Price was not deprived of his office without procedural due process.[192]

Gammage also rejected Price's argument that he was illegally classified and therefore denied equal protection under the Fourteenth Amendment by the city. Price was not a member of a suspect class, such as race, and the city's classification of Price as a person who was not entitled to represent himself before the zoning commission because he was an officer holder was not an illegal classification. Again, the City's actions bore a rational relationship the legitimate objective of preventing the appearance of impropriety.

Addressing an important, but secondary question in the lawsuit was whether Price's freedom of expression was unconstitutionally curtailed. Gammage argued that Price was *not* stripped of his First Amendment rights by being denied the right to speak before the zoning board. Price's motivation to speak before the board was for personal financial reasons, and not as a citizen speaking out on a matter of public concern, such as the need for a better education system. Gammage cited *Pickering v. Board of Education*,[193] in which the US Supreme Court narrowly upheld the First Amendment right of a public school teacher who was fired because she criticized the local school board for spending more tax money on athletics than academics.[194] Gammage also cited *Connick v. Myers*, in which the court ruled that the First Amendment protects the speech of public employees in the workplace if that speech is of public concern but not if the employee criticizes office operations or somehow undermines an organization's mission.[195] However, the two cases seem to have little bearing on what Price attempted to do. He didn't criticize fellow board members or his higher-ups. Nor did he try to convince the zoning board that the approval of the development of a high rise building was detrimental to the public good. His speech was purely self-serving.[196]

School Funding in Texas: The Beginning of the *Edgewood v. Kirby* Saga

The *Edgewood v. Kirby* public school funding lawsuit was actually a series of six rulings between the years 1989 and 1995 that were intended to force the Texas legislature to create a more equitable system of education funding. *Edgewood* appears in nearly every book written on Texas history or politics and was very aptly called a "saga," by Albert Kauffmman, who was one of the lawyers involved in the litigation.[197] The case involved hundreds of litigants and shifting alignments of judges and justices, each positing a distinct interpretation of the provisions of the Texas constitution that mandate a public education system. However, *Edgewood* is much more than a case dealing with the arcane issue of public school funding formulae; it must also be understood as a struggle for equal treatment under the law for Latino school children.

Edgewood has its deepest roots in the historic *Brown v. Board of Education* case, in which the US Supreme Court ruled that the doctrine of "separate but equal" has no place in public education: segregation in public education deprived African Americans of the equal protection of the laws guaranteed by the Fourteenth Amendment.[198] *Brown* is unquestionably one of the most pivotal rulings in American history, but the phrase "separate educational facilities are inherently unequal" is merely a statement of principles; at the time it offered no precise remedy to the problem of school segregation.[199] School systems were then (and are today) localized and traditionally autonomous institutions influenced by the customs and culture of the surrounding community. Noncompliance to the *Brown* ruling in the Deep South was expected, and although the Court voted unanimously to overturn segregation in the public schools, it was quite divided over the proper means of implementation. Because the case involved class actions and had wide applicability to a variety of local school systems, formulating solutions to the problem of unequal educational opportunities would not be simple.[200]

At the time of *Brown*, Texas segregated black and white school children under the Public Free Schools Act of 1893. Following the court's ruling in *Brown*, some Texas schools in urban areas were gradually desegregated by the 1960s; for others change would not come until after the federal courts placed all Texas school districts under a desegregation order in the 1970s.[201] Federal district court judge William Wayne Justice ordered the annexation of all-black school districts into contiguous white districts in order to equalize educational opportunities. Texas remained under this infamous court order until Judge Justice's order was lifted in the mid-1980s.[202]

Mexican-American students were not subject to *de jure* segregation under the Public Free Schools Act—which applied to Negro or children of mixed-race Negro ancestry—but they experienced it *de facto* throughout Texas. The state maintained separate schools by allowing parents of Anglo students to attend "American" schools while Hispanic children were required to attend "Mexican" schools, segregated on the basis of alleged language barriers. With such segregation came unequal funding for Anglo and Hispanic schools. To challenge discriminatory treatment, the League of United Latin American Citizens (LULAC) was formed in 1928, but little progress was made until after the Second World War. In 1947, seven years before *Brown*, the US Court of Appeals for the Ninth Circuit ruled in *Mendez v. Westminster School District* that California's segregation of Anglo and Mexican public school students violated the equal protection clause of the Fourteenth Amendment.[203] Following the *Mendez* ruling the Attorney General of Texas, Price Daniel, declared in an opinion that the segregation of Anglo and Mexican children in public schools was no longer permissible under law. In 1948 a federal district court ruled in *Delgado v. Bastrop Independent School District* that the equal protection clause of the Fourteenth prohibited the segregation of students of Mexican (or of Latin American descent) and Anglo students. Even after *Mendez* and *Delgado*, LULAC and other advocacy organizations continued to file discrimination cases against school districts throughout the decades of the 1950s and 1960s.[204] In 1970 in *Cisneros v. Corpus Christi*

Independent School District a federal district court adopted the position of LULAC and the Mexican-American Legal Defense and Education Fund (MALDEF) that because Hispanics were not "other white"—as they had been previously classified under law—but a distinct ethnic group, they were therefore protected against discrimination in public schools under the *Brown* decision. The ruling resulted in a number of imposed legal remedies, including thousands of Mexican-American students being bused to different schools in the area order to implement the desegregation order. Busing as a remedy for illegal race-based segregation was upheld by the US Supreme Court in *Swann v. Charlotte-Mecklenburg Board of Education.*[205]

The public school finance litigation in the Texas state courts began in the late 1960s, when parents of children attending school in the Edgewood Independent School District in San Antonio believed that their children were being denied equal educational opportunities in violation of the Equal Protection Clause of the Fourteenth Amendment. The parents argued that if schools in a given district are funded largely on the basis of the taxable value residential property, then the schools in property-rich districts will have more money to spend on each student's education. In essence, they argued that there was a direct relationship between money and quality education. Edgewood ISD was a poor district comprised of 90 percent Hispanic students and 6 percent black students. Alamo Heights ISD was a wealthy district, with a student population that was 80 percent white. In 1971, the parents won a victory in *Rodriguez v. San Antonio Independent School District,*[206] when a federal district court ruled that the state's system of school funding constituted wealth discrimination, and required the state to show a "compelling state interest" to justify continuance of the funding scheme.[207] The court argued that wealth, like race, is a suspect classification subject to strict scrutiny; and that education is a fundamental right. The disparate amounts spent by the state per student violated the rights of the students in the poor school districts.

However, in *San Antonio Independent School District v. Rodriguez*, the US Supreme Court voted 5-4 to reverse the lower court's ruling, categorically refusing to recognize that education is a fundamental right that is necessary for citizens to exercise other fundamental rights, such as freedom of speech and the right to vote.[208] Further, the high court reasoned, the state's funding system did not disadvantage any suspect class, nor did it even discriminate against any "definable class" of people. Wealth, the justices held, is not a suspect class like race. Simply because the state's financing system disadvantaged those who happened to live in a comparatively poor school district, it cannot be plausibly argued that the poorer class is subject to discrimination under the equal protection under the equal protection clause.[209]

After *Rodriguez*, the Texas legislature did make adjustments in the manner in which public schools were funded, but litigation began anew in the state courts, this time arguing in *Kirby v. Edgewood Independent School District* that the state's system financing public schools was in violation of the Texas constitution. Gammage played a pivotal role in *Edgewood*, first in 1988 on the Third Court of Appeals and then in cases from 1991 to 1995 as a justice on the Texas Supreme Court. Most importantly here, it must be pointed out that his dissenting opinion in *Kirby v. Edgewood Independent School District* in 1988 was the very first time that a state appellate court judge in Texas argued that education was a fundamental right, and that the state's system of school funding was unconstitutional because it deprived students in poor school districts of equal educational opportunities.[210] Gammage's dissent not only had a significant impact on the *Edgewood* case, but it also stands out as an intellectually forceful call for equality and the most comprehensive and detailed explication of his equal protection jurisprudence. However, few Texans had heard of the lawsuit in 1988, but *Edgewood* would ultimately become one of the most well-known and fiercely debated court cases in Texas history. The *Dallas Morning News* noted in April 1988 that "this high stakes legal battle," begun when a trial court ruled that the state's funding method was unconstitutional, was now in the hands of Justices Shannon, Gammage, and Aboussie on the Third Court of Appeals in Austin.[211]

Kirby v. Edgewood Independent School District originated when the MALDEF filed a lawsuit in 1984 against William Kirby, the Commissioner of Education, representing the Edgewood Independent School District. Edgewood ISD, one of the poorest school districts in the state. Edgewood ISD had $38,854 in property wealth per student, whereas Alamo Heights, in the same county, had $570,109 property wealth per student. Statewide, the wealthiest school district had over $14 million of property wealth per student and the poorest district had $20,000 of property wealth per student. Edgewood ISD was ultimately joined by sixty-seven other districts in the suit.[212] The lawsuit alleged that the State of Texas' public school funding system violated the principle of equal protection by discriminating against students in low-income school districts.[213]

The state and the school districts shared the cost of basic operations, but the cost of facilities and personnel was funded largely by the independent districts utilizing property taxes.[214] Based on this formula, school districts in property-rich areas were able to provide students with better academic and athletic facilities, more up to date curriculum, and better-trained teachers.[215] The lawsuit alleged that there was a heavy concentration of families living below the poverty line in the poorer districts.[216] Census data from 1980 showed that while "twenty-one percent of the State's population was Mexican-American, eighty-four percent of the population in the poorest [school] districts was Mexican-American."[217] The state did have a "Foundation" program that was intended to equalize funding across all districts so that poor districts received substantially more state funding than wealthy districts, but the property-rich districts still spent more money per student.[218]

After a bench trial in Austin, state district court Judge Harley Clark[219] ruled that the existing school finance system in Texas was unconstitutional.[220] He reasoned that the existing funding system violated the Texas constitution's requirement for an efficient educational system; and wealth is a suspect classification in terms of school-finance policy.[221] Thus, strict scrutiny had to be applied to the state's policy because it allowed for major disparities in per-student spending, disproportionally harming lower-income students. Judge Clark further ruled "that the Texas [c]onstitution demands 'fiscal neutrality' in public school funding," meaning that "the level of expenditures per [student] in any district may not vary according to the property wealth of that district."[222] The state's reliance on local property taxes to fund education created an inherently unequal system because huge differences in property values across school districts.[223] Judge Clark ordered the legislature to formulate a new school-financing plan by September 1989.[224]

Austin Judge Harley Clark is an interesting and important actor in the saga. Appointed in 1977 by Governor Dolph Briscoe, and then reelected several times until his return to a private law practice in 1989, Clark may be best known to Austinites as the man who invented the University of Texas "hook-'em" hand sign, but his ruling in *Edgewood* was nothing short of historic. Even before this controversial case proceeded on appeal, proponents and opponents were battling it out in the court of public opinion. Republican governor Bill Clements and legislative leaders publicly stated that this was a legislative matter and hoped to avoid a ruling declaring education a fundamental right. Clements even audaciously proposed a constitutional amendment that would strip the courts of jurisdiction to hear lawsuits dealing with public school funding. Wealthy school districts were cautiously optimistic that Judge Clark's ruling would be overturned.[225] But Judge Clark ignored the political storm and ruled that that the existing school finance system in Texas was unconstitutional.

The Third Court of Appeals at Austin reversed Judge Clark's ruling by a 2-1 vote.[226] Writing for the majority, Chief Justice Shannon argued that education was *not* a fundamental right, wealth was *not* a suspect classification, and that the state's system of school financing did *not* violate equal-protection rights, the due course of law, or the efficient school system provisions of the Texas constitution.[227] Furthermore, the majority argued that the court of appeals believed—given the complexity of a vast school system, which educated three million students—that the question of educational efficacy was fundamentally a political question that should not be subject to judicial review.[228] Shannon rejected the trial court's application of a Fourteenth Amendment equal protection analysis, on the grounds that in the 1973 case

San Antonio Independent School District v. Rodriguez, the US Supreme Court refused to recognize education as a fundamental right. He also rejected the "nexus" argument that education is necessary for citizens to exercise fundamental rights, such as freedom of speech and the right to vote.[229] Several years before, in *Spring Branch Independent School District v. Stamos*,[230] the Texas Supreme Court had rejected the idea that education is a fundamental right.

In a long dissenting opinion, Gammage argued in support of the trial court's ruling, and articulated his position on equal protection as it applies to school funding and educational opportunity. He began by noting that "[t]he Texas constitution imposes on the State the burden of . . . providing for public education."[231] As an alternative to a centralized system of school funding, the legislature created school districts and allowed for local property taxation for the support of schools within those districts.[232] He argued:

> Nowhere, however, does the Constitution permit the creation or adoption of any school system other than one which is efficient and which comports with the requirements of equal rights under the law.[233] The adequacy of a child's education in a competitive, free-market economic and political system such as ours is relative; it is a function of what *other* children are getting. A program of instruction available to one child cannot truly be deemed adequate or efficient if other children are afforded a better educational program and are thereby consistently advantaged in the lifelong competition for money, status, and political influence. [234]

He noted that four provisions of the Texas constitution provide a solid foundation for equality in education. First, Article I, section 3 provides that "all free men," in forming "a social compact, have equal rights, and no man" or group "is entitled to exclusive separate public emoluments, or privileges."[235] Second, Article I, section 3(a) requires that "equality under the law shall not be denied or abridged because of sex, race, color, creed, or national origin."[236] Third, focusing on public education, Article VII, section 1 comments that "a general diffusion of knowledge being essential to the preservation of the liberties and rights of the people," makes it a "duty of the Legislature . . . to establish and make suitable provisions for the support and maintenance of an efficient system of public free schools."[237] Finally, and specifically with respect to funding, Article VII, section 3(a) provides that tax revenue "shall be set apart annually for the benefit of the public free schools."[238]

Gammage cited *Spring Branch Independent School District v. Stamos*, in which the Texas Supreme Court held that the state legislature is free to determine the "'methods, restrictions, and regulations' necessary to administer public schools, 'so long as that determination is not so arbitrary as to violate the constitutional rights of Texas' citizens.'"[239] He also relied on *Stout v. Grand Prairie Independent School District*, where the Texas Fifth Court of Appeals ruled that education was a fundamental right guaranteed under Article VII of the Texas constitution.[240]

While the majority correctly understood that *San Antonio Independent School District v. Rodriguez* held that education was not a fundamental right under the Fourteenth Amendment, Gammage pointed out what seems to be obvious: the majority failed to recognize—or chose to ignore—the fact that the *Rodriguez* case was relying on the US Constitution, which *does not* include a specific provision for education.[241] The claim in *Edgewood* relied on the Texas constitution, which expressly recognizes education as indispensable to the exercise of fundamental rights and liberties, and mandates that the legislature make "'suitable' provision for an 'efficient' education system."[242] Of course, education as a fundamental right is not enumerated in the Bill of Rights of either the federal or state constitutions. However, Gammage concluded that even though a fundamental right may not be enumerated or have a "specific textual [basis] in our State Constitution," does not mean it does not exist.[243] Texas courts have repeatedly protected implied fundamental interests such as the right to privacy,[244] the rights of a parent in a family setting,[245] and the right to pursue an occupation.[246] Certain unarticulated rights are implicit in enumerated guarantees and are necessary to the protection or enjoyment of rights that are explicitly guaranteed.[247] The majority conceded the existence of unarticulated fundamental rights, but argued that government has no obligation to provide the money necessary to exercise such rights or liberties.[248] This is a common notion advanced by many conservatives, who argue that may be a right to speak out or to have an abortion but that the government has no affirmative obligation to fund these rights.[249]

If government was required to fund the exercise of fundamental rights, it would need to do so equally, and in doing so, would be a drain on the taxpayer. Many taxpayers might object to funding education equally, especially where local school taxes in wealthy suburbs were siphoned-off to fund schools in poorer districts. However, Gammage pointed out what he saw to be another error made by the majority, the Texas constitution "explicitly and prominently" obligates the state government to provide for a "suitable" and "efficient" educational system in order "to preserve other liberties and rights of the people."[250] Public education, with a few exceptions, is compulsory. Children must attend school; therefore, the government is required to fund education in a suitable, efficient, and equal manner.[251] The US Supreme Court ruled, in *Plyler v. Doe*, that Texas' denial of access of free public schools to the children of illegal aliens violated the Equal Protection Clause of the Fourteenth Amendment.[252] While the nation's highest court did not rule that education was a fundamental right, neither did it dismiss education as "some governmental 'benefit' indistinguishable from other forms of social welfare legislation."[253] As US Supreme Court justice William J. Brennan once wrote:

> It is difficult to understand precisely what the State hopes to achieve by promoting the creation and perpetuation of a subclass of illiterates within our boundaries, surely adding to the problems and costs of unemployment, welfare, and crime.[254]
>
> If the State is to deny a discrete group of innocent children the free public education that it offers to other children residing within its borders, that denial must be justified by a showing that it furthers some substantial state interest.[255]

Since the state law at issue in *Plyler* severely disadvantaged the children of illegal aliens by denying them the right to an education, and because Texas could not prove that the regulation was needed to serve a "compelling state interest," the US Supreme Court struck down the law.[256] Gammage conceded the *Edgewood* majority's point that wealth had never been held to be a suspect classification for purposes of equal-rights analysis.[257] However, the particular set of "undisputed findings of fact made by the trial court" in *Edgewood* have never been before either the US Supreme Court or the Texas Supreme Court.[258] The trial court found that poor people are heavily concentrated in low-wealth school districts—the majority of which are districts not fully accredited because they do not meet basic minimum state standards.[259] Thus, poor residents in those districts "might well be a 'suspect classification.'"[260] Gammage reasoned: "The relative powerlessness of these people to alter their situation through political means indicates strongly that they should be considered a suspect class in the education context."[261] He concluded:

> The majority opinion implies, by its reasoning, that the Texas Constitution places no limit whatsoever on the power of the legislature to establish school district boundaries. Such reasoning dangerously erodes that most precious of political rights—the right to be treated with respect and equality by the government, the right to full and participating citizenship in the state.[262]

If the people were powerless, as Gammage pointed out, state officials were ebullient with the decision to overturn trial court Judge Harley Clark's radical decision. Texas education commissioner W. N. Kirby, the lawsuit defendant, said that "ruling correctly interprets the Texas Constitution and state laws and affirms the authority of the legislature." Governor Clements applauded the appeals court's ruling.[263]

However, less than one year after *Kirby v. Edgewood*, the Texas Supreme Court reversed the court of appeals in *Edgewood Independent School District v. Kirby* (*Edgewood I*) in 1990 and adopted the principles set out in Gammage's dissenting opinion in *Kirby* ruling.[264] Gammage's dissent not only had a significant impact on the *Edgewood* cases, but it also stands out as an intellectually forceful call for equality and the most comprehensive and detailed explication of his equal-protection jurisprudence.

In Edgewood I the unanimous Court relied mainly on the position that the school-financing system violated the Texas constitution's obligation to provide an efficient and free public education in Article VII, section 1, and noted the strong nexus between inefficiency and the denial of equal rights.[265] The funding system at issue provided for a limited and unbalanced diffusion of knowledge contrary to the intent of the framers of the Texas constitution.[266] Justice Oscar Mauzy[267] wrote:

> Property-poor districts are trapped in a cycle of poverty from which there is no opportunity to free themselves. Because of their inadequate tax base, they must tax at significantly higher rates in order to meet minimum requirements for accreditation; yet their education programs are typically inferior . . . The amount of money spent on a student's education has a real and meaningful impact on the educational opportunity offered that student.[268]

The majority also rejected the court of appeals' claim that this case was a nonjusticiable political question because the Texas constitution vests exclusive discretion in the legislature.[269] The constitutional mandate that the legislature provides for free public schooling, is accompanied by standards such as the requirement that schools must be efficient and suitable for the "essential purpose of a general diffusion of knowledge."[270] While the standards are imprecise, the court nevertheless has the interpretive power to use these terms as a measure of the legislature's actions.[271]

Politically and logistically troublesome, however, is that the court neither provided the state legislature with the specifics of the remedial legislation that it should enact nor ordered the legislature to raise taxes. The legislature was ordered to have a plan in place by the 1990–1991 school year to eliminate the "gross inequalities" and "vast disparities" among the districts.[272] These inequalities resulted from concentrations of resources in property-rich school districts that taxed at low rates, while property-poor school districts taxed at high rates but were still unable to generate the sufficient revenues to meet the minimum state-education standards.[273] School "districts must have substantially equal access to similar revenues per pupil at similar levels of tax effort."[274]

Following the Texas Supreme Court's 1989 *Edgewood I* ruling, the legislature met in six special sessions called by the governor. On June 7, 1990, the legislature passed Senate Bill 1—a new funding plan that would increase state support for public schools, and establish a benchmark whereby 95 percent of Texas' students would ultimately attend school in an equalized system; however, the bill did not authorize the state to use revenue from the wealthiest school districts to fund the proposed equalized system.[275] Judge Scott McCown, who replaced Judge Clark, ruled that the new plan was unconstitutional because it did not provide "substantially equal" access to public school funds, as ordered by the Court in its 1989 *Edgewood* I ruling.[276] The State of Texas appealed the district court's ruling and *Edgewood II* was on the docket to be heard by the Texas Supreme Court early during its 1991 term.[277]

In the November 1990 general election, one of the major issues raised was the status of the school finance litigation. The high court had heard arguments in the midst of the election in November 1990, and a quick decision was expected. However, two influential and progressive Democrats, C. L. Ray (1980–1990) and Franklin Spears[278] (1979–1990), in the majority in Edgewood I, announced their retirement. The *Austin America-Statesman* wrote that the case was now in "limbo," and that the swearing in of two new justices—Democrat Gammage and Republican John Cornyn—created uncertainty over the outcome of the case.[279] The new justices could either read the transcripts of the previous oral argument or ask that the case be reargued. Gammage had gone on record on the school funding issue since he wrote the long dissent in *Kirby* while on the court of appeals. It was more uncertain how Cornyn would vote. With Gammage and Cornyn poised to take their seats on the Texas Supreme Court, we will return to the discussion of the *Edgewood* saga in the next chapter.

1990 ELECTION TO THE SUPREME COURT

In 1988, Gammage decided to launch a campaign for a seat on the Texas Supreme Court in the 1990 general election. He knew from experience in legislative politics that any decision to make a run for a statewide office does not occur in the vacuum of space. All of the planets in the political system must be aligned just so before a candidate stands for election; a nod from the state party organization, support from members of the bench and bar, endorsements and money from a range influential professional and political organizations, and positive media coverage are all necessary. Of course, weak primary opponents are helpful as well.

The Texas constitution calls for the election of justices on the Texas Supreme Court for six-year terms of office with staggered elections, so that every two years an average of three of the nine justices are up for reelection.[280] If elected, Gammage would hear appeals only in civil cases, because Texas is one of only two states (the other is Oklahoma) that bifurcates its highest appellate courts into separate bodies: the Texas Supreme Court hears civil appeals and the Court of Criminal Appeals possesses jurisdiction over criminal appeals.

The mid- to late-1980s was one of the most politically tumultuous periods for the Texas judiciary since Reconstruction. As discussed in detail in chapter 4, Texas Supreme Court elections were no longer low-key events but were becoming exponentially more expensive and hyper-competitive. In addition, the election of Ronald Reagan to the presidency in 1980, along with the left-ward ideological drift of the Democratic Party, and the influx of newcomers into the sprawling suburbs in the state, produced down-ballot benefits for Texas Republicans for the first time in decades. But Gammage knew that he was considered to be a serious contender for the court at least four years prior to the 1990 election. For instance, speculating about his political fortunes as early as 1986, *The Dallas Morning News* called Gammage "the unannounced gorilla in the room from the trial lawyer's standpoint . . . who also is a former state legislator and one of the state's most politically astute judges."[281] According to court watchers in the media, it was correctly predicted that the 1986 election might weaken the pro-plaintiff orientation of the court and "bring new blood to the defense-oriented minority."[282] In other words, conservatives might win more seats on the Supreme Court. Four, rather than the usual three, seats would be up for grabs on the court in 1986 because of the appointment of conservative Democrat Raul Gonzales[283] in 1984 by Governor Mark White. After a gubernatorial appointment to fill a vacancy, the appointee must run in the next general election to stay on the bench. Gonzales, the first Hispanic to be appointed to the high court, was considered to be vulnerable to a Republican challenge because of his ethnicity and the possibility of straight-ticket Republican voting that had already shaken up Democratic officeholders in the 1984 election.

In 1985, Democrat Oscar Mauzy, then a state senator, announced his intention to run for a seat on the high court. Mauzy, a trial lawyer, was first elected to the Texas Senate in 1966. Mauzy's decision to run in 1988, put Gammage's decision on hold until 1990 because the two men were close friends and political allies. Had Mauzy not run, Gammage would have joined the court two years earlier. Gammage's decision in to run in 1990 was also influenced by tenacious news coverage of the ethical lapses of many judges and justices, as well as by academic studies showing historically low public confidence in the state's judicial system. In 1987, *Texas Monthly* published an influential investigative piece providing empirical evidence that the Texas Supreme Court was controlled by wealthy trial lawyers.[284] A scathing 1987 *Wall Street Journal* piece pointed out that Texans doubted integrity of the justices of the Texas Supreme Court after the justices rejected an appeal in an $11 billion judgment against Texaco, while openly accepting campaign contributions from both Penzoil and Texaco lawyers who were involved in the lawsuit. Penzoil lawyers contributed more than $355,000 to the nine justices from 1984 to 1987.[285] The scandal was featured on a 60 *Minutes* segment titled "Justice for Sale?" which aired in 1987.

Interestingly, in 1989 while serving on the Third Court of Appeals Gammage participated in a case involving a dispute between two candidates for the Texas Supreme Court. As the November 1986 general election approached, candidates were playing hardball politics. Charles Ben Howell, the Republican nominee, sued the Democratic nominee, Oscar Mauzy. Howell claimed that Mauzy violated several campaign finance limitations mandated by the state election code. Mauzy denied these charges and filed a counterclaim seeking to have the case dismissed and sought attorney fees from Howell. By the time the trial court made an interlocutory ruling in March 1988, granting summary judgment in favor of Mauzy, Justice Mauzy had been on the high court for a little over a year. In May 1989, the court of appeals in *Howell v. Mauzy* dismissed the appeal on the grounds that the trial court's judgment was interlocutory and not appealable.[286] Gammage joined the majority's opinion. The case was illustrative more of hardball politics than anything else. There's no way to know if these allegations were based in fact, or if the suit was part of a creative campaign strategy. Mauzy would later trade barbs with Thomas Phillips and file Judicial Conduct Commission complaints during the 1990 campaign for the chief justice seat.

In 1988, Gammage's reputation had also been bolstered by the Clean Slate '88 campaign funded by the Texas Medical Association (TMA). The plan was heralded as an attempt to elect a bipartisan slate of impartial and honest justices but was in fact intended to rid the Supreme Court of justices who were unduly influenced by trial lawyers. As we shall see in chapter 4, the TMA and the civil defense bar were locked in an epic struggle with trial lawyers for control of the court. The objective of the Clean Slate '88 campaign was to elect Republicans Thomas Phillips and Nathan Hecht, and Democrats Eugene Cook, Lloyd Doggett, Raul Gonzalez, and Jack Hightower. It was a brilliant campaign—the first of its kind in Texas. All of the candidates supported by the TMA were elected in the 1998 race. Gammage was also included on the Clean Slate '88 ballot even though he was running as an incumbent on the Third Court of Appeals in 1988. Placing him on the Clean Slate ballot was an attempt to "groom" him for a high court run in 1990. Gammage would also appear on the red Clean Slate '90 ballot cards (with Republicans Thomas Phillips and John Cornyn) two years later. The Clean Slate '88 winning candidates for the high court in 1988 joined incumbents Democrats Oscar Mauzy, Franklin Spears, and C. L. Ray who had not been up for reelection that year. Ironically, the two Clean Slate campaigns ('88 and '90) worked in Gammage's political favor, because he benefited from support from the TMA and other pro-business groups, but the campaign also concomitantly represents the beginning of a pro-business Court. We will return to this tumultuous period in chapter 4.

The 1988 Supreme Court election was the most expensive and partisan judicial election in the history of the Lone Star State. That year, the twelve major candidates for the court raised $10 million ($20 million in 2019 dollars[287]). In addition, a political action committee formed by trial lawyers raised $1.4 million primarily for a barrage of television commercials.[288] Chief Justice Phillips raised $2 million ($4 million in 2019 dollars)[289] for his successful reelection bid even in light of his self-imposed limit of $5,000 on campaign contributions from attorneys and law firms. Phillips, a district court judge in Houston, was appointed by Governor Bill Clements in 1987 to replace retiring Chief Justice John Hill. Phillips was the first Republican to be elected (1988) to the court in the twentieth century. As mentioned earlier, he and Mauzy locked horns in 1990 in one of the most brutal campaigns for chief justice in history, with each candidate running negative TV ads and Mauzy filing complaints with the Judicial Conduct Commission. Phillips would prove to be the most successful campaign fundraiser in the court's history, raising over $2 million in his 1988 campaign and around $2.5 million in 1990 in his effort to maintain his position as chief justice.[290] However, Phillips, as we will see in chapter 4, would prove to be the most tenacious and effective reformer in the history of Texas judicial politics. His efforts culminated in the Judicial Campaign Reform Act of 1995 and other major reforms.

Gammage announced his candidacy for the Texas Supreme Court in 1989, pledging that he (like Phillips) would not accept contributions from individuals of more than $5,000. "We must avoid any appearance that our courts are for sale to the highest bidder," he said. In 1989 Gammage was also on record opposing calls by reformers to replace the state's system of electing judges in partisan elections with a merit plan that would allow gubernatorial appointment followed by retention elections—a position he would reverse soon he witnessed the rise of hyper-partisanship after 1990. "Retention elections don't take money or politics out of it," he said in an interview at the time.[291]

A 1990 campaign contribution flier bore a photo of Gammage, his wife Lynda Hallmark, and six-year-old son Sam relaxing in a park. It read "Bob and the entire Gammage family appreciate your support." A two-page advertisement touted Gammage's "independence" as a soldier, naval officer, teacher, lawyer, lawmaker, and judge.[292]

Red cards (Figure 2.2) the size of business cards and index cards were distributed by the Texas Medical Political Action Committee and Texas Restaurant Association PAC. One "clean slate" card read informed voters that the Texas Supreme Court elections are "the best kept secret on the November ballot. No public office does more to drive the cost of medical care or determine the Texas business climate." It continued, "Far too many of us don't take the

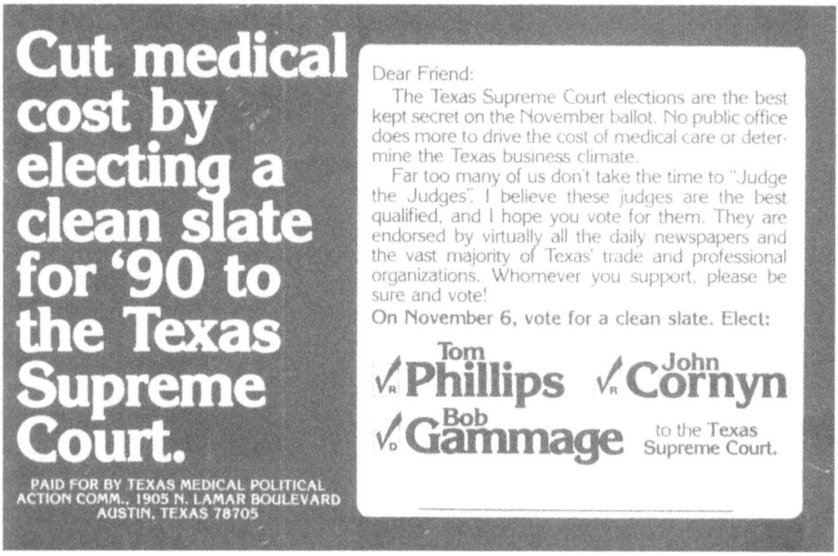

Figure 2.2 Gammage Clean Slate '90 Card. *Source:* Robert A. Gammage Collection. SHSU Special Collections, Newton Gresham Library, Sam Houston State University, Huntsville, Texas.

time to "Judge the Judges."[293] The card went on to say that electing a clean slate for '90 to the Texas Supreme Court would be a way to cut medical costs, alluding to the allegation that medical malpractice suits drive up the coast of care.

Gammage—who called himself "an independent Democrat — stated: "Justice is best served when the law serves all the people." One of his campaign fliers (Figure 2.3) explained his role in the *Edgewood v Kirby* school finance equity lawsuit:

> One judge, Judge Bob Gammage, disagreed with his colleagues [on the court of appeals] and wrote a strong opinion supporting Edgewood . . . In October 1989, the Texas Supreme Court agreed with Judge Gammage's opinion and ruled 9-0 in favor of Edgewood.[294]

Gammage ultimately won the Democratic primary in 1990, the race to choose C. L. Ray's successor. The *Austin American-Statesman* opined that 1990 would be a relatively "low-key" year compared to the wild 1988 election.[295] In the Democratic primary in April 1990, a runoff election between Gammage and Ross Sears was characterized as a bitter fight. The March 13 primary had reduced the original field of candidates to two. Sears had nearly 40 percent of the vote, Gammage's 35 percent, and Clifton "Scrappy" Holmes with 27 percent.[296] The runoff was scheduled for April 10. Gammage

BOB GAMMAGE

For The Texas ★ Supreme Court

Judge Harley Clark decided in favor of Edgewood in the landmark Edgewood v. Kirby school funding lawsuit.

When Clark's decision was appealed, a majority of the Court of Appeals ruled against Edgewood.

ONE JUDGE, JUDGE BOB GAMMAGE, DISAGREED WITH HIS COLLEAGUES AND WROTE A STRONG OPINION SUPPORTING EDGEWOOD. JUDGE GAMMAGE WROTE IN HIS OPINION THAT:

> **"Education is critical to an individual's participation in today's society; as a constitutional right it is hollow if its possessor is deprived of the opportunity to pursue it on a relatively equal basis with others in our open political system and labor market."**

In October 1989, the Texas Supreme Court agreed with Judge Gammage's opinion and ruled 9-0 in favor of Edgewood.

LET'S SUPPORT A CANDIDATE FOR SUPREME COURT WHO HAS PROVEN HIS COMMITMENT TO FAIRNESS AND EQUALITY.

Texans for Bob Gammage PO Box 13226 Capitol Station Austin, Texas 78711

Pd. Pol. Adv. by Texans for Bob Gammage, PO Box 13226 Capitol Station, Austin, Texas 78711

Figure 2.3 Gammage *Edgewood v. Kirby* Flyer for 1990 TXSC Election. *Source:* Robert A. Gammage Collection. SHSU Special Collections, Newton Gresham Library, Sam Houston State University, Huntsville, Texas.

led in the State Bar of Texas poll and was highly regarded by the major newspapers, including the *Dallas Morning News.*[297] In the midst of the race, allegations surfaced that Ross Sears physically assaulted another lawyer in a mid-1970s bar room brawl, that he had several judgments against him for not paying debt, and was forced to settle a legal malpractice suit for $25,000. In the runoff Gammage ran a negative television ad pointing out Sear's problems. Gammage was quoted in the *Austin American-Statesman* as saying, "I had never done any negative media in 20 years in politics . . . but I felt this time it was necessary."[298] Sears retorted that Gammage's attacks were untrue and a result of desperation. He called Gammage a lifelong politician and not a judge.[299] Gammage predicted accurately that it would take about $500,000 to win the primary and other $500,000 to win in the general election, but he said he would not accept more than $5,000 from any contributor, following Chief Justice Phillips's lead in voluntarily limiting the amount that he would accept from lawyers and law firms. "We must avoid any appearance that our courts are for sale to the highest bidder, that money or special interest can purchase preferential treatment in our courthouses," Gammage said. In the Republican primary in March that year Thomas Phillips won renomination as chief justice and was now gearing up for a battle with Justice Oscar Mauzy in November. John Cornyn easily defeated George Barbary in that primary.[300]

Gammage was seen as the strongest candidate so it was no surprise when the State Bar poll ranked him favorably and the *Austin American-Statesman* endorsed him for a seat on the court.[301] Gammage and Cornyn's victories in their respective primaries were reported to be a positive development for the integrity and prestige of the court after years of scandals.[302] In the November general election, Gammage defeated Republican Charles Ben Howell. A Dallas appeals court justice, Howell rode his bicycle 1,000 miles across Texas as a publicity campaign. He ran three times for a seat on the court without success. When asked to comment on his opponent, Gammage quipped, "he is trying to ride into office on a bicycle because he could never get there on his credentials."[303] Gammage, however, was sympathetic to Howell's publicity stunt because "it's hard to get anyone to express interest in the judicial races," he stated in an interview. "When groups do invite statewide candidates to speak, the judicial candidates are always last. By that time, most of the audience has left, so we do a lot of talking to each other. " He did call Howell a "kook" in a campaign ad for going to court in pajamas wearing a sign that read "Judge Kook" on it after Howell was branded as such by a former political opponent.[304]

Less than a month before the 1990 November general election the *Austin American-Statesman* endorsed Gammage as the best candidate to return dignity and honor to the court. His predecessor, Justice C. L. Ray, a Democrat who was the recipient of large campaign contributions from highly successful trial lawyers, once assured a litigant attending a 1984 fundraiser that if he did not win a current case he would win the next one. Ray also discussed the court's internal deliberations with the litigant and obliquely inferred he would try to pull strings with the associate justices. These actions led to the public reprimand of Ray by the Texas Commission on Judicial Conduct in 1987.[305] Ray did not seek reelection in 1990.

Although Gammage was touted by the conservative TMA as part of the Clean Slate '90 campaign, he was also endorsed by a number of influential liberal groups including the Progressive Voters League, Mexican-American Democrats, Mexican-American Bar Association, the Association of Women Attorneys, Travis County Democratic Women. Newspaper endorsements included the *Houston Post*, *Dallas Times-Herald*, *Fort Worth Star-Telegram*, and *Austin American-Statesman* (Figure 2.4).[306]

When the votes were counted Gammage easily defeated Howell (57 percent to 43 percent) for Place 2 on the court. Gammage spent about $900,000 overall in his campaign for a seat on the high court. Howell spent about $60,000.[307] Chief Justice Phillips defeated Justice Mauzy (59 percent to 41 percent) for the chief justiceship. Republican district court judge John Cornyn—who received solid endorsements from all major Texas newspapers—was easily victorious (56 percent to 44 percent) over Democrat Gene Kelly. Cornyn was elected to the court as a "reform candidate" that year, as well. He advocated legislation that would make judges' records available to the public, require a full financial disclosure policy, and place strict limits on campaign contributions to judicial candidates. Democratic candidate Kelly, a divorce lawyer who had no experience in Texas courts and had no endorsements, hoped that his name shared by the famous song and dance man alone would prompt voter support. One of the least qualified candidates to run for the Supreme Court, Kelly still received nearly 44 percent of the vote statewide.

In January 1991, Gammage was sworn in as a justice, joining incumbent Democrats Raul Gonzalez, Oscar Mauzy, Jack Hightower, and Lloyd Doggett. John Cornyn joined Republican Chief Justice Thomas Phillips, Eugene Cook, and Nathan Hecht. The court was narrowly split 5-4 in favor of the Democrats—the last time Democrats would have a majority on the Texas high court. Chief Justice Phillips returned for his second term in 1990, having first been appointed by Republican governor Bill Clements in 1987 to serve out the rest of retired Chief Justice John Hill's term and then winning election in November 1988. For the first time since Reconstruction, Republicans held four seats on the court. We will return for a closer examination of a tumultuous period of judicial politics along with the discussion of the judicial reform movement in chapter four.

Gammage now possessed the prestige and influence that came with a seat on the state's highest civil appellate tribunal. As a justice he was now poised

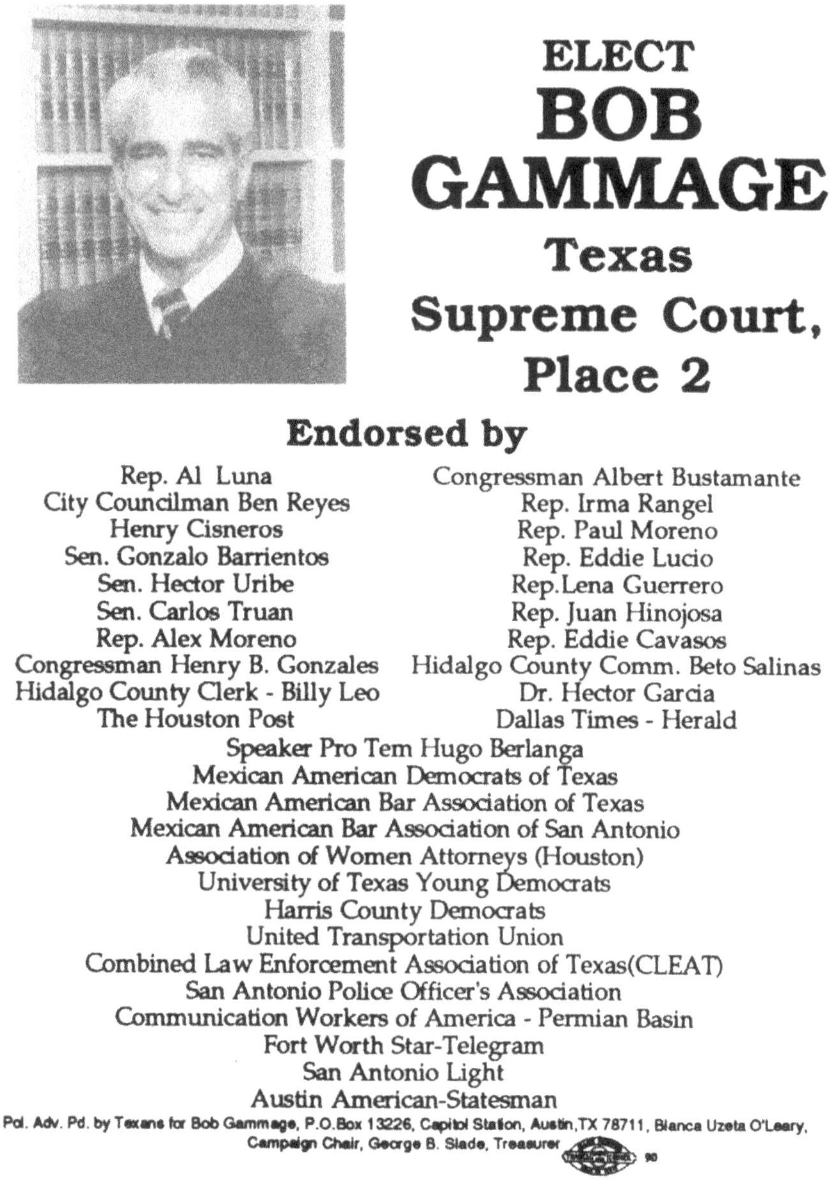

Figure 2.4 '90 Endorsement Card. *Source:* Robert A. Gammage Collection. SHSU Special Collections, Newton Gresham Library, Sam Houston State University, Huntsville, Texas.

to shape the law and, through the high court's administrative functions, to influence the canons of judicial conduct and rules of civil procedure. Gammage, his family, and friends were ebullient, but he was somewhat dispirited by the system. Looking back, Gammage's campaigns for his seat on the

Texas Court of Appeals at Austin were quiet and largely dignified affairs, often with no serious challengers. At most, judicial candidates needed a few endorsements, favorable State Bar rating, face-time with lawyers and state party members. But beginning in 1988 he knew he had entered a new era. Even as he looked forward to his swearing in, he knew that to maintain his seat on the high court he would need to be a one-man fundraising machine, especially toward the end of his six-year term. He knew that Tom Phillips spent over $2 million to get elected in 1990. As a Democrat, even a moderate one, Gammage also understood that he and others with a progressive, or even centrist, philosophy had become an endangered species. But celebrating at his home on election eve, that wasn't Gammage's main concern; in January 1991 he would be sworn in as a Texas Supreme Court justice.

NOTES

1. *Kirby v. Edgewood Independent School District,* 761 S.W.2d 859, 867–869 (Tex. App.—Austin 1988) (Gammage, J., dissenting), *rev'd,* 777 S.W.2d 391 (Tex. 1989).
2. Robert A. Gammage Collection, 1956–2012 at Sam Houston State University. Campaign literature. Series 2, Sub-Series 1, Box 1, Folder 9.
3. *Kirby v. Edgewood Independent School District.*
4. Senate Joint Resolution 36. 1980.
5. Deborah D. Powers, *The Court of Appeals at Austin: 1892–1992* (Austin: State House Press, 1992).
6. See James L. Haley, *The Texas Supreme Court: A Narrative History, 1836–1986* (Austin: University of Texas Press, 2013).
7. Id., at 3–4.
8. http://www.statutes.legis.state.tx.us/?link=EL.
9. Id., at 1–7.
10. Bruce Hight, "Democratic judicial race pits 2 Austin attorneys," *Austin American-Statesman,* May 29, 1982.
11. "Criss concedes judicial race to Gammage," *Austin American-Statesman,* June 7, 1982, p. 19.
12. Press Release, Office of Governor William P. Clements, Jr., August 11, 1982. Briscoe Center, Clements Texas papers.
13. Candice Hughes, "Republicans duck court races: Democrats face primary challenges," *Austin American-Statesman,* February 4, 1982.
14. Kim Tyson, "Democrats edging up in courts," *Austin American-Statesman,* November 3, 1982.
15. Powers, *The Court of Appeals at Austin: 1892–1992.*
16. Tomie Young, "Appeals court judge trying to find home for dog he accidently struck," *The Paris News,* August 20, 1986.
17. See Third Court of Appeals, http://www.txcourts.gov/3rdcoa/; and Powers, *The Court of Appeals at Austin: 1892–1992.*

18. Westlaw search on December 2018.
19. 790 S.W. 2d 819.
20. *Jones v. Texas,* 680 S.W.2d 499 (1983)
21. *Jones v. Texas,* at 500.
22. *Id.*
23. *Id.*, at 501.
24. *Id.* at 502–503.
25. *Id.,* at 504–505.
26. *Id.*
27. *Id.,* at 504, citing *Greene v. Massey,* 437 U.S 19 (1978).
28. *Id.,* at 505.
29. *Jacobson v. Texas*, No. PD-1466-11 (2013).
30. *England v. Texas,* 727 S.W.2d 810 (Tex. App.—Austin 1984).
31. England is considered to have precedential status and is cited in 17 subsequent rulings. Westlaw search conducted in 20180.
32. *England v. Texas,* 727 S.W.2d 810, 811 (Tex. App.—Austin 1984).
33. *England v. Texas*, at 812, Gammage citing *Jackson v. Virginia,* 443 US 307, 319, n. 12 (1979).
34. *Id.*, at 812.
35. Gammage also cites the Texas Court of Criminal Appeals ruling in *Wilson v. State,* 654 S.W.2d 465 (Tex. Cr. App. 1983).
36. *Drew v. State,* 735 S.W.2d 655 (1987).
37. "New trial ordered in slaying attempt," *The Dallas Morning News,* August 13, 1987.
38. See *Schmuck v. United States*, 489 U.S. 705 (1989) and *Hall v. State,* 225 S.W.3d 524 (Tex. Crim. App. 2007).
39. See Amanda Peters, "Thirty-one years in the making: Why the Texas Court of criminal appeals' new single-method approach to lessor-included offense analysis is a step in the right direction," *Baylor Law Review,* 60 (Winter 2008): 231.
40. *Drew v. State,* 735 S.W.2d 655, 656 (1987).
41. *Aguilar v. State*, 682 S.W.2d 556 (Tex. Cr. App. 1985) and *Royster v. State,* 622 S.W.2d 442 (Tex. Cr. App. 1981).
42. *Drew v. State.*
43. *Thompson v. State*, 521 S.W.2d 230 (Tex. Cr. App. 1980) and *Lugo v. State*, 667 S.W.2d 144 (Tex. Cr. App. 1984).
44. *Drew v. State,* at 657, Gammage citing *Thomas v. State,* 701 S.W. 2d 653, 656 (Tex. Cr. App. 1985). Following the court of appeals ruling Drew was indicted again, tried and convicted. On appeal for the second time, the Third Court of Appeals agreed that Drew's second conviction was void, 765 S.W. 2d 533 (1989). The Texas Court of Criminal Appeals affirmed, 805 S.W.2d 451 (1991).
45. *Id.*
46. *Id.*, at 657–658.
47. See generally Michael H. Hoffheimer, "The rise and fall of lesser included offenses," *Rutgers Law Journal,* 36 (2005): 351.
48. See *Hall v. State*. The court of criminal appeals has addressed the lessor included offence doctrine again since 2007, but the court's opinion in *Hall* is a good

exegesis of what has been characterized as a state of confusion among the courts regarding the doctrine.

49. *Port v. Texas,* 736 S.W.2d 865 (1987).

50. Gary Cartwright, "Everyone a victim," *Texas Monthly*, November 1987, at 140; Debbie DeLoach, "Port gets 75-year sentence," *New Braunfels Herald*, March 17, 1985; Arlene Battista, "Judge refuses to suppress murder confession, evidence," *Galveston Daily News*, July 1, 1987.

51. See Brian Rogers, "Infamous Houston killer walks out of prison a free man," *Houston Chronicle,* June 5, 2014.

52. *Port v. Texas.*

53. *Id.*

54. *Id.*, at 868.

55. *Port v. State,* 736 S.W.2d 865 (Tex. App. 1987).

56. Justice Aboussie, joined by Justices Smith and Gammage.

57. Associated Press, "Appeals court overturns murder conviction, sentence," *Longview Morning Journal*, August 13, 1987.

58. Tex. Code Cr. P. Ann. Art. 38.22 sect. 3 (Sup. 1987).

59. *Selman v. State*, 663 S.W.2d 838 (Tex.Cr.App. 1984) and *Dunn v. State*, 721 S.W. 2d 325 (Tex.Cr.App. 1986).

60. See George E. Dix, "Texas 'Confession' law and oral self-incriminating statements," *Baylor Law Review,* 1 (Winter 1989): 41; and Robert R. Barton, "The code means what it says: Revisiting the admissibility of corroborated unwritten custodial statements," *Texas Tech Law Review* 26 (1995): 779. These two articles were written during a time span following the *Port* verdict and appeal. They are an excellent overview of the law but may not reflect recent changes.

61. *Port v. Texas*, at 74.

62. "Schatz' mother furious at ruling; DA vows fight," *Houston Chronicle,* August 13, 1987, at 1, column. 1.

63. "Holmes seeks changes in Texas confession law," *Houston Post*, August 13, 1987, at 10A, column 1.

64. See Dix, "Texas 'Confession' law and oral self-incriminating statements".

65. *Id.*, at 13.

66. *Port v. State,* 738 S.W.2d 787 (1987).

67. *Briddle v. State*, 742 S.W.2d 379 (Tex. Cr. App. 1987).

68. Tex. Code Cr. P. Ann. At 38.22 section 3(c) (Supp. 1987).

69. *Port v. State,* 738 S.W.2d 787, 790 (1987).

70. *Port v. State,* 738 S.W.2d 787 (1987) at 792 (Gammage, J., dissenting).

71. *Port v. State,* 738 S.W.2d 787.

72. 791 S.W. 2d 103, 107 (1990).

73. *Bryant v. Texas*, 793 S.W.2d 59 (1990).

74. *Bryant v. Texas*, at 61.

75. Scot Meyer, "Girl's death linked to dope stash in trial," *Austin American-Statesman*, May 13, 1987; and "Murder conviction upheld in tot's death," *Austin American-Statesman*, Local Briefs, June 14, 1990.

76. *Bryant v. Texas,* at 61.

77. *Id.*

78. *Id.*, at 62.
79. *Id.*
80. Tex. Const. Ann. article I, sec. 9 reads: "The people shall be secure in their persons, houses, papers and possessions, from all unreasonable seizures or searches, and no warrant to search any place, or to seize any person or thing, shall issue without describing them as near as may be, nor without probable cause, supported by oath or affirmation."
81. 793 S.W.2d 59, 62. Gammage citing *Katz v. United States,* 389 US 347, 357 and Juarez v. State, 758 S.W.2d 772,775 (Tex.Cr.App.1988)
82. 793 S.W.2d 59, 65.
83. See *Walker v. Texas*, 701 S.W.2d 316 (1985).
84. *Brown v. State,* 657 S.W.2d 797, 799 (Tex.Cr.App.1983).
85. See Kimberly S. Keller, "Privacy lost: Comparing the attenuation of Texas Article I, Section 9 and the fourth amendment," *St. Mary's School of Law Journal* 429 (2003): 34.
86. *Brown v. State.*
87. *Id.*, at 807 (Judge Clinton concurring).
88. Dick Stanley, "3-term appeals jurist defended Ruby and O'Hair," *Austin American-Statesman*, October 7, 2004, 13.
89. *Colquette v. Forbes*, 680 S.W.2d. 536 (Tex. App.—Austin 1984).
90. *Colquette v. Forbes* has been cited in numerous cases, including *Magallanez v. Magallanez,* 911 S.W.2d 91 (1995),
91. *Id.,* at 537–538.
92. *Id.,* at 537.
93. *Id.*, at 537–538.
94. *Id.,* at 538.
95. *Id.,* at 538–539 (citing Griswold v. Connecticut, 381 U.S. 479 (1965)).
96. *Id.*
97. *See Id.,* at 539.
98. 540 S.W.2d 668 (Tex. 1976).
99. *Id.*
100. *Id.*
101. *Id.*
102. *Id.*
103. *Id.*
104. *Id.* (discussing Shelley v. Kraemer, 334 U.S. 1 (1948)).
105. *Shelley*, 334 U.S. at 23.
106. *See generally Colquette v. Forbes,* at 539.
107. *Colquette v. Forbes.*
108. *Id.,* at 537.
109. *Id.,* at 539.
110. *See generally Billings v. Atkinson,* 489 S.W. 2d 858, 859 (Tex. 1973) (recognizing that an invasion of privacy is a legal injury).
111. *City of Sherman v. Henry*, 928 S.W.2d 464 (Tex. 1996); *Texas State Employees Union v. Texas Dept. of Mental Health and Mental Retardation,* 746 S.W.2d 203

(Tex. 1987); *In re H.E.B. Grocery Co.*, L.P., 2014 WL 700749 (Tex. App. Corpus Christi 2014).

112. *Industrial Foundation of the South v. Texas Industrial Accident Board,* 540 S.W.2d 668 (Tex. 1976).

113. *Texas Comptroller of Public Accounts v. Attorney General of Texas*, 244 S.W.3d 629 (Tex. App. Austin 2008), judgment affirmed in part, reversed in part, (Dec. 3, 2010) and judgment affirmed in part, reversed on other grounds in part, 354 S.W.3d 336 (Tex. 2010).

114. *Roberts v. Houston Independent School District*, 788 S.W.2d 107, 60 Ed. Law Rep. 251 (Tex. App. Houston 1st Dist. 1990), writ denied, (June 27, 1990).

115. *Billings v. Atkinson*, at 858, 861.

116. *Billings v. Atkinson*, at 859.

117. *Id.* (citing *Milner v. Red River Publishing Company*, 249 S.W. 2d 227 (Tex. Civ. App.—Dallas 1952, no writ)).

118. *Id.*, at 860 (discussing *Milner v. Red River Publishing Company*, 249 S.W.2d 227, 229 (Tex. Civ. App.—Dallas 1952, no writ)).

119. *Id.*, at 860–861.

120. James Gray Denton (1917–1982), Associate Justice, Texas Supreme Court, 1971–1982.

121. *Id.*, at 859–860.

122. Samuel D. Warren and Louis D. Brandeis, "The Right to Privacy," *Harvard Law Review,* 4 (1890): 193. The Warren and Brandeis article is arguably the most well-known and oft-cited law review article in American legal history. The article can be found by searching most law-content or social science databases; or see Samuel D. Warren, and Louis D. Brandeis, *The Right to Privacy*, with a forward by Steven Alan Childress (New Orleans: Quid Pro Books), *Legal Legends Series* (2010).

123. *Billings v. Atkinson*, at 860.

124. *Id.*, at 860.

125. *Id.*

126. 540 S.W.2d 668, 682 (Tex. 1976).

127. *Id.*

128. *Id.*, at 672.

129. *Id.*, at 678.

130. *Id.*

131. Ross E. Doughty, Associate Justice, Texas Supreme Court, 1975–1976. Elected as a Democrat.

132. *Id.*, at 680–681.

133. *Id.*, at 682.

134. *Industrial Foundation*, 540 S.W.2d at 682.

135. 746 S.W.2d 203 (1987).

136. *Id.*, at 204.

137. 381 U.S. 479, 484 (1965).

138. Texas Constitution, article 1, section 19.

139. Texas Constitution, article 1, section 8.

140. Texas Constitution, article 1, section 10.

141. Texas Constitution, article 1, sections 9 and 25.
142. Texas Constitution, article 6.
143. John L. Hill, Jr., Chief Justice, Texas Supreme Court, 1985–1988. Elected as a Democrat.
144. *Industrial Foundation*, at 205.
145. *Id.*, at 206.
146. 53 Tex. Jur. 3d Negligence § 5.
147. *Figure World v. Farley*, 680 S.W.2d 33 (1984).
148. *Id.*, at 36.
149. Texas Tort Claims Act. Tex.Rev.Civ.Stat.Ann. (Supp.1982).
150. *Rawlings v. Angelo State University,* 648 S.W.2d 430 (1983).
151. *Rawlings v. Angelo State University*, at 433.
152. *City of Austin v. Davis,* 693 S.W.2d 31 (1985).
153. *City of Austin v. Davis* (citing *Landreth v. Reed,* 570 S.W. 2d 486 (Tex.Civ. App.1978, writ dismissed).
154. See *Landreth v. Reed,* 570 S.W.2d 486 (Tex.Civ.App.1978, writ dism'd).
155. *City of Austin v. Davis,* 693 S.W. 2d 31 at 33 (1985)
156. *Id.*
157. *Hill v. Kimball,* 76 Tex. 210, 13 S.W. 59 (1890).
158. *Twyman v. Twyman,* 855 S.W.2d 819 (Tex. 1993).
159. *Id.*, at 819.
160. *Id.*, at 822 (emphasis added) (quoting *Underwriters Life Ins. Co. v. Cobb,* 746 S.W.2d 810, 819 (Tex. App.—Corpus Christi 1988, no writ)).
161. *Bounds v. Caudle*, 560 S.W.2d 925 (Tex. 1977).
162. *Price v. Price*, 732 S.W.2d 316 (Tex. 1987).
163. *Price v. Price*, at 821 citing *Page v. United States,* 729 F.2d 818, 821–822 (D.C. Cir. 1984).
164. *Id.*, at 820 citing *Creswell ranch & Cattle Co. v. Scoggins*, 39 S.W. 612 (Tex. Civ. App. 1897, no writ).
165. *Twyman v. Twyman*, 790 S.W.2d 819 (Tex. App. Austin 1990).
166. *Twyman v. Twyman*, 855 S.W.2d 619.
167. *Id.*
168. John Cornyn, Associate Justice, Texas Supreme Court, 1991–1997. Elected as a Republican.
169. *Boyles v. Kerr,* 855 S.W.2d 593 (Tex. 1993) is discussed in chapter 4.
170. See David Crump, "Negligent infliction of emotional distress: An unlimited claim, but does it really exist?" *Texas Tech Law Review,* 49 (2017): 685.
171. *Twyman v. Twyman*, 855 S.W.2d 621–622.
172. Thomas R. Phillips, Chief Justice, Texas Supreme Court, 1988–2004. Elected as a Republican.
173. *Id.*, at 627 (Phillips, J., dissenting).
174. *Id.,* at 629–630 (Hecht, J., dissenting).
175. *Texas State Teacher's Association v. State*, 711 S.W.2d 421 (1986).
176. H.B. 72, 68th Leg., 2d Called Sess. (1984).
177. In 1984 the legislature amended the Texas Education Code, adding section 13.047 requiring that public schools teachers must pass the examination on or before June 30, 1986 as a condition for continued certification.

178. *Texas State Teacher's Association v. State*, at 421, 423.

179. For a comprehensive overview of the policy and comprehensive analysis of the legal issues attached to it see Beverly M.M. Charles, "First they came for the teachers . . . ," *Thurgood Marshall Law Review,* 12 (Fall 1986): 1.

180. *Id.*, at 424.

181. *Id.*, at 425.The majority citing *City of Coleman v. Rhone,* 222 S.W.2d 646, 648 (Tex. Civ. App. 1949, writ ref'd) and *City of Breckinridge v. Cozart*, 478 S.W.2d 162, 165 (Tex. Civ.App. 1972, writ ref'd n.r.e).

182. See Debbie Graves, "State Supreme Court sets review of issues on teacher literacy test," *Austin American-Statesman*, June 4, 1986; and "Texas teachers take basic-skills examination," The *New York Times,* March 11, 1986.

183. Terrance Stuutz, "Texas appeal court upholds literacy exam for educators," *The Dallas Morning News*, June 14, 1986.

184. Debbie Graves, "Justices back literacy tests for educators," *Austin American-Statesman,* February 19, 1987.

185. See John C. Domino, *Civil Rights & Liberties in the 21st Century*, 4th ed. (New York: Routledge, 2018), chapter 2.

186. See *Garcetti v. Ceballos,* 547 U.S. 410 (2006).

187. *Price v. City of San Marcos*, 744 S.W.2d 349 (1988).

188. *Price v. City of San Marcos.*

189. Citing *Tarrant County v. Ashmore*, 635 S.W.2d 417, 422 (Tex. 1982).

190. Citing *Massachusetts Indemnity and Life Insurance Co. v. Texas State Board of Insurance,* 685 S.W.2d 104 (Tex. App.1985, no writ).

191. See Hon. Harvey Brown and Sarah V. Kerrigan, "42 U.S.C. S 1983: The vehicle for protecting public employee's constitutional rights," *Baylor Law Review,* 47 (Summer 1995): 619, 638. This article is a comprehensive treatment of the rights of public employees. *Price v. City of San Marcos* is cited in note 112.

192. Brown and Kerrigan, "42 U.S.C. S 1983," at 352.

193. *Pickering v. Board of Education*, 391 U.S. 563 (1968).

194. *Id.,* at 353 (Gammage citing *Pickering v. Board of Education.*

195. *Id.*, at 353 (Gammage citing *Connick v. Myers* 461 U.S. 138 (1983)).

196. *Id.*, at 353.

197. *See generally* Albert H. Kauffman, "The Texas School finance litigation saga: Great progress, then near death by a thousand cuts," *St. Mary's Law Journal,* 40 (2008): 511, 514.

198. *Brown v. Board of Education*, 347 U.S. 483 (1954).

199. See J. Kluger, *Simple Justice: The History of Brown v. Board of Education and Black America's Struggle for Equality* (New York: Knopf, 1975); and see John C. Domino, *Civil Rights and Liberties in the 21st Century,* 4th ed. (New York: Routledge, 2018), chapter 6.

200. For a fascinating account of the interpersonal dynamic of this case, see Bernard Schwartz, *Super Chief: Earl Warren and His Supreme Court—A Judicial Biography* (New York: New York University Press, 1983), chapter 3.

201. See Michael Ariens, *Lone Star Law: A Legal History of Texas* (Lubbock: Texas Tech University Press, 2011), 242–247.

202. Ariens, *Lone Star Law.*

203. *Mendez v. Westminster School District*, 161 F.2d 774 (9th Cir. 1947).

204. Ariens, *Lone Star Law,* at 244.
205. *Swann v. Charlotte-Mecklenburg Board of Education,* 402 U.S. 1 (1971).
206. 337 F. Supp. 280, 282 (W.D. Tex. 1971).
207. 337 F. Supp. 280, 282.
208. *San Antonio Independent School District v. Rodriguez,* 411 U.S. 1 (1973).
209. *San Antonio Independent School District v. Rodriguez,* at 18–20.
210. *Kirby v. Edgewood Independent School District,* 761 S.W.2d 859, 867–869 (Tex. App.—Austin 1988) (Gammage, J., dissenting), *rev'd,* 777 S.W.2d 391 (Tex. 1989).
211. Terrance Stutz, "Justices to decide school funding case," *Dallas Morning News,* April 7, 1988.
212. *Kirby v. Edgewood Independent School District,* at 860.
213. *Kirby v. Edgewood Independent School District,* at 860–861; *see also* Tex. Educ. Code Ann. § 16.001 (West 1994), *repealed by* Act of May 30, 1995, 74th Leg., R.S. ch. 260, § 58(1).
214. *Kirby v. Edgewood Independent School District,* at 861.
215. *Id.*
216. *Id.,* at 868 (Gammage, J., dissenting).
217. *Id.*
218. *Id.,* at 861 (majority opinion).
219. Harley Ray Clark, Jr., District Court Judge (250th District Court), 1977–1989.
220. *Kirby v. Edgewood Independent School District,* at 860.
221. *Id.*
222. *Id.*
223. *Id.,* at 860–861.
224. *See generally Id.*; and see *Edgewood Independent School District. v. Kirby* (*Edgewood I*), 777 S.W.2d 391, 399 (Tex. 1989) (stating that a remedy by the Texas legislature was long overdue while giving the legislature more time to achieve a more efficient system. The Texas Supreme Court reinstated the trial court's decision and only modified the final date of the stay of the injunction).
225. Terrance Stutz, "School decision reversed—State funding system found constitutional," The *Dallas Morning News,* December 15, 1988.
226. *Kirby v. Edgewood Independent School District,* at 860, 867.
227. *Id.* (joined by Justice Aboussie, and with Justice Gammage dissenting) (discussing Tex. Const. art. I, §§ 1, 3, 19).
228. *Id.,* at 867.
229. *Id.,* at 862–863 (citing *San Antonio Independent School District v. Rodriguez,* 411 U.S. 1 (1973)).
230. *Spring Branch Independent School District v. Stamos,* 695 S.W.2d 556, 695 S.W.2d 556, 560 (Tex. 1985).
231. *Kirby v. Edgewood Independent School District.*
232. *Id.*
233. *Id.*; *see also* TEX. CONST. art. I, § 3 ("All free men, when they form a social compact, have equal rights, and no man, or set of men, is entitled to exclusive separate public emoluments, or privileges, but in consideration of public services.").
234. *Kirby v. Edgewood Independent School District,* at 867 (Gammage, J., dissenting).

235. *Id.,* at 869 (quoting Tex. Const. art. I, § 3).
236. *Id.* (quoting Tex. Const. art. I, § 3(a)).
237. *Id.* (quoting Tex. Const. art. VII, § 1).
238. *Id.* (quoting Tex. Const. art. VII, § 3(a)).
239. *Id.* at 869–870 (quoting *Spring Branch Independent School District v. Stamos*).
240. *Id.* at 871 (citing *Stout v. Grand Prairie Independent School District.*, 733 S.W.2d 290, 294 (Tex. App.—Dallas 1987, writ ref'd n.r.e)).
241. *See Id.*
242. *Id.,* at 870.
243. *Id.*
244. *Texas State Employees Union v. Texas Department of Mental Health & Mental Retardation.*
245. *Holick v. Smith,* 685 S.W.2d 18, 20 (Tex. 1985).
246. *Waller v. State,* 68 S.W.2d 601, 604 (Tex. Civ. App.—Amarillo 1934, writ ref'd).
247. *Richmond Newspapers, Inc. v. Virginia,* 448 U.S. 555, 579 (1980).
248. *Kirby v. Edgewood Independent School District,* at 863 (majority opinion).
249. *See DeShaney v. Winnebago County Department of Social Services,* 489 U.S. 189, 190, 196 (1989); *Poelker v. Doe,* 432 U.S. 519, 521 (1977) (per curiam).
250. *Kirby v. Edgewood Independent School District,* at 870–871 (Gammage, J. dissenting) (quoting Tex. Educ. Code Ann. § 21.032 (1987)).
251. *Id.,* at 871.
252. *Plyler v. Doe,* 457 U.S. 202, 215 (1982), *superseded by statute,* Personal Responsibility and Work Opportunity Reconciliation Act (PRWORA), Pub. L. No. 104-193, 110 Stat. 2105 (1996); Illegal Immigration Reform and Immigrant Responsibility Act (IIRIRA), Pub. L. No. 104-208, 110 Stat. 3009 (1996).
253. *Plyler v. Doe.,* at 221.
254. *Id.*
255. *Id.,* at 230.
256. *Plyler v. Doe,* at 209–210.
257. *Kirby v. Edgewood Independent School District,* at 872, 874 (Gammage, J., dissenting) ("Read fairly and in the proper historical perspective, article VII, [section] 3 and article I, [sections] 3 and 3a—in conjunction—do not permit disparities between school districts to be substantial unless the State can show a compelling reason for such disparity. Here, the State has shown no compelling reason.").
258. *Id.,* at 872.
259. *Id.*
260. *Id.*
261. *Id.*
262. *Id.,* at 51.
263. Peggy Fikac, *Associated Press.* Austin (AP), December 15, 1988.
264. *Edgewood Independent School District v. Kirby* (*Edgewood I*), 777 S.W.2d 391, 399 (Tex. 1989).
265. *Edgewood Independent School District v. Kirby* (*Edgewood I*), at 397.
266. *Id.,* at 395, 397.

267. Oscar Holcombe Mauzy, Associate Justice, Texas Supreme Court, 1987–1992. Elected as a Democrat.

268. *Id.*, at 393.

269. *Id.*, at 393–394.

270. *Id.*, at 394.

271. *Id.*, at 394.

272. *Id.*, at 394–395.

273. *Id.*, at 395–396.

274. *Id.*, at 397.

275. *Edgewood Independent School District v. Kirby* (*Edgewood II*), 804 S.W.2d 491, 493, 495 (Tex. 1991).

276. *See Id.*, at 495.

277. *Id.*, at 491.

278. Franklin S. Spears, Associate Justice, Texas Supreme Court, 1979–1990. Elected as a Democrat. See Thomas R. Phillips, "Justice Franklin S. Spears: Unsung hero of Texas Justice," *St. Mary's Law Journal,* 28 (1997): 341.

279. Debbie Graves, "Change in Court keeps school finding case in Limbo," *Austin American-Statesman*, January 3, 1991.

280. Tex. Const. art. I, section 1. The number of justices was set at nine by the legislature in 1945.

281. Sam Kinch, Jr., "Judiciary contests in Texas," *The Dallas Morning News*, August 16, 1985.

282. Kinch, "Judiciary contests in Texas".

283. Raul A. Gonzales, Jr., Associate Justice, Texas Supreme Court, 1984–1988 . Elected as a Democrat.

284. Burka, "Heads, we win, tails, you lose," *Texas Monthly.* May 1987.

285. Thomas Petzinger, Jr. and Caleb Solomon, "Texaco Case spotlights questions on ingratiate of the Courts in Texas," *Wall Street Journal*, November 4, 1987, at 1.

286. *Howell v. Mauzy,* 744 S.W. 2d 274 (1989).

287. https://money.cnn.com/calculator/pf/inflation-adjustment/.

288. Anthony Champagne, "Campaign contributions in Texas Supreme Court Races," *Crime, Law and Social Change,* 17 (1992): 91 at 95–99; and see generally Kyle Cheek and Anthony Champagne, *Judicial Politics in Texas: Partisanship, Money and Politics in State Courts* (New York: Peter Lang, 2005).

289. https://money.cnn.com/calculator/pf/inflation-adjustment/.

290. Bruce Hight, "Texas court contest low-key compared to 1988 campaigns," *Austin American-Statesman*, February 4, 1990,

291. *Victoria Advocate,* November 3, 1989, 10.

292. 1990 Texas Supreme Court Campaign materials, SHSU Gammage Collection.

293. Texas Medical Political Action Committee Clean Slate '90 card, SHSU Gammage Collection.

294. 1990 Texas Supreme Court Campaign materials, SHSU Gammage Collection.

295. Bruce Hight, "Texas court contest low-key compared to 1988 campaigns."

296. George Kuempel, "Incumbent Phillips will face Mauzy in race for chief justice." *The Dallas Morning News*, March 14, 1990.

297. Sarah Bly, "Bar association results of member's poll on judicial races," *The Dallas Morning News*, June 9, 1990.

298. Bill Collier, "Gammage get high court nod; Appeals race close," *Austin American-Statesman*, April 11, 1990.

299. George Kuempel, "Fistfight, racism charged in Texas judge campaigns—High court, appeals bench seats are at stake," *The Dallas Morning News,* April 1, 1990.

300. Kuempel, "Fistfight, racism charged in Texas judge campaigns".

301. The *Austin American-Statesman* wrote that Gammage's "depth of experience in the political, judicial and business worlds should give him an edge with Democratic voters in the March 13 primary." Editorial, *Austin American-Statesman*, February 23, 1990.

302. "Gammage, Cornyn deserve support of Texas voters," editorial, *Austin American-Statesman,* October 19, 1990.

303. George Kuempel, "Balance of power at stake in 3 high court contest," *The Dallas Morning News*, October 21, 1990.

304. Kuempel, "Balance of power at stake in 3 high court contest".

305. State Comm'n on Judicial Conduct, Findings, Conclusions and Public Reprimand Relating to Certain Activities of Justice C.L. Ray of the Supreme Court of Texas (1987).

306. Robert A. Gammage Collection, 1956–2012 at Sam Houston State University. Campaign literature. Series 2, Sub-Series 1, Box 1, Folder 9.

307. George Kuempel, "Phillips defeats Mauzy for court justice," *Dallas Morning News*, November 7, 1990.

Chapter 3

Texas Supreme Court

> Much of the demonstrators' conduct cannot be considered integral to their ability to deliver their message. Indeed, the record reveals that some of their conduct involved not just "mere advocacy, but . . . overt act[s] of intimidation" unrelated to protected expression. The presence of such conduct tends heavily to support the jury's finding that the demonstrators caused the Aquinos' mental anguish.
>
> —Justice Gammage dissenting in *Valenzuela v. Aquino*.[1]

Bob Gammage was sworn in as a justice on the Texas Supreme Court on January 2, 1991. US Supreme Court justice Antonin Scalia administered the oath.[2] Gammage and Scalia could not have been further apart ideologically, but the mood was collegial in the capacious House chambers in the state capitol. Senator Ralph Yarborough introduced Gammage as a man with vision, character, and integrity. Gammage commented:

> I took my first oath of public office in this chamber 20 years ago [elected to the state legislature]. During the course of my campaign, I promised to be fair, impartial, and independent. I can't promise I will never make mistakes, but they will be my own. I look forward to the challenge, and thanks for the opportunity.[3]

A second freshman justice—John Cornyn, a conservative Republican—was also sworn in that day, raising the number of Republicans on the Texas Supreme Court from three to four. As former district court judge and "reform" candidate, Cornyn advocated higher ethical standards for all judges and proposed legislation that would require limits on campaign contributions to judicial candidates. As discussed in the previous chapter, Gammage and Cornyn joined incumbent Democrats Raul Gonzalez, Oscar Mauzy, Jack Hightower, and Lloyd Doggett; and Republicans Thomas Phillips, Eugene Cook, and Nathan Hecht. Chief Justice Phillips returned for his second term in 1990, having first been appointed by Republican governor Bill Clements in 1987 to serve out the rest of retired Chief Justice John Hill's term, and then winning election in November 1988. In January 1991, the court was now narrowly split 5-4 in favor of the Democrats—the last time Democrats would have a majority on the Texas High Court. Gammage was joining a divided court that was in the last years of a progressive era in the state that began in the late 1960s and ended in the 1990s.

The liberals on the court were sometimes joined by conservative-leaning Democrat Raul Gonzales, the first Hispanic to serve on the Texas Supreme Court. Gonzales was first appointed to the court by Governor Mark White (D) in 1984, after serving on the court of appeals and district court. Lastly, in 1993, Democrat Rose Spector became the first woman to be elected to the Texas Supreme Court. She would be the last Democrat to survive the Republican electoral sweep and domination of the judicial branch that continues to exist today. Table 3.1 shows the composition of the Texas Supreme Court in January 1991.

This chapter examines Gammage's record as a justice on the Texas Supreme Court. It analyzes pivotal and landmark decisions dealing with civil rights and liberties, the *Edgewood* school finance saga, balancing the First Amendment rights of abortion protests with the privacy of individuals, a challenge to the state's sodomy law, and high-profile tort law decisions. What follows is an exegesis of Gammage's jurisprudence primarily in selected cases, but it is also an account of legal thought of other jurists with whom he served on the court.

Table 3.1 Texas Supreme Court: 1991 Term

Justice	*Dates Served*	*Party*	*Ideology*
Gonzales, Raul	1984–1998	Democrat	Moderate to Conservative
Mauzy, Oscar	1987–1992	Democrat	Liberal
Hightower, Jack	1988–1996	Democrat	Moderate to Conservative
Doggett, Lloyd	1989–1994	Democrat	Liberal
Gammage, Bob	1991–1996	Democrat	Liberal
Phillips, Thomas (CJ)	1988–2004	Republican	Conservative
Cook, Eugene	1988–1992	Republican	Conservative
Hecht, Nathan	1989–present	Republican	Conservative
Cornyn, John	1991–1997	Republican	Conservative

Figure 3.1 Justices of the Texas Supreme Court: 1991 Term. Courtesy of the Supreme Court of Texas.

EDGEWOOD V. KIRBY: EDUCATION AS A FUNDAMENTAL RIGHT

As freshmen justices in 1991, Gammage and Cornyn now would have the opportunity to participate in one of the most protracted litigation sagas in Texas legal history: the school funding equity cases collectively known as *Edgewood v. Kirby.* Recall from the previous chapter that Gammage was serving on the Third Court of Appeals at Austin when it ruled 2-1 in *Kirby v. Edgewood* in 1988 (with Gammage dissenting) that the state's funding system was constitutional.[4] Then, on appeal in 1989, the Texas Supreme Court reversed the court of appeals ruling and ordered the legislature to devise an equitable plan for school funding. In November 1990 the justices heard oral argument on the constitutionality of the legislature's new plan in this second round of litigation. With the two new justices on the court, there was a great deal of statewide anticipation about the outcome of this case. Potentially every school district in the state would be affected. The *Austin American-Statesman* observed Justices-elect Gammage and Cornyn in the courtroom audience listening attentively, as skeptical justices peppered the state's attorneys with questions.[5]

Gammage played a pivotal role in *Edgewood*, first in 1988 on the Texas Third Court of Appeals and then from 1991 to 1995 as a justice on the Texas Supreme Court. His dissenting opinion in *Kirby v. Edgewood Independent School District* in 1988 was the first time an appellate court judge in Texas argued that education was a fundamental right, and that the state's system of school funding was unconstitutional because it deprived students in poor school districts of equal educational opportunities.[6] Gammage's dissent not only had a significant impact on the *Edgewood* cases, but it also stands out as an intellectually forceful call for equality and the most comprehensive and detailed explication of his equal protection jurisprudence.

The *Edgewood* case was in actuality six rulings between the years 1988 and 1995. The intent of the litigation was to compel the Texas legislature to adopt an equitable system of education funding. *Edgewood* involved hundreds of litigants, numerous judges, changing compositions of courts, and evolving or shifting alignments of justices, each positing a distinct interpretation of the provisions of the Texas constitution which mandate a public education system.[7]

In Edgewood I the unanimous court relied mainly on the position that the school-financing system violated the Texas constitution's obligation to provide an efficient and free public education in article VII, section 1, and noted the strong nexus between inefficiency and the denial of equal rights.[8] The funding system at issue provided an unbalanced diffusion of knowledge, contrary to the intent of the framers of the Texas constitution,[9] argued Justice Oscar Mauzy. He wrote:

> Property-poor districts are trapped in a cycle of poverty from which there is no opportunity to free themselves. Because of their inadequate tax base, they must tax at significantly higher rates in order to meet minimum requirements for accreditation; yet their education programs are typically inferior. . . . The amount of money spent on a student's education has a real and meaningful impact on the educational opportunity offered that student.[10]

The majority also rejected the court of appeal's argument that this case was a nonjusticiable political question, because the Texas constitution vests exclusive discretion over education in the legislature.[11] The constitutional mandate that the legislature provide for free public schooling is accompanied by certain standards, such as the requirement that schools must be efficient and suitable for the "essential purpose of a general diffusion of knowledge."[12] The court has the power of judicial review to use these imprecise terms as a measure of the constitutionality of the legislature's actions in the area of education policy.[13]

What was politically and logistically troublesome was that the court neither provided the state legislature with the specifics of the remedial legislation that it should enact nor ordered the legislature to appropriate money for the equalization of funding. The legislature was ordered to have a plan in place by the 1990–1991 school year to eliminate the "gross inequalities" and "vast disparities" among the districts.[14] These inequalities resulted from concentrations of resources in property-rich school districts that taxed at low rates, while property-poor school districts taxed at high rates but were still unable to generate the sufficient revenues to meet the minimum state-education standards.[15] Justice Mauzy argued that school "districts must have substantially equal access to similar revenues per pupil at similar levels of tax effort."[16]

Following the 1989 *Edgewood I* ruling, the legislature met in six special sessions called by the governor. On June 7, 1990, the legislature passed Senate Bill 1—a new funding plan that would increase state support for public schools, and establish a benchmark whereby 95 percent of Texas' students would ultimately attend school in an equalized system. However, the bill did not authorize the state to use revenue from the wealthiest school districts to fund the proposed equalized system.[17] The Mexican American Legal Defense and Educational Fund rejected the new legislation and asked the district court for another hearing.[18] Judge Scott McCown, who replaced Judge Harley Clark, who presided over the *Kirby v. Edgewood* case in 1988, ruled that the new plan was unconstitutional because it did not provide "substantially equal" access to public school funds, as ordered by the court in its 1989 *Edgewood I* ruling.[19] The State of Texas then appealed the district court's ruling, resulting in the court hearing *Edgewood II*.[20]

It was anticipated that the swearing in of two new justices—Gammage and Cornyn—would create uncertainty over the outcome of the case. This high-profile case was now in "limbo," wrote court-watcher Debbie Graves of the *Austin American-Statesman*.[21] The two new justices could either read the transcripts of the previous oral argument or ask that the case be reargued. Gammage had already gone on record on the school funding issue, since he wrote the long dissent in *Kirby v. Edgewood* while on the court of appeals. It was more uncertain how Cornyn would vote.

In January 1991, with Gammage now on the Texas Supreme Court, the justices ruled unanimously in *Edgewood II*[22] that the legislature's plan (Senate Bill 1)[23] was unconstitutional. The court gave the legislature three months to come up with a new proposal compatible with the standard set out in *Edgewood I*, which had called for the elimination of gross inequalities in funding.[24] The funding disparities between high-wealth and low-wealth districts were not ameliorated by the new law.[25] Chief Justice Phillips wrote:

> Senate Bill 1 does make certain improvements in public school finance . . . [including] a mandate for biennial adjustment, based upon information from a battery of studies, with the intention of preventing the opportunity gap between poor and rich districts from re-widening each time legislative action narrows it.

> However, Senate Bill 1 leaves essentially intact the same funding system with the same deficiencies we reviewed in *Edgewood I*.[26]

Senate Bill 1 focused primarily on increasing the state's contributions to reduce some of the existing discrepancies between school districts. The majority called this a "Band-Aid" that would not sufficiently change the system.[27] *Edgewood II* strengthened the requirement in *Edgewood I* that a "direct and close correlation must exist between a district's tax effort and the educational resources available to it."[28] *Edgewood II* also suggested remedies that would allow districts equal access to funds, such as consolidating school districts and tax bases.[29]

Edgewood I and *II* were progressive rulings by a unanimous court that had potential to create a more equitable system of public education. At this point, the various actors in the lawsuit and the legislature were repeatedly asking the court for clues about the type of system that would pass muster, but the court refused to issue what it believed to be an advisory opinion on the nature of a specific plan that might be constitutional.[30] The court suggested that the legislature needed to "change the boundaries of . . . the current 1,052 school districts, the wealthiest of which continue[d] to draw funds from a tax base roughly 450 times greater per weighted pupil than the poorest district."[31] Senate Bill 1 did not do this, nor did it attempt to equalize funding among the districts or change the way revenue was collected (from local property taxes as opposed to state revenue).[32] The legislature needed to devise a plan that provided "a direct and close correlation between a district's tax effort and the educational resources available to it."[33]

On April 11, 1991, the legislature passed Senate Bill 351 (SB 351) based on the court's suggested parameters for a remedy in *Edgewood II*.[34] The law created a new plan calling for the consolidation of the state's 1,058 school districts into 188 county education districts (CEDs), with each CED spending $2,200 per student.[35] The CEDs had the power to tax and distribute tax revenue to school districts existing within the CEDs.[36] The plan would generate new revenue from the wealthiest districts and then make it available statewide to decrease the disparities between the richest and poorest districts.[37] While three district courts found the bill to be constitutional, in *Carrollton-Farmers Branch Independent School District v. Edgewood Independent School District* (*Edgewood III*),[38] the Texas Supreme Court held that the law violated article VIII, section 1-e by levying a statewide *ad valorem* tax and article VIII, section 3 by levying an *ad valorem* tax without a required local election.[39]

Reading the massive and complex opinion, one senses the deep amount of frustration shared by the nine justices. While Gammage concurred with the majority's position that the tax imposed by the law was unconstitutional, in a separate dissent he expressed doubt that the court had honored its commitment to funding equity set forth in *Edgewood I* and *II*, and he accused the majority of striking down the same plan that the court had once supported.[40]

An angry Texas legislature[41] responded to *Edgewood III* by passing Senate Bill 7 (S.B. 7), a complex multi-option plan by which school districts would equalize per-student spending by choosing among several approaches.[42] The law set a cap on a school district's taxable property at a level of $280,000 per student. Any district exceeding the $280,000 cap could choose one or more of the following actions to bring its taxable property within the cap: "(1) consolidation with another district . . . (2) detachment of territory . . . (3) purchase of average daily attendance credit . . . (4) contracting for the education of nonresident students . . . or (5) tax base consolidation with another district . . . ."[43]

A number of both property-rich and property-poor school districts challenged Senate Bill 7 on a number of constitutional grounds in *Edgewood Independent School District v. Meno* (*Edgewood IV*)[44] in 1995. Prior to the court's response to Senate Bill 7, a growing number of voices around the state expressed skepticism about the justice's ability to solve the "school-finance mess." During oral argument on May 25, 1994, the justices appeared to be evenly divided along partisan lines and expressed their skepticism about the current iteration of the "Robin Hood" plan's leveling down formula, which took money from a handful of wealthy school districts and redistributed the funds to a large number of poor school districts—arguably hurting everyone and helping no one. The main point of contention was whether the "Robin Hood" plan was a statewide property tax, which is explicitly forbidden by the Texas constitution. *Texas Monthly* aptly characterized the *Edgewood* litigation as "a game of chicken between the Texas Supreme Court and the Legislature."[45]

Along the oak-lined walkways that crisscross the capitol complex, exasperated or angry legislators would stop the startled justices and plead for guidance on what the court wanted.[46] Gridlock had occurred between Republican chief justice Thomas Phillips and the legislature that, at the time, was dominated by Democrats. Gammage, who had served in both the House and Senate, was criticized by some legislators for lobbying for a separate bill for funding for judicial education and training while the two branches were at odds over the school funding plans. After that, Gammage, and other justices, no longer felt welcome in the statehouse and retreated to the Supreme Court building. Several legislators threatened to defund the court. Chief Justice Nathan Hecht recalled that initially he wanted nothing to do with the case because it was probably a political question best left to the legislature, but then he came around to believe that the court had an important role to play in creating an equitable system of education funding. Eventually, the storm passed, and the *Edgewood* litigation was "old hat," and not "a constitutional impasse or crisis."[47]

In *Edgewood IV*, the court ruled that the formula was constitutional, reasoning "the State's duty to provide districts with substantially equal access to revenue applies *only* to the provision of funding necessary for a general diffusion of knowledge."[48] The court held that Senate Bill 7 established an efficient system of public schools that equalized funding, which is required only to the point that efficiency is achieved, and that "unequalized" supplementation thereafter is constitutionally permissible.[49] The majority pointed out that the efficiency clause of article VII, section 1 contains a qualitative component—efficiency must be measured not only by financial efficiency but also by its qualitative component.[50] The court also backed away from the political fray by refusing to "prescribe the structure for 'an efficient system of public free schools,'" called for by *Edgewood III*.[51] That was a duty best left to the legislature, the majority opined, but "if the cost of providing a general diffusion of knowledge rises to the point that a district cannot meet its operations and facilities needs within the equalized program, the State will, at that time, have abdicated its constitutional duty to provide an efficient school system."[52] Justice Gammage joined the majority opinion in *Edgewood IV*, but he had not written separately on the issue since his dissent in *Edgewood III* in 1992.

Much of the news coverage and commentary was critical of *Edgewood IV*. The *Houston Post* called the decision a victory for the state and a loss for the property-tax-poor districts who challenged the law.[53] *Texas Lawyer* aptly quipped that an odd coalition upheld the law, with Cornyn and Phillips shifting away from their Republican colleagues to join "centrist Democrats" Jack Hightower, Raul Gonzales, and "liberal" Bob Gammage to produce a "confusing" and "contradictory" opinion.[54] This was the last of the *Edgewood* decisions in which Gammage participated, although school funding litigation continued through 2015.[55]

NEGLECT AND NEGLIGENCE: THE TRAGIC CASE OF OPAL PETTY

In 1995, the court heard one of the most heart-rending cases in Texas legal history, involving a long-forgotten woman named Opal Petty.[56] At age sixteen, she was committed to the Austin State Hospital. There, she languished forgotten for fifty years until Linda Kauffman learned, through a chance conversation at a family reunion in 1985, that her husband's aunt, Opal Petty, had been involuntarily committed for fifty years to a state mental hospital (as it was then called). The tragic tale began when Opal's parents, fundamentalist Baptists, were so exasperated by their sixteen-year-old daughter's recalcitrant and unusual behavior (which included dancing and dating), and what they believed to be intellectual impairment, committed her to the Austin State

Hospital in 1934. In 1971, Ms. Petty was then transferred to the San Angelo State School where she remained until 1985. Although the case turned on arcane questions of negligence and sovereign immunity, at the heart of the dispute lies the bitter truth than an innocent woman was confined for a half century.

Linda Kauffman contacted the institution and discovered that Opal Petty was indeed still there, long forgotten by her family. When the Kaufmans first visited Opal they found her listless, dirty, and wearing rags. She could barely communicate. With each visit, school officials became more uncooperative and taciturn. Kauffman finally arranged for Petty's release into her custody in 1985. Opal began to regain normal speech with the help of a speech therapist, played the piano for the first time since she was a child, and made clothing for her collection of dolls. She lived happily with Kauffman and her husband until her death at age eighty-six.[57]

Medical records dating back to her initial commitment in 1934 showed differing diagnoses made over a fifty-year period, ranging from schizophrenia, to mild retardation, to psychosis, to having no impairments or disability of any kind. Notwithstanding conflicting diagnoses, Opal Petty was confined for five decades without any meaningful periodic review by state officials. According to records the only treatment that was administered was employment in the hospital laundry at a salary of $2.00 per week. Even after Texas passed the Mentally Retarded Persons Act in 1978, and the US Supreme Court mandated review of involuntary commitment rules, Petty remained forgotten.

Opal Petty (through Linda Kauffman and Herbert Denson, as "next friends"), and with Jim Harrington of the Texas Civil Rights Project, sued the Texas Department of Mental Health and Mental Retardation.[58] They argued that the state wrongfully confined Petty because she was neither mentally ill nor intellectually deficient, and never received meaningful hearings to review her continued commitment. An Austin psychiatrist, Dr. Jefferson Nelson, testified that based on hospital records and his examination, she may have been psychotic when first committed in 1934 but should have been released shortly thereafter when her symptoms subsided.

The jury found in her favor. Petty had been injured as a result of the negligence of state personnel, whose actions deprived her of proper psychiatric care and treatment. Furthermore, her confinement deprived her of living skills that she possessed before confinement, as well as the skills that she would have developed had it not been for her institutionalization. The jury awarded Petty $505,000 in damages, but the trial judge reduced the award to $250,000 in accordance with the cap on damages imposed by the Texas Tort Claims Act.[59] The judge also ruled that under the Act, Ms. Petty could recover for damages only for the negligent actions that occurred after January 1, 1970, which was the effective date of the Tort Claims Act.

Aside from negligent treatment of Opal Petty at the hands of state employees—as well as the modest amount she was awarded for her suffering—the major issue addressed on appeal was whether Opal Petty had standing to sue the State of Texas. That is, did the doctrine of sovereign immunity bar the lawsuit? Sovereign Immunity is the doctrine that all government entities are presumed to have immunity from lawsuits. In Texas the only way to sue the state is to seek a waiver of sovereign immunity is under law. Under the Texas Tort Claims Act immunity can be waived if three conditions are met: (1) when a person is injured as a result of the use of public vehicles, (2) when there are defects in premises used or owned by the government, and (3) "personal injury and death so caused by a condition or use of tangible personal or real property if the government unit would, were it a private person, be liable to the claimant according to Texas law."[60] Although the law defines the conditions under which a waiver occurs, courts have the discretion to interpret the language of the law and to define the relevant tort law principles (such as negligence). As the Texas Supreme Court became more conservative, it limited waivers of liability so that plaintiffs could sue the government for damages.

In ruling for Petty, the trial court rejected the state's claim that her suit against the state was barred by sovereign immunity. In order for Ms. Petty to prevail, she had to prove that a state employee was negligent (using the traditional elements of common-law negligence) and that her injury was caused by "a condition or use of tangible personal or real property."[61] The Act does not define tangible property, however. Under precedent, the definition of tangible property includes the use or misuse of medical records, staff meeting results, notes on her progress, treatment plans, tests, evaluations or diagnoses. So, unlike a state employee negligently running over a pedestrian with a vehicle (tangible property), in Petty's case the tangible property would be the aforementioned medical records. The court of appeals affirmed the trial court's judgment and the state appealed to the Texas Supreme Court.[62] In 1992, a divided high court affirmed the court of appeals' decision in *Texas Department of Mental Health and Mental Retardation v. Opal Petty*.[63]

Gammage wrote the court's opinion that addressed the central issue in the appeal: Were the department's negligent actions encompassed within the conditions that must be met before the state allows a limited waiver of its sovereign immunity under the Tort Claims Act? During oral argument the justices and lawyers for both sides spent most of the time on this point. Were the totality of Opal Petty's medical records, which spanned fifty years, considered tangible property under the Act? Looking at this question from the standpoint of modern medical practices, one would need to ask whether a medical malpractice (negligence) suit could be brought against a surgeon for interpreting transcribed MRI results upside down. Would the MRI results be considered tangible property? The state's lawyers conceded that its employees acted negligently in their judgments but argued that Petty was not injured by the use of its property (as in the use of a vehicle). Since this condition was not met, it was argued, the department could not be sued. The department recognized "that the records are tangible in that they can be seen and touched, but nonetheless contended that Ms. Perry was not injured by the records themselves, but by their contents, consisting of intangible information." As the lawyer for the government stated, one cannot be injured by records unless a box of them falls on your toe. However, nearly a decade before Opal Petty's case, in *Salcedo v. El Paso Hospital District*,[64] the Texas Supreme Court *did* hold that the government could be sued because a physician who worked for the government acted negligently by misreading graphs produced by an electrocardiograph machine, and that the graphs were tangible property.[65]

Gammage noted that in *Petty*, the government insisted that no one could be harmed by medical records of any kind, just the harm resulting from incorrectly interpreting them. So if the state's reasoning prevailed, then Petty could not recover damages. The government also insisted upon drawing a distinction between *Salcedo* and *Petty*, based on the fact that the graph produced by an electrocardiogram machine was different from notes written down about Opal Petty by a hospital staff member. In sum, Gammage concluded, the jury correctly found that Ms. Petty was injured by the staff's use or misuse of property. In misusing her medical records, the state misdiagnosed her medical condition which in turn resulted in her prolonged confinement in mental institutions.[66]

In his dissenting opinion, Justice Cornyn[67] wrote that the *Petty* decision was without precedential value, because only four justices stated their reasons for affirming the lower court's decision. The majority relied on *Salcedo*, which he saw as a flawed decision. He admitted that there was no difference between the EKG graph in *Salcedo* and Ms. Petty's treatment records but argued that in both instances the tangible record or writing did not in itself cause the injury. Under the plurality's reasoning, any physical object could be identified and used to bring a claim within the waiver rule under the Act. Cornyn wrote, "while apparently motivated by the understandable concern that no one injured by the state's negligence go uncompensated, this would result in swallowing the rule whole."[68]

In the end, Ms. Opal Petty prevailed.[69] As a result of the ruling, the state modified its rules so that anyone who is confined receives an annual review of their condition. Opal Petty's case received very little media coverage: initially in 1992 by the *Dallas Morning News* and then in two 2005 obituaries that appeared in the *Los Angeles Times and New York Times*.[70]

FREEDOM OF SPEECH AND THE RIGHT TO PRIVACY AS COMPETING RIGHTS

The dilemma of competing rights has often been at its most intractable when tension exists between a woman's right to have an abortion and an anti-abortion activist's freedom to protest against the exercise of that right. According to the US Supreme Court, a woman's right to an abortion requires that no "undue burden" be placed on that right, and that she have access to a physician and facility where the abortion is to be performed.[71] Anti-abortion activists have long exercised their First Amendment rights in locations far removed from the traditional public forums of courthouses and state capitol buildings. Groups have demonstrated near medical facilities where abortions are performed, in front of the private residences of the physicians who perform abortions, and even in front of schools attended by the children of those physicians.[72] The motives of anti-abortion protestors include expressing moral outrage, shaming women who seek abortions, and intimidating abortion providers. There has also been violence, including fatal shootings and bombings, at abortion clinics.[73] It is estimated that over one thousand abortion clinics and facilities in the country have, at one time, been protected by court-ordered buffer zones.[74] The courts find themselves not only in the middle of two competing rights but smack in the middle of culture wars. It was in this context that, in 1993, the Texas Supreme Court heard the case of *Valenzuela v. Aquino.*[75] The *Austin American-Statesman* covered the case as one in which speech and privacy rights "collide in Courtroom."[76]

The case originated when a physician, Dr. Eduardo Aquino, sued Eliseo Valenzuela, Jr., and other anti-abortion protestors for negligent infliction of emotional distress and breach of privacy caused by incessant protesting outside of his home.[77] Aquino had an obstetrics and gynecological practice, a small part of which provided abortions. In 1982, a group called South Texans for Life began picketing at Aquino's offices. Even after the group threatened his personal safety, Aquino never attempted to enjoin them from protesting.[78] However, in 1988, the demonstrators began picketing the Aquinos' family home, often beginning their protest activities shortly after the Aquino children returned from school but before Dr. Aquino came home from work.[79] The group held signs bearing messages such as "Nice House Dr. Eduardo, How Many Babies Paid the Price," "Beware Abortionist in Your Block," and "God Gives Life, Aquino Takes Away."[80] Police cars were regularly parked on the street and Aquino's neighbors lined the streets to watch the demonstrations.[81] Protestors photographed the Aquino home, and on one occasion a protestor followed Ms. Aquino as she attempted to leave for the grocery store.[82] There was little doubt that this "circus-like" environment traumatized the family. Ultimately, Ms. Aquino was diagnosed with post-traumatic stress disorder and prescribed antidepressants.[83] The children were traumatized and suffered signs of emotional distress, and the oldest son was placed in a psychiatric hospital.[84]

At last, a temporary injunction was granted by the trial court, prohibiting the protestors from conducting a wide range of activities, "including all residential picketing within one-half mile of the Aquinos' home."[85] After the jury found for the Aquinos, the trial court awarded the Aquino family actual and punitive damages for infliction of emotional distress resulting from the breach of privacy caused by the demonstrators.[86] The trial court also issued a permanent injunction ordering the protestors to conduct their activities outside of a 400-foot buffer zone around the Aquino residence.[87] The district judge wrote:

> I believe Texas recognizes a right to privacy. This right, I believe, includes the right to be free from willful intrusions into one's personal life at home and at work—this right to be left alone from unwanted attention that may be caused by picketing or other unwanted demonstrations . . . is protected by injunctive relief.[88]

The court of appeals, in affirming the trial court's permanent injunction, found that there was a "significant governmental interest in protecting the privacy and domestic tranquility of the home," and the injunction was "narrowly tailored to serve [that] interest."[89] However, the court of appeals did reverse the jury's award of damages for the Aquinos' emotional distress because the court believed the monetary award constituted an infringement or "chill" on the protestors' freedom of speech.[90]

Oral argument before the Texas Supreme Court was complex and animated, focusing on a number of questions. First, should the justices analyze the dispute under the state or federal constitution? It was conceded that the Texas Constitution provided more speech protection than the US Constitution, but no one was aware of any existing state precedent directly related to the conflict before the court. Counsel representing Dr. Aquino, Frank Weathered, argued that the US Supreme Court made it clear in *Frisby v. Schultz* in 1988 that a "focused" and extended demonstration by anti-abortion protestors in front of a physicians' residence can be prohibited in the interest of the homeowner's privacy.[91] However, counsel for the antiabortion group, William Bundren, asked the justices to "work around" or downplay the importance of *Frisby* because the protestors had more speech protection at the state level than under the US Constitution. Justice Doggett seemed receptive to this line of reasoning. Another question was whether upholding the injunction imposed on nine of the group's more aggressive protestors would violate their constitutional rights. During oral argument, Justice Gonzales asked, "so anybody else can engage in the right to free speech except these

[nine] defendants?" and "does the right to privacy trump freedom of speech in all circumstances?" Justice Gammage interjected that the court should be mindful of the distinction between focused and unfocused expressive conduct. Focused conduct, in which the demonstrators targeted Dr. Aquino's family and home, as opposed to targeting his professional actions where he practiced, should receive less speech protection. Unfocused expressive conduct, such as flag burning in a public forum or protesting in the vicinity of an abortion clinic, should receive more protection. In the former instance *Frisby* would apply.[92]

Ultimately, the Texas Supreme Court reversed the permanent injunction and remanded the case back to the trial court.[93] Writing for the majority, Justice Nathan Hecht declined to address what he believed to be the "hypothetical" constitutional question of whether the award of damages constituted a chill on free speech on the grounds that no tort cause of action for negligent infliction of emotional distress exists in the state. Hecht argued that Dr. Aquino theoretically *could* have recovered damages for breach of privacy, but first, the trial court needed to determine whether the picketing "would be highly offensive to a reasonable person."[94] Dr. Aquino could have claimed that the protestors' acts resulted in an *intentional* intrusion on his privacy that was highly offensive to the average person, but the majority wrote that the testimony among the protestors and witnesses, relating to the presence of an intent to intimidate, was too ambiguous and contradictory to establish the second element of invasion of privacy.[95] The majority reasoned that, as horrible as the effects of the intense protesting might have been on the family, it could be argued that the demonstrators were not trying to intimidate Aquino but merely trying to express their heartfelt belief that abortion was morally wrong.[96]

It is somewhat unclear why the majority split hairs by focusing solely on the question of intentional versus negligent infliction of emotional distress, when the basis for Aquino's original petition was an invasion of privacy based on the US Supreme Court's ruling in *Frisby v. Schultz*.[97] Was the hair splitting a way of avoiding a thorny political issue in conservative Texas or was it an understandable reluctance to recognize a new tort? The Texas Supreme Court majority did recognize that *Frisby* allowed for limits to be set on residential picketing, but it did not believe that such picketing was illegal *per se*.[98] Notwithstanding a half-decade of protesting, Aquino's lawyers could not convince the majority that the breach of privacy was intentional and offensive. As a result, the majority refused to give serious consideration to the possible limits on such picketing.

In his dissenting opinion, Gammage agreed that under Article I, section 8 of the Texas Constitution's Bill of Rights, a person could not win damages from a group engaged in protected speech. However, the targeted individual may be allowed to recover damages that arise from conduct unrelated to protected expression.[99] He argued that the picketing of the doctor's home was "an assault on his family domain, not an assault on his professional activity that you (the protestors) object to."[100] It was doubtful that the group was interested in simply expressing their moral opposition to abortion, since the protestors targeted Aquino's home only at times when they knew *he* would not be home but his wife and children might be.[101] Instead, the protestors' intent was to intimidate and disrupt his family to the extent that he succumb to the pressure and stop performing abortions.[102] Even when the speech component of a group's demonstrations is protected, the conduct components—if they are aimed at intimidation—are not constitutionally protected and may permit recovery of damages. This is made plain in the draft card burning case, *United States v. O'Brien*, and other "speech-plus conduct" cases, where it has been established that a criminal conviction can be upheld if it stands on the noncommunicative impact of conduct.[103] Citing the Texas Supreme Court's ruling in *Casso v. Brand* in 1989, Gammage argued that under article I, section 8 of the Bill of Rights of the Texas Constitution, speech loses protection and may give rise to liability for damages where the conduct associated with the speech is "so excessive and intrusive" that it does not deserve protection.[104] In *Casso*, a mayoral candidate made allegedly defamatory statements against the incumbent mayor Brand, a public official, during a political campaign. The Texas Supreme Court ruled that absent actual malice, Brand could not recover damages for Casso's false statements about him.[105] However, the court recognized that unlike the US Constitution, the Texas Constitution expressly requires the speaker to be "responsible for the abuse" of the privilege to speak or publish, thus making it easier to seek damages for outrageous speech. Gammage added that liability for one's speech may arise only when "unprotected conduct is intertwined with protected expression," and the award for damages is based on that unprotected conduct.[106] He reasoned:

> Much of the demonstrators' conduct cannot be considered integral to their ability to deliver their message. Indeed, the record reveals that some of their conduct involved not just 'mere advocacy, but . . . [also included] . . . overt act[s] of intimidation' unrelated to protected expression. The presence of such conduct tends heavily to support the jury's finding that the demonstrators caused the Aquinos' mental anguish. To award damages as a consequence of unprotected collateral conduct does not chill free expression, and recovery should be allowed in this case.[107]

When the group of protestors realized that their constitutionally protected right to picket Dr. Aquino's clinic failed to meet their objectives, they went beyond expression and "intentionally engaged in conduct calculated to intimidate" the entire Aquino family by taking "outrageous actions at his private residence."[108] Gammage concluded: "What they could not win through the persuasion of protected free speech they sought to win through intimidation and coercion."[109]

The majority of justices believed that allowing the Aquinos to recover damages for the picketing that took place at their residence would create an unconstitutional chill on speech by sending the message to other protestors that they might be liable in some way merely for exercising their freedom of expression.[110] However, Gammage argued that damages awarded "as a consequence of unprotected collateral conduct" of the protestors, not because of their protected speech, do not chill the exercise of the freedom of expression.[111]

In a separate dissenting opinion, Justice Rose Spector (joined by Gammage) provided a lengthy analysis of the privacy interests at stake in this case.[112] Spector argued that the case originated as a breach-of-privacy claim.[113] By remanding the case back to the trial court, "the majority needlessly prolongs this litigation and effectively endangers a family's most basic rights."[114] When a violation of the right to privacy exists, injunctive relief is necessary—especially when legal remedies are inadequate, there are inadequacies with damages, or there is evidence of future violations.[115] Here, the evidence and the jury's finding that the picketing was "focused and directed" at the Aquino residence met the *Frisby* standard discussed earlier, which protects the right to residential privacy.[116] The dissenters relied on *Billings v. Atkinson*, which defines the right to privacy under Texas law as "the right of an individual to be left alone, to live a life of seclusion,"[117] to be free "from unreasonable intrusion,"[118] and "to preserve the sanctity of the home."[119] The conduct also threatened other privacy rights. By targeting and harassing doctors as the "weak link," anti-abortion rights groups know that they could make *Roe v. Wade* "an empty promise."[120] In the end, the dissenters agreed with the court of appeals that the award of damages in this case *would* inhibit debate on public issues but that an injunction is a reasonable restriction on expressive conduct.[121] The dissenting justices—a liberal to moderate bloc made up of Justices Gammage, Gonzales, and Spector—appeared puzzled by the absolute refusal of the majority to discuss the constitutional tension between Aquino's right to privacy and the expressive conduct rights of the pro-life group in question, South Texans for Life, even though this issue was brought up during oral argument and was mirrored by *Frisby*. In the end, the Aquino family suffered one of the most relentless and punishing campaigns even undertaken by an anti-abortion group.

In a second abortion protest case the same year as *Valenzuela*, *Ex parte Tucci*,[122] anti-abortion demonstrators challenged a temporary restraining order issued by a trial judge. Protestors were restricted from coming within 100 feet of any doorway or entrance, parking lot or driveway of any abortion clinic.

The protestors were then convicted of civil contempt after violating the order. The Texas Supreme Court ruling agreed with the protestors that the 100-foot restriction violated their right to engage in freedom of speech. Writing for the majority,[123] Justice Doggett relied on the Texas constitution, state precedent,[124] and the state's history to grant relief to the protestors.[125] He wrote:

> In reviewing the validity of the particular one-hundred foot limitation in these orders, we must look first to our Texas Constitution. With its broad command that "'every person shall be at liberty to speak . . . opinions on any subject,' article one, section eight . . . provides greater rights of free expression than its federal equivalent." "Its language demonstrates Texas' strong and longstanding commitment to free speech." [citing *Davenport v. Garcia*, 834 S.W.2d 4, 12 (Tex.1992)][126]

Doggett continued that unless such a restriction is demonstrated to be the least restrictive means of preventing an irreparable and imminent injury to persons at the clinic, it is an "impermissible infringement on our state constitutional right of free expression."[127]

Chief Justice Phillips joined the majority but approached the case from the standpoint of the First Amendment to the US Constitution, and not on independent state grounds. In rejecting Doggett's reliance on Texas history and precedent, Phillips wrote that "only because of the false construct of considering state constitutional issues first, pronounced by this Court in *Davenport*, has it been necessary for seven justices who join in the judgment to write three separate, time consuming opinions."[128] In *Davenport*, the court unanimously struck down a gag order as a violation of the speech protections found in the Texas constitution, article I, section 8. Doggett, in writing the majority opinion, again did not mention the First Amendment, over the objection of Justice Hecht. Gammage did not participate in either *Davenport* or *Tucci*.

PRESS FREEDOM AND THE RIGHT TO PRIVACY AS COMPETING RIGHTS

In 1995, the Texas Supreme Court returned to the issue of competing rights—in this instance the tension was between the freedom of the press and the right to privacy. One of the most challenging problems in adjudicating assertions of constitutional rights arises when rights must be balanced, not only with societal or governmental interests but also with other rights. A common example is when the freedom of expression and the right to privacy collide. When the news media obtains information about a crime or other event that is in the public's interest, freedom of the press must be weighed against the privacy of individuals, including a victim of crime or anyone else who might be harmed by the disclosure of private facts. Privacy suits are often brought against the media but they rarely prevail. If a news organization is held liable and punished for publishing the name or other information of a victim, then a chill on speech would occur giving pause to other news outlets which would then be fearful of lawsuits. The result would be self-censorship, leaving the news media unable or unwilling to play a pivotal role in a democratic society.

In the 1995 landmark ruling *Star-Telegram, Inc. v. Doe*, the Texas Supreme Court was asked to weigh the freedom of the press against the individual's right to privacy, and, more specifically, whether a newspaper may be held liable for disclosing private facts about a victim of sexual assault.[129] The case originated when *The Fort Worth Star-Telegram* published a news article based on a police report for the crime.[130] The attack occurred at the victim's home in the darkness of the early morning. Doe was bound with strips of her bedsheets but managed to free herself and call the police. The assailant was found driving the victim's car in Oklahoma and was apprehended by police. The news article did not name the victim, but it provided so much detail about her that it was almost impossible for acquaintances and neighbors not to know her identity.[131] The article disclosed Doe's age, her neighborhood, the fact that she drove a Jaguar, and even the medication she took.[132] A second published story gave an account of her sexual assault and added that she owned a travel agency.[133] The "police beat" reporter for the newspaper obtained information about the crime from an unredacted police report at the Fort Worth Police Department.[134]

Jane Doe sued the newspaper and the "police beat" reporter, Betsy Tong, for invasion of privacy and intentional and/or negligent infliction of emotional distress.[135] The newspaper responded that the information published was of legitimate public concern, citing the federal constitutional standard set adopted by the US Supreme Court in *Florida Star v. B.J.F.*, which provides that "if a newspaper lawfully obtains truthful information about a matter of public significance, then state officials may not constitutionally punish publication of the information absent a need to further a state interest of the highest order."[136] In *Florida Star*, a newspaper ran a similar story about a sexual assault victim based on an official police press report. However, the report actually identified B.J.F. by her full name and made it available to reporters in the sheriff's department's press room. A reporter-trainee copied the police report verbatim, including B.J.F.'s full name, and ran the story in the paper contrary to state law which made it unlawful to publish the names of sexual assault victims. B.J.F then won civil damages against the newspaper. The trial court denied the *Florida Star's* claim that civil sanctions against the newspaper violated the First Amendment. The verdict was upheld on appeal. The

US Supreme Court reversed, holding that imposing damages on the *Star* for publishing B.J.F.'s name did in fact violate the First Amendment.[137]

In *Star-Telegram* the Texas trial court granted summary judgment (in favor of the newspaper and reporter) without explaining the ground on which the judgment was based.[138] A state court of appeals reversed and remanded the case in order for the trial court to answer the question of whether the information had been lawfully obtained by the newspaper.[139] Even if the news articles contained information of legitimate public concern, the appeals court reasoned, the publications were not protected by the First Amendment because the information was unlawfully obtained. During oral argument before the Texas Supreme Court the justices all seemed very reluctant to challenge the newspaper's assertion of press freedom. Justice Gammage's only question had to do with the applicability of the Texas Open Records Act.[140] The court then unanimously reversed the court of appeals and held that no privacy violation had occurred, since the private facts disclosed about Doe, a crime victim, were of legitimate public concern.[141]

Writing the opinion for the unanimous court, Gammage began his analysis of the competing-rights claim by citing the famous 1890 Warren and Brandeis *Harvard Law Review* article. Warren and Brandeis argued for the first time that the right to personal privacy, or the "'right to be let alone' is as much a part of personal liberty as the right to be free from physical restraint and the right to possess property."[142] Gammage believed that this article provided the foundation for the modern constitutional right to privacy, including its articulation in *Griswold v. Connecticut*[143] and *Roe v. Wade*[144] decided by the US Supreme Court. Gammage wrote:

> The right to personal privacy was first articulated in 1890, in an article arguing that the "right to be let alone" is as much a part of personal liberty as the right to be free from physical restraint and the right to possess property. The concept has since been incorporated into a common-law tort in Texas and serves to protect individuals from invasion of privacy.[145]

This dimension of privacy is incorporated into a common-law tort in Texas that serves to protect individuals from invasions of their homes and disclosures of personal information.[146]

Returning to the issue of privacy in *Star-Telegram v. Doe*, Gammage cited *Industrial Foundation of the South v. Texas Industrial Accident Board*, a dispute which arose under the Texas Open Records Act.[147] A private nonprofit foundation had requested the State of Texas' Industrial Accident Board to furnish personal information of all workers who filed claims for workmen's compensation.[148] The Board argued that such information was protected by the right to privacy.[149] Several claimants for employment compensation had arrest records and the foundation sued to enjoin the release of these records.[150] The Texas Supreme Court ruled that the Board could not withhold information: "The State's right to make available for public inspection information pertaining to an individual does not conflict with the individual's constitutional right of privacy unless the State's action restricts his freedom in a sphere recognized to be within a zone of privacy protected by the Constitution."[151] The court found that no privacy interests were violated because the records dealt with public arrests and not personal information protected by the right to privacy, such as the nature of injuries or matters of marriage, procreation, or association. Nevertheless, in *Industrial Foundation*, the court did expressly recognize this second type of privacy tort—the right to "freedom from public disclosure of embarrassing private facts."[152]

Did the *Star-Telegram*'s detailed account of Jane Doe violate her right to privacy? The court said no. Justice Gammage wrote that although newspapers should take precautions to avoid the public disclosure of private facts, and that under Texas law the public had no legitimate interest in embarrassing facts about private citizens, a chilling effect on the freedom of press would occur if newspapers were required by law to take measures to avoid the publication of facts that may or may not subject innocent persons to unwanted or unpleasant notoriety.[153] During oral argument, the justices seemed to agree that Doe was correct in her argument that more personal information was published than necessary in the name of a legitimate public interest in newsworthy information. However, Gammage wrote that the media should *not* be expected to comb through all of the facts and "catalogue each of them according to their individual and cumulative impact." This would impose an onerous burden. Ultimately, information of legitimate public interest might be withheld.[154]

The justices were concerned that a ruling in favor of the newspaper might leave private citizens naked to media scrutiny simply because they were involved in a newsworthy event of legitimate public concern.[155] For example, if death penalty protestors incited a small riot in front of a courthouse, and a well-known attorney was inadvertently assaulted on the way to her car, does the media have the right to publish personal information about the lawyer? Gammage suggested that question such as these must be answered on a case by case basis. The determination of whether privacy could be sacrificed in the name of newsworthiness must be made "in the context of each particular case, considering the nature of the information and the public's legitimate interest in its disclosure.[156]

To untangle the competing rights issue in *Star-Telegram*, Gammage relied largely on *Florida Star* and, to a lesser degree, the state precedent of *Industrial Foundation*, stating that "there is a presumption under Texas law that the public has no legitimate interest in private embarrassing facts about private citizens."[157] There *is* a legitimate interest in factual information about a newsworthy event that may contain embarrassing facts. Of course, the claim of freedom of the press prevailed. Yet, of greater significance to Texas case law was Gammage's analysis of the right to privacy. He did not rely on federal precedent but instead built upon two Texas cases, *Billings v. Atkinson* and *Industrial Foundation*. These earlier cases are important because the Texas Supreme Court incorporated the concept of privacy into a common law that protects a range of interests, such as disclosure of private information about one's personal life. This common-law right protects individuals from invasions of their homes by electronic or other means of acquiring personal facts, and the subsequent disclosure of such information. This notion of privacy is distinct from federal precedent which focuses on three dimensions: marital privacy,[158] Fourth Amendment-based privacy,[159] and associational privacy.[160]

Recall from the lengthy discussion of the origin and evolution of right to privacy in Texas in chapter 2, Texas did not recognize any form of an invasion-of-privacy tort until *Billings*, when the Texas Supreme Court applied one of Prosser's[161] four distinct injuries under the tort of invasion of privacy—intrusion upon a person's right to be left alone in his or her own private affairs.[162] The second type of invasion, involving publicizing private information about a person, was recognized in *Industrial Foundation*.[163] The third involves the appropriation of a person's name, likeness, or personality for commercial gain, in *Kimbrough v. Coca-Cola/USA*.[164]

The fourth privacy doctrine, false light invasion, occurs when a person, acting with malice and reckless disregard as to the falsity of the publicized matter, gives publicity to a matter concerning another that places the other before the public in a false light which is highly offensive to a reasonable person.[165] False light was recognized but not adopted by the Texas Supreme Court in *Diamond Shamrock Refining*, when an employee brought an action against his former employer alleging false light invasion of privacy caused by the circulation of information regarding his termination for theft of nails from a construction site.[166] Writing for a divided court, Chief Justice Thomas Phillips argued that although the court had previously recognized in *Industrial Foundation* that false light was one of the four categories of tort action for invasion of privacy, it has never ruled on whether it existed in Texas. The employee's case should be remanded for a new trial without making a ruling in the affirmative or negative. A question related to false light would be whether recovery for damages would require the injured party to show actual malice or merely negligence. In practical terms, by recognizing the doctrine's existence the court would then allow for a range of lawsuits by injured persons by allowing them access to a new legal remedy. Interestingly, *amicus* briefs filed by members of the media—both print and electronic—urged the court not to adopt the false light doctrine for fear of the impact on press freedom, profits, or some combination of the two.[167]

In *Cain v. Hearst Corporation*, handed down in 1994 (a year before *Star-Telegram*), the court again refused to recognize the false light as an independent privacy tort, because it the justices felt that it "substantially duplicates the tort of defamation."[168] In *Cain*, a prison inmate sued the Hearst Corporation, claiming that the *Houston Chronicle* invaded his privacy by placing him in a false light.[169] The newspaper article stated that he had killed as many as eight people, but Cain complained only about his depiction as a member of the "Dixie Mafia."[170] In rejecting Cain's claim, the majority produced an impressive exegesis of the right to privacy, detailing the four privacy torts. The majority explained that even in light of several federal court rulings that permitted a cause of action for false light to be brought under Texas law, the Texas Supreme Court had been reluctant to adopt the "least-recognized and most controversial aspect of invasion of privacy."[171] Gammage, in joining Justice Hightower's dissenting opinion in *Cain*, agreed with the majority's analysis of the first three privacy doctrines but disagreed with its rejection of the false-light doctrine.[172] The dissenters[173] disputed the claim that "false light unduly increases the tensions between tort law and free speech law."[174] Hightower argued that the two torts were intended to protect different interests: "Defamation preserves individuals' reputational interests, but false light invasion of privacy extends to what people know and believe about them."[175] Defamation requires only publication of information to one person, who then changes his or her opinion about another person's good reputation, but false light requires widespread publicity of false information. For example, a newspaper article that maliciously and falsely reports that a person suffers from a deadly contagious disease would not be defamatory but could depict that person in a false light so that his friends and coworkers would avoid him like the plague. He might lose his job or clients based on false information. The fact that some overlap of the two torts occurs does not mean that the court shouldn't recognize both torts.[176]

On the matter of potential self-censorship by the media because of the possibility of a successful false light claim, the requirement that the injured party show actual malice safeguards press freedoms according to the US Supreme Court in *Time, Inc. v. Hill.*[177]

In November 1994, Justice Doggett resigned from the court to run for Congress. Doggett left behind a solid record supporting civil rights and liberties. Like Gammage, Doggett embraced a judicial philosophy that emphasized state constitutional law in resolving disputes, rather than automatically relying on federal precedent. He was replaced by Priscilla Owen, a Republican, who beat Democrat Jimmy Carroll in the November 1994 election. The *Houston Chronicle* reported the momentous event: Owen's election handed the GOP a solid majority on the Texas Supreme Court.[178]

INFLICTION OF EMOTIONAL DISTRESS: THE SEX TAPE CASE

In 1993, Gammage participated in the highly publicized sex tape case, *Boyles v. Kerr*.[179] Seventeen-year-old Dan Boyles, Jr. and his friends installed a hidden camera in his friend's home in order to record him and his nineteen-year-old girlfriend, Susan Kerr, having sexual intercourse.[180] Once the recording system was installed, Boyles and his two friends made crude commentary at the beginning of the tape as a prelude to the recorded sex act that was to follow. Boyles showed the tape to friends on three occasions and later shared with ten fraternity brothers, in some instances in exchange for money. Gossip spread among friends and acquaintances, in their hometown Houston and at the colleges that Kerr and Boyles attended college: she at Southwest Texas State University in San Marcos and he at the University of Texas at Austin. Boyles and Kerr had several previous consensual sexual encounters prior to the videotaping, but she did not know about the video recording.[181] This led to Kerr's reputation as a "porn queen" by many those who had seen the video or had knowledge of the recorded sex act. Her academic performance was adversely affected and she was later treated for depression as a result of PTSD.[182]

Kerr sued Boyles in a state trial court for willful invasion of privacy and negligent infliction of emotional distress. Before the case was submitted to the jury, and over the queries of a perplexed trial judge, Kerr's lawyers suddenly dropped the privacy complaint and pressed the negligent infliction of emotional distress action. A Houston jury returned a verdict for Kerr, awarding her $1 million—$500,000 in actual damages and $500,000 in punitive damages.[183]

The case soon reached even greater heights of infamy, as during the appeal phase in the lawsuit the firm representing Boyles violated a court order to keep the tape private, prompting *The New York Times* to write that the Houston law firm that represented Boyles—Hirsch, Glover, Robinson & Sheiness—should be renamed "Hirsch, Glover & Shameless."[184] Upon hearing the amount of the million-dollar judgment, which the firm thought would be higher, Boyles's lawyers decided to celebrate their "victory" at a retreat on Lake Conroe, north of Houston. While the partners partied, some members of the firm who were not invited to the party watched the tape again, ostensibly to prepare for the appeal. They were joined by secretaries, paralegals, and others, one of whom exclaimed, "Let's get to the good part!" The firm also sent a copy of the tape to Boyles's homeowner's insurance company, where five more people were able to enjoy it. Upon hearing of this breach of ethics, Judge Davis West fined the firm $2,000. The firm also settled with Kerr for an undisclosed amount for their carelessness.[185]

The court of appeals[186] affirmed the trial court's million-dollar judgment against Boyles, stating that Kerr had successfully established negligent infliction of emotional distress and negligent invasion of privacy. However, the Texas Supreme Court reversed the trial court's judgment, ruling that although Boyles's behavior was offensive, the tort of negligent infliction of emotional distress was not the proper remedy to pursue. Indeed, the majority refused to recognize this tort doctrine. Therefore, the court of appeals' decision was reversed. Kerr's case was sent back to Houston for a second trial—"in the interest of justice"—to give the Kerr an opportunity to have the case tried on other legal grounds, namely the doctrine of intentional infliction of emotional distress that the court had just adopted in the companion case of *Twyman v. Twyman*, handed down the same day.

Recall from chapter 2 that the sexual bondage case *Twyman v. Twyman* was heard by Gammage in 1990 while he served on the Third Court of Appeals. The dispute involved a pattern of coerced sexual bondage and alleged "deviate sexual acts" in which a wife sought to recover damages against her estranged husband for negligent infliction of emotional distress. Gammage, now on the Supreme Court when the *Twyman* appeal was heard, recused himself because he wrote the majority opinion in the case while he served on the court of appeals. He *did* however participate in *Twyman*'s companion case, *Boyles v. Kerr.*

Writing for the majority of the court in *Boyles*, Chief Justice Thomas Phillips rejected the doctrine of *negligent* infliction of emotional distress as an independent cause of action for a number of reasons. First, Phillips argued that this tort doctrine encompassed too broad a category of behavior, including actions that are merely rude or insensitive. Tort law is not intended to provide a remedy for every form insensitive or distasteful behavior, he argued. Its adoption by the court would create an avalanche of litigation in the state, especially by litigants seeking big settlements from insurance companies that cover homeowners in Texas. Second, a person can only recover damages for *negligent* behavior only when the alleged negligent action or inaction occurs in connection with the breach of some other legal duty owed to the plaintiff by the defendant. For example, a hospital owes a duty to a patient or landlord to a tenant. Third, the existence of this tort was by no means a settled matter—indeed, a body of scholarly and legal debate existed over whether a plaintiff needed to show a form of physical manifestation of the alleged emotional distress.

Was negligent infliction of emotional distress a legitimate tort doctrine or were Kerr's lawyers creating a legal fiction? In 1987, the Texas Supreme Court *did* recognize negligent infliction of emotional distress in *St. Elizabeth's Hospital v. Garrard.*[187] In that case, a husband and wife sued a hospital for disposing of the couple's stillborn baby in an unmarked common grave without their knowledge or consent. Prior to this ruling, Texas case law maintained that in order to recover for negligent infliction of emotional distress, a plaintiff needed to prove physical injury: in other words, an allegation of mental suffering alone was not actionable without proof of some form of physical manifestation of the mental suffering. However, in the *Garrand* case, the court, per Justice C. L. Ray, a liberal Democrat who served on the Supreme Court until 1990, found that the physical manifestation requirement was arbitrary and anachronistic and therefore abolished it. What resulted was the adoption of the doctrine of negligent infliction of emotional distress, defined as a general duty not to inflict reasonably foreseeable emotional distress.[188]

In *Boyles*, however, the majority held that *St. Elizabeth's Hospital v. Garrand* was wrongly decided and overturned it because, in Phillips's view, that decision was based on an incorrect interpretation of Texas case law. Phillips also wrote that due to the ambiguity of that decision, lower state courts were having difficulty determining whether the 1987 ruling created a new independent cause of action for emotional suffering, thus contradicting the notion that "tort law cannot and should not attempt to provide redress for every instance of rude, insensitive or distasteful behavior, even though it may result in hurt feelings, embarrassment, or even humiliation."[189] He rejected Kerr's argument that even if the court does not recognize recovery for negligent infliction of emotional distress, it should recognize a right to recovery for *grossly* negligent infliction of emotional distress.[190] Phillips further argued that:

> The liability standard under this new tort, however, was never entirely clear. *Garrand* seemed indicate that "trivial" emotional distress should not be compensated . . . and similarly that the law should protect against "severe" emotional distress. Rather than articulating any threshold level of severity, however, the Court concluded that "jurors are best suited to determine whether and to what extent the defendant's conduct caused compensable mental anguish by referring to their own experience."[191]

In a concurring opinion, Justice Raul Gonzalez expressed puzzlement why Kerr's lawyers gave up her right to recovery under two recognized theories of recovery: willful invasion of privacy and intentional infliction of emotion distress. Her lawyers made a poor "strategic decision to proceed only with the questionable theory of negligent infliction of emotional distress." Gonzales wrote:

> Ms. Kerr's lawyers may have believed that if they obtained a judgment declaring that Boyles' conduct came within the rubric of "negligence" (inadvertence or carelessness), they could tap the homeowners policies owned by the parents of Boyles and the other defendants'. Thus, this case has a lot to do with a search for a "deep pocket" who can pay.[192]

Justices Gammage and Spector joined Justice Lloyd Doggett's fiery dissenting opinion, which criticized the court's legal hair splitting over intentional versus negligent infliction of emotional distress. Boyles and his confederates may not have *intended* to cause emotional harm to Kerr but they did intend to videotape the sex act without her consent and intended to distribute it to their friends. The dissenters viewed the majority's ruling as nothing more than another attempt by the court to create barriers to prevent exploited people from recovering damages. According to the logic of the ruling, the dissenters argued, even though the injury was the same, and the behavior that caused the injury calculated and outrageous, Kerr could not recover unless it were shown that Boyles intentionally tried to cause harm. Doggett believed that the court was wrongly overturning the 1987 precedent of *St. Elizabeth Hospital.*[193] In its decision to make the standard for recovery more exacting,[194] the dissenters believed that the majority "recant[ed] the respect for human dignity affirmed by this court in *St. Elizabeth Hospital*"[195] Doggett also argued that the court should have held that Boyles owed a duty not to negligently inflict harm on Kerr rather than "belatedly discover[ing] a brand new, narrowly-drawn alternative intentional infliction cause of action." Doggett concluded:

> For her trouble, the majority imposes on Susan Kerr the obligation to pay court costs and reverses completely the judgement for damages awarded for the severe emotional distress she suffered when he most intimate act was videotaped and, with utter and complete disregard for her welfare, shared with others. Refusing to accept responsibility for overturning a century of Texas law in order to deny Susan Kerr recovery, then blaming the victim—this is not justice.[196]

In his notes from the court's oral argument in *Boyles*, Gammage wrote that Kerr could have sought a remedy under an *intentional* tort such as invasion of privacy, but he believed that *negligent* infliction of emotional distress was already an established remedy in Texas. Gammage was perplexed by the fact that the majority was eliminating a tort remedy and rejecting a precedent that was no more than six years old in order to protect insurance companies.[197]

Following the court's decision in *Boyles v. Kerr*, there was an onslaught of finger-pointing and contentious debate, not only among the justices but among journalists and legal scholars, as well.[198] Were the two sides of the court divided by legitimate jurisprudential differences, or was it purely ideological? Was the decision based on an accurate interpretation of tort law? As outrageous as the conservatives in the majority believed Boyles's actions to be, they could not bring themselves to make it easier for women to bring tort actions in sexual exploitation cases for fear of an avalanche of lawsuits. Liberals on the court, like Doggett, Spector, and Gammage, believed that in cases like *Twyman* and *Boyles*, conservatives instinctively sought to protect insurance companies and homeowners from million-dollar lawsuits brought by personal injury lawyers. Conservatives embraced the opposite position, believing that the liberal justices were reflexively supportive of plaintiffs in personal injury lawsuits. Many lawyers believed that Susan Kerr should have begun litigation anew but instead she settled with Boyles for $500,000 and with the firm representing Boyles for $600,000. A television mini-series about the case was proposed but never materialized.

Was the decision was a product of "maleness" and not legal precedent? The all-male majority sincerely believed that Kerr *was* horribly exploited, but from the standpoint of the "reasonable man" standard, she suffered no real injury under the law. Even in the era of #MeToo many women are still raising the issues presented in *Boyles* and *Twyman*—that is, men, conservative or liberal men—don't get it. Many who played a role in the litigation believed the court's ruling was as callous as Boyles's videotaping of the sex act. A number of advocacy groups, such as the Women's Advocacy Project, went on record that the court's decision was based purely on sexism and that it left victims of sexual abuse without a remedy, because the case law in Texas made it very difficult to recover damages for sexual exploitation.[199]

In contrast, a conservative Houston attorney named Kiri Martin agreed with the majority in blaming trial lawyers for Kerr's troubles. She opined in a *Houston Chronicle* article that Kerr's lawyers could have relied on intentional infliction of emotional distress but chose not to, purely because it would have been impossible to collect their contingency fee from the future earnings of college students; so they pursued the homeowner's insurance company under a negligence-based doctrine.[200]

Further evidence that the public was following the case was an unusual thank-you note that was sent to Justices Doggett, Mauzy, and Gammage from a woman in Garland, Texas. She wrote:

> On behalf of many people who either directly or indirectly have or will be affected by the recent decision . . . let me offer you and Justice Mauzy and Gammage a thank you for attempting to right a wrong. Please continue to fight to preserve the rights of the other citizens of the State of Texas. The women and minorities . . . Again, thank you for being in the dissenting vote. I know I made a right choice when I voted for you in the last elections.[201]

In chapter 2 we discussed the Third Court of Appeals ruling in *Twyman v. Twyman.* In that case a wife sought to recover damages against her husband for negligent infliction of emotional distress because he "intentionally and cruelly" attempted to engage her in "deviate sexual acts." The trial court ruled in favor of Shelia Twyman, and the court of appeals sustained the judgment.

Gammage wrote for the majority in that case, recognizing the existence of negligent infliction of emotional distress. However, on appeal two years later, with Gammage now on the Supreme Court, the majority reversed Gammage's decision in *Twyman*[202] refusing to recognize the tort of negligent infliction of emotional distress, just as it did in the companion case of *Boyles.* The court then remanded the case for a new trial under the tort of *intentional* infliction of mental distress as a possible remedy. Justice Gammage recused himself from the case since he wrote the majority opinion in the court of appeals' ruling.

Writing the high court's plurality opinion in *Twyman v. Twyman* in 1993,[203] Justice John Cornyn stated that while the appeal in *Twyman* was pending, the court, in the companion case of *Boyles v. Kerr*[204] discussed earlier, refused to recognize the tort of negligent infliction of emotional distress. However, in *Twyman*, the court *did* decide to expressly recognize that the tort of intentional infliction of emotional distress. Cornyn, writing for a plurality of justices, characterized the newly recognized doctrine as follows:

> As distinguished from the tort of negligent infliction of emotional distress, we believe the rigorous legal standards of the Restatement formulation[205] of intentional infliction of emotional distress help to assure a meaningful delineation between inadvertence and intentionality or recklessly outrageous conduct. The requirements of intent, extreme and outrageous conduct, and severe emotional distress before liability can be established will, we think, strike a proper balance between diverse interests in a free society. That balance, at minimum, must allow freedom of individual action while providing reasonable opportunity for redress for victims of conduct that is determined to be utterly intolerable in a civilized community . . . This holding represents a middle ground between the polar positions adopted by various members of the court.[206]

Cornyn was confident that individuals who have been subjected to sexual exploitation were definitely *not* left in in the cold. Armed with this new tort, women could seek damages for the type of harm endured by Sheila Twyman.

Justice Hecht, who has consistently demonstrated a philosophy of judicial restraint through the years, dissented from the majority's decision to adopt intentional infliction of emotional distress. He argued that "intentional or reckless infliction of emotional distress is too broad a rubric to describe actionable conduct, as this case illustrates." He feared that this new tort would be asserted not only in divorce litigation but in disputes involving employers and employees, patients and physicians, clients and lawyers, to name but a few.[207]

Dissenting, Justice Rose Spector was troubled by the plurality of the justice's rejection of infliction of emotional distress claims based on negligence. Short of calling the plurality of justices sexists, she did call their position on inter-spousal immunity "medieval." "Today, when the widespread mistreatment of women is being documented throughout the country for instance, in the areas of sexual harassment and domestic violence a majority of this court takes a step backward and abolishes one way of righting this grievous wrong." She reasoned that in many instances emotional distress was caused by a person who did not set out or intend to inflict harm and "who is even oblivious to the fact that such distress is certain, or substantially certain, to result from his conduct."[208] Perhaps William Twyman coerced Sheila into bondage activities only for the purpose of satisfying his own sexual desires, but he did cause severe harm to Sheila. Justice Spector concluded:

> While the plurality would allow some possibility of recovery for injuries like Sheila Twyman's, the dissenting opinions by Chief Justice Phillips and Justice Hecht would allow none at all. Adopting the medieval view of marital relations, Chief Justice Phillips argues that spouses should be shielded from liability for even the most outrageous acts against one another. This view echoes William Twyman's assertion at trial that, by consenting to marriage, Sheila Twyman assumed the risk of physical injury and emotional harm. Fortunately, in Texas, this archaic view has been soundly rejected; interspousal immunity has been abolished "completely as to any cause of action."[209]

The *Austin American-Statesman*, covering the rulings in *Twyman* and *Boyles*, stated that the Texas Supreme Court—in what constituted a setback for women—created a new standard in emotional distress lawsuits.[210] Did the court instantly adopt a new and novel doctrine? True, as the court stated, forty-six other states allowed recovery under the tort of intentional infliction of emotional distress, but this was not the first time the tort was recognized by a Texas appellate court.[211] Based on *Boyles* and *Twyman*, victims of sexual exploitation in some form would now need to use this new remedy.

SOCIAL HOST LIABILITY AND THE "EVOLVING COMMON LAW"

In 1993, the court handed down a ruling with broad legal and public policy ramifications. *Graff v. Beard*[212] addressed the question of whether a social host serving alcohol could be found liable for the injuries of a third party caused by a guest. Examples of a social host include a couple inviting a few friends over for wine and cheese, a Fourth of July barbeque, and a fraternity keg party that serves 200 imbibers. Groups such as MADD, individuals who had been injured, or those seeking to reign in fraternity parties hoped that the Texas Supreme Court would rule that social hosts were liable for the injuries of third parties.

The case in question originated when a Mr. Houston Moos left a party that was hosted by the Graff and Hausmon families. Driving from the party while in an intoxicated condition, Moos's vehicle collided with a motorcycle operated by Brett Beard. Beard sued both Moos and his hosts for his injuries. The trial court dismissed Beard's lawsuit against the hosts, but the court of appeals reversed and remanded the case for trial. Although no Texas court had ever held that social hosts were liable for the injuries of third parties caused by intoxicated party guests, the court of appeals held that the Graff and Hausmon families were liable for Beard's injuries. The foreseeable risk posed by the drunk driver justified imposing a common-law duty on social hosts.[213] In essence, for the first time in Texas legal history, an appellate court held that a social host violated a common-law legal duty to a third party when the host served an alcoholic beverage to a guest the host knew was intoxicated and would be driving. The duty of the host, then, is either to prevent the guests who will be driving from becoming intoxicated or limiting his or her access to a motor vehicle or any machine that might cause harm if operated by an intoxicated person.

Insurance companies braced for impact. An adverse ruling could open the floodgates for personal injury lawsuits which would be paid out of homeowner insurance policies. A segment of the bench and bar were concerned that the state's Dram Shop law would be extended to backyard barbeques, creating a nightmare scenario where mom and dad were obligated to ascertain who had too much to drink or from whom to take away the keys to the pickup truck. Texas, like most states, has a Dram Shop law. Enacted by the state legislature in 1987, the law defines the legal liability that bars and other establishments that serve alcohol have to persons who are injured by the actions of an intoxicated person. The law allows victims of alcohol-related accidents to sue bars and restaurants for negligence.[214]

During oral argument and conference discussion, three justices were clearly inclined toward establishing a social host cause of action—Justices Gammage, Doggett, and Hightower—although Hightower expressed reservations about how the court could justify this decision in its opinion. Chief Justice Phillips and Justices Cook, Hecht, Cornyn, and Gonzales were inclined against. Phillips's focus was on the Dram Shop law. He believed that it was up to the legislature to resolve this question, not the courts. The majority of justices were clearly worried that a decision for establishing a social host liability doctrine would alter the conduct of every backyard barbeque in Texas. Gammage mused that although it might affect the level of fun at backyard barbeques, "it should be remembered that the innocent and sober guest en route to the party is entitled to the same legal protection from a drunken and dangerous departing guest as any other member of the driving public." "If circumstance do not permit the social host to adequately monitor and control the quantity of alcoholic beverages a guest consumes, the host still retains absolute control over whether alcoholic beverages should be served at all."[215]

However, in *Graff v. Beard* in 1993, the Texas Supreme Court reversed the court of appeals, rejecting a "judicially created duty" to injured third parties on the part of social hosts.[216] Writing for the 6-2 majority, Justice Cornyn argued that the Texas Dram Shop law which imposed a statutory duty on commercial providers (such as restaurants and bars) does not impose such a duty on noncommercial social hosts.

Cornyn pointed out in *Graff* that the highest courts in only four states had recognized a social host's duty to guests when alcohol was served.[217] Historically, tort law never recognized a common-law duty of the providers of alcohol to third parties, because the consumption of alcohol by the drunkard, rather than the provision of it by the host, proximately causes the injury. The social host could not be held liable, because the host could not reasonably know the guest's alcohol consumption and possible intoxication; nor did the host have the right to control the conduct of the guest. Under Texas law, in the absence of a relationship between parties that gives the right to control, such as that which exists between an employer over an employee, the average person is under no duty to control the conduct of another. So, although an employer might be held liable because of the employers' negligent exercise of control over the employee (allowing him to drink at work or at lunchtime), there is not a general duty to prevent intoxicated individuals at social gatherings from driving. Cornyn argued that the court of appeals erred by focusing not on whether the host had the duty to control the guest but on the host's duty to control the alcohol supply. If alcohol were made available to the guest, then under the new standard established by the court of appeals, the host would not be liable if he cut off the alcohol at some point before the guest became intoxicated. How could a host gauge this threshold? "The guest, on the other hand," argued Cornyn, "is in a far better position to know the amount of alcohol he has consumed, his state of sobriety, and the consequential risk he poses to the public."[218] The second problem was that should the guest become intoxicated the host then must prevent the guest from driving. What would the host need to do to fulfill his duty? Give a warning? Take car keys? Forcibly restrain the guest?[219] Cornyn concluded that the implications of these unaddressed questions "demonstrate the frail foundation upon which the court of appeals has constructed social host liability." "The guest . . . is in a far better position to know the amount of alcohol he has consumed, his state of sobriety, and the consequential risk he poses to the public." Cornyn continued, "We cannot assume that guests will respond to a host's attempts, verbal or physical, to prevent the guest from driving."[220]

Prior to *Graff*, the Texas Supreme Court had already held in *Smith v. Sewell* earlier in its 1993 term that when the legislature enacted the 1987

Texas Dram Shop law, it declined to create a common-law duty on the part of social hosts to guests, such as the one asserted by Beard.[221] A version of the bill that ultimately became the 1987 law, provided for social host liability, but the law which passed both houses did not contain the social host liability provision.[222] The law also superseded the court's 1987 ruling in *El Chico Corporation v. Poole*[223] that commercial providers owed a common-law duty to injured third parties as a result of serving alcohol.[224] The 1987 Dram Shop law made it even more difficult to sue vendors than it was under the common-law standard, stating that vendors could be held accountable only when it could be proved that at the time of the service the patron was "obviously intoxicated to the extent that he presented a clear danger to himself and others."[225]

In his dissenting opinion, Gammage (joined by Justice Doggett) rejected Cornyn's contention that the only the legislature could "create" a duty for social hosts not to send their intoxicated guests "driving in our streets to maim and kill."[226] The legislature, Gammage argued, may or may not enact a law to create a duty, but the legislature's failure or reluctance to do so does not eliminate an existing duty that is already created by the common law. A duty based on the common law exists until the legislature takes action to eliminate it, which it has not. Thus, the common-law duty applies to the defendants in this case. This is another example of Gammage's emphasis on the common law as a higher law, and how the common law often offers more guidance in matters of social obligations. He held the position that the majority sought to repudiate the principles established in *Poole* and "stop the evolving common law dead in its tracks."[227]

In *El Chico v. Poole* in 1987, Justice Franklin Spears argued for a common-law duty of commercial vendors of alcoholic beverages not to serve patrons when the vendor knew, or should have known, that the patron was intoxicated and going to drive in that condition.[228] However, it did *not* extend this duty to social hosts. Despite this, Gammage argued that the fact that the court did not address the matter of a social host's liability should not have been construed to mean that the common law of Texas did not apply or "may not be reasonably deduced from *Poole's* language."[229] Gammage wrote:

> The majority fails to acknowledge *Poole's* rationale that the most important factor in recognizing a duty under the common law of negligence is the foreseeability of the risk . . . Probably the most important quotable line from Poole suggests the foreseeability here is analogous to letting a rattlesnake loose on an unsuspecting public: "The risk and likelihood of injury to serving alcohol to an intoxicated person whom the licensee knows will probably drive a car is as readily foreseen as an injury resulting from setting loose a live rattlesnake in a shopping mall."[230]

If the word "social host" is substituted for "licensee," the statement remains equally true, argues Gammage. Logically, no distinction should be made, especially when as the court recognized in *Poole* the public policy considerations of driving while intoxicated. It is no less tragic to die in an accident caused by a drunk driver served by a commercial vendor than by a drunk driver who was served by a social host. The danger is equally as great. The only difference between the social host and commercial vendor is the nature of the relationship to the driver. The risk and foreseeability of harm are the same. "Balancing the relationship factor, in determining whether a duty exists, must tip in favor of the public interest."[231]

In addition to the court's ruling in *El Chico v. Poole*, there was the 1983 case of *Otis Engineering Corp. v. Clark*,[232] where an employer, seeing that his employee was intoxicated, sent him home knowing that he was going to drive while intoxicated. In *Otis* the court found that the employer was liable because of the employer's negligent exercise of control over the employee. The *Graff* majority believed that this fact distinguished *Otis* from *Graff*. In *Otis*, the control was sending the drunk employee home while in Graff the host served alcohol to an intoxicated driver knowing that he or she would drive. Either way, wrote Gammage, the risk was "knowingly letting the rattle-snake loose."[233] Gammage argued that the majority was overly concerned with the host's difficulty in preventing injury—that is, difficultly in placing a duty on the host to prevent the intoxicated guest from driving—but it ignored the fact that the injury was a consequence of intoxication. The host may not have been in a relationship of control (like an employer over the employee) but the host did control the flow of alcohol and therefore had the duty to make every reasonable effort to keep the inebriated guest from driving. If the guest resisted those efforts and drove away then it would be up to a jury or factfinder to determine "whether the host's efforts were all that reasonably could have been done under the circumstances." Furthermore, Gammage took issue with the majority's assertion that the guest was in a far better position to know the amount of alcohol he had consumed than the host because "from personal observation we know that most persons, as they become intoxicated . . . gradually become less and less cognizant of how much they've had and how badly intoxicated they are."[234]

The majority was obviously troubled by what Gammage called the "evolving common law" that ought to place liability on social hosts as well as commercial vendors. Gammage believed that the majority wanted to stop this evolution in its tracks and return to an old common-law doctrine that a person's decision to drink is the only proximate cause of the harm—that is, it is the "drinkers fault only" rationale. The state's Dram Shop law addressed liability of commercial servers but did not address social host liability. So, for Gammage, the court‘s duty was to resolve this omission by applying the evolving common law to a real societal problem.

Gammage concluded by recalling the television commercial that stated: “Friends don’t let friends drive drunk.”[235] He argued, the majority was saying, “Intoxicate your friends and send them out upon the public streets and highways to drive drunk. Don’t worry, you won’t be liable.” He believed that this was unsound policy contrary to the court’s earlier decisions and the decisions of other state courts. The court refused to impose a common-law duty on social hosts and believed that the legislature must do so, not the court. Gammage said the duty already existed in the common law regardless of the legislature’s or court’s inaction. Gammage argued that social hosts bore the same responsibility as bartenders or establishments who sold drinks.

The *Austin American-Statesman*, several days after the decision, cited Gammage’s dissenting opinion. It wrote that according to the court, party hosts had no legal liability for deaths, injuries, or property damage caused by their guests who left the party drunk. The article noted that according to Justice Cornyn, liability would remain with guests at social gatherings and not be extended to their hosts.[236] Published shortly after the decision was a *Texas Bar Journal* article, titled “Friends Can Let Friends Drive Drunk.” Written by two civil litigators, the article supported Gammage’s dissent in *Graff* and took issue with the majority’s conclusions.[237]

Four years after *Graff*, in *Smith v. Merrit*,[238] a unanimous Texas Supreme Court held that according to the Texas Dram Shop law, there is no liability for social hosts who served alcohol to guests who were 18 years old or older. The court rejected outright the plaintiffs’ argument that *Graff* did not apply because the host gave alcoholic beverages to a guest below twenty-one, the legal drinking age in Texas. In *Reeder v. Daniel*[239] in 2001, a unanimous supreme court ruled that no common-law cause of action may be brought against a social host, even if that host served alcohol to a guest under eighteen years old. The justices refused to extend liability to a social host under a theory of negligence based on the penal section of the Alcohol Beverage Code, which is bifurcated into civil and penal sections. The penal section extends criminal liability to persons serving alcohol to minors, but the Dram Shop provision is found in a different section of the Code. Four years after *Reeder*, the legislature amended the Dram Shop law by adding a provision that would allow a civil cause of action to be brought against adult social hosts who served alcohol to “true minors,” persons under eighteen years old.[240] As of this writing, the Texas Supreme Court has not handed down any rulings on social host liability since the 2005 amendments and *Graff* is still precedent.[241]

THE TEXAS SODOMY LAW

In 1994, nine years before the US Supreme Court's historic ruling *Lawrence v. Texas*,[242] which struck down sodomy laws nationwide, Gammage participated in a case that had the potential to overturn Texas' sodomy law.[243] The law was rarely, if ever, enforced, and there was no evidence that it would be in the near future.[244] Nevertheless, the law was used to stigmatize and discriminate against homosexuals in areas such as housing, family law, and employment.[245] In *State v. Morales*, three lesbian women and two gay men[246] challenged the law on the grounds that it violated the Texas constitution.[247] The case took five years to work its way through the Texas court system, although similar laws had been challenged in a number of states for two decades.[248] At the time of the *Morales* decision in 1994, sodomy was a criminal offense in over twenty states and the District of Columbia.[249] *Bowers v. Hardwick*,[250] the 1986 US Supreme Court which upheld Georgia's sodomy law, was still the law of the land but the *Morales* plaintiffs challenged the sodomy statute based on state grounds: the constitutional right to privacy, due course of law[251] and equal-protection[252] provisions of Texas constitution.[253]

The fact that the criminal law was not currently being enforced made it more difficult to challenge its constitutionality. Unless a person was prosecuted for an act of sodomy, the case would not proceed to Texas' highest criminal court, the Texas Court of Criminal Appeals. In a criminal court, a constitutional challenge to the sodomy law could be used as a defense, so that an affirmative or negative vote on its constitutionality would take place.[254] Since there were no pending prosecutions under the law, the only feasible strategy for the *Morales* plaintiffs was to challenge the law in a civil court. The *Morales* case could also have been brought in one of four federal district courts in Texas. Then, on appeal, a ruling by either the US Court of Appeals for the Fifth Circuit or the US Supreme Court could overturn the law.[255] However, at the time of *Morales*, Texas civil courts had only twice reviewed the constitutionality of unenforced criminal statutes.[256]

In a surprise ruling, a Texas trial court declared the sodomy statute (section 21.06 of the Texas Penal Code) unconstitutional and enjoined the enforcement of the law.[257] The state countered with a procedural argument that the civil court was precluded from deciding the case because the court's equity jurisdiction did not extend to questions regarding the constitutionality of criminal statutes.[258] The Third Court of Appeals at Austin rejected the state's procedural argument and affirmed the trial court's ruling,[259] relying on the landmark Texas Supreme Court privacy ruling, *Texas State Employees Union (TSEU) v. Texas Department of Mental Health & Mental Retardation*, in which the justices ruled that the policy of requiring certain employees to take mandatory polygraph tests violated the right to privacy found in the Texas

Bill of Rights. Recognizing that the right to privacy contained in the Texas constitution offered broader protections than the right to privacy under the US Constitution, the court of appeals held that the sodomy law violated the fundamental right of two consenting adults to engage in private sexual behavior.[260] The court of appeals added in *Morales* that since the sodomy law did not advance any compelling governmental interest.[261]

During oral argument before the Texas Supreme Court, and in the conference that followed, the justices appeared to be willing to accept that there was a violation of the right to privacy, but many could not get past the jurisdictional and standing issues. Justice Cornyn seemed to be on the fence regarding the standing question.[262] Cornyn asked the Attorney General during oral argument how it was that he could argue the state's case if he conceded that Morales was harmed. The Attorney General responded that the issue was not whether there was harm but whether there was a rational basis for the law. Cornyn asked whether it should be a compelling rather than a rational interest if a constitutional right were violated, but the attorney general responded that he did not think a constitutional right applied in this case.[263] Justice Enoch appeared concerned that by granting standing the court was opening the door to a review of criminal statutes by the Texas Supreme Court, thus usurping the jurisdiction of the court of criminal appeals. Justice Doggett commented that he believed that the state was criminalizing behavior between people of the same sex but not between people of the opposite sex. Gammage stated during the conference following oral argument that it was clear that the court had authority to determine the constitutionality of criminal statutes because: (1) personal rights were at stake, (2) irreparable harm occurred, (3) there was no adequate remedy for that harm, and (4) there was sufficient case law that supported the authority of the court to rule on the constitutionality of a provision of the penal code.[264]

The Texas Supreme Court had the opportunity to make history by striking down the invidious law, but it narrowly decided (5-4) to reject the appellate court's holding on procedural grounds and remanded the case back to the trial court with orders to dismiss.[265] The narrow majority argued that when no actual or threatened enforcement of a criminal statute occurs, a civil court could not enjoin the enforcement of the statute.[266] Writing for the majority, Justice Cornyn[267] circumvented the constitutional question and framed the challenge to the sodomy law solely in procedural terms. Focusing on the scope of equity jurisdiction of a civil court, Cornyn stated: "Civil equity courts have no jurisdiction to enjoin the enforcement of criminal statutes in the absence of irreparable harm to vested *property* rights."[268] The majority rejected the appellate court's interpretation of *Passel v. Fort Worth Independent School District*, which held that equity power *did* extend to the protection of personal rights violated by a criminal statute. *Passel* involved a lawsuit brought against an unenforced criminal statute prohibiting fraternities, sororities, and secret societies in public schools below college level. Because the law itself was never enforced, nor was anyone punished by it, the lawsuit challenged Fort Worth ISD's student policies that were based on the statute on the grounds that it deprived students of their personal rights.[269] The majority reiterated that legal precedent has long recognized that the equity jurisdiction of civil courts is limited to violations of vested property rights and not to personal rights.[270]

Courts of equity can intervene in a case where a criminal statute is enforced, only if the statute is unconstitutional and its enforcement will result in an injury to property rights.[271] The majority argued that if civil courts extended their jurisdiction to challenges of criminal statutes, conflicting decisions on the constitutionality of laws would occur between the civil and criminal courts of last resort.[272] In sum, by dismissing the challenge on procedural grounds, the majority upheld the sodomy law. Citing the Attorney General's position, Cornyn concluded:

> There is no record of even a single instance in which the sodomy statute has been prosecuted against conduct that the plaintiffs claim is constitutionally protected; none of the plaintiffs claims a specific instance of career or employment opportunities having been restricted by the existence of the statute; none of the plaintiffs alleges having been the victim of a hate crime, or a fear of becoming the victim of any specific threatened future event.[273]

In his dissenting opinion, Gammage, joined by Chief Justice Phillips, and Justices Doggett and Spector,[274] challenged the majority's assertion that there was an absence of harm. He reasoned that the majority "confuses harm with prosecution" by its insistence that the sodomy statute caused no harm, merely because there was no actual or imminent prosecution.[275] The question of whether the prosecution of gays and lesbians was imminent, rather than a possibility, was relevant only if the allegations made were based on anticipated or hypothetical harm rather than an injury that has already occurred.[276] Gammage wrote:

> This court set forth a confusing discussion of lack of jurisdiction because reaching the merits would be an advisory opinion, which is somehow linked to this absence of harm. . . . The State *stipulated* that plaintiffs' job choices are limited, that they face discrimination in housing, family, and criminal justice matters, and that *they suffer psychological harm to their relationships because they are labeled criminals by the very existence of the statute*.[277]

As the appellate court acknowledged, the *Morales* plaintiffs suffered actual harm under the statute independent of the threat of criminal prosecution.[278]

The dissent criticized what they saw as the majority's procedural maneuvering to prevent the court from ruling directly on the constitutionality of the sodomy law. The court *did* have the power to address *Morales*' challenge to the sodomy law, argued Gammage and the other dissenters (including Phillips, who usually voted with the conservative bloc).

Gammage pointed out that an equity court's primary concern in enjoining the enforcement of a criminal statute is not whether there are property rights involved but whether there is irreparable harm to a person's rights.[279] Equity courts usually declined to interfere with a criminal prosecution because an individual could challenge the unconstitutionality of a law as a defense in a criminal case.[280] However, "the power of a [civil] court to assume jurisdiction of a cause on the ground of irreparable injury is the fundamental characteristic of equity jurisdiction."[281] The jurisdiction of a court of equity did not depend on the nature of the right harmed—whether personal or property—but on "the existence of a justiciable right for which there is not" an adequate legal remedy.[282]

Morales and the other respondents could seek a remedy in a civil court, even though there was no pending or anticipated prosecution, because they were harmed by the statute. The harm was not hypothetical, and "to hold otherwise would disregard the fundamental principle upon which such courts are established."[283] Gammage indicated that the standard established in *Passel* is that the meaning and interpretation of a criminal statute should ordinarily be determined by courts exercising criminal jurisdiction unless the law were unconstitutional, there was no way to test its constitutionality because the law was not being enforced, and its enforcement would result in irreparable injury to vested property *and* personal rights.[284] He argued that the majority was rewriting the *Passel* standard, which is established law.[285] As he stated in previous cases where individual rights were threatened, Gammage concluded that the majority abdicated its duty to apply judicial scrutiny to laws that infringe upon the rights of citizens.[286] He wrote:

> Under the court's analysis, the State may adopt all manner of criminal laws affecting the civil or personal rights of any number of citizens, and by declining to prosecute . . . them, ensure that no court ever reviews them.
>
> Declining to even *consider* the merits of the pleas for equitable relief before us today could have an impact far beyond the class of citizens immediately affected. . . . The court effectively denies standing in Texas courts to *any* individual or group of citizens who seek equitable relief under the Texas [c]onstitution, because of an unenforced Texas criminal statute, for the alleged deprivation of *any* personal liberty or civil right which does not also involve what the court may perceive as an adequate vested property interest.[287]

Gammage further argued that judicial scrutiny should be appropriately applied to all "criminal laws affecting the civil or personal rights of any number of citizens."[288] To prevent individuals from seeking remedies in a civil court, simply because there was no pending or anticipated prosecution under a criminal statute, "disregard[s] the fundamental principle upon which such courts are established."[289] This gives us another glimpse into Gammage's understanding of the role of the judiciary.

The sodomy law and homosexual rights were lightning rod issues in Texas. The justices may have wanted to act to uphold basic human rights, but perhaps they did not have the desire to face the electoral consequences of voting to uphold the court of appeals ruling. Two justices (Hecht and Gonzales) who voted to reverse the court of appeals and one (Doggett), who voted to affirm, would have had to justify their positions to voters the following year in 1994 general election.

The *Morales* decision was one vote short of overcoming a procedural wall intentionally erected to avoid ruling on the constitutionality of a highly controversial law. Research shows that the sodomy law was not (and is not) just languishing, ignored, and dusty in the penal code but has been modified and preserved by social conservatives.[290] As of now, the law is still on the books despite the US Supreme Court's ruling in *Lawrence v. Texas*—although there is a proposal in the Texas legislature for its repeal.[291] The majority of justices took great comfort from the fact that the law was unenforced, and that there was no evidence gays and lesbians ever suffered from any form of employment discrimination or hate crimes. Gammage was incredulous at these assertions. Even if the statute as written were never enforced, the very existence of the law classified LGBT Texans as criminals, and in doing so allowed discrimination against them. Gammage raised the frightening prospect that under the "unenforced law" concept, the state could pass all kinds of criminal laws which single out groups of people and violated their constitutional rights, as long as the laws went unenforced.[292]

Had the court been willing to overcome the procedural and jurisdictional questions and address the sodomy law directly, we would have a more complete picture of how Gammage (and his associates on the bench) might have analyzed the substantive issue—whether from the standpoint of equal protection, the right to privacy, or both, as the appellate court did in *Morales*. Recall that in *Barber*, Gammage argued that the Texas Equal Rights Amendment (ERA) of 1972 offered broader protection than the Fourteenth Amendment to the US Constitution.[293] In *Morales*, he argued that homosexuals constitute a class of people who face discrimination in housing, family law, and criminal justice matters.[294]

The Texas ERA was adopted by voters in 1972 after nearly a decade of debate in the state legislature. Many members of both the bench and bar were hesitant to support the amendment, preferring instead to reform rules governing community property in particular and family law generally. Others supported dealing with sex discrimination legislatively, or to rely on existing federal protections. Legislators were reluctant to support the amendment for a variety of reasons, ranging from fear of a conservative backlash to an avalanche of litigation. Eventually, progressive legislators like Gammage prevailed, and the amendment was sent to voters for ratification. As originally proposed the ERA banned discrimination on the basis of sex, but the constitutional amendment adopted by voters in November 1972 states, "Equality under the law shall not be denied or abridged because of sex, race, color, creed, or national origin."[295]

Returning to *Morales*, the fact that the court did not even decide on whether the state's 115-year-old law prohibiting homosexual sodomy was unconstitutional prompted the headline "State High Court Mum on Sodomy Law" in the *Austin American-Statesman*.[296] Quoted in that article, Martin Hiraga, director of the Gay and Lesbian Task Force Privacy Project in Washington, D.C., stated that the court "has passed over an opportunity to change a ludicrous law which fosters an environment of hatred, bigotry and discrimination in Texas towards gay men and lesbians." The state's only openly gay legislator at that time, Glen Maxey (D-Austin), suggested that the ruling was irrelevant. Maxey said that the Third Court of Appeals in 1993 had already set an important precedent in *City of Dallas v. England*.[297] Police departments across the state had routinely invoked the sodomy law to deny employment to openly gay and lesbian job applicants, on the grounds that they *might* potentially be engaged in criminal behavior.[298] When Mica England applied for a position with the Dallas Police Department in 1989, she was informed by the chief of police that under the department's hiring policy she was ineligible for employment because of her homosexuality, which she freely admitted during the interview. The trial court struck down the law as an unconstitutional violation of the right to privacy under the Texas constitution[299] and enjoined the city from enforcing the statute in a discriminatory manner. The court of appeals upheld the trial court's decision, but the Texas Supreme Court did not rule on the merits of the case because the city never filed a motion for rehearing within the required deadline.[300] Had it done so, the Supreme Court might not have been able to avoid ruling on the merits of the case, because of the fact that Mica England had suffered real employment discrimination, which would have fallen under the Supreme Court's civil jurisdiction. However, since the case was dismissed by the Supreme Court, the court of appeals ruling became the final judgment on whether the law could be used to discriminate in hiring, and ended the Dallas Police Department's discriminatory hiring practices. Since *Bowers v. Hardwick* was still the law of the land, gays and lesbians were still at risk for criminal prosecution or discrimination in housing, family law, and employment.

It would be nearly a decade before the US Supreme Court would overturn *Bowers* in *Lawrence v. Texas* in 2003.[301] *Lawrence* originated when

Houston police officers, responding to a complaint about "a man going crazy with a gun," entered Lawrence's apartment and saw him and another adult man engaging in a consensual sexual act. The two men were arrested and convicted in a state district court of deviate sexual intercourse in violation of Texas' sodomy law, and were each fined $200. They argued that their convictions "impermissibly discriminate on the basis of sex" under the Texas constitution.[302] Citing *Bowers*, the Texas Fourteenth Court of Appeals, with a Republican majority, rejected the petitioners' arguments under both the Equal Protection and Due Process Clauses of the Fourteenth Amendment and affirmed the convictions.[303] The Texas Court of Criminal Appeals, and later the Texas Supreme Court, refused to give the case a full review.

By a 6-3 vote, the US Supreme Court held in *Lawrence* that the Texas statute making it a crime for two persons of the same sex to engage in certain intimate sexual conduct violated the due process clause of the Fifth and Fourteenth Amendments of the Constitution. Finding it "necessary to reconsider" *Bowers*, the Court ruled that the two men, as adults, were free to engage in private conduct in the exercise of their liberty. Writing for the majority, Justice Anthony Kennedy (joined by justices Stevens, Souter, Ginsburg, and Breyer) argued that this case, as well as *Bowers* before it, dealt not merely with the right to engage in certain kinds of sexual conduct but whether the state could regulate "the most private human conduct, sexual behavior, in the most private of places, the home." Through the sodomy law, the State of Texas was seeking to control a personal relationship—whether heterosexual or homosexual—which was within the liberty of persons to choose without being punished as criminals. The liberty protected by the constitution allowed homosexual persons the right to choose to enter upon relationships in the privacy of their homes and their own private lives and "still retain their dignity as free persons."[304]

Ever since the Texas Supreme Court first recognized the right to privacy in *Billings v. Atkinson* in 1973 (discussed in chapter 2), the question has been this: How broad is this right and to what types of activities and dimensions of human existence does it extend? Interestingly, nine years after *TSEU* (and the year after Gammage resigned from the Texas Supreme Court), the justices unanimously ruled that the right to privacy does not confer a right to commit adultery, something that the *Austin American-Statesman* felt obligated to clear up.[305] *City of Sherman v. Henry*, originated when Otis Henry, a Sherman, Texas, police officer, was denied a promotion because he was sexually involved with another officer's wife.[306] Before he was denied the promotion, the police chief authorized an extensive investigation to determine if the rumors of the affair were true. Colleagues were interviewed and love letters discovered. A district court ruled in favor of Henry and a court of appeals court agreed that the investigation and denial of promotion because of this admittedly morally wrong but distinctly private and intimate matter violated his right to privacy. However, the Texas Supreme Court reversed in a 7-2 vote.

Writing for the majority, Justice Greg Abbott[307] reaffirmed the constitutional right to privacy established in the *Texas State Employees Union* decision, but wrote that the right to privacy under the Texas constitution or US Constitution does not include a right to maintain a sexual relationship with the spouse of another person. Abbott stated, however, that the decision "does not mean . . . that the government is free to engage in intrusive investigation methods to determine the sexual practices of individuals" but what was at issue here was not governmental intrusion into his life but a matter of the "autonomy aspect of privacy—the right to make certain fundamental decisions and engage in certain conduct without state interference."[308]

In a concurring opinion Justices Rose Spector and Priscilla Owen agreed with Abbott that the denial of the officer's promotion was not a violation of a constitutional right but that the majority "shriveled" the right to privacy "to the point that the most personal aspects of our lives are the government's business . . . " One can only speculate how Gammage would have ruled in this case—whether he would have joined the concurring justices in arguing for a broader concept of privacy or perhaps been able to persuade members of the majority to not necessarily rule in Henry's favor but to refrain from narrowing the right to privacy. Of course, the decision was handed down prior to the US Supreme Court ruling in *Lawrence v. Texas*, so the majority's decision relied in part on the discredited precedent, *Bowers v. Hardwick.*[309] At the time of *Henry*, laws criminalizing adultery in Texas had been repealed since 1973,[310] but the court ruled that adultery as a positive act is not protected by the concept of privacy as autonomy which extends to such activities as marriage, procreation, contraception, and parenting.[311]

In 1996, the year that *City of Sherman* was handed down, Gammage was a visiting professor at Sam Houston State University where he taught constitutional law and gave several lectures to general audiences on the origins and development of the right to privacy. He stated that long before *Griswold v. Connecticut* in 1965, guarantees of limited privacy interests were found in a body of case law surrounding the common-law tort doctrines of trespass, defamation, and nuisance. This early expression of privacy was very narrow and the full legal expression of the right of privacy in its modern form developed slowly, incrementally building upon this existing body of tort law as it had in Texas. Privacy as autonomy, however, is a more comprehensive definition of privacy. Not merely the right to be let alone, privacy as autonomy is the right to be free from governmental invasions—the personal right to determine for oneself whether to perform a specific act or undergo a particular experience free from governmental scrutiny. He recalled his efforts to expand privacy while on the court of appeals and supreme court and his unsuccessful attempt to persuade the majority to rule on the Texas sodomy law.[312]

THE POPPY SEED MUFFIN CASE: NEW TORT REMEDIES

In 1995, the last year that Gammage was on the court, he participated in what became known as the poppy seed muffin case. Drug testing as a condition of employment became more commonplace in the 1980s and 1990s, as the government and private businesses ramped up the War on Drugs. The argument in support of this policy was that the minor inconveniences caused by drug testing are offset by society's interest in drug-free workplace. Employers do not wish to be held legally liable if their employees, who may be impaired by drugs, cause harm through unprofessional or negligent behavior. While some may have shrugged off drug testing as a small price to pay for employment and a safe workplace, others contended that compelling a person to give blood samples or subjecting them to supervised urination was the worst intrusion on a person's dignity and privacy. In addition to the initial intrusion, drug testing further implicates privacy rights by necessitating the creation of data files that persist long after the test itself. Of course, the issue in the poppy seed case was much narrower: Do employees, or prospective employees, have legal protections if a drug testing company acts in an irresponsible or negligent manner? What happens if a lab mixes up samples or shares a false-positive result with a prospective employer? Does the drug testing lab owe a legal duty to the person tested?

The poppy seed muffin case, *SmithKline Beecham Corporation v. Doe*,[313] received both media and academic attention after a woman claimed that poppy seeds caused her to test positive for drugs and lose her job.[314] Less than a year after the decision, an episode of the television program *Seinfeld* dealt with a false positive caused by poppy seeds.[315] The case originated when "Jane Doe," a twenty-four-year-old graduate student, was offered a job by the Quaker Oats Company in their marketing department. The offer was contingent on her passing a routine drug screening test administered by a third-party drug testing lab, SmithKline Beecham Clinical Laboratories (SmithKline). The laboratory produced a promotional brochure that stated "a positive result from SmithKline can be accepted with *virtual certainty* as evidence of drug use" and "[a] confirmed positive result offers 100 percent assurance that the specified drug is actually present in the urine specimen."[316]

Quaker's policy stated that any individual who tested positive for illegal drugs would not be hired. Furthermore, if an applicant tested positive for *any* drug and failed to disclose current medications on a medical history form, he or she would not be hired. The only medication that Jane Doe listed on a medical history form were birth control pills, for which she had a prescription from her physician. However, the test showed the presence of opiates in her urine and SmithKline reported the results of her test to Quaker.

Upon learning of Doe's positive results, Quaker confronted her. She attempted to attribute the positive results to a Vicodin given to her by her roommate; however, Quaker then withdrew their offer of employment to Doe, explaining that she took a drug for which she did not have a prescription and that she failed to report taking the drug on her medical history form. Doe later admitted to Quaker that she lied about taking the Vicodin because she was "under extreme duress" and "completely, essentially out of her mind."[317] After conducting her own research on the effect of poppy seeds on the outcome of a drug test, Doe then claimed that she tested positive because of several poppy seed muffins she had eaten prior to the test.

SmithKline did not dispute the fact that poppy seeds eaten in large quantities might indicate the presence of morphine or codeine in a urine sample but admitted that it had not shared this information about the foods that might cause false positives in a brochure with Quaker or Doe. In fact, SBCL argued that it did not have a duty to share this information but only to competently conduct the test and report the results of the urinalysis to Quaker. SmithKline ultimately revised the language in its advertising materials, stating that "certain types of poppy seeds, if consumed in sufficient quantity, can produce a positive result for opiates."[318]

Doe sued SmithKline Beecham for negligence, breach of the duty of good faith and fair dealing, defamation, and tortious interference with a prospective contract. Doe also sued Quaker but later settled out of court. A favorable ruling for Doe would mean drug testing labs have a legal duty to warn test-takers and employers prior to the test that eating poppy seeds might affect the outcome of a person's drug test. The trial court granted summary judgment in favor of SmithKline and Quaker. The court of appeals affirmed the summary judgment for Quaker but reversed the summary judgment for SmithKline on the negligence and tortious interference claims. Therefore, Doe's negligence lawsuit against SmithKline could proceed.

Much of the oral argument was dominated by the question of whether a "special relationship" existed between Doe and the lab. Jane Doe was not employed by the lab, nor under contract with it for services. A majority of the justices seemed reluctant to create a new duty—a duty to warn employers and employees about the possible misrepresentation of drug test results.[319] In his notes from oral argument, Gammage was willing to consider that the court might need to rethink negligence doctrine in light of a growing trend to require employees to submit to drug testing. In the absence of statutory protections in Texas, there needed to be some way that employees accused of positive results could hold drug testing labs accountable. Gammage also seemed to be the only justice concerned with the impact that poppy seeds sprinkled on food or herbal teas might have on the drug test. As a joke, on the day of the conference Gammage showed up with a tray of poppy seed muffins and pastries for his colleagues.[320]

The Texas Supreme Court ruled 6-3 that the lab owed neither Doe nor Quaker a legal duty to warn of the possible causes of a false-positive drug test, and that the lab had no duty to inquire into whether the employee had eaten poppy seed muffins or anything else that might have created a false-positive result. The lab was *not* responsible for Doe being denied a job at Quaker or being harmed or inconvenienced in any way.

Writing for the majority, Justice Nathan Hecht[321] argued that state and federal courts have held that the only legal obligation a drug testing lab owes to a person tested is "a duty to perform its services with reasonable care."[322] Based on an analysis of case law (which included *Boyles v. Kerr*) and the common law, Hecht concluded that SmithKline did *not* have the duty to warn Doe or Quaker. SmithKline merely performed a urinalysis and duly reported the presence of opiates in its report. The lab was in no way responsible for the way that Quaker responded to the results of the drug testing. Hecht wrote:

> We assume that there is some significant likelihood, which Smith Kline could and did foresee, that a person will have a positive drug test due to having eaten poppy seeds . . . Foreseeability alone, however, is not sufficient to create a new duty . . . Without precedent and without the support of our own jurisprudence, we decline to recognize the duty Doe alleges in this case.[323]

Dissenting, Gammage wrote that the court *should* recognize the existence of a new common-law duty to warn. Quaker and Doe should have been made aware by SmithKline of the possibilities of false positives. SmithKline misrepresented the accuracy of its tests and failed to inform Quaker and Doe about the poppy seed factor. He pointed out that in depositions, several Quaker employees stated that if SmithKline had told Quaker about the possibility of false positives then the incident would never had occurred and Doe's offer of employment would not have been rescinded. Gammage wrote:

> Contrary to the majority's analysis, this Court should recognize a duty from the drug testing company to Doe to not affirmatively misrepresent the significance of the test results to Quaker, her employer. The majority miscasts the controversy. It analyzes this case as a traditional negligent failure to disclose case . . . [which is a tort] meant to apply only to commercial and business transactions that do not fit the employment drug testing context.[324]

SmithKline, according to the dissenters, had a duty to Doe because the lab was not simply a bystander to the relationship between Doe and Quaker. The lab created the harmful situation by its negligent misrepresentation and had a "special relationship" to Doe, whose urine they tested at her risk of loss of employment. In sum, they had a duty to Doe.[325] Gammage concluded that with the growing prevalence of drug testing in the workplace, and potential of harm to employees as a function of false positives, the court should have recognized the duty of drug testing companies to explain the causes of false positives and be responsible if they negligently misrepresented the accuracy of their tests or incorrectly interpret the results of tests.

Subsequent Texas case law on the liability of drug testing labs is scant. In 2003 the Texas Supreme Court reversed a court of appeals ruling which held that employers who conducted in-house urine specimen collection under government guidelines owed a common-law duty to employees to conduct the test with reasonable care.[326] The court of appeals believed that *SmithKline Beecham* left open the question of whether such a duty existed, but the Supreme Court rejected that finding because of existing federal regulations that govern the collection and processing of urinalysis.

"GET A HAIRCUT . . . BECAUSE!" THE RIGHTS OF STUDENTS AND THE TEXAS CONSTITUTION

In 1995, his last year on the Texas Supreme Court, Gammage expounded one his strongest affirmations of individual rights in *Barber v. Colorado Independent School District*, a class-action suit in 1995 that challenged the constitutionality of hair-length restrictions for male students imposed by a school district.[327] Most people would be surprised to learn that hair-length and dress-code cases constitute a substantial body of law, and *Barber* was one of the most influential of these cases in Texas.[328] Decades before *Barber*, federal circuit courts handed down a large number of conflicting rulings on the constitutionality of hair-length regulations and on the question of whether federal courts could justifiably make rulings on local school policy.[329] For example, in 1970 a student successfully challenged the constitutionality of a hair-length regulation based on the liberty interest to determine one's personal appearance.[330] In 1971 the US Court of Appeals for the Ninth Circuit argued that the school need not even prove that hair length caused a disruption to the educational process in order to discipline a student.[331] A year later, the US Court of Appeals for the Fourth Circuit ruled that it was impermissible under the US Constitution for public schools to mandate hair lengths.[332] Even in light of a number of conflicting federal court rulings,[333] the US Supreme Court would not grant *certiorari* to reconcile these decisions.[334] State courts were just as divided on hair-length regulations.

The Colorado Independent School District (CISD) in Texas established a dress code to "teach grooming and hygiene, instill discipline, prevent disruption, avoid safety hazards, and teach respect for authority."[335] Boys were only allowed to wear their "hair to the bottom of [their] collar, the bottom of the ear and combed out of [their] eyes."[336] They were not allowed to wear earrings.[337] There was no hair or earring rule for girls but the policy stated that "unbecoming fashions or anything designed to attract undue attention to the individual or activities are not acceptable."[338]

When a student named Austin Barber turned eighteen, his family requested that the school board suspend enforcement of the policy for him and other students who were his age and older. At the time of the case Barber wore his hair touching his shoulders. The Barber family argued that the application of the hair-grooming and earring policy to males, but not females, violated their son's constitutional rights. The school board voted 4-2 to uphold the enforcement of the policy. Barber still refused to cut his hair and was given in-school suspension as his punishment. He received instruction, but it was in a segregated setting outside of the regular classroom setting. Barber was also barred from all extracurricular activities because of the length of his hair.[339]

At the trial there was testimony from a wide range of school officials about hair and dress codes. Some schools in the state chose to "get out of the hair business" out of uncertainty of whether there was authority to regulate such matters.[340] Other schools did not have rules regarding hair-length regulations for the general student population but allowed coaches to set hair-length rules for athletes.[341] One high school principal testified that his high school had an earring policy, allowing boys to wear a stud earring but not dangling earrings. However, a principal for CISD testified that there was a compelling reason for grooming rules. Schools must have rules to carry out its business. He stated, "I think that that is part of our responsibility to educate kids. I think it's an educational tool to teach students that they must comply with rules even if they don't agree with the rule."[342] CISD also called one expert witness, a professor of psychology at Abilene Christian University, who testified that more than ever, due to the breakdown of the family, it was imperative that schools teach students how to live in society. Grooming rules were a way of teaching students not only about proper hygiene but respecting authority. The professor did not explain how haircuts might mitigate the effects of the disintegration of the American family, but nevertheless the school district was suggesting that in the absence of parental guidance school officials needed to step in.[343]

The trial court held for Barber, stating that the grooming policy violated the ERA of the Texas constitution,[344] the right to privacy, and the right to freedom of expression.[345] The trial court also granted a permanent injunction against the school district, contending that the objectives of the grooming code could be accomplished by less restrictive means—that is, other than gender-based discrimination.[346] However, the court of appeals reversed the trial court's ruling, finding that Barber's suit did not warrant judicial intervention into the school district's policy.[347]

During oral argument before the Texas Supreme Court, Jim Harrington of the Texas Civil Rights Project, and Pat Barber, father of Austin Barber, framed the dispute as a classic case of individual freedom and a "confluence of various individual rights," including the right to privacy as autonomy, symbolic expression, the right to be free from discrimination under the Texas ERA and the right to an education. "You cannot intrude upon the rights absent a showing of compelling state interest," Harrington argued. A blanket rule would be unconstitutional—each instance of disruption would need to be examined individually. The school district would have to show that hair length was directly related to the disruptive behavior in order to show a compelling interest in the restrictions. Disruptive conduct could be punished but the mere expression of individuality could not.[348]

Many justices were skeptical of Harrington's argument and attempted to frame the issue differently. Justice Raul Gonzales asked Harrington eleven questions during oral argument—more than any other justice except Gammage (who asked lawyers from both sides thirty-seven questions).[349] Gonzales suggested that Barber's challenge was frivolous, and asked Harrington whether this case was really about the authority and responsibility of school boards to set rules based on accepted community standards. In light of this responsibility, Gonzales suggested, some constitutional rights should not be enforced in the public school. He was doubtful that the Texas ERA stripped the public schools of their authority to impose traditional dress codes. Gonzales also attempted to get Harrington to concede that the rule was not arbitrary but based on the need to promote discipline. Harrington agreed that discipline is important but doubted that the need for it was compelling enough to supersede a person's right to privacy and to be free from gender-based discrimination.

Justice John Cornyn raised the question of whether there would be an interest in regulating hair if a certain hairstyle was related to gang membership. At the time, most schools in Texas had rules pertaining to gang colors. Still, Harrington insisted that clothes were covered by dress codes are different than hair, because during the day you could easily change your clothes upon arriving at school, but you couldn't change your hair length. Hair is not something one can take off and put on like sneakers; it is more closely related to self-expression and personal autonomy.

T. L. Rees, the attorney for the CISD, argued that the school district's policies reflected the traditional values of the community. If students wanted to get jobs after graduation, their hair and manner of dress needed to reflect those values. In response to this, Gammage quipped that two justices on the court, John Cornyn and Raul Gonzales, wouldn't be able to get jobs in Colorado City because of their rather shaggy hair length, a comment that was picked up by the *Austin American-Statesman* during the case.[350] Indeed, the case drew a surprising amount of statewide press coverage. When Rees used a judicial activism argument as an attempt to play to the conservative justices, by stating that the "heavy-hand of the courts" should stay out of these matters, Gammage sternly corrected him, stating that it wasn't the courts that were violating Barber's rights but the "heavy hand" of the school district. "We don't go out and get cases. They are brought to us by people in the community," Gammage stated. "And here you have a young man and his family in the community that took this case to court because they were dissatisfied with the treatment they received." Gammage also interjected when Rees argued that the hair-length rule taught students societal values: "What I am hearing from you is it teaches them conformity with arbitrary rules and regulations . . . We are not teaching them about liberty. We are not teaching them about due process. We are not teaching them about mutual regard for one another's autonomy and individuality, are we?" Gammage's exchange with both Harrington and Rees was an attempt to frame the argument in terms of the complete arbitrariness of the rule and the fact that the school district flagrantly disregarded the Texas constitution. But the majority would not go there, and ultimately voted 7-2 to reject Barber's claims as not substantial enough to "merit . . . intervention in this case."[351]

Relying on several federal cases in the Fifth Circuit from the 1960s and 1970s that rejected challenges to high school dress codes, the majority, per Justice Gonzalez, reasoned that unlike adults in other settings, a high school student's right to be unfettered by school-grooming regulations had never been recognized.[352] The majority cited *New Jersey v. T.L.O*, in which the US Supreme Court made it easier for school officials to suspend the Fourth Amendment rights of minors in order to conduct random locker searches in the name of safety and discipline.[353] In supporting the decision against judicial intervention, Gonzales also cited a number of unsuccessful Texas ERA challenges to grooming regulations in Texas schools.[354] Given the vulnerability of children, as well as their inability to make important decisions in an informed and mature manner, the majority concluded that students did not have the same constitutional rights as adults.[355] Justice Gonzales also considered it "a matter of common sense that the state judiciary is less competent to deal with students' hair length than a parent, school board, administrator, principal, or teacher."[356] The majority was very reticent to have the courts intervene in local dress-code politics, since there was precedent supporting nonintervention. Their judicial reluctance—or restraint—might also have been based on the view that requiring only boys to cut their hair is hardly sex discrimination. Nevertheless, what is significant is the majority's avoidance of the equal-protection issue. Justice Gonzales does not mention it; instead, the entire majority opinion focused on the rights of minors—or lack thereof—in the public schools.

In his dissenting opinion, Gammage argued that the majority's dismissal of Barber's claim without the benefit of providing a full legal analysis was more a matter of judicial abdication than "nonintervention."[357] He seemed puzzled as to why the majority relied exclusively on federal precedent when Barber had "pleaded his case exclusively on state constitutional grounds."[358] Gammage recognized the validity of Barber's privacy and free-speech claims under the Texas constitution but chose to analyze the CISD policy under the Texas ERA.[359] The record shows that, up to this point, everyone had framed the issue as the rights of minors versus the need for discipline in schools.[360] It was also accepted as legal and appropriate that the CISD regulation mandated a different treatment of males and females.[361]

Adopting an equal-protection analysis, Gammage relied on the 1976 Texas case *Mercer v. Board of Trustees, North Forest Independent School District*, where a state court of appeals, in reviewing a hair-length policy, held that "any classification based [on] sex is a suspect classification" and was subject to a strict-scrutiny standard of review but then stopped short of intervening and granting relief.[362] Gammage also relied on *In re McLean*, where the Texas Supreme Court recognized in 1987 that the Texas ERA provided broader protection against sex discrimination than the Equal Protection Clause of the Fourteenth Amendment.[363] Given this broader protection, and using a strict-scrutiny analysis, Gammage argued the court needed to analyze the CISD grooming policy from the standpoint of whether the regulation of hair length promoted a compelling governmental interest that could not be achieved by other means.[364] Recall that the purpose of the CISD policy was "to teach grooming and hygiene, instill discipline, prevent disruptions, avoid safety hazards, and teach respect for authority,"[365] which were seemingly good reasons. However, Gammage observed that the school district admitted that their sole purpose was to prevent the "disruptions" that long hair on male students might cause, even though no evidence was offered of these "disruptions."[366] Counsel for the school district even noted this in clear terms: "How do we prove that [a long-haired student] is disruptive? We can't."[367] Thus, in addition to being an intrusion into Barber's privacy, the sex-based classification was upheld by the majority of the court without discussion of the compelling interest needed to justify such a distinction based on sex alone. CISD did suggest that the rule was also a "'teaching device,' reflecting 'the community's societal values. [It was] harder for a person in Colorado City, Texas to get a job if they [had] long hair.'"[368] Gammage responded to that purported justification as follows:

> The majority of this Court chooses, without the requirement or offer of any proof, to accept this specious explanation for a gender-based, discriminatory regulation without any concern for its infringement of constitutionally guaranteed personal liberties. While dress and grooming codes do not, per se, violate the constitution, they must be based upon compelling educational goals and may not be arbitrary and without foundation in furthering the educational mission of schools or avoiding disruptions. By its own admission, CISD's gender-based hair length policy [was] "arbitrary" and [did] not achieve the rule's purported educational goal.[369]

For that reason, he wrote, the grooming code "cannot withstand analysis under the Texas Equal Rights Amendment."[370]

Gammage pointed out that "because CISD [could] offer no proof that any purported objectives of educational policy [were] met by regulating the hair length of male students only, the hair-length rule cannot survive even minimum rationality scrutiny."[371] A female student's Rapunzel-like hair might be down to her ankles; it might get stuck in the bus door or trip the cheerleaders. Her hair may even be dirty and, thus, implicate the hygiene requirement. Since girls engage in the same activities in chemistry or physical education classes, Gammage argued,[372] the classification here was based upon assumptions and stereotypes about the appropriate gender appearance of students.

For Gammage, the policy set out to accomplish two things: obedience for the sake of obedience and respecting authority for authority's sake. The policy did not punish behavior that might endanger others but did punish personal choice in one's manner of dress or appearance—thus "significantly intrud[ing] into the private lives of students with proportionately little justification" and "without any concern for its infringement of constitutionally guaranteed personal liberties."[373] The intrusion or regulation also existed beyond the school, since it is impossible to control hair length only during a school day. Unlike the wearing of clothing, hair cannot be one length for school and one length for home, so the hair-length requirement affects one's life after school and on the weekend. The nature of this kind of intrusion demands a compelling justification.[374]

Gammage understood that his colleagues were by no means against the right of self-expression in the form of hair length or fashion, but they were fearful of igniting some form of riotous or anarchical environment in the public schools. The kind of culture that promotes obedience and authority in the public schools is anathema to civil libertarians. Students unaccustomed to freedom of expression in high schools have difficulty adjusting to the give-and-take of ideas in college or in a democracy. Raised in a culture of conformity, and often authoritarianism (on both ends of the political spectrum), they are intolerant of new ideas and different viewpoints. *Barber* was decided in 1995, not in the 1950s, so one would think that society—even in Texas—would have progressed beyond the emphasis on conformity. In fact, the public schools have changed little since then; censorship by the right and left has reigned in freedom of expression. Students, themselves, also expect an environment free from unpleasant or offending ideas—a right not to be offended, if you will.

Much ink has been spilled in the Texas legal community over school districts being autonomous entities that should be largely unfettered by judicial intrusion—free not only to determine what is best for their students but also from being held to overly burdensome standards when constitutional challenges are made. Gammage agreed with the majority's view that courts ought to use the "heavy hand of justice" *sparingly* in local school matters, "but when the heavy hand of local government arbitrarily" violates constitutional protections, courts are required to act.[375] He rejected the majority's over-reliance on the Fifth Circuit Court of Appeals' "judicial nonintervention policy."[376] In contrast, Gammage viewed the case not as a federal cause of action but as a state matter, as it was brought in a Texas court and argued under the Texas constitution.[377] Gammage reminded the majority that for all the discussion of local autonomy, a school district was not an autonomous branch of government but a legislatively created political subdivision.[378] A school district has only those powers granted to it by the legislature, and a school district's actions are the actions of the state, not that of some abstract autonomous entity. And "absent some permissible basis founded upon an adequate standard, government may not violate constitutional prohibitions or intrude upon citizens' constitutionally protected liberties."[379] Since "the [l]egislature has no power to act in violation of the constitution and it may not grant [CISD's] Board the power to do so," the school district must be held accountable under the Texas ERA.[380]

The majority noted that the Fifth Circuit Court of Appeals declined to rule on challenges to school-grooming codes.[381] But as Gammage observed, the Texas Supreme Court is bound to enforce the Texas constitution, as there was no federal equivalent to the Texas ERA—which goes further than the federal constitution in specifically prohibiting gender discrimination.[382] Therefore, Barber's claim against the school district had to "stand or fall" on the Texas Supreme Court's interpretation of the ERA.[383] Barber was unable to rely on the Fifth Circuit Court of Appeals' judicial-nonintervention standard in hair grooming cases.[384] Gammage wrote:

> This case is not a federal cause of action, however, but was brought in Texas courts under the Texas Constitution. We are aware that some state courts adopt wholesale the federal judiciary's approach to federal constitutional issues in interpreting their own state constitutions, disregarding whether their state constitutions contain the same clauses or provisions as the federal constitution. But state courts *are not* bound to follow the analysis or approach of federal courts, and state governments *are* bound by the constraints of their own constitutions.[385]

In the final analysis, the majority took a two-pronged approach to the dispute, invoking first "judicial nonintervention"—which one supposes is an emanation of judicial restraint—and second, by not framing the issue as a constitutional violation.[386] In the end, Gammage lamented the majority's "gratuitous judicial nullification" of the expressed will of the people in passing the Texas ERA to outlaw sex-based classification *and* for what he saw as an abdication of the state courts' authority to that of the federal courts—particularly where a clear state remedy was available.[387] He wrote:

> Baseless and irrational discrimination in all its forms, at whomever directed and whatever its source or motivation, is still baseless and irrational discrimination. In a free society we may not always be able to prevent its private exercise, but in Texas our fundamental law does not permit it in our public schools and other governmental institutions. They should not teach it, condone it, or engage in it, and our courts and other legal institutions should not—even passively and benignly—enforce it. I dissent.[388]

Gammage's frustration with the majority's indifference to Barber's claims is demonstrated not only by his comments during oral argument and set forth in his dissenting opinion but in notes he made on court stationery. He observed that the question before the justices was a clear and simple one: Would the Supreme Court of Texas enforce provisions of the Texas constitution to protect an individual from a constitutionally prohibited government intrusion? "The majority's answer is just as clear and simple: No!" He also mused that while parents often had to invoke arbitrary rules in dealing with their children, "public schools are not parents, they are government."[389] Gammage hoped in vain that the court would come down on the side of individual rights and thus forge new precedent in an area of law where many courts were reluctant to tread.

In 1997, just two years after *Barber*, the Texas Supreme Court revisited the hair-length issue in *Bastrop Independent School District v. Toungate*,[390] upholding a hair-length regulation that applied only to male students. By this time Gammage had retired and was succeeded by Justice James A. Baker, a Republican appointed by Governor George W. Bush. In the case, an eight-year-old third-grade student was suspended from school for three days for having a five-inch-long "rat tail" haircut. At the end of the suspension period, young Zachariah Toungate was given in-school suspension and placed in isolation from his classmates. His mother refused to force him to cut his hair. During in-school suspension Zachariah was not allowed to interact with classmates, was taught by a substitute teacher, was not permitted to have lunch or recess with other students, and was barred from choral activities or the Christmas program, all because of his "rat tail."

After four months of segregation, his mother withdrew him from school on the advice of a psychologist and then home-schooled Zachariah. His mother, September Toungate, sued Bastrop Independent School District (BISD) but the trial court granted summary judgment for the school district. The Third Court of Appeals reversed and remanded for a jury trial. The trial court ultimately held that BISD violated Toungate's rights under the Texas ERA as well as under state anti-discrimination law,[391] thus permanently enjoining BISD from enforcing the hair-length rule. The court of appeals then upheld the lower court's ruling on statutory grounds but dismissed Toungate's assertion of rights under the Texas ERA in light of the *Barber* precedent. BISD appealed. The Texas Supreme Court reversed (7-1) the appeals court ruling, holding that constitutional challenges to hair-length regulations were nonjusticiable, and did not violate Texas' ERA because such regulations did not favor one sex over another by denying educational opportunities based on sex. Furthermore, as Republican justice Priscilla Owen argued for the majority, the anti-discrimination statute was never intended to prohibit the adoption and enforcement of grooming standards by the public schools.[392] Had the legislature intended the phrase "denying any benefit because of sex" to extend to hair-grooming rules or dress codes, it would have stated so, wrote Justice Owen. It was unlikely that "because of sex" was intended to prohibit dress codes "that recognize a difference between the sexes in light of the history of these statutes."[393] In sum, in applying *Barber* the court ruled that constitutional challenges to hair-length policies promulgated by elementary and secondary schools did not rise to the level of infringement of a student's right which would warrant judicial intervention. Concurring, Justice Baker, Gammage's successor, reiterated the majority's position in *Barber* that "this Court should not involve itself in hair length disputes."

With Gammage now retired, the lone dissenter (and last Democrat to serve on the court) was Justice Rose Spector. She argued that, as in *Barber*, the school district had adopted the "obedience for obedience sake" mind-set. While dress codes serve legitimate purposes, such as fostering respect and unity and avoiding distractions, school districts did not have the "license to impose unjustified, discriminatory standards." The school's principal only supported the rule out of the need for boys to look like boys and girls to look like girls. The hair-length rule was not gender-neutral, as a rule requiring cleanliness or prohibiting immodest clothing would be. Zach had already completed the second grade with his tail and there was no disruption. The only disruption came after he was isolated from other students. It was then that the other students began to tease and taunt him. There was no evidence that the third-grader's tail caused or promoted gang activity. Lastly, the reinforcement by the school of the view that only girls had long hair was a stereotype based on outdated notions of gender. Indeed, Zach's "girlish" hairstyle was based on his father's ponytail—a form of male identification.[394] Justice Spector concluded:

> Two years ago in *Barber v. Colorado Independent School District,* this Court left it within the discretion of parents, school administrators, and the Legislature to choose appropriate hair length policies. Sometimes, however, parents and administrators disagree. As the trial judge wrote, "Shame should be heaped generously on both the plaintiff's parents, and the school officials for not working out some way to remove the child from [in-school suspension] before it reached the absurd level it did." It became necessary for a court to protect the child caught in the crossfire. This court has failed to give that protection.[395]

Texas Monthly pointed out that Texas schools remain in the hair business. In 2014 a five-year-old named Malachi Wilson in Seminole, Texas, was sent home from kindergarten because he wore his hair in a long, braided ponytail. His parents sought an exemption to the policy because Malachi was Navajo. Once the parents provided documentation that the child was truly Navajo and his hair was an expression of religious belief—as opposed to mere self-expression—the school granted him an exemption to its hair policy.[396]

The actual impact of the Texas ERA on state civil rights law is subject to debate. According to many scholars, it has had only modest successes in guarding against discriminatory practices and laws.[397] In 1987 the Texas Supreme Court struck down a section of the Family Code as discriminatory under the Texas ERA, because the code allowed an unmarried biological father to seek "legitimization" of his child that had been given up for adoption by the unmarried biological mother, if it was in the "best interests" of the child. However, no "best interests" provision existed in the code that allowed the mother to legitimize her child.[398] The court applied strict scrutiny in that case, but then in a subsequent case in 2002, the court—which had grown even more conservative—ruled that the Texas ERA did not require that strict judicial scrutiny be applied in *all* cases alleging sex discrimination. Instead, laws that are "facially neutral"—even though they place a burden on one sex over another—merely require that said laws are presumed to be constitutional unless the state discriminates based on sex.[399]

COURT WARS AND JUDICIAL RECUSAL

One of the last major cases heard by Gammage raised several of the issues that have plagued the Texas courts: the influence of powerful groups on judicial elections, campaign contributions, and judicial ethics. Following the most expensive judicial campaign in Texas history in 1988, and as a part of the strategy to elect pro-business justices and offset the influence of Texas trial lawyers, the Texas Medical Association (TMA) and TEX-PAC produced a remarkable television campaign infomercial for the 1992 Supreme Court election. The TV ad—at that time unprecedented in Texas—was a combination documentary-campaign ad focused on an actual pending appeal in a high-profile malpractice lawsuit. At the time, Dr. Benjamin Bradley, a surgeon, was fighting a malpractice judgment. An appeal of the judgment was heading to the Texas Supreme Court just as the campaign ad aired prior to the general election. The ad urged doctors to vote in November to alter the composition of the Supreme Court, not only so Dr. Bradley would prevail in the pending appeal but also so that a new court would be seated whose bias would favor physicians and the lawyers who defended them against harsh judgments. The video contained statements by the sitting justices who were supported by the medical profession, although is no evidence that the justices or their campaign committees authorized the ad. The producers simply pieced together footage of the justices speaking at various public events and explained that several of the sitting justices had received campaign contributions from the PAC.

TEX-PAC lobbyists also orchestrated an unprecedented grassroots campaign, holding briefings and rallies. They provided training, talking points and form letters to physicians and their spouses. Doctors would leave slick pre-prepared brochures—and the famous small red ballot cards—in their waiting rooms suggesting that patients' health care costs would skyrocket or that their family doctors would be driven from practice.[400] The TMA donated money to favorable judicial candidates, including incumbent and prospective justices that would hear Bradley's appeal. Interestingly, one judge who was *not* supported by the TMA was surprised to find one of these ubiquitous red campaign cards when he took his daughter to her doctor's office.

In the 1992 campaign infomercial *Court Wars III: The Fight to Defend the Court*—a loose parody of *Star Wars*—the TMA analogized the Texas trial lawyers as Darth Vader's evil empire, aggressively bringing endless unwarranted medical malpractice suits against heroic physicians who were simply trying to heal the sick and injured.[401] As a part of the strategy to take back the courts, the TMA, and a political action committee called TEX-PAC, moved far beyond Clean Slate '88-type canvassing and red ballot cards to produce this remarkable television campaign infomercial. The commercial was a combination documentary-style campaign ad focusing on an actual pending appeal in a high-profile malpractice lawsuit. With dramatic theme music eerily similar to the *Star Wars* movie soundtrack playing in the background, the narrator states:

> In the early 1970s, a handful of the richest, most powerful personal injury lawyers in Texas devised a scheme to seize control of the Texas Supreme Court, using big-money politics to rewrite Texas law and tilt justice unfairly in their favor. By 1976, they had succeeded. The Texas legal system became their hunting ground. Business and health care were forced to run for cover under the threat of an activist Supreme Court with a legislative agenda. Insurance premiums soared. Hospitals and doctors were forced out of business. Corporations fled Texas. New Businesses stayed away. And the people suffered.[402]

After bemoaning the obscene amount of money spent by trial lawyers, the TEX-PAC video specifically endorsed incumbent Justice Jack Hightower, candidate Craig T. Enoch's (Fifth Court of Appeals) challenge to incumbent Justice Oscar Mauzy, and supported incumbent Justice Eugene A. Cook's reelection campaign against challenger Judge Rose Spector (131st District Court). Clips featuring all of the endorsed candidates appeared in the video. None of the candidates were filmed expressly for the video nor gave TEX-PAC permission to use their image or words from the various events for the campaign spot. The TEX-PAC video also contained brief comments by two incumbents not on the ballot in 1992, Justices John Cornyn and Nathan Hecht.

To bolster its reputation as an organization with political clout, the video then highlights the names of other justices that TEX-PAC had successfully supported in the past: Chief Justice Phillips and Justices Gonzales, Hightower, Hecht, Cornyn, and Gammage. There was no mention of the voting patterns or political party of these justices—they were depicted simply as qualified, honest, and unbiased.

Dr. Bradley, the doctor appealing the judgment, appears in the video and makes an emotional plea for a "fair" court. So, the campaign video was not merely a plea to voters to support a particular judicial candidate whom TEX-PAC deemed friendly to the medical profession but was an elaborate and not-so-thinly veiled plea to actual sitting justices, and viable judicial candidates, to consider Dr. Bradley's unfair jury verdict which was currently on appeal. While the video speaks of fair and independent justices, the whole tone of the video suggests not only that particular justices are good for the medical profession but that Dr. Bradley's fate was inextricably tied to the presence of particular justices on the court whom TEX-PAC supported.[403] There is an eerie Machiavellian cynicism and lack of self-awareness in the whole production in that in seeking a "fair" court, the producers of the video ignored (or perhaps were not even aware of) notions of judicial independence and impartiality.

The case at the center of *Court Wars III, Rogers, et al. v. Bradley*,[404] originated when plaintiffs (the family of woman who died and another woman who was permanently disfigured after a liposuction procedure) sued Dr. Bradley in a Houston trial court. She won a multi-million-dollar jury award in a malpractice suit against Brian Bradley, MD. The court of appeals reversed the trial court's judgment, on the jury verdict and the appellants filed a writ of error to reverse the court of appeals. The appellants also filed a motion to recuse several justices on the Texas Supreme Court, including Justices Hightower, Hecht, Cornyn, and Enoch. The basis for the motion to recuse was the video produced by TEX-PAC because it depicted which sitting justices were supportive of the needs of the medical profession in face of lawsuits brought by trial attorneys.[405]

Judicial disqualification and recusal involves a body of law and rules that to most would seem painfully dull. Matters concerning conflict of interest, pecuniary interest, states of mind of judges, and the plethora of norms inherent in recusal jurisprudence are hardly lively topics compared to million-dollar contributions and *quid pro quos*. However, people begin to pay attention when recusal law and judicial campaign contributions intersect. In other words, when judges preside over high-profile cases involving parties and lawyers who contributed money to their campaign, the media take notice.

Responding to the motion for recusal brought by Rogers, Justice Gammage argued for the recusal of *all* nine justices, including himself, based on the fact that the video made a direct and express association between support for certain candidates and the probable result in a pending case. At that time the state's recusal law[406] stated that "a judge shall recuse himself in any proceeding in which his impartiality might reasonably be questioned." Did the video calling for voter support of justices who are or might be friendly to the medical profession require any named incumbent or candidate to recuse him or herself in that case? Gammage answered in the affirmative, arguing that recusal law, which in 1995 said nothing about campaign ads run by a third party, should apply in a pending or impending case. Recusal law at that time applied *not* only to judges who have engaged in obvious biased or prejudicial conduct and speech but also to judges whose "impartiality might reasonably be questioned," regardless of the circumstances giving rise to the question of impartiality even if the circumstances "may be beyond the judge's volition or control."[407] Gammage concluded:

> Because I believe a reasonable member of the public at large, knowing all the facts in the public domain, would doubt that the justices portrayed favorably in the TEX-PAC video are actually impartial I recuse myself from participation in all matters related to this cause.[408]

Gammage touched a raw nerve, not only with associates but with members of the bench and bar. Justice Craig Enoch responded somewhat testily that he saw no basis for Gammage's or any other justice's recusal, and he took issue with Gammage's "declaration," as Enoch called it. If Gammage's reasoning was followed, Enoch argued, all nine of the current justices would need to recuse solely on the basis of the political speech of a third party. Recusal would then be required where there was no questionable conduct on the part of the judge solely because of a political action committee's endorsement of or opposition to sitting justices on the court. Gammage reasoned that TEX-PAC was not merely engaged in political speech but was attempting to use the ongoing case as part of its strategy to elect certain kinds of judges, including the ones currently serving on the court. However, Enoch correctly argued that nothing in state or federal law required recusal of any justice in this case,[409] and inferred that Gammage was unilaterally rewriting the state's recusal law.

In the end, the court rejected the motion to recuse,[410] with the exception of Gammage who used the opportunity to push for the adoption of a radical change in the state's recusal philosophy. For him, these kinds of campaigns constituted another form attack on the independence of the judicial branch. Many factors can weaken independence, ranging from judicial candidates promising a particular kind of outcome cases, to expensive campaigns that send the message to judges that they cannot win office without the support of a powerful cartel of professional interests, to third-party attack ads of the "Court Wars" variety that drive home the point that justice is for sale.

In his separate recusal opinion, Justice Enoch, who had joined the judicial reform movement (discussed at length in chapter 4) by publishing a 1995 article in *Southern Methodist University Law Review* critical of the state's method of selection, went on record that while he personally deplored the current system under which Texas judges were selected,[411] no justice should be expected to recuse because TEX-PAC or any other PAC sought to raise campaign funds to support the election of justices. According to Enoch, Gammage's reasoning would "totally disrupt the efficient administration of justice in Texas," and only justices who faced no election opposition would be able to carry out their responsibilities without regularly recusing themselves. If the written or electronic statements of a PAC or clips of justices' speeches used by PACS were grounds for recusal because they compromised the perceived impartiality of justices, then few judges would remain on the bench. Enoch concluded that:

> The vice lies . . . in the Texas judicial selection system, which places intolerable tensions between the process by which judges are chosen and the obligations they must discharge once in office. This Court has unanimously supported

> efforts to reform judicial elections in Texas. It is the Texas legislature that has failed to respond.[412]

Under the Texas Code of Judicial Conduct, no judge in this case was obligated to recuse. In legislative politics, we would be surprised if there were not a link between contributors and the behavior of legislators; but as Gammage had argued consistently before he left the bench, judges were different: legislators owe no duty to be impartial but judges do. Gammage benefited from campaign contributions—he had to if he wanted to stay on the bench—but big money PAC videos featuring sitting justices and parties in a pending dispute making a statewide pitch to influence thinking on lawsuits went far beyond the "rough and tumble" of political campaigning, as Justice Enoch had called it.

Rogers v. Bradley received coverage by the *Austin American-Statesman* as a "Case [that] Leads Supreme Court to Push for Judicial Reform."[413] That year, judicial selection reform was on the legislature's agenda, but despite Lt. Governor Bob Bullock's support, bills that would reform the system of judicial selection died. The failure of the legislative measure was responsible in part for Justice Enoch's exasperated comment that "the vice lies . . . in the Texas judicial selection system."[414]

GAMMAGE RESIGNS FROM THE COURT

In 1995, after thirteen years on the appellate bench, Gammage unexpectedly announced that he would not seek a second term on the Texas Supreme Court. Resigning from one of the most coveted offices in the state was bad news for Democrats and progressives who saw their influence quickly diminishing on the court with each passing election cycle. Gammage had bipartisan support and was regarded as a fair, capable and impartial judge who had helped return integrity to the court after a number of scandals. In his August 23, 1995, letter to Governor Bush he wrote that:

> I am honored and deeply grateful for the many opportunities of public service the people of Texas have entrusted to me during the last 25 years. I have worked hard to earn their trust and hope that I have lived up to their aspirations for the quality of my service. They, in turn, have afforded me challenges, adventures, opportunities and experiences of which most people can only dream.[415]
>
> The time has come, however, for me to move on—to focus on my family, our personal financial security, and to pursue long neglected personal goals and challenges.[416]

His resignation garnered state and national media attention after he appeared on Bill Moyers's PBS *Frontline* documentary, "Justice for Sale."[417]

The question, however, was whether this attention would infuse the judicial reform movement with new vigor. Gammage stated in the interview that judicial candidates should not make campaign promises or political speeches, which he felt was wholly inappropriate, unethical, and deleterious to the principle of judicial independence. His colleague and friend Chief Justice Thomas R. Phillips—a Republican who for decades was the most active and influential champion of judicial election reform in Texas[418]—once said that Gammage took up the issue of judicial election reform "before it became a popular topic in the Texas Legislature and editorial boards around the state" and that "Judge Gammage believed that a judiciary could only be truly independent if it was appointed rather than elected." Phillips, a conservative, called Gammage "a dedicated jurist who discharged his duties without fear or favor."[419]

Gammage was more than an ivory tower idealist resigning on principle. He was a highly pragmatic politician who saw the proverbial writing on the wall. By the mid-1990s, a Republican majority had won control of most courts, as well as most other elected offices statewide. At the end of his first term he faced an uphill battle of fending off challenges for his seat. Though very well respected and capable of maintaining a strong base of supporters, an article in the *Texas Weekly* in April 1995 predicted that if he were to run for reelection in 1996, assuming he won the primary, Gammage's name would appear as the first Democratic incumbent candidate on the ballot, directly below the candidates for president and Congress. "Not a pleasant political place to be in a presidential election year."[420] Republicans were winning and straight-ticket voting was the norm. In Texas in 1996 Republican Robert Dole won 48.8 percent of the vote to Bill Clinton's 43.8 percent. Republican senator Phil Gramm won reelection and the Republican Party maintained majorities in the US House and Senate.

If Gammage decided to run in 1996 an aggressive fundraising campaign would need to commence immediately, since approximately $4 million would be needed—mostly for television ads. Millions of dollars would be spent by a growing coalition of conservative groups to unseat Gammage, one of the few Democrats remaining on the court. Dallas district judge David Brooks and Houston district judges Greg Abbott were likely Republican opponents for the upcoming election. The TMA and other conservative groups that had supported the Clean Slate '88 and '90 campaigns were disappointed with Gammage's record and were likely to turn against him. Democrats were pressuring Gammage to run for reelection for fear that Republicans would win a sixth seat on the court. If Gammage could raise enough money to win reelection, his victory could help other Democrats down ballot.

Gammage's comment that "It's all become so partisan and so polarized and so destructive," both in campaigns and on the bench, was a sentiment shared by many judges.[421] As a well-respected incumbent, Gammage believed that he could win reelection in 1996 but hated to put his friends and family through the arduous fundraising and election battle. Fundraising would be a full-time job now that conservative and pro-business groups had a taste of winning judicial elections. He had several options: he could be a fundraising juggernaut, shift to the right of the political spectrum in order to assuage the fears of those groups for one or two more elections, he could switch his party affiliation as many Texas politicians had done, or resign and join the reform movement.

Ken Herman of the *Austin American-Statesman*, quoted Gammage that his reason for leaving the court was to make a statement on the way Texans pick judges.[422] Wayne Slater, court-watcher from the *Dallas Morning News*, characterized Gammage's resignation as a "blow to Democrats, who found themselves in the minority on the high court for the first time in many years after last year's elections."[423] At the time of his announced resignation, the court consisted of five Republicans and four Democrats. Since Democrat Jack Hightower had announced in June 1995 that he also planned to retire, Governor Bush had the opportunity to fill two seats. The number of Democrats on the court would be down to two.[424]

Gammage may have had additional reasons for retiring, such as family and finances, but he used the publicity that his retirement created to air not only his views on reforming the state's judicial section method and campaign spending but also his deep frustration with the direction of what he felt was an ideologically driven court. "You only need to read my dissenting opinions in the last few years to appreciate what I think of the direction of the court." As someone who had held numerous political offices since the 1970s, Gammage understood politics and was not naïve to the role it could play in judicial decisions, but he felt that the court had turned the corner where ideology trumped law. He wrote that "I have an idea of what the administration of justice should be and at this point in time this court and the judiciary in Texas, through the selection process, doesn't fit the pattern."[425]

In October 1995 Governor Bush announced the names of two Republican judges to fill the vacancies left by Hightower and Gammage: James A. Baker and Greg Abbott. Espousing the standard conservative mantra when appointing (or criticizing) judges, Bush said his appointees share "my conservative philosophy about the judiciary . . . It is a philosophy that says judges should interpret the law as passed by the Legislature, not make laws from the court." This is a standard talking points line that has been used by every Republican since Nixon. Bush, a businessman and political novice, had never thought about judges beyond whether or not they were good for business. Republicans now had a 7-2 majority on the Texas Supreme Court. If there had been a progressive era in the long history of the Texas Supreme Court, it had come to an end.

The high court from which Gammage retired at the end of 1995 was much different than the one to which he was elected in 1990. When Gammage was sworn in in 1991, the court had a 5-4 Democratic majority, down from a 6-3 majority in 1990. When the Republican justices gained a majority for the first time on the court after the 1994 elections, Gammage increasingly became a dissenter,[426] a role that played to his strengths at pointing out not just substantive legal differences but attempts to advance a conservative agenda that put ideology over law. One can see in his arguments his use of the law and constitution to protect individual liberties, to help ordinary Texans and to promote equality, while many of the conservatives seemed increasingly reluctant to challenge traditional cultural norms. Of course, with an electorate growing more conservative, to continue to do so would be political suicide.

In 1999, a little over three years after retiring from the Texas Supreme Court—now involved in arbitration and university teaching—Gammage was interviewed alongside judges, scholars, and campaign consultants by Bill Moyers on *Frontline.*[427] The video is still shown in classrooms and referenced in dozens of articles. The theme of the show was that in thirty-nine states judges were elected, and like all candidates they needed money to win. Bill Moyer's investigation focused on who was contributing and what they got in return. While most Americans weren't particularly interested in the arcane subject of judicial elections, *Frontline* had an impact. For decades scholars had written papers and reformers had introduced legislation, but *Frontline* was intended to shock the public in order to help get voters behind reform. We now turn to judicial politics and the reform movement in chapter 4.

NOTES

1. *Valenzuela*, 853 S.W.2d at 520.

2. Each justice is assigned a circuit, in this instance Scalia was responsible for the Fifth. See https://www.supremecourt.gov/about/circuitassignments.aspx; and https://www.supremecourt.gov/about/circuitassignments.aspx.

3. Melinda Smith, "New justices hailed at swearing in ceremonies," *Texas Bar Journal*, February 1991, 148.

4. *Kirby v. Edgewood Independent School District,* 761 S.W.2d 859, 867–869 (Tex. App.—Austin 1988) (Gammage, J., dissenting).

5. Debbie Graves, "Change in court keeps school funding case in Limbo," *Austin American-Statesman*, January 3, 1991.

6. *Kirby v. Edgewood Independent School District*, 761 S.W.2d 859, 867–869 (Tex. App.—Austin 1988) (Gammage, J., dissenting), *rev'd*, 777 S.W.2d 391 (Tex. 1989).

7. *See generally* Albert H. Kauffman, "The Texas School Finance Litigation Saga: Great progress, then near death by a thousand cuts," *St. Mary's Law Journal,*

40 (2008): 511, 514. Kauffman was involved in the case as attorney for Mexican American Legal Defense and Education Fund.

8. *Edgewood Independent School District v. Kirby (Edgewood I),* 777 S.W.2d 391 (Tex. 1989) at 397.

9. *Edgewood Independent School District v. Kirby (Edgewood I),* at 395, 397.

10. *Id.,* at 393.

11. *Id.,* at 393–394.

12. *Id.,* at 394.

13. *Id.,* at 394.

14. *Id.,* at 394–395.

15. *Id.,* at 395–396.

16. *Id.,* at 397.

17. *Edgewood Independent School District v. Kirby (Edgewood II),* 804 S.W.2d 491, 493, 495 (Tex. 1991).

18. *Edgewood Independent School District v. Kirby (Edgewood II),* at 496.

19. *See Id.,* at 495.

20. *Id.,* at 491.

21. Debbie Graves, "Change in court keeps school finding case in Limbo," *Austin American-Statesman*, January 3, 1991.

22. *Edgewood Independent School District v. Kirby (Edgewood II).*

23. Act of June 7, 1990, 71st Leg., 6th C.S., ch. 1, 1990 Tex. Gen. Laws 1.

24. *Id.,* at 498–499; *Edgewood Independent School District v. Kirby (Edgewood I),* at 395–396.

25. *See Edgewood Independent School District v. Kirby (Edgewood II),* at 500.

26. *Id.,* at 494–495.

27. *Id.,* at 496.

28. *Id.,* at 397.

29. *Id.*

30. *See Id.,* at 496, 500–501.

31. *Id.,* at 496.

32. *Id.*

33. *Id.* (quoting *Edgewood Independent School District v. Kirby (Edgewood I)* at 397).

34. *Carrollton-Farmers Branch Independent School District v. Edgewood Independent School District* (*Edgewood III*), 826 S.W.2d 489, 492 (Tex. 1992); *see also* Act of Apr. 11, 1991, 72nd Leg., R.S., ch. 20, 1991 Tex. Gen. Laws 381 *amended by* Act of May 27, 1991, 72. Leg., R.S., ch. 391, 1991 Tex. Gen. Laws 1475.

35. *Carrollton-Farmers Branch Independent School District v. Edgewood Independent School District* (*Edgewood III*) at 498.

36. *Id.*

37. *See Id.* at 543 (Doggett, J., dissenting) (quoting Act of Apr. 11, 1991, 72nd Leg., R.S., ch. 20, § 2, 1991 Tex. Gen. Laws 381 *amended by* Act of May 27, 1991, 72. Leg., R.S., ch. 391, 1991 Tex. Gen. Laws 1475).

38. *Carrollton-Farmers Branch Independent School District v. Edgewood Independent School District* (*Edgewood III*), 826 S.W. 2d 489 (Tex. 1992).

39. *Id.,* at 524 (majority opinion).

40. *Id.,* at 536–537 (Gammage, J., concurring and dissenting).

41. See Janet Elliott, "At the Capitol, Court Wore a Dunce's Cap: Hamstrung by Edgewood Backlash," *Texas Lawyer,* June 7, 1993.

42. *See generally* Act of May 28, 1993, 73rd Leg. R.S., ch. 347, § 1.01, 1993 Tex. Gen. Laws 1479.

43. *Id.*

44. *Edgewood Independent School District v. Meno* (*Edgewood IV*), 917 S.W.2d 717, 727 (Tex. 1995).

45. Paul Burka and David McCormick, "Hung Jurists," *Texas Monthly,* 22, no. 7, July 1994.

46. Chief Justice Nathan Hecht recalled this scene taking place in the 1990s during the *Edgewood* saga. Hecht spoke at an April 12, 2019, panel discussion about *Edgewood* held by the Texas Bar and Texas Supreme Court Historical Society in Austin.

47. *Edgewood Independent School District v. Meno* (*Edgewood IV*).

48. *Id.,* at 725, 731.

49. *See Id.,* at 730.

50. *Id.,* at 729 (quoting Tex. Const. art. VII, § 1).

51. *Id.,* at 747 (quoting *Edgewood III*, 826 S.W.2d 489, 523 (Tex. 1992)).

52. *Id.*

53. Gardner Selby, "Victory for state school finance," *Houston Post*, January 1995.

54. Janet Elliott and Richard Connelly, "Odd group crafts New Edgewood," *Texas Lawyer* February 6, 1995.

55. See Albert Kauffman, "The Texas Supreme Court retreats from protecting Texas students," *Scholar,* 19 (2017): 145.

56. *Texas Department of Mental Health and Mental Retardation v. Opal Petty,* 848 S.W.2d 680 (1992).

57. Opal Petty's case received some media attention. See Scott Rothschild, "The Dallas Morning news, Justices hear case of woman institutionalized for 51 years—state fighting award on suit over wrongful confinement," *The Dallas Morning News*, April 1, 1992; and Myrna Oliver, Obituaries: "Opal Marie Petty, 86: Won lawsuit over 51 years in mental hospitals," *Los Angeles Times*, March 16, 2005.

58. *Texas Department of Mental Health and Mental Retardation v. Opal Petty,* 848 S.W.2d 680 (1992).

59. Tex. Civ. Prac. & Rem. Code Ann. Sections, 101.001-.109 (Vernon 1986 & Supp. 1992).

60. Tex. Civ. Prac. & Rem. Code Ann. Section 101.021 (Vernon 1997).

61. *Id.*, at section 101.021 (B)(2).

62. *Texas Department of Mental Health and Mental Retardation v. Opal Petty,* 848 S.W.2d 680 (1992).

63. *Texas Department of Mental Health and Mental Retardation v. Opal Petty.*

64. 659 S.W.2d 30 (Tex. 1983).

65. *Texas Department of Mental Health and Mental Retardation v. Opal Petty,* at 682.

66. *Id.*

67. Joined by Chief Justice Phillips and Justices Gonzales and Hecht.

68. *Id.,* at 688 (Cornyn, J., dissenting).

69. However, the Court virtually overturned *Petty* two years later in 1994 in *University of Texas Medical Branch at Galveston v. York.* The Court, now dominated by a conservative majority, and with Gammage dissenting, ignored the *Petty* ruling completely.

70. See Scott Rothschild, "Justices hear case of woman institutionalized for 51 years—state fighting award on suit over wrongful confinement," *The Dallas Morning News*, April 1, 1992; Myrna Oliver, Obituaries: "Opal Marie Petty, 86: won lawsuit over 51 years in mental hospitals," *Los Angeles Times,* March 16, 2005; and Christopher Lehmann-Haupt, "Opal Petty, 86, patient held 51 years involuntarily in Texas, des," *New York Times,* March 17, 2005.

71. *See Planned Parenthood of Pennsylvania v. Casey*, 505 U.S. 833, 877–878 (1992) (plurality opinion).

72. *See* Elizabeth J. Hall, "Protecting California's abortion clinic workers from harassment and violence," *McGeorge Law Review,* 36 (2005): 797, 800, 802; and *see also Valenzuela*, at 521.

73. *See* John Alan Cohan, "Civil disobedience and the necessity defense," *Pierce Law Review,* 6 (2007): 111, 153.

74. *See generally* Hall, "Protecting California's abortion clinic workers from harassment and violence," note 117, at 797, 800; *see also* Cohan, "Civil disobedience and the necessity defense," note 118, at 153.

75. *Valenzuela*, at 512.

76. Bruce Hight, "Speech, privacy rights collide in courtroom," *Austin American Statesman*, October 23, 1991.

77. *Id.,* at 513.

78. *Id.*, at 520–521.

79. *Id.,* at 521.

80. *Id.,* n.2.

81. *Id.,* at 521.

82. *Id.*

83. *Id.*

84. *Id.*

85. *Id.,* n.3. The temporary injunction was subsequently dissolved for being overly broad, *see Valenzuela v. Aquino*, 763 S.W.2d 43, 45–46 (Tex. App.—Corpus Christi 1988, no writ).

86. *Valenzuela*, at 521 (Spector, J., dissenting).

87. *Ibid.*

88. *Id.,* at 522.

89. *Valenzuela v. Aquino*, 800 S.W.2d 301, 305 (Tex. App.—Corpus Christi 1990) *aff'd in part, rev'd in part*, 853 S.W.2d 512 (Tex. 1993).

90. *Id.,* at 309. Justice Gonzalez, in agreeing with the court of appeals' reversal, stated that "[t]he uncertainty of not knowing where one might be penalized for expressive speech would have an unacceptable *chilling effect* on the right of free speech." *Valenzuela*, at 519 (Gonzalez, J., dissenting) (emphasis added).

91. *Valenzuela*, at 517 (Gonzalez, J., dissenting) (discussing *Frisby*, 487 U.S. at 486).

92. Oral argument quotes from Gammage's notes taken during oral argument. Robert A. Gammage Papers, Dolph Briscoe Center for American History, University of Texas at Austin, Box D-0740.

93. *See Valenzuela*, at 514 (majority opinion) (affirming the court of appeals' judgment "insofar as it sets aside the trial court's award of damages, and revers[ing] in all other respects").

94. *See Id.,* at 513 (quoting Restatement (Second) of Torts § 652B (1977)). In discussing the two elements for an invasion of privacy cause of action, the Texas Supreme Court noted that Aquino failed to request that *either* element be submitted to the jury; furthermore, the evidence presented failed to conclusively establish either element. *Id.*

95. *Id.*, n.1.

96. See *Id.*

97. *Frisby v. Schultz,* 487 U.S. 474 (1988).

98. *Frisby v. Schultz,* at 513–514 (majority opinion) (citing *Frisby v. Schultz*, at 474).

99. *Id.,* at 519–520 (Gammage, J., dissenting) ("every person shall be at liberty to speak, write or publish his opinions on any subject, *being responsible for the abuse of that privilege*" (emphasis in original) (quoting Tex. Const. art. I, § 8)) (citing *Hustler Magazine, Inc. v. Falwell*, 485 U.S. 46, 56–57 (1988); United States v. O'Brien, 391 U.S. 367, 382 (1968)).

100. Bruce Hight, "Speech, privacy rights collide in courtroom," *Austin American Statesman*, October 23, 1991.

101. Hight, "Speech, privacy rights collide in courtroom," at 519.

102. *See Id.,* at 519.

103. *United States v. O'Brien,* 391 U.S. 367, 382 (1968) (O'Brien's criminal conviction was affirmed because he was convicted for the impact of burning his draft card.).

104. *Valenzuela*, at 520 (Gammage, J., dissenting) (citing *Casso v. Brand*, 776 S.W.2d 551, 556 (Tex. 1989)).

105. *Casso v. Brand*. (Chief Justice Phillips citing *New York Times v. Sullivan*, 376 U.S. 254 (1964)).

106. *Id.* (citing *James v. Brown*, 637 S.W.2d 914, 917 (Tex. 1982)).

107. *Id.* (alteration in original) (footnote omitted) (citation omitted) (quoting United *States v. Lee*, 935 F.2d 952, 956 (8th Cir. 1991)).

108. *Id.*

109. *Id.* (footnote omitted).

110. *See Valenzuela v. Aquino*, 800 S.W.2d 301, 308–309.

111. *Valenzuela*, at 520 (Gammage, J., dissenting).

112. *Id.,* at 519.

113. *Id.,* at 522 (Spector, J., dissenting).

114. *Id.,* at 520.

115. *Id.,* at 522 (citations omitted).

116. *Id.,* at 523 (citing *Frisby v. Schultz,* 487 U.S. 474, 486–887 (1987)).
117. *Id.,* at 524 (quoting *Billings v. Atkinson*, 489 S.W.2d 858, 859 (Tex. 1973)).
118. *Id.* (citing *Texas State Employees Union v. Texas Department of Mental Health & Mental Retardation*, 746 S.W.2d 203, 205 (Tex. 1987)).
119. *Id.* (citing *Iken v. Olenick*, 42 Tex. 195, 198 (1874)).
120. *Id.,* at 524–525 (quoting David A. Grimes, "Clinicians who provide abortions: The thinning ranks," *Obstetrics & Gynecology,* 80 (1992): 719, 721–722)); see *also* Angela Christina Couch, "Wanted: Privacy protection for doctors who perform abortions," *American University Journal of Gender and Law,* 4 (1996): 361, 361–362.
121. *Valenzuela*, at 525 (Spector, J., dissenting).
122. 859 S.W.2d 1 (Tex. 1993).
123. Justice Doggett was joined by Chief justice Phillips, and Justices Cornyn and Gonzales. Justice Enoch and Hecht dissented.
124. *Davenport v. Garcia*, 834 S.W.2d 4 (Tex. 1992).
125. See *Ex parte Tucci*, 859 S.W. 2d at 5.
126. *Ex parte Tucci.*
127. *Id.*, at 6.
128. *Id.*, at 33 (Phillips, C.J., concurring).
129. *Star-Telegram, Inc. v. Doe,* 915 S.W.2d. 471, 472 (Tex. 1995).
130. *Star-Telegram, Inc. v. Doe,* at 472–473.
131. *Id.,* at 473.
132. *Id.,* at 472.
133. *Id.,* at 472–473.
134. *Id.,* at 472.
135. *Id.,* at 473.
136. *Id.* (quoting *Florida Star v. B.J.F.*, 491 U.S. 524, 533 (1989)).
137. *Id.*
138. *Id.*
139. *Id.*
140. Recording of the oral argument in *Star-Telegram v. Doe* accessed on Texas Supreme Court website, http://www.txcourts.gov/All_Archived_Documents/SupremeCourt/oralarguments/1993/D-4578.mp3.
141. *Id.,* at 474–475. The Texas Supreme Court did not address the question of whether the information was or was not legally obtained.
142. *Id.,* at 473 (citing Samuel D. Warren and Louis D. Brandeis, "The right to privacy," *Harvard Law Review,* 4 (1890): 193.
143. *Griswold v. Connecticut,* 381 U.S. 479 (1965).
144. *Roe v. Wade,* 410 U.S. 113 (1973).
145. *Star-Telegram, Inc. v. Doe*, at 473.
146. *Id.,* at 473–474.
147. *Star-Telegram, Inc. v. Doe*, at 473–474 (citing *Industrial Foundation of the South v. Texas Industrial Accident Board*, 540 S.W.2d 668, 682 (Tex. 1976)).
148. *Industrial Foundation of the South v. Texas Industrial Accident Board*, at 672.
149. *Id.,* at 678.
150. *Ibid,*

151. *Id.,* at 680–681.

152. *Id.,* at 682.

153. *See Star-Telegram, Inc. v. Doe*, at 474–475.

154. *Id.,* at 475.

155. See *Dallas Morning News v. Fifth Court of Appeals*, 842 S.W.2d 655 (Tex. 1992), which was similar to *Star Telegram v. Doe,* in that a newspaper sought access to trial exhibits in a case against a pharmaceutical company that were barred by the trial court because they contained information protected by the right to privacy. The Texas Supreme Court refused to decide the case on the merits. Justice Gonzales argued that there is nothing in the constitution or laws that give the press unlimited access to trial exhibits. Justice Doggett wrote the dissenting opinion, joined by Justices Gammage, Hightower, and Mauzy, attacking the majority reluctance to hear the case and refusal to protect the freedom of the press.

156. *Industrial Foundation of the South v. Texas Industrial Accident Board*, at 685.

157. *Star-Telegram, Inc. v. Doe*, at 4774.

158. *Griswold v. Connecticut,* 479, 484.

159. *Katz v. United States,* 389 U.S. 347, 353 (1967), *superseded by statute*, N.Y. Crim. Proc. Law § 700 (Consol. 2013).

160. *NAACP v. Alabama ex rel Patterson*, 357 U.S.449, 462 (1958).

161. See William L. Prosser, "Privacy," *California Law Review,* 48 (1960): 383; and see generally Neil M. Richards and Daniel J. Solove, "Prosser's Privacy Law: A mixed legacy," *California Law Review,* 98 (2010): 6.

162. *Cain v. Hearst Corp*., 878 S.W.2d 577, 578 (Tex. 1994) (discussing Billings v. Atkinson, 489 S.W.2d 858, 859–860 (Tex. 1973)).

163. *Industrial Foundation of the South v. Texas Industrial Accident Board*, 668, 682–683.

164. *Kimbrough v. Coca-Cola/USA*, 521 S.W.2d 719, 722 (Tex. Civ. App.—Eastland 1975, writ ref'd n.r.e.).

165. Restatement (Second) of Torts sec. 652E.

166. *Diamond Shamrock Refining and Marketing Company v. Roque Mendez,* 844 S. W.2d 198 (1992).

167. Amicus brief submitted jointly in this case included the "Reporters Committee for Freedom of the Press," the A.H. Belo Corporation, the National Association of Broadcasters, the Houston Chronicle Publishing Company, and others.

168. *Cain v. Hearst Corp*., at 577 (Tex. 1994).

169. *Id.*

170. *Ibid.*

171. *Id.,* at 579. The majority cited several federal cases that did recognize false light, including *Moore v Big Picture Co.*, 828 F.2d 270 (5th Cir. 1987) and *Wood v. Hustler Magazine, Inc.*, 736 F.2d 1084 (5th Cir. 1984), *cert. denied*, 469 U.S. 1107 (1985). *See also* Diane Leenheer Zimmerman, "False light invasion of privacy: The light that failed," *New York University Law Review,* 64 (1989): 364, 452.

172. *Id.,* at 584 (Hightower, J., dissenting, joined by Justices Doggett, Gammage, and Spector).

173. *Id.*

174. *Id.,* at 586.

175. *Id.* (citing *Godbehere v. Phoenix Newspapers, Inc.*, 783 P.2d 781, 787 (Ariz. 1989)).

176. See Gary T. Schwartz, "Explaining and justifying a limited tort of false light invasion of privacy," *Case Western Law Review,* 41 (1991): 885.

177. 385 U.S. 374, 387-90 (1967).

178. See John Williams, "Election '94: GOP gains majority in State Supreme Court," *Houston Chronicle*, November 10, 1994, at 29.

179. *Boyles v. Kerr*, 855 S.W.2d 593 (Tex. 1993).

180. Bruce Hight, "Court vacates woman's award in sex tape case," *Austin American-Statesman,* December 3, 1992.

181. *Id.* (discussing *Boyles v. Kerr*, at 593).

182. *Id.,* at 595–596.

183. *Id.,* at 594.

184. David Margolick, "Law: At the bar: For Texas firm, the price of circulating a videotape roves quite steep," *New York Times*, June 1, 1990.

185. *Id.*

186. Sixth Court of Appeals (Texarkana).

187. *St. Elizabeth Hospital v. Garrard,* 730 S.W.2d 649 (Tex. 1987).

188. *Id.*

189. *Id.*, at 602.

190. *Boyles v. Kerr*, 595, 600.

191. *Id.,* at 596.

192. *Id.,* at 603 (Gonzales, J., concurring).

193. *St. Elizabeth Hospital v. Garrard.*

194. *Id.*, at 605, 606.

195. *Id.*, at 605 (Doggett, J. Dissenting).

196. *Id.*, at 611.

197. Gammage's notes from oral argument and conference in *Boyles v. Kerr*, Gammage (Robert A.) Papers, Dolph Briscoe Center for American History, the University of Texas at Austin, Box D-0963.

198. See generally Mae C. Quinn, "The garden path of Boyles v. Kerr and Twyman v. Twyman: An outrageous response to victims of sexual misconduct," *Texas Journal of Women and the Law,* 4 (1995): 247.

199. *Id.*

200. Kiri Martin, "Lawyers, not court, deprived woman of justice," *Houston Chronicle,* December 30, 1992.

201. December 4, 1992 letter from Ms. Nancy Rae Ortiz of Garland, Texas. Gammage (Robert A.) Papers, Dolph Briscoe Center, University of Texas. Call no.; 2008-318/5. Retrieved by author in 2016.

202. *Twyman v. Twyman*, 855 S.W.2d 619 (Tex. 1993).

203. *Id.*

204. *Boyles v. Kerr,* 593 is discussed in chapter 4.

205. Restatement (Second) of Torts section 46 (1965).

206. *Twyman v. Twyman*, at 619, 622,623.

207. *Id.*, at 629, 630, 631 (Hecht, J., concurring and dissenting).

208. *Id.*, at 644 (Spector, J., dissenting).

209. *Id.,* at 644.

210. Bruce Hight, "Emotional distress' suits face new standard-2 justices accuse court majority of sexism," *Austin American-Statesman,* May 16, 1993.

211. See Richard R. Orsinger, "Asserting claims for intentionally or recklessly causing severe emotional distress in connection with divorce," *St. Mary's Law Journal,* 25 (1994): 1253; and see Richard A. Ginsburg, Note, "The Supreme Court giveth, and the Supreme Court taketh away: Negligent infliction of emotional distress is not an independent cause of action in Texas," *Texas Tech Law Review,* 24 (1993): 1247, 1248.

212. *Graff v. Beard,* 858 S.W.2d 918 (Tex. 1993).

213. *Id.*, at 918.

214. Tex. Alco. Bev. Code section 2.03 (Supp. 1993).

215. Gammage's notes on oral argument and conference in *Graff v. Beard,* Robert A. Gammage Papers, Briscoe Center for American History, University of Texas at Austin, Box D-0756.

216. *Graff v. Beard,* at 918.

217. *Id. at* 919 (California, Massachusetts, Iowa and New Jersey).

218. *Id.*, at 921.

219. *Id.*, at 921, 922.

220. *Id.*

221. 858 S.W.2d 350 (Tex. 1993).

222. *Id.*

223. *El Chico v. Poole,* 732 S.W.2d 306 (Tex. 1987).

224. Tex. Alco. Bev. Code section 2.03 (Supp. 1993). The Dram Shop law supersedes the Court's ruling in *El Chico v. Poole,* at 306 and thus became the exclusive basis for the civil liability of commercial providers. https://statutes.capitol.texas.gov/Docs/AL/htm/AL.2.htm.

225. *El Chico v. Poole* at 919.

226. *Id.*, at 922.

227. *Id.*, at 927.

228. Spears was a progressive on the court (1979–1990) who invoked the needs of a changing society to make changes to the common law. See Chief Justice Thomas Phillips tribute to Spears in "Justice Franklin spears: Unsung hero of Texas justice," *St. Mary's Law Journal,* 28 (1997): 341.

229. *El Chico v. Poole*, at 922.

230. *Id.*

231. *Id.*

232. *Otis Engineering Corp. v. Clark*, 668 S.W.2d 307 (Tex. 1983).

233. *Graff v. Beard*, at 918, 923.

234. *Id.*, at 926.

235. *Id.*, at 927.

236. Bruce Hight, "Party hosts not liable for drunken guests, Court Rules," *Austin American-Statesman*, May 20, 1993

237. Randal O. Sorrels and Benny Agosto, Jr., "Social host liability: Friends can let friends drive drunk!" *Texas Bar Journal,* 58 (1995): 560.

238. 940 S. W. 2d 602 (Tex. 1997).

239. 61 S.W.3d 359 (Tex. 2001).

240. Tex. Alco. Bev. Code Ann. Section 2.02 (West 2005).

241. 76 Tex. B. J. 419, May, 2013.

242. *Lawrence v. Texas*, 539 U.S. 558 (2003).

243. *See State v. Morales*, 869 S.W.2d 941 (Tex. 1994); *see also* Tex. Penal Code Ann. § 21.06 (2003). It provides: "A person commits an offense if he engages in deviate sexual intercourse with another individual of the same sex." The statute defines "[d]eviate sexual intercourse" as follows:

"(A) any contact between any part of the genitals of one person and the mouth or anus of another person; or

"(B) the penetration of the genitals or the anus of another person with an object." §21.01(1).

244. *Id.,* at 203, 205.

245. *Id.,* at 203.

246. Linda Morales, Tom Doyal, Patricia Cramer, Charlotte Taft, and John Thomas.

247. *See State v. Morales* at 942 n.4 (citing Tex. Const. art. I, §§ 3(a), 13, 19).

248. Michael H. Garbarino, "Homosexuality and Texas Law: An analysis of Texas v. Morales and its implications," *Texas Law Journal on Civil Liberties & Civil Rights,* 1 (Spring 1994): 50.

249. *See Lawrence v. Texas,* at 572 (explaining that at the time of the *Bowers v. Hardwick* decision, over twenty states and the District of Columbia had sodomy laws); *see also* Carlos Maza, "State Sodomy Laws continue to target LGBT Americans," *Equality Matters Blog*, August 8, 2011, http://equalitymatters.org/blog/201108080012 (noting that in 2013, sodomy was still a criminal offense in 18 states).

250. *Bowers v. Hardwick,* 478 U.S. 186 (1986), *overruled by Lawrence v. Texas*, at 558.

251. Tex. Const. art I, sections 13, 19.

252. Tex. Const. art I, sections 3, 3A.

253. *See State v. Morales*, 826 S.W.2d 201, 202 (Tex. App.—Austin 1992), *rev'd*, 869 S.W.2d 941 (Tex. 1994).

254. *See State v. Morales* at 953.

255. For a detailed discussion of challenges to the Texas sodomy law and the procedural hurdles that were faced, see generally Christopher R. Leslie, "Procedural rules or procedural pretexts?: A case study of procedural hurdles in constitutional challenges to the Texas Sodomy Law," *Kentucky Law Journal,* 89 (2001): 1109, 1115.

256. *See City of Austin v. Austin City Cemetery Association,* 28 S.W. 528, 528–529 (Tex. 1894) (discussing whether it was constitutional for a city to enforce an ordinance regulating the burial of the dead by prohibiting funerals on specific property); *see also Passel v. Fort Worth Independent School District*, 440 S.W.2d 61, 62 (Tex. 1969) (questioning whether a statute prohibiting school-age children from joining clubs constituted an unwarranted interference with their constitutional rights to free speech and private association).

257. *State v. Morales*, at 202.

258. *Id.*

259. *Id.,* at 202–203.

260. See *Texas State Employees Union v. Texas Department of Mental Health & Mental Retardation,* 746 S.W.2d 203, 204 (Tex. 1987), in which the Texas Supreme Court ruled that the policy of requiring certain employees to take mandatory polygraph tests impermissible violated the right to privacy found in the Texas Bill of Rights.

261. *Texas State Employees Union v. Texas Department of Mental Health & Mental Retardation,* at 205.

262. See Gammage's notes from oral argument and conference. Robert A. Gammage Papers, Briscoe Center for American History, University of Texas at Austin, Box D-0756.

263. See *Id.*

264. See *Id.*

265. *State v. Morales*, at 941, 942.

266. *See Id.*

267. Joined by Justices Gonzales, Hightower, Hecht, and Enoch. *Id.*

268. *Id.,* at 943.

269. *Id.,* at 946–947 (citing *Passel v. Fort Worth Independent School District*, at 61, 63–64. *Id.,* at 62–63.

270. *State v. Morales*, at 944–945.

271. *Id.,* at 945.

272. *Id.,* at 948 (citing Dearing v. Wright, 653 S.W.2d 288, 290 (Tex. 1983)).

273. *Id.,* at 943 (footnote omitted).

274. Joined by Chief Justice Phillips, Justice Doggett, and Justice Spector. *Id.,* at 941.

275. *Id.,* at 953.

276. *Id.*(citing *Frey v. DE Cordova Bend Estates Owners Association,* 647 S.W.2d 246, 248 (Tex. 1983)).

277. *Id.,* at 953–954 (Gammage, J., dissenting) (emphasis added) (footnote omitted).

278. *Ibid.*

279. *Id.,* at 949.

280. *Id.,* at 953.

281. *Id.,* at 949 (citing *Sisco v. Hereford,* 694 S.W.2d 3, 7 (Tex. App.—San Antonio 1984, writ ref'd n.r.e.)).

282. *Id.* (quoting Joseph R. Long, "Equitable Jurisdiction to Protect Personal Rights," *Yale Law Journal,* 33 (1921): 115, 116); *see also* 27 AM. JUR. 2D *Equity* § 21 (1966).

283. *State v. Morales* at 949 (Gammage, J., dissenting) (citing *City of Austin v. Austin City Cemetery Association*).

284. *Id.,* at 950–951. Justice Gammage also cited a federal district court ruling that supports the proposition that Texas law sanctions injunctive relief to protest both property and personal rights. *Id.,* at 951 (citing *Dreyer v. Jalet*, 349 F. Supp. 452, 466–467 (S.D. Tex. 1972), *aff'd*, 479 F.2d 1044 (5th Cir. 1973)).

285. *Id.,* at 952.

286. *Id.,* at 954.
287. *Ibid,*
288. *State v. Morales* at 954 (Gammage, J., dissenting).
289. *Id.,* at 949 (citing *City of Austin v. Austin City Cemetery Association*).
290. *See* Leslie, "Procedural rules or procedural pretexts?" note 203, at 1114, 1130–1132, 1140.
291. *See Press Release*, Sito Negron, Rodríguez Bill to repeal unconstitutional law against homosexual conduct passed by Senate Committee (April 18, 2013), available at http://www.senate.state.tx.us/75r/Senate/members/dist29/pr13/p041813a.pdf (stating how the Texas Senate Criminal Committee passed a bill that will eliminate section 21.06 of the Texas Penal Code).
292. *Id.,* at 954.
293. *Barber*, 901 S.W.2d at 452 (Gammage, J., dissenting).
294. *State v. Morales* at 953–954 (Gammage, J., dissenting).
295. Article I, section 3a.
296. James E. Garcia, "State High Court Mum on Sodomy Law," *Austin American-Statesman,* January 13, 1994.
297. *England and Morales* were decided at roughly the same time in the Texas court system. In *Morales* the supreme court stated that it was not addressing the merits of *England.* See *Texas v. Morales,* 869 S.W. 2d 941, 942 n. 5.
298. *See City of Dallas v. England*, 846 S.W.2d 957, 958 (Tex. App.—Austin 1993, writ dism'd w.o.j.).
299. In *Texas v. Morales,* at 201, 205 (Tex. App.—Austin 1992), the Third Court of Appeals in Austin ruled that although the right to privacy is not expressly contained in the Texas Constitution, it is created or implied by sections 6, 8, 9, 10, 19, and 25 of the Texas Bill of Rights.
300. *State v. Morales,* at 941, 942, n. 5.
301. *Lawrence v. Texas*, at 123.
302. See Dale Carpenter, *The Story of Lawrence v. Texas: How a bedroom arrest decriminalized gay Americans* (New York: W.W. Norton & Company, 2012).
303. 41 S.W. 3d 349 (Tex. App. 2001).
304. *Lawrence v. Texas*, at 123.
305. Peggy Fikac, "Privacy rights don't protect adultery, court rules," *Austin American-Statesman*, July 9, 1996.
306. *City of Sherman v. Henry*, 928 S.W.2d 464 (1996).
307. Greg Abbott, Associate Justice, Texas Supreme Court, 1996–2001. Elected as a Republican.
308. *Id.*, at 468–469.
309. For a scholarly commentary of the case shortly after it was handed down see Shelly L. Skeen, "*City of Sherman v. Henry*: Is the Texas Constitutional Right of privacy still a source of protection for Texas citizens?" *Texas Wesleyan Law Review,* 4 (Fall 1999): 99.
310. Act of June 14, 1963, 63rd Legislature, R.S. chapter 399, 3, 1973 Texas General Laws 883, 992 repealing Texas penal Code article 499 (1925).
311. See *City of Sherman v. Henry*, at 470–471.

312. Gammage's lectures (during the 1996–97 academic year) on privacy as recalled by the author and his colleagues at Sam Houston State University.

313. *SmithKline Beecham Corporation v. Jane Doe*, 903 S.w.2d 347 (Tex. 1995).

314. Peggy Fikac, "Court says warning not required in drug tests: Woman loses suit in claim that Poppy seeds caused her to test positive for drugs," *Austin American-Statesman*, 1995; and see Scott P. Callahan, "Liability in employer-mandated drug testing—Drug laboratories have no duty to warn employees that ingestion of certain substances could cause false positive test results," *South Texas Law Review,* 38 (May 1997): 823.

315. *Seinfeld* television series, Season 7, Episode 16, "The Showerhead," February 15, 1996.

316. *SmithKline Beecham Corporation v. Jane Doe*, 349.

317. *Id.*, at 350

318. *Id.*

319. *Id.*, Oral argument recording accessed on Texas Supreme Court website, http://www.txcourts.gov/All_Archived_Documents/SupremeCourt/oralarguments/1993/D-4131.mp3

320. As told to the author by Bob Gammage's wife, Linda Hallmark Gammage in a 2013 interview.

321. Justice Hecht was joined in the majority opinion by Chief Justice Phillips and Justices Gonzales, Cornyn, Enoch and Owen.

322. *SmithKline Beecham Corporation v. Jane Doe*, 351.

323. *Id.*, at 353.

324. *Id.*, at 359.

325. *Id.*, at 360, 361. Gammage cited an Illinois case, *Stinson v. Physicians Immediate Care, Ltd.*, 269 Ill.App.3d 659 (1995) which held that a drug testing company owes a prospective employee duty not to contaminate the urine sample and to report a false positive result.

326. *Mission Petroleum Carriers, Inc. v. Solomon,* 106 S.W.3d 705 (2003).

327. *Barber v. Colorado School District*, 901 S.W.2d 447, 448 (Tex. 1995).

328. *See* Higinio Gamez, "Comment, son, get a haircut or leave my school? Hair length restriction for male students upheld by Texas Supreme Court in *Barber v. Colorado Independent School District,*" *Thurgood Marshall Law Review,* 21 (1996): 185, 186–188.

329. *Barber v. Colorado School District.*

330. *Richards v. Thurston,* 424 F.2d 1281 (1st Cir. 1970).

331. *Olff v. East Side Union High School District,* 445 F. 2d 932 (9th Cir. 1971), cert denied, 404 U.S. 1042 (1972).

332. *Massie v. Henry*, 455 F.2d 779 (4th Cir. 1972).

333. *See, e.g., Richards v. Thurston*; *Massie v. Henry*; *Holsapple v. Woods*, 500 F.2d 49, 52 (7th Cir. 1974) (per curiam); *Bishop v. Colaw*, 450 F.2d 1069, 1077 (8th Cir. 1971).

334. See *Holsapple v. Woods*, cert. denied, 491 U.S. 901 (1974).

335. *Barber v. Colorado School District* at 448.

336. *Id.*

337. *Id.*
338. *Id.*
339. *Id.*, at 448.
340. *Id.*, at 448.
341. *Id.*
342. Testimony of James McSwain, the high school principal of CISD.
343. *Id.*
344. Tex. Const. art. I, § 3(a).
345. *Barber v. Colorado School District*at 449.
346. *Id.*, at 449–450.
347. *Id.*, at 450.
348. Oral argument transcripts in *Barber et al. v. Colorado ISD*, 94-0054, 11/16/94, Robert A. Gammage papers, Dolph Briscoe Center for American History, University of Texas at Austin, Call No.: 2008-318/22.
349. *Id.*
350. Chip Brown, "West Texas student's hair dispute makes way to court," *Austin American-Statesman,* November 17, 1994.
351. *Id.*, at 447, 450 (coming to a 7–2 decision).
352. *Id.*, at 450 (citing *Karr v. Schmidt,* 460 F.2d 609, 611 (5th Cir. 1972); *Lansdale v. Tyler Junior College*, 470 F.2d 659 (5th Cir. 1972)).
353. *Barber v. Colorado School District*, at 450 (citing *New Jersey v. T.L.O.,* 469 U.S. 325, 347–348 (1985)).
354. *Id.*, at 450–451 (citing *Mercer v. Board of Trustees,* 538 S.W.2d 201, 206 (Tex. Civ. App.—Houston [14th Dist.] 1976, writ ref'd n.r.e.); *Eanes Independent School District v. Logue*, 712 S.W.2d 741, 742 (Tex. 1986)).
355. *Id.*, at 451.
356. *Id.*, at 450.
357. *Id.*, at 451 (Gammage, J., dissenting).
358. *Id.*
359. *Id.*
360. *See generally Id.*, at 450–451(majority opinion) (discussing the difference in constitutional rights between public school students and adults through a litany of Texas and federal cases).
361. *Id.*, at 455 (Gammage, J., dissenting).
362. *Id.*, at 451 (Gammage, J., dissenting) (citing *Mercer v. Board of Trustees*).
363. *Id.*, at 452 (citing *In re* McLean, 725 S.W.2d 696, 698 (Tex. 1987)).
364. *Id.*
365. *Id.*
366. *Id.*
367. *Id.*
368. *Id.*, at 453.
369. *Id.*
370. *Id.*
371. *Id.*, at 452.
372. *Id.* (citing *Crews v. Cloncs*, 432 F.2d 1259, 1266 (7th Cir. 1970)).
373. *Id.*, at 453.

374. *Id.*, at 453 citing *Independent School District No. 8 of Selling, Dewey County v. Swanson*, 553 P.2d 496 (Okla. 1976).

375. *Id.*, at 453–454.

376. *Id.*, at 453–454 (discussing *Karr v. Schmidt,* 460 F.2d 609, 611 (5th Cir. 1972); *Ferrell v. Dallas Independent School District,* 392 F.2d 697 (5th Cir. 1968)); *cf. Lansdale v. Tyler Junior Coll.*, 470 F.2d 659 (5th Cir. 1972).

377. *Barber v. Colorado School District,* at 454 (Gammage, J., dissenting).

378. *Id.,* at 453.

379. *Id.*

380. *Id.*

381. *Id.,* at 450 (majority opinion) (citing *Karr*, 460 F.2d at 611; *Ferrell*, 392 F.2d at 702–04).

382. *Id.,* at 451–452 (Gammage, J., dissenting).

383. *Id.,* at 454 (quoting *Mercer v. Board of Trustees*, 538 S.W.2d 201, 203 (Tex. Civ. App.—Houston [14th Dist.] 1976, writ ref'd n.r.e)).

384. *Id.,* at 454.

385. *Id.* (citation omitted). In 1995, when *Barber* was decided, fifteen other states had equal rights amendments in their state constitutions.

386. *Id.,* at 450–451 (majority opinion).

387. *Id.,* at 455 (Gammage, J., dissenting).

388. *Id.*

389. Robert A. Gammage Papers. Dolph Briscoe Center for American History, University of Texas at Austin.

390. 958 S.W. 2d 365 (1997).

391. Tex. Civ. Prac. & Rem. Code Sec. 106.001 prohibits an officer or employee of the state or political subdivision of the state from denying any public benefit, including employment and licensure, or denying participation in any public event on the basis of race, religion, color, sex, or national origin. The law, originally passed in 1971, was amended in 1983 to encompass discrimination on the basis of pregnancy, childbirth, or related medical conditions. These amendments ultimately became part of the Human Rights Act, Ex. Lab. Code Secs. 21.001-.306.

392. 958 S.W. 2d 365, 367–368.

393. *Id.*, at 368.

394. *Id.*, at 378.

395. *Id.*, at 379.

396. Dan Solomon, *Texas Monthly,* September 3, 2014, http://www.texasmonthly.com/daily-post/navajo-kindergartener-west-texas-who-was-sent-home-his-first-day-school-long-hair-back.

397. Michael Ariens, *Lone Star Law: A Legal History of Texas* (Lubbock: Texas Tech University Press), 176–177.

398. *In re McLean,* 725 S.W. 2d 696 (1987).

399. *Bell v. Low Income Women of Texas*, 95 S.W. 3d 253 (Tex. 2002); and see Linda J. Wharton, "State equal rights amendments revisited: Evaluating their effectiveness in advancing protection against sex discrimination," *Rutgers Law Journal,* 67 (2005): 1201.

400. Frontline interview with Kim Ross, Lobbyist for the TMA (1999). https://www.pbs.org/wgbh/pages/frontline/shows/justice/interviews/ross.html).

401. Video "Court Wars: The fight to defend the courts," video and transcript of the video filed in the Supreme Court of Texas, October 20, 1994 (94-0861). Exhibit B. Case files, Records, Texas Supreme Court. Archives and Information Services Division, Texas State Library and Archives Commission.

402. *Id.*

403. *Id.*, at 874–875.

404. 909 S.W. 2d 872 (1995).

405. *Id.*, at 873.

406. Tex. R. App. P.15a, Tex. R. Civ. P. 18b.

407. 909 S.W. 2d 872, 874.

408. *Id.*

409. See Tex R. App. P. 15a (incorporating by reference Rule 18b which states "A judge shall recuse himself in any proceeding in which . . . his impartiality might reasonably be questioned . . . " Tex R. Civ. P 18b (2) (a)).

410. When a party files a motion to recuse a justice on the Texas Supreme Court he or she must either recuse from participation in the case or certify the question to the rest of the court sitting en banc, which then decides the disqualification question by majority vote. Tex. R. App. P. 16.3. If a justice is disqualified the chief justice will certify to the governor who can appoint a replacement justice. Tex. Gov't Code Ann. Sec. 22.005. http://www.statutes.legis.state.tx.us/Docs/GV/htm/GV.22.htm

411. See Craig Enoch, "1995 Annual survey of Texas Law: Forward," *Southern Methodist University Law Review,* 48 (1995): 723.

412. 909 S.W. 2d 872 (Tex.1995), 882–884.

413. Dean Stevens, *Austin American–Statesman,* August 3, 1995.

414. 909 S.W. 2d 872 (Tex.1995), 884.

415. Letter of resignation from the Texas Supreme Court. Robert A. Gammage Collection. SHSU Special Collections, Newton Gresham Library, Sam Houston State University, Huntsville, Texas.

416. *Id.*

417. http://www.pbs.org/wgbh/pages/frontline/shows/justice/etc/press.html.

418. Chief Justice Thomas Phillips was elected as a reformer. A Republican, Phillips received bipartisan support, put a voluntary limit on campaign contributions, and campaigned with the intent of receiving votes from a broad base of voters. Phillips was one of the most efficacious fund raisers in the state even while consistently advocating reform. He felt like he was trapped by the system, believing that raising money was inappropriate for a judicial candidate yet knowing full well that without it he would be defeated. He was appointed chief justice in January 1988, ran for election that same year, and ran for reelection in 1990, 1996, and 2002. In the 1990 election Phillips and his opponent each spent well over $2 million on the campaign.

419. Press advisory from the Texas Supreme Court, http://www.supreme.court.state.tx.us/advisories/pdf/.

420. "Champing at the Supreme Court Bit," *Texas Weekly,* April 10, 1995.

421. Dave McNeely, "Partisanship drove away Gammage," *Austin American-Statesman*, August 29, 1995.

422. Ken Herman, *The Austin American Statesman,* August 24, 1995.

423. George Kuempel, "Gammage to resign from the supreme court—decision called setback for Democrats—Gov. Bush to have 2 vacancies to fill," *The Dallas Morning News*, August 24, 1995.

424. Ben Wear, "Texas Court tilts right, upends '80s decisions: Plaintiffs less likely to prevail in today's Supreme Court statistics show," A*ustin American-Statesman,* September 13, 1995.

425. Ken Hermann, "Justice Gammage to resign from high court; With two seats open, Bush has chance to strengthen GOP majority," *Austin American-Statesman,* August 24, 1995.

426. According to "Amicus Curiae and Dissenting Votes at the Texas Supreme Court," by Ryan Rebe, Gammage dissented in 23 percent of the decisions while on the Court, compared to Thomas Phillips who dissented in 0.05 percent of the cases. Gammage's ideology score was 32.35 on this scale of 0–100, 0 being the most liberal, and 100 the most conservative. Across a range of all cases—*not* just civil rights and liberties—Gammage scored 32.35, placing him right of center with John Cornyn, a Republican, with an identical score. Chief Justice Phillips, a Republican, scored 22.18. The mean was 36.48. I used a similar methodology to calculate Gammage's dissent rate (0.40) and ideology score (18.76) in civil rights and civil liberties cases.

427. *Frontline*, "Justice for sale," November 23, 1999, https://www.pbs.org/wgbh/pages/frontline////shows/justice/etc/script.html.

Chapter 4

Court Wars

Judicial Politics and Reform in Texas

> People don't go pour money into campaigns because they want fair and impartial treatment. They pump into campaigns because they want things to go their way. Why else would the contributors be there? They have interests to pursue. In some cases they have ideologies to pursue. They're not just bland, benign philosophies. They want results.[1]
>
> —Bob Gammage

Bob Gammage served on the Third Court of Appeals (1982–1990) and the Texas Supreme Court (1990–1995) during one of the most tumultuous times in the history of the Texas judiciary. Through the 1970s and early 1980s, judicial elections were generally sedate and dignified, drawing the attention of mainly members of the bench and bar. At the beginning of his judicial career in 1982, incumbents, most of whom were Democrats, very rarely faced a viable opponent in primary or general elections.[2] However, within the span of a decade, elections suddenly became more competitive, and a nascent two-party system threatened the Democratic Party's domination of statewide elected offices.[3] By the mid-1980s, millions of dollars in campaign contributions were being poured into judicial campaigns by trial lawyers, unions, the petrochemical industry, and medical profession. As Bob Gammage recalled, seemingly overnight, judges were forced to become fundraising machines. Worse than that, campaign contributions came with strings attached. As Gammage aptly stated in the aforementioned passage, "people don't go pour money into campaigns because they want fair and impartial treatment."[4] Contributors want to elect judges who not only reflect preferred partisan ideologies but specific outcomes in cases.

By the late 1980s, the tort reform movement was in its ascendancy, allowing the defense bar to challenge trial lawyers for control of the courts.

Democrats and progressives were losing seats on the bench, and Republicans were poised to dominate the Texas judiciary for the next three decades. The 1988 Supreme Court race was the most expensive in history, with many candidates spending over $2 million to retain their seats on the court. Judicial candidates were now under extraordinary pressure to make campaign promises, run negative television attack ads, and spend a disproportionate amount of their time and energy raising campaign money. Suddenly, judicial races were highly partisan, competitive, and among the most expensive in the nation. This perfect storm threatened judicial independence and further undermined public confidence in the judicial system. Conversely, the judicial politics of the time also gave rise to a robust reform movement. Reforms that were considered included replacing the state's system of partisan elections with an appointive system or a merit plan. There were also plans to diversify the bench, limit campaign contributions and spending, adopt a system of public funding of campaigns, and enact tougher judicial recusal and ethics rules, to name but a few. This chapter transcends Gammage's record on the bench and examines the history of judicial politics and reform in the Lone Star State.

THE POLITICS OF JUDICIAL SELECTION

The history of judicial selection in Texas reflects the centuries old tension between two fundamental principles: judicial independence and accountability. For as long as there have been judges, a disagreement has existed between those who endeavor to protect the decisional independence of judges from political pressure and those who contend that judges must be held directly accountable to the king, the people, or powerful interests. Long before the founding of the American Republic, English jurists argued that because judges need to be impartial, they should serve during "good behavior"—an indefinite term of office—and not merely at the "pleasure of the king," subject to removal when the monarch or his minions were displeased with rulings. The theoretical underpinnings of the Founders' understanding of the importance of life tenure for judges, as well as the function of the judiciary in a constitutional republic, has been attributed to many sources, the most influential being William Blackstone's commentaries on the common law of England.[5] The Founders' views on judicial independence were also influenced by the 1701 English Act of Settlement,[6] and from their own experiences with British interference with colonial courts.[7]

So important was the need for an independent judiciary that Thomas Jefferson wrote in the Declaration of Independence that one of the "repeated injuries and usurpations" committed by the king was making "judges dependent on his Will alone for the tenure of their offices, and the amount and payment of their salaries."[8] In that momentous year, John Adams argued in his 1776 political pamphlet *Thoughts on Government* that:

> The judicial power ought to be distinct from both the legislative and executive, and independent upon both, that so it may be a check upon both, as both should be checks upon that. The judges, therefore, should always be men of learning and experience in the laws, of exemplary morals, great patience, calmness, coolness, and attention. Their minds should not be distracted with jarring interests; they should not be dependent upon any man, or body of men. To these ends, they should hold estates for life in their offices; or, in other words, their commissions should be during good behavior, and their salaries ascertained and established by law.[9]

Crafted during the constitutional convention of 1787, Article III of the US Constitution was intended to address the "injuries and usurpations," of which Jefferson wrote, as well as secure the qualities Adams deemed fundamental, by vesting judicial power in a separate and independent branch of government consisting of federal judges, federal judges that "shall hold their Offices during good Behavior."[10] During the ratification debate, in support of life tenure for judges, Alexander Hamilton wrote in his Federalist #78:

> Adherence to the rights of the Constitution, and of individuals, which we perceive to be indispensable in the courts of justice, can certainly not be expected from judges who hold their offices by a temporary commission. Periodical appointments, however regulated, or by whomsoever made, would, in some way or other, be fatal to their necessary independence.[11]

Americans, and then, later, Texans, accepted the fact that judicial appointments would never be entirely apolitical, but sharing the power of selection between an executive and the upper chamber of a legislature would ideally foster a well-qualified judiciary and impartial system of justice. The election of judges who served at the pleasure of voters, in contrast, would lead to a judiciary accountable not to the law but to party machines and popular passions.

Mirroring the Constitution of the United States, the Constitution of the Republic of Texas (1836–1845) created legislative, executive, and judicial branches of government, vesting the judicial power in a supreme court. Much like Article III of the US Constitution, the Republic's constitution said little about the judicial branch beyond delegating to the Texas Congress the power to establish the judiciary, and to enact laws governing the selection of judges. The chief justice of the Texas Supreme Court and district judges were elected by both houses of Congress on a joint ballot, and served for renewable four-year terms.[12] Texas was divided into four judicial districts, each having four district judges traveling throughout the assigned circuit. The Supreme Court was not a permanent body but consisted of the four district judges and chief justice sitting *en banc* to hear appeals once a year in a single session.[13] However, it was not until four years after the founding of the Republic in 1836, that the Supreme Court held its first session.[14] The number of judicial districts would later be increased. Yet, due to the sheer vastness of the young nation, as well as primitive roads and transportation systems, disease, murders, and low salaries, the nation's new judicial branch was plagued by low prestige and a high turnover rate.[15]

The first chief justice was James T. Collingsworth (1836–1838), an ally of Sam Houston, who was the first president of the Republic of Texas. However, since the court did not convene under Collingsworth, and he tragically drowned in Galveston Bay in 1840, the first session of the court was convened under Chief Justice Thomas Jefferson Rusk (1838–1840). The Rusk Court had a cautious reputation when it came to constitutional interpretation, as well as a deference to the legislative and executive branches of government.[16] Rusk had an opportunity to assert judicial review in a dispute that involved the constitutionality of electing chief justices of county courts, an office not mentioned in the constitution, ruling that the Texas Congress had broad discretion to establish new courts and judicial offices.[17] Rusk resigned in 1840 to start a private law practice.

His successor, John Hemphill—often called the John Marshall of Texas—served as chief justice of the Republic from 1840 to 1845, and then in the same capacity for over a decade after Texas was annexed by the United States (1845–1858).[18] Hemphill had a profound impact not only on defining the role and function of the Texas judiciary but also on the state's nascent jurisprudence. The state's constitution demanded that the principles and precedent of the English common law provide the foundation of the Texas legal system, but the vestiges of Spanish civil law—in force in Mexico before Texas independence—continued to have an impact on the development and practice of law in the early Republic.[19] Hemphill passionately supported one of the better known Spanish civil law concepts, retained by Texas today—that wives possessed rights and could own property, independently of their husbands. Under the English common law, once a woman married, she gave up her property rights to her husband. If she divorced her husband, she forfeited her property—even that property which she owned prior to the marriage. By forfeiting her property, she also gave up her rights and independence. Thus, the origin of the concept of community property in Texas is rooted in the civil law as it was practiced in Mexico.[20] Because the civil law granted more protection to women, barred the jailing of debtors, and simplified pleadings in civil cases, Hemphill preferred it over the common law. The civil law also emphasized the equity power of judges to resolve civil disputes without the use of lay juries. Hemphill was criticized for his embrace of the civil law over the common law by those who believed that the two systems of law were incompatible and by those who harbored a general antipathy toward Mexico after independence.[21]

Under Chief Justice Hemphill's nearly two decades of leadership, the Texas judiciary asserted its independence and the office of judge rapidly gained prestige.[22] Hemphill believed that as the composition of the court became more stable, confidence in the legal system would rise, and a distinct and coherent body of law would emerge.[23] In 1841, the Supreme Court wielded the power of judicial review for the first time in *Morton v. Gordon*, striking down an act of the Texas Congress that attempted to impose limits on the right to appeal in certain cases. Then, in *Stockton v. Montgomery* in 1842, the Texas Supreme Court again voided an act of Congress which created a new territory, and in doing so, cited Chief Justice John Marshall's reasoning in *Marbury v. Madison*.[24] In *Allen v. Scott* in 1844, the Hemphill Court ruled that a law enacted by the Texas Congress that altered a judicial district was repugnant to the constitution because it "violate[d] the spirit of the constitution and is at war with its plain meaning and intent."[25] In short, under Hemphill, the supreme court of the republic had found its footing as a coequal branch of government.

As a delegate to the 1845 constitutional convention, during the process by which Texas was annexed to the United States, Hemphill's plan for the new state's judicial branch included a supreme court consisting of three judges, appointed by the governor with the advice and consent of the state Senate.[26] Justices would serve a six-year term of office, before facing the reconfirmation process. In addition, the new constitution established district courts and "inferior courts," such as probate and justice courts. Over the fierce objections of many delegates at the constitutional convention of 1845 who argued for the popular election of judges, Chief Justice Hemphill convinced a majority of delegates that an appointive method of judicial selection, mirroring that which exists at the national level, would best secure the independence and integrity of the judiciary. Hemphill, and his predecessor, Thomas Rusk, "considered the Judicial Department the most important branch of government"[27]and that the election of judges would lead to a "weak and vacillating judiciary, destitute of talent and integrity."[28] Rusk further stated in 1845:

> If we have . . . a judiciary . . . which is swayed by popular clamors, you are on a sea without compass; your rights as a person are not safe; your property is not safe; the reputation of your country is endangered; all is anarchy and confusion.[29]

Rusk's prophetic words have been echoed by modern opponents of judicial elections, and ring true 170 years later. James L. Haley writes in his authoritative narrative history of the Texas Supreme Court:

> Rusk and Hemphill had no idea, of course, that in taking up the cause to find a better way to select judges than subjecting them to the "popular clamors," they were firing the opening salvo in a debate still unresolved after a century and half.[30]

Supporters of the popular election of judges would eventually prevail. Caught up in Jacksonian populism, a constitutional amendment was ratified in 1851 that granted Texans the right to vote for judges. Under Jacksonian democracy, the idea of appointing judges was regarded as elitist and antidemocratic. Formally educated people who advocated for an independent judiciary were viewed with suspicion by the majority of voters. The populist argument then—as today—grudgingly acknowledges the importance of judicial independence, as long as this abstract concept does not interfere with the people's right to hold judges directly accountable—as opposed to indirectly accountable through the popular election of representatives.[31]

Following the Civil War, for a short brief period of time under the 1869 Reconstruction constitution, Texas embraced gubernatorial appointment of judges but then quickly returned to a system of electing judges for four-year terms under the 1876 constitution (present constitution) following what was perceived as abuses of power by Governor Edmund Davis and his appointed judges. The 1876 constitution added an intermediate appellate court—the court of appeals—which would hear, almost exclusively, criminal appeals. The Supreme Court of Texas retained its appellate jurisdiction to hear appeals in civil cases tried in the district courts, but no longer possessed criminal jurisdiction. The number of justices was set at three and they would serve a term of six years. All judges were to be elected by the people. Interestingly, the Texas constitution is silent on whether elections should be partisan or nonpartisan, but under state election law judicial candidates run for office as a nominee of their party, thus effectively promoting partisan elections.[32]

THE REFORM MOVEMENT

Distain for an elected judiciary existed among many members of bench and bar ever since the days of Chief justices Rusk and Hemphill, but it was not until nearly a century later, in the mid-1900s, that serious discussions of reforming the system resurfaced. In 1943, Charles T. McCormick, the dean of the University of Texas School of Law, wrote in a widely read *Texas Law Review* article that

> no constitutional mechanism can be devised which will make certain the choice of the best qualified men as judges, but we should strive for the method of selection, which in the light of reason and experience is most likely to produce this result.[33]
>
> The elected judges of this and other states are in the main capable, honest and fair minded men. But it seems probable that they do not attain quite the same level of efficiency or inspire quite the same degree of public confidence as the judges of England, Massachusetts, or of the federal courts. Moreover, in recent decades two influences have conspired to weaken the system of election.[34]

Dean McCormick encouraged members of the bench and bar to oppose all forms of popular elections, which, he argued, contradicted the ideal of the impartial and qualified judge who is not bound to a particular constituency. *If* popular elections were to be held, he reasoned, then political parties should use conventions, rather than direct primaries to choose candidates.[35] McCormick wrote that party primaries were "circuses," and he admitted that Texans had accepted the fact that many judges elected would be unqualified; but their ability to remove judges with whom they disagreed superseded concerns about their qualifications. McCormick offered a wide range of methods of selection, including the appointment of judges by either the chief justice, or by a panel of sitting judges, for a term of service followed by a popular referendum—or what we would call today a retention election.[36] However, distain for change prevailed, and no action was taken following McCormick's proposals.

Following the publication of McCormick's article in 1946, a body called the Texas Civil Judicial Council proposed a constitutional amendment that would require the merit selection of all judges. The legislature approved the amendment, but it was defeated by a majority of voters who viewed it with suspicion.[37] Reform efforts stalled during the 1950s and 1960s, largely due to internecine battles between New Deal progressives and anti-New Deal/segregationists in the Democratic Party. Tension between these two factions was further exacerbated by the US Supreme Court's landmark desegregation rulings in *Sweatt v. Painter*[38] in 1950 and *Brown v. Board of Education*[39] in 1954. These rulings, and other Warren Court decisions during the 1960s in the areas of due process and civil liberties, became the backdrop for the emergence of political campaigns in which judicial candidates either supported or opposed the Court's "activist" agenda. These liberal rulings also fueled grassroots calls for even greater judicial "accountability" to the voters.

In 1971, Chief Justice Robert Calvert[40] announced his support of an amendment to the Texas constitution that would establish merit selection of appellate judges.[41] Under Calvert's plan, judges would be initially appointed by the governor and then run in retention elections after a designated term of office. The prospect for reform was good. Younger members of the bar, who were critical of the quality, impartiality, and integrity of the older generation of judges, supported Calvert's proposal. A major taskforce was formed, and support for the amendment was enthusiastic, but, ultimately, the effort died in the state legislature.[42] Calvert's successor, Chief Justice Joe Greenhill,[43] also called for reforms in the 1970s, lobbying the legislature to adopt nonpartisan election of judges. The bench and bar rallied around the respected Greenhill, but once again the legislature would not budge.[44]

Early in Greenhill's tenure, judicial candidate's names rarely even appeared in newspapers, so candidates relied mainly on support from leaders of the legal profession and the business community. A well-respected attorney or judge might be asked to stand for election, or receive a recommendation by peers for a gubernatorial appointment, if a vacancy arose due to retirement or death. The prospective nominee would then make the rounds at professional meetings and community organizations, before filing to appear on the ballot. Incumbents very rarely faced an opponent, and primary challenges were almost unheard of.[45] By the late 1970s, as elections became more competitive, campaign contributions poured in from groups and organizations from both sides of the political spectrum.[46] The use of aggressive and negative television campaign commercials by Democrats and Republicans in the late 1970s pushed the total amount of campaign contributions past the million-dollar mark for the first time.[47]

By the mid-1980s, embarrassing newspaper headlines, such as "Supreme Court Probe," appeared regularly in state newspapers,[48] thus bolstering claims by reformers that unregulated campaign contributions, primarily from trial lawyers, was corrupting the system of justice. Aggressive news coverage of these problems further fueled low confidence in the state's judicial system. In 1987 *Texas Monthly* published a controversial investigative piece on how the Texas Supreme Court was controlled by trial lawyers,[49] proving to average citizens that problem was real and not merely political hyperbole by Republicans and the defense bar. An influential article appearing in the *Wall Street Journal* that same year cited empirical studies revealing that a vast majority of Texans doubted integrity of the justices of the Texas Supreme Court. Confidence further plummeted when the public learned that justices of the Texas Supreme Court rejected an appeal in an $11 billion judgment against Texaco, while openly accepting campaign contributions from Texaco and Pennzoil lawyers involved in the lawsuit. Pennzoil's lawyers contributed more than $355,000 to the nine justices from 1984 to 1987.[50] The scandal was featured on a 1987 segment on the popular national television program *60 Minutes*. The program, titled "Justice for Sale?" examined the cozy relationships between plaintiff lawyers and judges, as well as the direct impact of campaign contributions on court decisions in Texas.[51]

Adding fuel to the simmering controversy surrounding allegations of corruption was a Texas House Judicial Affairs Committee investigation. The committee uncovered ethical lapses by a number of justices through the testimony of former court employees. Several justices and their staffs had been told to avoid inappropriate contact with attorneys with cases pending before the court. In 1983, Chief Justice Jack Pope warned about "information-seeking attorneys" prowling around the Supreme Court building. A former briefing attorney testified that he had overheard a justice discussing a pending appeal with an attorney. The committee was also told by a former litigant who had business before the court, that Justice C. L. Ray, a Democrat, told him at a fundraising event that he (Ray) would help him with a case pending before the court.[52]

One notorious 1984 case that further sullied the reputation of the Texas Supreme Court was *Manges v. Guerra*.[53] The case originated when a jury awarded the Guerra family $382,000 in actual damages and $500,000 in exemplary damages against Clinton Manges, a successful San Antonio trial lawyer who served as an executive manager of mineral leases on 70,000 acres owned by the Guerra family. A court of appeals upheld the judgment and Manges appealed to the Texas Supreme Court. Manges hired a defense attorney named Pat Maloney, Sr., to represent him before the court. Presiding in the appeal was Justice C. L. Ray, a Democrat, who was the recipient of large campaign contributions from both Manges and Maloney. Behind the scenes, Ray drafted an opinion in favor of Manges and encouraged other justices to support his position. When the other justices rejected the opinion, Ray wrote another opinion in favor of Manges. Then, two justices recused themselves from the case after it was discovered that Manges and Maloney contributed over $100,000 to the justices' reelection campaigns. The justices then voted 4-3 to reverse the trial court's judgment against Manges, but Chief Justice Jack Pope decided that the votes of five of the nine votes were required for reversal, therefore, the court of appeals ruling was upheld. Justice Ted Z. Robertson then un-recused himself and voted for reversal. The Guerras filed a motion for a rehearing and a motion to recuse Justices Kilgarlin, Robertson and Ray because each had received campaign contributions from both Manges and Maloney.[54]

In another instance, Justice Ray assured a litigant, who was attending a 1984 fundraiser for Ray, that if he did not win a pending case, then he would win the next one. Ray also discussed the court's internal deliberations with the litigant, and obliquely inferred he would try to pull strings with the associate justices. Then, in 1985, Justice Ray tried to transfer two cases from one court of appeals to another at the request of Pat Maloney. These actions led to the public reprimand of Ray by the Texas Commission on Judicial Conduct,[55] and public admonition of Kilgarlin.[56]

Justice Ray was disciplined for attempting to transfer the cases at the request of Maloney, for improper receipt of air transportation, for the receipt and consideration of *ex parte* private communication, for the improper solicitation of funds, for the *ex parte* disclosure of confidential information to a litigant, and for the initiation of an *ex parte* private communication.[57] Justice William Kilgarlin, a Democrat, was admonished publicly by the commission. Two of Justice Kilgarlin's briefing attorneys had accepted a weekend trip to San Antonio from Pat Maloney, Jr., of *Manges* case fame. Kilgarlin was admonished to "make certain in the future that all staff working under him be required to observe the standards of fidelity and diligence that apply to him." Kilgarlin blamed all of his troubles not on himself but on a man named Larry Thompson, who in 1985 had founded an organization called the "Supreme Court Justice Committee." The purpose of the organization was to counter the influence of plaintiff's attorneys. Kilgarlin referred to this pro-defense organization as "19 lawyers who hate my guts."[58] Personal animosity toward Kilgarlin may or may have not been the sole motivating force, but the reformers, media and defense bar were now aggressively exerting pressure on judges and justices who once considered themselves untouchable and who arrogantly and openly cultivated close ties with campaign contributors.

That controversy was also showcased in a second *60 Minutes* program about contributions to Texas judicial candidates by lawyers and clients with cases before the court. One of the justices who was a subject of the program was Kilgarlin, who eventually lost his seat to a Republican Nathan Hecht in 1988. That year, three Republicans, Hecht, Thomas R. Phillips, and Eugene Cook, were elected to the Texas Supreme Court, the first time since Reconstruction. Kilgarlin was off the bench in 1988. Justice C. L. Ray, the subject of allegations by the Commission on Judicial Conduct for improper contact with lawyers who had cases before the court, resigned in 1990. In 1990 Gammage, serving his last term on the Third Court of Appeals in Austin, won the Democratic primary, the race to choose Ray's successor. Gammage then went on to win in the general election in November, defeating Republican Will Garwood.[59]

In the midst of these scandals, former chief justice John Hill, a Democrat, argued that these ethical problems were caused by the method of judicial selection. Hill was well-known across the state. He had been a successful lawyer, Texas attorney general, and 1978 candidate for governor. So, he believed he possessed all the requisite qualities to lead a movement for judicial reform. However, resistance to Hill's proposal was fierce. Hill had resigned the chief justiceship in 1988 and was succeeded by Thomas Phillips, a district court judge appointed by Governor Clements, a Republican. Phillips was an independent-minded judge and tireless reformer. At Phillips's swearing-in ceremony, outgoing Hill announced his support for adopting merit selection. Under Hill's "Texas Plan," which he originally proposed in 1986, the governor would choose from a list of candidates compiled by a nominating commission. The appointed judge, after serving a term of office, would stand for a popular retention election.

Vowing to fight Hill, Justice Robert Campbell was said to have resigned on the spot just so that he could work against the merit selection movement.[60] Campbell had many allies in his opposition to Hill's plan. Most of the state's incumbent judges in Texas opposed merit selection. The Democratic and Republican parties opposed merit selection, and lauded the benefits of the elective system. Trial lawyers, who backed Democrats, had enjoyed a great deal of success with the no-holds-barred partisan election system. There was no reason to give this up for the uncertainty of a merit plan. Democrats also recognized that the growth of the percentage of Latino voters in the state, as well as the strength of African American voters in Houston and Dallas, meant that the Democratic Party might ultimately mitigate the recent success of the Republican Party. Advocacy groups representing Latinos and African Americans wanted a greater say in the election of judges through the creation of smaller districts within densely populated urban counties from which judges were elected. Even the American Civil Liberties Union opposed reform.[61] Chief Justice John Hill's quixotic reform movement was moribund from the start.

The question of whether the state should reform the method of judicial selection was *even* put to the voters in 1988. Of those voters who cast ballots in the March 1988 Democratic primary, 86 percent voted "yes" to nonbinding measure appearing on the ballot asking whether "Texans shall maintain their right to select judges by a direct vote by the people rather than change to an appointment system created by the legislature."[62] Sixty-five percent of Texans polled believed that the elective system was "working all right as it is." Eighty-six percent of voters in the Democratic primary opposed merit selection of judges.[63] Seventy-one percent of those polled in 1989 showed that citizens were in favor of electing judges.[64] Furthermore, 1986 State Bar of Texas poll also showed that a majority of lawyers objected to a merit system for either trial or appellate judges. Attorneys responding to a 1988 survey were asked to choose their preference of selection methods from a list of five systems used across the country: partisan election, nonpartisan election, merit selection, gubernatorial appointment, and legislative appointment. Eighty-five percent of the lawyers agreed with the statement that the method of judicial selection has an impact on the neutrality of the judge, and 90 percent agreed that selection method has an impact of the quality of judges. After this, however, the results were opaque. Of all of the methods of selection, 27 percent of the attorneys surveyed preferred merit selection above others methods, followed by nonpartisan election (18 percent), partisan election (17 percent), gubernatorial appointment (5 percent), and legislative appointment (0 percent). However, they were nearly equally split on whether they believed merit selection was "excellent" versus "poor."[65]

The Clean Slate '88 and '90 Campaigns

The influence of trial lawyers on the state's judiciary, the willingness of juries to award damages to plaintiffs, and the concomitant expansion of tort law remedies for persons injured by powerful corporations and medical professionals were at their zenith. Texas, especially in trial courts in Harris County, earned the reputation as the best place to bring a personal injury lawsuit.[66] The Clean Slate '88 campaign was undertaken by a coalition of the medical profession and the business community to wrest control of the Texas Supreme Court from trial lawyers and Democrats. Employing the expertise of Republican political consultant Karl Rove, the Texas Medical Association (TMA) in 1988 initiated a politically savvy and highly successful campaign to "take back" the courts. Rove later went on to become the "Architect" of George W. Bush's 2000 presidential campaign. In 1988, six of the nine justices on the court were up for election, thus the proposal for a "clean slate." The notion of "taking back" branches of government, or the whole state for that matter, went over big in Texas, tapping into the state's anti-government mind-set. Rove possessed the savvy for tapping into the innate desire of many voters to perceive the world in black and white or us versus them. The genius of the campaign was that Rove and the TMA framed the issue in such a way as to appeal both to elites and ordinary voters alike. They argued that the court was aligned with greedy plaintiffs and trial lawyers who were seeking outrageous malpractice judgments against honest doctors. These lawsuits led to higher malpractice insurance costs for health care providers. Rove pitched this argument to doctors, who then opened their wallets. The TMA also promoted the populist argument that malpractice suits cause lower quality and more expensive healthcare for patients, because doctors either leave the profession (or a medical specialty) or pass along the cost of higher insurance premiums to patients.[67]

As a part of his overall agenda, Rove also began a populist "tort reform" movement. Through his own brand of political magic, "tort reform" became a panacea for a range of problems, including low wages and high unemployment. Tort reform was a program of legislation aimed at imposing caps on the dollar amount of damages that juries could award injured plaintiffs. Beat up pickup trucks and 1976 "exploding" Ford Pintos[68] bearing "tort reform" bumper stickers could be seen driving south of Houston on Interstate 45 near oil refineries. Most of the largest judgments against the petrochemical industry came out of the Beaumont area, east of Houston, where the big oil refineries and plants are located. Dangerous and toxic, this region has killed or injured thousands of Texas workers, but it was also a font of lawsuits that made hundreds of plaintiff attorneys rich and famous. Many of the big trial court judgments against petrochemical companies had forced CEOs to think twice about neglecting worker safety, but again Rove and Republicans were successful in convincing both blue and white-collar voters alike that holding irresponsible corporations accountable for their actions would somehow lead to the layoff of workers.

During the Clean Slate '88 campaign, the TMA methodically vetted potential judicial candidates by studying their voting records, looking for possible ethics violations, and using experts to analyze judicial philosophies and predict voting behavior. To counter this strategy, consumer groups, labor unions, and Democrats argued that the TMA and business associations were judge shopping—attempting to buy the outcome of cases. The TMA-led coalition sought not only to recruit judges with a pro-business legal philosophy but also to convince voters that their interests were best served by these judges.[69] Red Clean Slate '88 cards and brochures were left in physician's waiting rooms around the state, tucked in among frayed magazines.[70] Appearing on the Clean Slate '88 red ballot were Republicans Thomas Phillips and Nathan Hecht and Democrats Eugene Cook, Lloyd Doggett, Raul Gonzalez, and Jack Hightower. As noted in chapter 3, Bob Gammage was included on the red Clean Slate '88 ballot, even though he was running as an incumbent on the Court of Appeals (Austin) in 1988. Gammage would appear on the red card again in the 1990 election for a seat on the Supreme Court.

The TMA was successful in electing five of their endorsed candidates. By 1990, they had "taken back" six seats.[71] The 1988 campaign was the most expensive judicial election in the history of the Lone Star State. The twelve candidates for the six open seats on the court raised $10,092,955 in direct contributions ($20.8 million in 2019 dollars[72]).[73] By comparison, eight years earlier, in 1980, the total amount of contributions to all Texas Supreme Court candidates running for election or reelection was a paltry $155,033 ($439,712 in 2018 dollars). One-third of all money contributed to the candidates in 1988 came from the TMA and fifty law firms. A trial lawyer political action committee (PAC) spent $1.4 million for television commercials.[74] Chief Justice Phillips (R) raised over $1 million, and his opponent Ted Z. Robertson (D) raised nearly $2 million.[75] Justice Kilgarlin (D) raised over $2 million and Nathan Hecht (R) raised $650,000. Lloyd Doggett (D) raised close to $700,000 is his campaign to remain on the court that year. Following this 1988 campaign contributions arm race, Phillips and others were stunned, fearful not only for their own political fortunes but for the court as an institution.[76]

Winners in the Clean Slate election in 1988 were Republicans Thomas Phillips and Nathan Hecht and Democrats Eugene Cook, Lloyd Doggett,

Raul Gonzalez, and Jack Hightower. The newly elected justices joined Oscar Mauzy (D), Franklin Spears (D), and C. L. Ray (D). Two years later, Gammage would spend close to $1 million to win a seat on the Supreme Court in 1990. Looking back to his tenure on the Third Court of Appeals, Gammage spent a minimal amount of time raising campaign money. A few rudimentary "meet the candidate" campaign commercials were run during the Democratic primaries in 1982, but he spent most of the time doing face-to-face events in and around Austin. His total expenditures in 1982 amounted to about $25,000, with his largest contribution of $2,500 coming from the political action committees of the Houston Builders Association and Texas Business Political Action Committee.[77]

As races for seats on nearly all appellate courts became more competitive in the mid-1980s, televised attack ads became sophisticated and expensive. Judicial candidates were at first reluctant to adopt this form of political campaigning ("going negative"), but at the same time, they were not going to unilaterally disarm. In the 1988 "Clean Slate" race, Chief Justice Phillips and his challenger Ted Z. Robertson ran some of the first negative attack ads in the history of Texas Supreme Court races. Outside groups ran attack ads against Chief Justice Philips and Justices Eugene Cook and Barbara Culver, all Republicans initially appointed by Governor Clements. Culver, the first Republican woman to serve on the high court, was appointed by Clements in January 1988 to fill a vacancy but was defeated by Democrat Jack Hightower in November 1990.[78]

In the 1990 election for chief justice, Thomas Phillips and Oscar Mauzy both ran merciless negative attack ads. As the stakes were raised, candidates even resorted to filing grievances against their opponents with the Judicial Conduct Commission. In one now-infamous televised ad in 1994, Republican challenger Rene Haas ran an ad claiming that Democratic justice Raul Gonzales refused to issue a death sentence while serving on the Supreme Court. Of course, few voters actually questioned whether or not the Supreme Court, which possesses exclusively civil jurisdiction, could sentence a person to death. What records we do have from that period documenting television ads show that the most contested elections tended to generate more negative ads, but during periods of only moderate competitiveness, fewer negative televised ads were produced and run.[79]

John Cornyn's election in 1990 increased the number of Republicans on the Texas Supreme Court from three to four. Two years later in the 1992 election, Rose Spector (D) became the first woman elected to the high court, defeating incumbent Eugene Cook (R). Justice Mauzy (D) was then defeated by Republican court of appeals judge Craig Enoch. Lloyd Doggett (D) left the court in 1994 to serve in the legislature, and Priscilla Owen (R) won election that year. Republicans gained a majority of seats in 1994 for the first time since the 1870s.

In 1993, Lt. Governor Bob Bullock, a powerful Democrat, created a diverse bipartisan reform committee consisting of appellate judges, state senators, representatives from the African-American and Latino communities, prominent attorneys, and members of the business community.[80] The group sought to reach a compromise between those who wanted election of urban-area judges by district and those who advocated for a merit system in which the governor appoints judges who then face nonpartisan retention elections.[81] Bullock's group included sitting-justices Gammage, Phillips, and Hightower. The final proposal called for the appointment of appellate judges, with a retention election at the end of a prescribed term, and the election of trial judges. The group further proposed that in urban areas, judges would be elected from precincts within counties so to maximize the possibility of seating more minority judges. All elections would be nonpartisan—that is, no candidate would bear a party label. There was cause for optimism when the plan was drafted into legislation and passed by the Texas Senate. However, the bill died in the House.[82]

In 1993 Mauzy (D) was replaced by Enoch (R) but Cook (R) was defeated by Spector (D) so Democrats maintained a 5-4 majority. However, in 1995, Doggett (D) did not seek reelection in order to run for Congress. He was replaced by Priscilla Owen (R), giving Republicans a 5-4 majority. As the leverage of trial lawyers was offset by the medical and business community, and Republicans were successful in winning seats on the supreme court, the number of progressive and liberal justices on the bench diminished and then disappeared. The *Austin American-Statesman* predicted that by 1995, the supreme court would be packed with justices who were reflexively pro-business and ideologically less supportive of civil rights and liberties and consumer protections.[83] The Republicans had formed a conservative bloc that was often joined by Democrats Gonzales, Hightower, and, on occasion, Spector. "Only Doggett and Gammage are counted on as solidly liberal," reported the *Austin American-Statesman.*[84]

Gammage's retirement at the end of the 1995 term handed Governor George W. Bush an opportunity to appoint Republican James Baker, increasing Republican majority to 6-3 majority. In 1996 Hightower (D) retired and was replaced by Greg Abbott (R), increasing the Republican majority to 7-2. In 1997 Cornyn retired and Governor Bush appointed Deborah Hankinson (R). Then, in 1998 the last Democrat to be elected to the court, Rose Spector (D), was defeated in her reelection bid by Harriet O'Neill (R), increasing the Republicans' majority to 8-1. In 1998, Raul Gonzales (D), the last Democrat to serve on the Texas Supreme Court, retired and Governor Bush appointed

Alberto Gonzales (R). All nine seats on the court were now solidly conservative. Republican judges, in general, would grow more conservative with each election cycle as a result of highly competitive party primaries that pushed candidates to the right, to the exclusion of moderates.

CAMPAIGN CONTRIBUTIONS DURING THE COURT WARS ERA

Returning to the issue of campaign contributions during this period, the question was just how much money flowed into the coffers of judicial candidates. The answer depends on who you ask. The most authoritative source for data on judicial campaign finance is the Texas Ethics Commission; however, the records from the 1990s are incomplete. According to reports filed by candidates with the Texas Ethics Commission between 1994 and 1998 (the period in which the reporting is the most complete), the nine Texas Supreme Court justices raised over $11 million, 48 percent from lawyers and law firms and 15 percent from two powerful pro-business tort reform political action committees, Texans for Lawsuit Reform and the Texas Civil Justice League.[85]

According to a much-publicized report by a private reform group called Texans for Public Justice (TPJ), $12.8 million was contributed to candidates for the Texas Supreme Court between 1994 and 1998.[86] Seven of the nine Texas Supreme Court justices that were elected after 1994 (Justices Gonzalez, Hecht, Phillips, Cornyn, Owen, Baker, and Abbott) raised $9.2 in total contributions (as mentioned in chapter 3, Gammage spent close to $1 million in 1990, but the exact amount of contributions to his campaign is not available). Lawyers and law firms contributed 42 percent of all money ($3.8 million), with the mega-firm Vinson and Elkins contributing the most ($244,018). Eighty percent of this money came from sources that had pending cases on the court's docket. Fifteen percent ($1.4 million) of the contributions came from PACs and executives of fifty corporations, including Enron, HEB (the grocery store chain), Coastal, Houston Industries, Texas utilities, DOW Chemical, and Exxon. The seven justices took 9 percent ($854, 825) in contributions from the PACs and employees of thirty trade groups, many of which file supporting briefs in litigation. One-time bundled contributions to a single justice often come from employees of the law firm or business. Some of these bundles amounted to $10,000 to a single justice.[87]

Professor Anthony Champagne, who is the leading authority on the issue of money in Texas Supreme Court elections, including the most expensive partisan judicial election in history in 1988,[88] found that money raised, more than any other factor, appears to have the most impact on the outcome of supreme court elections.[89] The average contributions to *all* Texas Supreme

Court candidates running for election or reelection were $155,033 in 1980, increasing to almost $ 1.5 million in 1994, before dropping off to $521,516 in 1998 as elections became less contested.[90] The average campaign war chest for each winning candidate increased from nearly $300,000 in the late 1980s to over $1.5 million in 1994, with a drop off to $829,794 in 1998.[91]

Lawyers with cases before the court from 1994 to 1997, as well as parties "closely linked" to these litigants, were responsible for 40 percent ($3.7 million) of the $9.2 million that the seven justices raised. Many justices took money from litigants with cases on the court docket even though it was not politically necessary to do so. For example, only two justices faced opponents in the primary and only two had opponents in the general reelection between the years 1994–1997. TPJ also caused a furor by announcing that it had found that campaign contributors are four times more likely to have their appeals granted by the Texas Supreme Court that those petitioners who make no contributions to the justices' campaigns.[92] In nearly 4,000 appeals filed, the court granted 11 percent of all petitions. Of the 11 percent it granted 56 percent of the appeals filed by contributors who gave individual justices at least $250,000.[93] Sixty percent of the 530 opinions that the court delivered from 1994 through October 1997 involved at least one of the seven justices who took money from a contributor with "close links" to a party or lawyer involved in that case.[94]

It is safe to say that TPJ was a major headache for both Texas Supreme Court candidates and campaign contributors alike. While TPJ's activities were too numerous to document here, a brief review of a few of their studies and reports will provide an idea of why TPJ was an important player in the reform movement. TPJ was definitely an outsider; few if any state officials aligned themselves with the organization. Nevertheless, TPJ's flashy reporting caught the attention of the media in Texas and around the country. TPJ was even called to testify before the American Bar Association's Commission on Public Financing of Judicial Campaigns, asserting that justice is in crisis in Texas because what many regard to be an appearance of impropriety is in reality corruption. Citing the fact that on average winners of Texas Supreme Court seats are spending an average of $1.2 million, TPJ stated that "it's a lot of money, and the current system is very disturbing because even when justices don't face an opponent, they still raise money hand over fist, and most of that money comes from those with cases on the docket."[95]

Two of TPJ's more highly publicized reports," Checks and Imbalances," and "Pay to Play," highlighted the amount that justices on the Texas Supreme Court raised in judicial races in the 1990s, emphasizing the amounts that lawyers and law firms contributed to the justices. The report found that between 1994 and 1998 Texas Supreme Court justices raised a total of $12.8 million in campaign contributions. Fifty-two percent of those contributions ($6.7

million) came from lawyers and law firms. During that period the amount of money contributed by lawyers increased by 63 percent. The greatest percentage of the money contributed by lawyers and law firms overwhelmingly consisted of business and defense attorneys. Business and defense firms accounted for nineteen of the Texas Supreme Court's top twenty-five campaign contributors. Only 13 percent of contributions came from plaintiffs' attorneys, while 79 percent of the justice's contributions from lawyers and law firms came from business and defense attorneys. After lawyers and law firms, the largest contributors to the Supreme Court justices came from the Energy and Natural Resource sector. The report also addressed the issue of "war chests." The study reported that the candidates who raise the most money win their judicial election races. "The average war chest raised by these Republican justices (who have enjoyed the most success) was $1.4 million, or almost three times the average war chest of their opponents ($463,109)." TPJ also brought to the attention of the media that two pro-business tort reform political action committees, Texas for Lawsuit Reform and the Texas Civil Justice League, contributed $1.6 million to the most recent campaigns of the current justices, accounting for $15 out of every $100 the justices raised.[96]

Another TPJ project, "Payola Justice: How Texas Supreme Court Justices Raise Money from Court Litigants," reported on the amount of money contributed by lawyers who have business before the court. Between 1994 and 1997 seven Supreme Court justices raised 40 percent ($3.7 million out of $9.3 million) of their contributions from parties and lawyers that had official business on the court's docket. Eighty percent of the lawyers and law firms that contributed to the court had cases on the docket before the court. The top corporate contributor was Enron, donating $78,700 to seven justices and having three court cases on the docket of the Texas Supreme Court during the study period. Houston Industries had six cases on the court's docket and contributed a total of $36,350 to the seven justices that were studied. PAC's and executives of fifty corporations contributed a total of $1.4 million. This constituted 15 percent of the money the justices raised. PAC's and employees of business and professional associations contributed a total of $854,825, or 9 percent of the total amount. The Texas Society of CPA's and its members contributed $116,450 and members of the TMA contributed a total of $98,217. "Payola Justice" also addressed the practice of employees of law firms contributing to a candidate on the same day, a practice known as bundling. For example, as stated by the report, forty-eight members of the law firm Baker and Botts contributed $10,950 on November 13, 1995. Similar practices demonstrated by the members of law firms such as Vinson and Elkins, Fullbright and Jaworski, and Susman Godfrey are just a few examples.[97]

Justices were 7.5 times more likely to accept the petitions filed when the group had contributed at least $100,000. When contributions were more than $250,000 the court was ten times more likely to accept petitions that have been filed. Baker and Botts, Chief Justice Phillip's former law firm, had a petition acceptance rate of 74 percent. They had contributed more than $250,000. The report's findings seemed to reconfirm the existing perception that justice was for sale in Texas. TPJ cited the existence of independent studies and national media attention in investigative programs by *Frontline* and *60 Minutes* to corroborate their findings.[98]

"Pay to Play" and other TPJ reports received considerable criticism from members of the bench and bar. The main complaint was that TPJ's conclusion that large contributions were directly related to the court's acceptance of petitions for appeal was based on a misuse or misunderstanding of the term "correlation." TPJ found a correlation between petition acceptance rate and contributions, but critics, such as the *Texas Lawyer*, pointed out that TPJ failed to consider the impact of other variables that might account for the relationship.[99] Such other variables might include the amount of experience that lawyers had in drafting petitions for appeal. Critics also argued that in 60 percent of the cases among those top-donor petitions, the side that gave the least amount of campaign contributions won, either by arguing that the court should not accept the petition or by the court's eventual decision.[100] Chief Justice Phillips condemned the "Pay to Play" study conducted by TPJ as "worse than junk science" and denied any link between contributions and the granting of appeals. He believed that all the study showed was that lawyers who were involved with a large number of appeals have a somewhat greater chance of having their petitions for appeal granted.[101] At the time, Justice Hecht made an important point about the need to raise money. "The fundamental flaw [with judicial elections] is that this just puts the court and candidates between a rock and a hard place," Hecht stated. "There is no responsible way to get elected without sending some message to the public about who you are. And there's no way to this without money."[102]

What impact did the publication of these reports and exposes have on public confidence in the fairness of the system? In the late 1990s, the Texas Supreme Court, Texas Office of Court Administration, and State Bar of Texas conducted a study entitled "Public Trust and Confidence in the Courts and the Legal Profession in Texas." The study found that there was a significant weakening of support and respect for the courts and legal profession.[103] Half of the respondents (52 percent) indicated a positive overall impression of the Texas court system and believed (71 percent) that judges were "very" or "somewhat" honest and ethical. However, the overwhelming majority of Texans (83 percent) believed that campaign contributions made to judges have a "very significant" (43 percent) or "somewhat significant" (40 percent) influence on the decisions made in the courtroom. The reform received much attention in the state, particularly in light of a decade of critical reports about the campaign contributions in judicial races by the news programs, such as *60 Minutes* and *Frontline*.

At the time, another statewide study conducted by the Office of Court Administration and the Texas Bar, "The Insider's Perspective: A Survey of Judges, Court Personnel, and Attorneys," found that most judges (68 percent), court personnel (77 percent), and attorneys (69 percent) believed that the Texas courts suffer from a negative public image; and that about half (48 percent) of all judges, 69 percent of court personnel, and 79 percent of attorneys believed that campaign contributions had a "fairly" or "very" significant influence on judicial decisions. Forty-three percent of judges, 50 percent of court personnel, and 53 percent of attorneys favored a change in the way district and appellate judges are selected in Texas.[104] Reformers hoped that these studies would strengthen the case for the adoption of a new method of judicial selection. By the end of the 1990s, even in light of this damning evidence the reports did little to move the needle toward a higher likelihood that reform measures would gain the support of voters.

THE JUDICIAL CAMPAIGN FAIRNESS ACT OF 1995 AND OTHER PROPOSED REFORMS

In 1994, the obstacles to reforming the method of selection appeared to be insurmountable, especially after Governor Bush made clear his opposition to any reform plan that would abolish the popular election of judges. Recognizing that it was virtually impossible to change the method of judicial selection, the focus was redirected to attempting to place limits on campaign contributions to candidates for judicial office. Several state legislators were instrumental in keeping the judicial campaign funding reform on the agenda. Senator Rodney Ellis, D-Houston, was at the forefront of the movement to reform the system. Ellis was elected to the Texas Senate in 1990, serving as chairman of the Senate Finance Committee and as a member of the Senate Redistricting and the Jurisprudence Committee. Ellis has joined forces with Chief Justice Phillips on numerous occasions to address the runaway costs of judicial campaigns. He maintained since the early 1990s that "the quality, impartiality, and moral authority of the Texas judiciary are severely undermined by the shortcomings of the judicial election system"; that his primary goal of judicial reform is, "to promote a fair, diverse and accountable system of justice in Texas"; and that "we must ensure that there is not even the appearance that justice is for sale in Texas."[105] Ellis has also publicly stated, "All of the people of Texas must have faith in the judicial system"[106] and that "my issue was then, is now and always will be, how do we enhance the quality of the people in the judiciary and how do we increase the diversity."[107]

Ellis hammered the embarrassing point that it is the widespread perception among Texas citizens that "justice is for sale" in Texas.

Senator Ellis and Chief Justice Phillips attended a well-publicized conference coordinated by the National Center for State Courts. Participating in the conference were teams of judges, legislators, and academics from the eighteen most populous states that used judicial elections at that time. The conference was intended to discover ways in which the influence of money and partisan politics could be curtailed.[108] For Ellis the problems of the Texas judicial system had long been ignored to the point where "the influence of politics and money in the administration of justice is harming public confidence in our most sacred branch of government."[109]

Ellis and Representative Jerry Madden, a Republican from Plano, reached a compromise on a bipartisan bill placing limiting individual and law firm contributions. The bill addressed what was seen as the biggest threat to the integrity of the judiciary. Lawyers from both sides (plaintiff and defense) joined various reform groups and judges who supported the bill because they felt they were being outspent in a kind of arms race. The Judicial Campaign Fairness Act of 1995 (SB 94) was passed. In arguing for the law's passage Ellis stated:

> No Texan is well served by our current judicial system. Judicial Elections are very expensive, and candidates are forced to raise huge sums of money from attorneys who appear before them in court. We must ensure that there is not even the appearance that justice is for sale in Texas.[110]

The Judicial Campaign Fairness Act (JCFA) set limits on contributions from individuals at $5,000 for each statewide election, with lower amounts for judges who are running for non-statewide judgeships. For non-statewide candidates, contributions are limited on the basis of population of the election district. This included justices on the supreme court and court of criminal appeals. Individual contributions to non-statewide judicial candidates are limited to $1,000 to $5,000 depending on the population of the judicial district. Law firms and individual members of law firms are limited by a complex formula: contribution's by law firms and individual lawyers in law firms is limited to $30,000 for statewide candidates. PACs are limited to 15 percent of the voluntary expenditure limits for that judicial office, so candidates for statewide office may accept up to $300,000 in PAC contributions. The law requires that donors be identified by name, address, and job title. Expenditures by candidates for statewide judicial office are limited to $2 million; court of appeals candidates are limited to between $350,000 and $500,000 depending on the population of the judicial district. Candidates for all other offices are limited to between $100,000 and $350,000 depending on the population of the judicial district. Contributions from corporations and labor unions were already prohibited prior to the passage of JCFA.[111] Governor Bush signed the bill into law on June 17, 1995.[112] The legislation also places limits on the practice of reimbursing personal funds with political contributions and encourages, through voluntary limits, candidates not to spend over $2 million in statewide races and not over $100,000 in district races where there were less than 250,000 people. Candidates not abiding by these spending limits must note that fact on all political advertisements.[113] A candidate is not obligated to comply with the limits if any one of his or her opponents does not comply.

The spirits of reformers were buoyed by the passage of JCRA. A year later in 1996, the Texas Supreme Court created a number of new task forces with the intent of developing plans for judicial selection reform that might spur legislative efforts in the 1997 legislative session. Bills were proposed in the Senate providing for plans for the appointment of appellate judges and election of district court judges in nonpartisan elections. However, no agreement could be reached.

In 1997, Senator Duncan sponsored a plan that called for the initial partisan election of appellate judges who would then stand for a retention vote in subsequent nonpartisan retention elections. A gubernatorial appointment with Senate confirmation would be provided to fill vacancies. This selection would have to reflect the ethnic, racial, and geographic composition of the districts. The plan also called for the elimination of straight-party voting in judicial elections.[114] Duncan argued that the plan would resolve the two most pressing problems that currently exist—judicial candidates running as partisan politicians and raising money from lawyers and business interests who appear before their courts. Although the plan drew support from around the state,[115] the measure was never passed.

Seeking any type of modest reform, in 1999 Duncan he pushed for the creation of a voter information guide for judicial election available to the public on the Internet. The assumption was that the guide would reduce the amount of money that judicial candidates would have to raise in order to get their names out to voters.[116] This modest measure passed both houses but was vetoed by then-governor Bush. No information could be found on why Bush vetoed this bill.

Duncan proposed the merit plan again in the 1999 legislative session and also called for the elimination of a straight-party vote for district judges[117] but neither measure was voted on. In the seventy-sixth and seventy-seventh Legislature, Duncan supported proposed constitutional amendment that called for a major overhaul of the system. All justices and judges would be appointed by the governor followed by nonpartisan retention elections. The retention elections would take place after the judge or justice had served an initial term of six years. The proposed amendment applied to members of the Texas Supreme Court, Court of Criminal Appeals, and fourteen courts of appeals. As reported by the House Judicial Affairs committee the supreme court and court of criminal appeals would be merged into a single high court with fourteen justices and one chief justice. The fourteen justices would have been elected from seven districts established by the legislature. The initial election would be partisan. Once elected they would have faced retention elections every six years. The chief justice would be held to a twenty-year term limit, appointed by the governor. The governor would not be able to appoint a chief justice from the same district as the last chief justice.[118] Neither proposed amendment was passed.

Legislators Henry Cuellar (D) and Robert Duncan (R) cosponsored a bill that would allow the Texas secretary of state to post information distributed on the Internet in order to increase voter understanding of judicial campaigns. The proposed legislation, which would have reduced the cost of campaigning for name recognition, had the support of Chief Justice Tom Phillips, the American Bar Association, and Professor Anthony Champagne, the most visible and influential scholar in the reform movement in Texas.[119] However, then-governor George W. Bush vetoed the legislation, saying that it would place the secretary of state in an "inappropriate role." No information could be found on why Bush thought it was inappropriate. Of course, voters already have some information on the Internet provided by bar polls and organizations such as the League of Women's Voters. It was rumored that Bush opposed this modest reform based on Karl Rove's advice that if voters had more information on judicial candidates, more split-ticket voting would occur and, thus, mitigate the Republican Party's success in judicial races.

State senator Mario Gallegos (D-Harris County) was also a key player in judicial campaign reform. First elected to the Texas House of Representatives in 1991, where he served until 1994, Senator Gallegos became a member of the Texas Senate in 1995. Gallegos sponsored legislation and constitutional amendments supporting the appointment (and subsequent retention election) of appellate justices and the nonpartisan election of district judges.[120] He further proposed that in a judicial district composed of a county with a population of 2.5 million or more half would be elected from the state representative districts. For judicial districts with more a population exceeding one million, but less than 2.5 million people, the judges would be elected from the commissioner's court precinct. At the end of the district judge's term they will face a retention or rejection vote. After a judge has been retained he or she would be entitled to remain in office for four years.[121] None of Gallegos's proposals passed.

Another actor in the reform movement was Senator Royce West (D-Tarrant County). In the seventy-seventh Legislative session (2001) Senator

West proposed a measure that would prohibit judicial candidates from using political contributions that they received to make contributions to other candidates.[122] The bill placed limits on the amount of collected donations that judicial candidates can contribute to political parties but would allow them to contribute to political parties for the return of services or goods provided by the party. Officeholders would also be prohibited from contributing to political committees a total of more than $250 in a given calendar year. Senate Bill 720 was signed by Governor Rick Perry on June 14, 2001. The law went into effect on November 1, 2001.[123] West also sponsored a bill that would have prohibited judicial candidates who ran unopposed in an election from knowingly accepting political contributions.[124] No action was taken on this bill.[125]

TWENTY-FIRST-CENTURY JUDICIAL POLITICS AND REFORM

After two decades of ethical and political scandals, intense media criticism, and a powerful cadre of reformers who kept these issues on the legislative agenda, as Texas entered the twenty-first century there remained little grassroots or voter support for changing the method by which judges were selected. Although polls showed low public confidence in the courts, that voters were admittedly ill-informed about judges, and there was abysmally low voter turnout in judicial elections, Texans still stubbornly balked at reforms and clung to the prerogative of electing judges. Chief Justice Phillips wrote in 2002 that "voters cherish their franchise and in elected states they generally prefer to retain it by a two to one margin."[126] So, any attempt to change the method of selection from partisan election to appointment or the merit plan had completely run out of steam, especially after Republicans gained a solid majority on the supreme court.

As Phillips and others have pointed out, just one of the reasons that the much-heralded merit plan is politically unpalatable to many actors in the process has to do with the question of who makes the initial appointment. Or to paraphrase George W. Bush's comment about being the "Decider," who decides on the deciders? Many merit plans use a nominating commission chosen by the governor, legislature, or some combination of the two. The nominating commission consists of legal and lay experts who provide the governor with a list of potential nominees. So the nominating commission adds more political complexity to the system, which is why Chief Justice Phillips endorsed gubernatorial appointment with retention elections, but was not a proponent of a merit plan with a nominating commission.[127]

When Chief Justice Phillips retired in 2004, Wallace B. Jefferson, the first African American to serve both as a justice and chief justice on the Texas

Supreme Court, embraced the role of reformer. Jefferson was first appointed by Governor Rick Perry in 2001 and was elevated by Perry to the chief justiceship in 2004. Jefferson, a moderate Republican who often publicly bristled about party labels for judges and roundly criticized partisan elections, continued a push for reform during his tenure on the court (2001–2013). Jefferson's primary strategy as a reformer was to reach beyond elites and educate the public about the shortcomings of partisan election. Jefferson's speeches, interviews, and writings are all damning accounts of judicial elections. In one piece on straight-ticket party voting in judicial elections, he admitted that his own electoral success was a function of the state's straight-ticket partisan voting. As long as he had an "R" next to his name "even if I never appeared in court, lost every endorsement and fared poorly in polls that assess qualifications, I would still have won in Texas." He continued:

> The state voted for [John] McCain [in 2008], and I was the down-ballot beneficiary. Currently, merit matters little in judicial elections. We close our eyes and vote for judges based on party affiliation even though a party label does not ensure a judicial committed to the rule of law. We reject worthy judicial candidates whose names are hard to pronounce. The men and women we elect in this arbitrary process make decisions that affect all of our lives. We don't know who they are.[128]

Reaching a national audience in an interview published by *Atlantic* magazine in 2013, Jefferson stated that in a presidential election year there are at least sixty to seventy judges on the ballot in Harris County (Houston) alone, including candidates for the supreme court, court of criminal appeals, district courts, county court, and municipal court. "The voters have no clue about the experience or background of these candidates for office," Jefferson stated, "and so what happens in Texas is that voters increasingly vote based upon partisan affiliation."[129] "It is a broken system. We shouldn't have partisan elections. I do not like the concept of a Republican or Democratic judge. I think fundraising undermines the confidence in a fair and impartial judicial system."[130] Jefferson summed up the traditional resistance to reform:

> The Harris County Democrats, they say: "Well, we're doing fine. We don't want to change. We're winning now." There are thousands of judges who breathe life into the party and they are winning, so they don't want to change it when they are winning. And Republicans, we are winning statewide, we don't want to change it. So that's one of the problems.[131]

According to scholars and observers of judicial politics, straight-ticket voting undermines the legitimacy of judicial selection.[132] This method *does* provide voters who are largely unfamiliar with judges, and other down-ballot candidates, with a cue that makes voter choice somewhat less random than it would be absent party labels, but this kind of voting often leads to the election of candidates with little experience or often those more prone to ethical or legal problems.

When Jefferson retired from the court, Governor Perry elevated long-serving justice Nathan Hecht to chief justiceship in 2013. Hecht went on record in support of eliminating straight-ticket voting in Texas, for many of same reasons cited by former chief justice Jefferson but also because straight-ticket partisan sweeps adversely affect Republican judicial candidates in Democratic-leaning Bexar, Harris, and Travis counties. In fairness, Hecht's predecessors—former chief justices Wallace Jefferson, Thomas Phillips, and John Hill—were also critical of straight-ticket voting for judges; and under a law passed by the legislature in 2017 straight-ticket voting for all candidates on the ballot will no longer exist in Texas after 2020.[133] However, the elimination of straight-ticket voting in partisan elections may result in even lower voter impact on the outcome of judicial races, because higher rates of down-ballot voter "roll-off" will occur. Roll-off occurs when a voter reaches a point on a long ballot where judicial candidates (or other offices) are listed. The voter then determines that he or she is not interested or doesn't have the needed information to make a decision. The voter will then either walk away leaving these boxes unchecked or make decisions based on the sound of a candidate's name, perceived ethnicity, or gender.[134]

THE IMPACT OF THE US SUPREME COURT ON REFORM IN TEXAS: SELECTED RULINGS

Gammage was highly critical of judges who made campaign promises or statements that intimated how they might rule in future cases. Yet, realistically, in a system that elects its judges, voters need information other than simply party labels to make decisions at the ballot box. Shouldn't judges have the same First Amendment protections as any other candidate for office? In August 2002, just prior to the November general election, the Texas Supreme Court amended the Texas Code of Judicial Conduct,[135] removing from the code a provision that prohibited a candidate from making statements of opinion on issues that might come before the court to which the candidate sought election. This action followed *Republican Party of Minnesota v. White*[136] in which the US Supreme Court declared that such codes of judicial conduct violate the First Amendment.

Minnesota elects is judges using nonpartisan elections. Prior to *White*, the state's canon of judicial conduct prohibited judicial candidates from "announcing" their views on disputed legal or political issues. Gregory

Wersal, a candidate for the Minnesota Supreme Court in 1998, challenged the constitutionality of the canon's restriction on speech. He argued that under the law he was unable to respond to questions asked by the either the media or the public regarding his views on "disputed legal or political issues." Both a federal district court and federal circuit court of appeals upheld the constitutionality of the law, recognizing its role in protecting an impartial judiciary, but on appeal the US Supreme Court narrowly struck down the law on the grounds that it violated Wersal's First Amendment rights. Writing for the 5-4 majority, Justice Antonin Scalia argued that the state law placed a content-based restriction on core political speech, without advancing a compelling state interest in preserving the impartiality of judges.[137]

At first panic ensued in Texas, because *White* was initially interpreted to mean that every state code of conduct that placed restrictions on the speech of judicial candidates or sitting judges would be subject to strict judicial scrutiny. State codes of judicial conduct would have to be scrapped or rewritten so that they did not limit the political speech of judges. Of course, making political statements is different than making promises that would lead to the reasonable person doubting the judge's impartiality. So, after *White*, in most instances campaign statements on "disputed legal issues" by judicial candidates cannot be grounds for disqualification or sanction. *White* allows candidates for judicial office to raise as issues in their campaigns matters that may come before them if they are elected; however, "a statement made during a campaign for judicial office . . . may cause a judge's impartiality to be reasonably questioned in the context of a particular case and may result in recusal."[138] *White* seemed to have had resolved the issue of candidate speech, but the question of other forms of political activity still needed to be addressed. In 2006 and 2008 two important post-*White* rulings,[139] dealing with judges who engaged in political activity, were handed down by Texas appellate courts: *In re Hecht*[140] and *Ex Parte Ellis.*[141]

In re Hecht was an unusual and highly publicized case that sheds light on the degree to which judges can campaign not for themselves but for other judicial candidates.[142] The case originated when in October 2005 the State Commission on Judicial Conduct voted to initiate an investigation of long-serving Texas Supreme Court justice Nathan Hecht based on his statements appearing in the *New York Times* and *Texas Lawyer* endorsing his friend Harriet Miers, George W. Bush's 2005 nomination to the US Supreme Court to replace retiring Sandra Day O'Connor. Hecht is a highly respected conservative jurist who is currently the longest-serving high court justice in Texas history. Hecht was initially elected in 1988 and served with Gammage and Thomas Phillips during the tumultuous 1980s and 1990s, and was later appointed chief justice in 2013 by Governor Perry after Wallace Jefferson stepped down from that office.

Hecht and Miers were very close friends for thirty-five years and had practiced in the same law firm from 1976 to 1981. Miers became White House Counsel when George W. Bush became president. Hecht was also a longtime friend of Karl Rove, Bush's "Architect" and White House Deputy Chief of Staff. Always attentive to detail, Rove asked Hecht to speak to Dr. James Dobson, the founder of Focus on the Family (a conservative religious organization) about Miers's faith, which Rove believed would appeal to an important segment of Bush supporters, who in turn might exert political pressure on wavering senators during her confirmation hearings. Rove also asked the articulate and telegenic Hecht to speak to the media about Miers's qualifications and accomplishments. He was in the spotlight nearly every day, the "go-to" man for interviews and pithy quotes. At the time, no one thought that this activity seemed inappropriate in any way, but the commission believed that Hecht had inappropriately acted as a one-man campaign team for Miers.[143]

Hecht exercised due diligence before consenting to help garner support for Miers's nomination, consulting with former chief justice Tom Phillips and former justice Priscilla Owen about whether his statements of support to the media would violate the Code of Judicial Conduct. Since Hecht was assured by both former justices that the statements in question were not inappropriate, he was broadsided with news of the conduct commission's investigation. He answered the commission's questions and voluntarily appeared at a hearing before eight members of the commission. The commission concluded that Hecht violated Canons 2B and 5(2) of the Texas Code of Judicial Conduct and issued a public admonition. Canon 2B states that "A judge shall not lend the prestige of judicial office to advance the private interests of the judge or others" and Canon 5(2) states, "A judge shall not authorize the public use of his or her name endorsing another candidate for any public office."[144]

Miers ultimately withdrew her name from consideration, after it was unlikely that she would make it past the Republican-controlled Senate Judiciary Committee, much less the full Senate. Indeed, even at an early junction of the Miers nomination, many prominent Republicans were urging Bush to withdraw her name. Perceived to be unqualified for a seat on the high court, her nomination had the appearance of blatant Texas cronyism.[145]

The commission's public admonition stung Hecht, so he requested a *de novo* review of the decision.[146] Texas Supreme Court chief justice Wallace Jefferson then appointed (by random selection) members of a Special Court of Review[147] to review the commissions' decision. The Special Court conducted an evidentiary hearing calling Justice Hecht as the sole witness. Expert testimony was given by a range of experts, including former chief justice Tom Phillips, a well-respected expert on judicial ethics. The court also reviewed the codes of judicial conduct from other states, Senator Arlen

Specter's oral deposition, and official transcripts from numerous Senate confirmation hearings. The Special Court then vindicated Hecht by overturning the commission's ruling.[148]

Writing for the majority of the special court, Justice Fitzgerald recognized that contrary to the commission's allegation there was no evidence that Hecht "authorized" the public use of his name in endorsing Miers. True, Hecht may have "supported" her but he did not "authorize" his name to be used in support. In its 1990 amendments to the code of conduct, the Texas Supreme Court did not reinstate the 1974 "endorsement" prohibition. It deleted "endorse" and added "authorize."[149] So Hecht wasn't authorizing the use of his name and position to support Miers. What then is an authorization? When does a judge cross the line? A judge is in violation of the Canon 5(2) if he or she gives the candidate express permission to include the judge's name on a publicly distributed campaign brochure or list of persons endorsing the candidate.[150]As a public figure, Hecht anticipated his name being used as the person who gave the interview, if the media chose to identify him. But he did not authorize the media to use his name to publicly endorse Miers.

In his testimony Hecht admitted that "of course you're endorsing in the sense that you're supportive, but that's not what the canon means." He felt that much of what was being said in the media about his friend was negative and untrue and that he had to set the record straight. Hecht testified that he was present on the Texas Supreme Court when the canons were amended in 1990: "There was not the slightest thought that it would ever apply to comments made in respect to a nomination to the United States Supreme Court. That was not a concern, it never crossed anybody's mind, and it hasn't since until this case."[151] The rule was intended to prevent sitting judges from endorsing other Texas judges up for election. The Special Court concluded that Hecht's statements did not constitute an "endorsement" and that judges are permitted to speak out on political matters.[152]

The commission's second charge alleged that Hecht violated the prestige of his public office to advance the interests of his personal friend Harriet Miers in violation of Canon 2B, which provides that "A judge shall not lend the prestige of judicial office to advance the private interests of the judge or others."[153] The Special Court disagreed with the commission's position that Miers was pursuing private interests as opposed to public service. A judge campaigning or supporting another candidate is engaged in political speech under *Republican Party of Minnesota v. White*,[154] and is not advancing a private interest, even though a judge who is being endorsed receives compensation, and in the case of Miers, employment for life.[155] In the end, Justice Hecht was vindicated.

Hecht's vindication was somewhat pyrrhic, however. The Code of Judicial Conduct, coupled with what appeared to be hardball politics, proved to be a minefield. During the commission's hearings, Hecht was advised to retain a First Amendment attorney named Chip Babcock. The attorney successfully argued, that under the *White* precedent, the First Amendment superseded the judicial canons of conduct in Hecht's case. The only problem was that Babcock allegedly gave Hecht a discount on his legal fees, which, according to the Texas Ethics Commission, amounted to an in-kind political contribution of $100,000 in violation of JCFA that the justice failed to report.[156]

The Ethics Commission ordered Hecht to pay a hefty $29,000 fine in 2008. Hecht appealed, and in 2014 with the fine still not paid, the liberal public interest group, TPJ, filed a suit to require the Texas Attorney General Greg Abbott to collect the fine, which, according to the *Austin American-Statesman*, he appeared reluctant to do.[157] TPJ alleged that Abbott's reluctance to collect the fine over a six-year period was due to the longtime friendship of the two men. Finally, in 2015 Hecht negotiated a settlement which closed the matter.[158]

The second high profile post-*White* recusal case is *Ex parte Ellis.*[159] The 2009 case originated when Travis County (Austin) district attorney Ronnie Earle[160] filed a motion to recuse court of appeals justice Alan Waldrop[161] from an ongoing criminal case against James Ellis and John Colyandro for election code violations and money laundering. Both Ellis and Colyandro worked for former US House of Representatives majority leader Tom DeLay, a Republican, who was ultimately convicted for conspiracy and money laundering. Earle had filed the charges against Delay in 2005. The recusal motion argued that while he was engaged in private practice before his 2005 appointment[162] to the court of appeals, Justice Waldrop served as counsel for a Republican tort reform group called Texans for Lawsuit Reform (TLR). Members of TLR regularly attended campaign strategy sessions with Colyandro with the intent to continue the effort in the legislature to cap awards in civil lawsuits. Justice Waldrop filed a number of pleadings in a separate civil case on TLR's behalf involving issues similar to those raised in the Ellis/Colyandro criminal proceeding that was currently before the court.[163] Earle's motion to recuse was based entirely on statements Waldrop made as an attorney in a civil suit and not on anything he said or wrote as a justice on the court of appeals.[164] The plaintiffs (Democrats) in this earlier civil suit attempted to serve TLR with a subpoena seeking documents and records of TLR's communications with another group called Texans for a Republican Majority Political Action Committee (TRMPAC). Jim Ellis and John Colyandro were affiliated with TRMPAC.[165] In his successful effort to fight the subpoena Waldrop, as TLR's attorney, signed and filed pleadings on behalf of TLR referring to the case as a "politically motivated lawsuit" without merit and simply a means of harassing a political opponent.

The court of appeals ruled 3-2 against the motion to recuse. Writing for the majority, Justice David Puryear argued in a lengthy opinion that when the basis for a recusal motion originates from events occurring from a judge's legal career before appointment to the bench, it must be recognized that when representing clients lawyers are required to express the beliefs of their clients and advocate their clients' interests. Therefore, statements made by a lawyer representing a client, without more, "can only rarely serve as legitimate reasons for excluding a judge from fulfilling his sworn duties."[166] Puryear reasoned:

> Were the rule otherwise, judges would be recused from presiding over all cases that present issues similar to the ones that they confronted in their prior careers as advocates . . . judges would face recusal from all cases involving the same areas of law or types of claims regardless of the identity of the parties involved. Moreover, this rule would lead to the paradoxical result that the more expansive a judge's prior practice are and experience, the more limited his judicial role could be.[167]

Precedent recognizes that judges are obligated to decide matters before them and not unnecessarily recuse themselves even in cases in which the judges might prefer not to participate because of embarrassing criticism or mere allegations of bias.[168] The need for recusal exists only when a judge displays an attitude or a state of mind that is closed to fairness that the reasonable person would question the judges' impartiality.[169] Just as *Republican Party v. White* extends First Amendment protection to judges' political statements, so too does it protect opinions expressed by individuals prior to becoming judges.[170] Judges should not be expected or required to recuse simply because of the personal statements previously expressed.

In her dissenting opinion Justice Patterson cited Justice Gammage's dissent in *Rogers v. Bradley* in 1995, where members of the Texas Supreme Court were asked to recuse because of the actions of a powerful PAC. Judge Patterson agreed with Gammage that the problem is perception. Would a reasonable member of the public, knowing all of the facts concerning the judge's conduct, have a reasonable doubt that the judge is actually impartial? Justice Patterson, in applying this standard concluded that Justice Waldrop should recuse himself from further participation in any appeals by Ellis and Colyandro. Waldrop's conduct as a private litigator in related civil proceedings was more than sufficient to cast reasonable doubt on his impartiality in these appeals. He represented a group that worked with, was ideologically aligned with, and had similar goals as the two defendants.[171]

Gammage's recusal philosophy, which states that the focus should not only be on the judge but on those with a disproportionate influence on the outcome on judicial elections, would not change Texas recusal law in the short term, but his progressive—and at times criticized—views on recusal were later reflected in the US Supreme Court's 2009 groundbreaking ruling in *Caperton v. Massey Coal Co.*[172] This byzantine landmark ruling began when a West Virginia jury awarded Hugh Caperton $50 million in damages against Massey Coal Company in 2002 for fraudulent misrepresentation and tortious interference with contractual relations. By the time the case reached the West Virginia Supreme Court on appeal in 2005 Don Blankenship, chairman, CEO, and president of Massey Coal, had contributed $3 million in campaign contributions to unseat an incumbent justice and to elect Brent Benjamin to the Supreme Court of Appeals of West Virginia (the state's highest court) in the 2004 judicial election.

Blankenship donated the legal state limit of a modest $1,000 to Benjamin's campaign committee but then spent over $2.5 million of his own money to support a PAC called "And for the Sake of Our Kids." Blankenship's donation constituted two-thirds of all money that the PAC raised. The PAC then ran a series of television and newspaper ads supporting Benjamin.[173] In addition, Blankenship spent $500,000 of his personal wealth on various independent expenditures related to the campaign.

With the appeal of the jury verdict heading to the state's supreme court in 2005, Hugh Caperton filed a motion to disqualify newly elected Justice Benjamin based on the Due Process Clause of the Fourteenth Amendment and State of West Virginia Code of Judicial Conduct. Justice Benjamin denied the motion in 2006, writing that he found "no objective information . . . to show that he has a bias for or against any litigant." In December 2006 Massey Coal filed its appeal, but in November 2007 the West Virginia Supreme Court (3-2) reversed Mr. Caperton's $50 million judgment against Massey Coal. Justice Benjamin was in the majority. Caperton then filed a motion for a rehearing and sought the recusal of three of the five justices who decided the appeal. The motion for the recusal of Justice Benjamin was not granted. On rehearing, the state supreme court once again reversed the jury verdict against Massey Coal with Justice Benjamin casting the deciding vote.

One after another, the motions for recusals continued through 2008, when the state supreme court again reversed the jury verdict against Massey Coal. Justice Benjamin reiterated his point that need not recuse himself because he had "no direct, personal, substantial, pecuniary interest in this case" and that adopting a recusal standard merely because of the action of a PAC would throw the whole judicial system into complete chaos. Caperton then successfully petitioned the US Supreme Court for a writ of certiorari.

As in the Texas case of *Rogers v. Bradley*, the question in *Caperton* was whether the action of a third party (Blankenship and his PAC) rather than the actions of a judge (Benjamin) demands recusal. This question hangs like a dark cloud over many similar situations in which an appearance of bias exists, yet technically no rule or law demands recusal. In *Caperton* in 2009, the

Supreme Court of the United States reversed the ruling of the Supreme Court of Appeal of West Virginia. Writing for the majority, Justice Anthony Kennedy argued that traditionally matters of judicial recusal and disqualification are settled by state statutes and codes of conduct and do not usually pose a constitutional question, however, in this case the millions of dollars spent by Massey Coal to elect a state supreme court justice violated the constitution's guarantee of a fair tribunal.[174] Even in cases where the bias is less glaring, Kennedy added, codes of judicial conduct should be more strictly enforced.[175]

Caperton, like *Rogers v. Bradley*, raised an issue not addressed in past precedent or codes of conduct: Does the behavior of a wealthy campaign contributor or well-funded PAC who is instrumental in electing a judge presiding in a case that will benefit said contributor create a constitutionally intolerable probability of actual bias of the judge? The inquiry in *Caperton* was not into Justice Benjamin's "subjective assessment" of his own impartiality. No one knows what was in Justice Benjamin's mind. There was no evidence of a bribe or bias. He believed he could remain impartial. However, Justice Kennedy reasoned that the guarantee of due process does not require proof of actual bias but that given an objective "appraisal of psychological tendencies and human weakness," there is a risk of actual bias or prejudgment.

The Court's ruling in *Caperton* was what Gammage and other reformers had advocated for decades—that the failure to recuse due to the action of third party actors or contributors in some instances amounts to a denial of due process. Texas rules for disqualification are based on the state constitution and its recusal rules are promulgated by the Texas Supreme Court. Texas disqualification and recusal jurisprudence was then, and is now, conservative and restrained. It is based on a narrow judicial interpretation of state constitutional provisions outlining disqualification and codes of conduct pertaining to recusal that are intended to promote impartiality and accountability without creating a net loss to judicial discretion and the stability of the judicial process. At a minimum, it ensures that the actions of the judge should not give rise to reasonable grounds to question the neutral and objective character of a judge's rulings or findings.[176]

The pressing question in Texas in the post-*Caperton* era was whether standards would change. Would there be an avalanche of *Caperton*-based motions for recusal? In 2010, the Texas Supreme Court Advisory Committee proposed reforms to recusal standards under Rules 18a and 18b of the Texas Rules of Appellate Procedure.[177] Minor changes were made by the court but nothing substantive that directly addresses the issues raised in *Caperton* was adopted. Nor has the Texas Supreme Court either cited or discussed *Caperton*[178] in any published opinion to date. *Caperton* has been cited in appeals from adverse recusal motions heard by the court of criminal appeals in *Gaal v. State* in 2011[179] and four Texas Court of Appeals decisions: *Villareal v.*

State in *2011*,[180] *Black v. 7-Eleven Convenience Stores* in 2014,[181] *McIntosh v. Texas State Board of Dental Examiners* in 2014,[182] and *Barfield v. Texas* in 2015.[183] In *Gaal*, the court of criminal appeals reversed the decision of the court of appeals that denied a motion to recuse a judge in a driving while intoxicated case. *Gaal* simply reiterated the existing grounds for recusal in Texas, but in a single footnote cited *Caperton* as setting out three situations that violate the Due Process Clause of the Fifth Amendment: first, when a judge has a financial interest in the case; second, when the judge acted as a "one-man grand jury" to bring charges in the case he is trying; third, "when a person with a personal stake in a particular case had a significant and disproportionate influence in placing the judge on the case by raising funds or directing the judge's election campaign when the case was pending or imminent."[184]

Similarly, in each of the four court of appeals cases discussed, appellants raised due process concerns under *Caperton* along with the recognized grounds for recusal. In *Black*[185] the court ruled that the trial judge did not abuse his discretion by denying Black's recusal motion because it was not established that the judge's alleged biases arose from an extrajudicial source or that Black was denied due process under the *Caperton* standard.[186] In *Villareal*[187] the court rejected a recusal motion alleging the trial judge harbored prejudice against the defendant contrary to a ground for recusal established by *Caperton:* that the "probability of actual bias on the part of the judge . . . is too high to be constitutionally tolerable."[188] *McIntosh* held that a judge's mere disagreement of party's legal position did not demonstrate a bias or prejudice amounting to a violation of due process and requiring recusal.[189] In *Barfield* the court ruled that displaying a Mother's Against Drunk Driving plaque in the courtroom did not violate the Code of Judicial Conduct, thus casting doubt on the impartiality of the judge amounting to a denial of due process under *Caperton.*[190]

The *Caperton* probability of bias standard has become part of the dialogue on recusal and disqualification in Texas; however, the actual impact of *Caperton* in the state has been limited by several factors. The fact that recent motions for recusal based on *Caperton* were viewed skeptically and ultimately denied with little or no discussion by appellate courts suggests continued resistance to judicially driven changes in the state's recusal jurisprudence. A presumption exists that the state's Code of Judicial Conduct offers more protection against judicial bias than the *Caperton* standard requires. This would explain the reluctance of Texas Supreme Court to use its rule-making authority to rewrite recusal guidelines. In addition, in a state that elects its judges state recusal precedent still adheres to the position that campaign contributions *alone* do not create grounds for recusal, nor necessarily are the actions of a powerful PAC or contributor *automatic* grounds for disqualification of a judge presiding in that case unless the circumstances created by the campaign contributions give rise to an unconstitutional probability of bias. Texas' Judicial Campaign Fairness Act of 1995[191] thus tempers the impact of *Caperton* because it imposes a strict $300,000 ceiling as the maximum donation from a political action committee to a candidate for statewide judicial office. This is the highest contribution permitted from any category of donor in Texas—well below the $3 million spent by Don Blankenship and his PAC to elect Brent Benjamin to the West Virginia Court of Appeals in the *Caperton* case.

It is uncertain whether *Caperton* challenges will prevail in the near future because many members of the bench and bar share the belief that the state's judicial campaign contribution restrictions and recusal jurisprudence create a firewall against violations of the Due Process Clause like the kind that existed in *Caperton.* However, continued resistance to change may further erode confidence in existing ethical safeguards. Texans hold a deep-seated lack of confidence in the fairness of the judicial system since the days of "Court Wars" and the million-dollar judicial elections in the early 1990s. Concerns that wealthy donors continue to exercise disproportionate influence on the judiciary have not yet been assuaged.

LITIGATION TO INCREASE MINORITY REPRESENTATION ON THE BENCH

A series of lawsuits have been brought in federal courts over the past three decades alleging that Texas' method of judicial selection limits minority representation on the bench and weakens the political influence of the state's Latino population. As far back as the late 1980s, Voting Rights Act litigation alleging minority vote dilution has had an impact on earnest efforts to enact judicial reform legislation. The litigation originated when ten voters and the League of United Latin American Citizens (LULAC) filed suit under section 2 of the Voting Rights Act alleging that at-large county-wide election of district court judges diluted the votes or voting strength of Hispanics and African Americans. LULAC and others were hopeful when, in 1991, a federal district court ruled in favor of the plaintiffs and ordered the state legislature to develop a plan to address the problem or else be subject to a court-ordered remedy. Republican governor Bill Clements called a special legislative session to address the issue but stipulated to legislators that he would veto the single-member district plan advocated by LULAC. According to the *Austin American-Statesman*, that closely followed the litigation, Clements promised instead to support a merit-selection plan in the next regular legislative session.[192] LULAC opposed merit selection as a way increasing minority representation on the bench and criticized Clements's weak record of appointing minorities when vacancies arose.[193] The federal district court rejected both proposals and ordered nonpartisan elections in nine of Texas' most populous counties, causing the *Dallas Morning News* to optimistically report that a favorable ruling would likely alter judicial campaigns in the state.[194] However, the US Court of Appeals for the Fifth Circuit reversed the district court ruling, holding that section 2 of the Voting Rights Act does *not* extend to judicial elections.[195] The US Supreme Court reversed the court of appeals, ruling that judicial elections *were* covered by section 2 and remanded the case back to the court of appeals.[196] The court of appeals again ruled against LULAC, holding the organization had failed to prove a violation of the law,[197] but the US Supreme Court denied to rehear the case on appeal.

Two decades after the LULAC lawsuit, two nonprofit consumer advocacy organizations, Public Citizen and the Gray Panthers, sued the state in a federal district court in 2000 challenging the constitutionality of Texas' system of electing judges. The plaintiffs' argument was that because of large campaign contributions to judges by lawyers and businesses with cases pending before the courts, the current system of financing judicial elections creates the appearance, if not the reality, of partiality and impropriety of Texas state judges. There was intense media coverage of the case, with most major newspapers in the state supporting the litigation.[198] Hoping that a federal court ruling might be the impetus for the legislature to take action, the plaintiffs cited a state bar survey that found that 83 percent of the Texas public, 79 percent of Texas lawyers, and 48 percent of the state's judges believed that campaign contributions had a significant influence on the outcome of judicial decisions. TPJ submitted evidence that the nine justices on the Supreme Court raised $11 million for the 2000 election cycle The plaintiffs did not allege that improper influence or even the appearance of such influence, existed in any present or future case, but the lawsuit was a "systemic challenge to Texas' system for financing the election of state-court judges."[199]

The federal district court dismissed the lawsuit for lack of jurisdiction because the plaintiffs had failed to show a specific injury. The court further held that "campaign contributions by parties with cases pending before the judicial candidate . . . is not so irregular or 'extreme' as to violate the Due Process Clause of the Fourteenth Amendment."[200] On appeal,[201] in *Public Citizen, Inc. v. Bomer* in 2002,[202] the US Court of Appeals for the Fifth Circuit affirmed the district court's ruling, arguing that a trial before an unbiased judge is essential to due process, but only in the most extreme of cases does the Due Process Clause require the disqualification of a judge. The plaintiffs failed to show that they suffered a real injury rather than a hypothetical or conjectural one. Although a trial before an unbiased judge is essential to due process, argued the court of appeals judge, only in the most extreme cases does the constitution require disqualification of a judge. Most matters of judicial disqualification simply do not rise to a constitutional level.[203] For a denial of due process to be proved, a party would have to show that a judge has a "direct, personal, substantial, pecuniary interest in reaching a conclusion against him in his case."[204] Writing for the majority, Judge Barksdale wrote:

> Plaintiffs, however, do not allege—nor could they do so, that every lawsuit in Texas state court involves a situation in which one or more of the parties and/or attorneys have made campaign contributions to the presiding judge. Indeed, none of the Plaintiffs has alleged that one or more of the Plaintiffs, or any member of the two plaintiff organizations, or any client represented by one of the five plaintiff lawyers has ever been involved in a case in which an opposing party or lawyer has contributed money to the presiding judge.[205]

The plaintiffs in this case, or any lawsuit challenging the constitutionality of a system of judicial selection, would have had a stronger case if they had been able to show harm—that is, provide hard evidence that the system resulted in an improper judgment or verdict. At the time, many commentators believed that the lawsuit was far-fetched, and that legislative action, rather than lawsuits or judicial self-regulation, was needed to solve the problem.[206]

In 2016, another vote dilution lawsuit, *Lopez v. Abbott*, alleged that the state's at-large statewide elections for the Texas Supreme Court and Court of Criminal Appeals violate the section 2 of the Voting Rights Act of 1965 by diluting the impact of Latinos voters.[207] Latinos, who make up over 25 percent of the state's electorate, have never won an election to either the supreme court or court of criminal appeals, without first having been appointed by the governor to fill a vacancy. According to the suit, of the seventy-six justices to have served on the Texas Supreme Court since 1945 only 5 (6.6 percent) were Latino. Similarly, of the forty-eight justices to have served on Texas Court of Criminal Appeals since that date, only two (4.2 percent) of the justices were Latino. During the period of 2002 to 2014, ten Latino candidates sought election to the supreme court, but only two candidates (who were initially appointed) were successful. During that period, Latino candidates sought election to the court of criminal appeals in five elections. The system of electing judges to the state's two highest courts, coupled with the historical and socioeconomic factors that have existed in Texas for a century and a half, dilute the political influence of the Latino population.[208]

The remedy that the lawsuit sought was a federal court order compelling the state to adopt single-member districts for each of the nine seats on the two highest appellate court. Arguably, if this were to occur, there would be a greater likelihood that judicial candidates supported by Hispanic voters in these districts would be elected to the two highest courts because Latino voters would constitute majorities in at least two of the hypothetical single-member districts. Further, it is no secret that Republican candidates for those courts rarely ever campaign in areas of the state with majority Hispanic populations because Hispanic voters generally support Democratic candidates.

In voter dilution lawsuits the argument is *not* that minority voters are prevented from voting in an election but that the minority group's influence to successfully elect a member of that group to a specific government body—legislative, executive, or judicial—is weakened or thwarted because of the at-large or statewide election scheme. For example, a minority group might make up 40 percent of a state's voting population but is unable to elect any (or only a small number) to any statewide offices. In effect, the inability of a sizeable voter bloc to ever elect one of its members to a court causes vote dilution and, therefore, the inability to influence public policy. Under the principle of one-person, one-vote the minority voter's vote counts less than the white voter's vote in a system where dilution exists. This is not a question of a political majority versus a political minority, such Democrat versus Republican in a red state. If you happen to be one of the few Democrats in a red state, then it is not because of discrimination that you cannot win but bad luck. However, if a system or method of election—either *de jure* or *de facto*—dilutes voter strength of a minority group, then you may have an actionable claim under the Voting Rights Act. Section 2 of the Voting Rights Act prohibits any "standard, practice or procedure" that "results in a denial or abridgement of the right of any citizen of the United States to vote on account of color."[209]

The state's counterargument in *Lopez* was that creating such districts would deprive the state's entire electorate of the opportunity to select all justices on the state's highest courts. District-based elections would in actuality disempower more Hispanic voters because the totality of all Hispanic voters would never be able to vote for *all* nine justices on each of the state's highest appellate courts. Opponents of the lawsuit further argued that the system does not discriminate based on race but only on the basis of political party. Since Republicans dominate party primaries—as well as the general election—minority voters are not losing court elections due to their race but because of their preferred party. Since Democrats are unlikely to win at-large elections, minority candidates should run as Republicans in primaries. In sum, the state maintained that the Voting Rights Act does not apply. However, even Latino candidates who run as Republicans in statewide Republican primaries face an uphill battle. For example, Justice Elsa Alcala, a Republican, was one of two Hispanics on the state's highest criminal appeals courts. She was appointed in May 2011 by then-governor Rick Perry and confirmed unanimously by the Texas Senate. She then ran unopposed in the Republican primary in 2012 and won the general election later that year against a little known third party candidate. However, she did not seek reelection in 2018 after one term based on her belief that she would be defeated in the Republican primary because of her Hispanic surname.[210]

In September 2018, US district judge Nelva Gonzales Ramos granted the state's motion to dismiss the *Lopez* case, arguing that Latino candidate's lack of success in at-large elections for the state's two highest appeals courts was due to partisan voting in the state rather than race. Citing *Thornburg*, the judge recognized that the system works to the disadvantage of Latino candidates, who are typically Democrats, but that partisanship rather than race explains the Hispanic defeat at the polls.[211] Once more, an attempt to reform the system was thwarted.

In conclusion, this chapter documented a long and complex history of judicial politics and reform efforts in the Lone Star State. Texas has faced many problems, including low public confidence in the justice system, ethical lapses of judges, runaway campaign contributions, questionable recusal standards, and a lack of gender and racial diversity on the bench. Reformers have had some success, most notably the Judicial Campaign Finance Act of 1995, as well as more effective recusal rules and procedures, but competing or entrenched interests, lack of grassroots support, political parties, and the inability to reach a consensus on the nature of the reforms have prevented many problems from being resolved. There *is* widespread consensus about the root cause of most of these intractable problems: the method by which judges are selected in the state. Texas remains one of only seven states that steadfastly clings to the use of partisan election as a method of judicial selection, and as of this writing, the only change that will take effect in 2020 is the elimination of straight-ticket voting. We will return to this issue and discuss a number of trends in judicial politics at the state and national levels in chapter 5.

NOTES

1. Bob Gammage interview on PBS *Frontline*, air date November 23, 1999.

2. *Id.*, at 210–212; and see generally, Anthony Champagne and Kyle Cheek, "Judicial Independence: The cycle of Judicial Elections: Texas as a case study," *Fordham Urban Law Journal,* 29 (2002)*:* 907–940.

3. Champagne and Cheek, "Judicial Independence," 911–913.

4. Bob Gammage interview on PBS *Frontline*, air date November 23, 1999.

5. William Blackstone, *Commentaries on the Law of England* (4 volumes 1765–69).

6. See Scott Douglas Gerber, *A Distinct Judicial Power: The Origins of an Independent Judiciary, 1606–1787* (New York: Oxford University Press, 2011).

7. See G.W.C Ross's classic article, "'Good behavior' of Federal Judges," *University of Kansas City Law Review,* 12 (1944): 119–120.

8. The Declaration of Independence.

9. John Adams, "Thoughts on Government," (1776), in *The Works of John Adams*, ed. Charles Francis Adams, 10 vols. Boston, 1850–56, 4; 193, 198–199.

10. United States Constitution, Article III, Section 1.

11. The *Federalist Papers,* by Alexander Hamilton, James Madison, and John Jay (New York: Bantam Books, 1982), 393–394.

12. See James L. Haley's definitive history of the state's high court, *The Texas Supreme Court: A Narrative History, 1836–1986* (Austin: University of Texas Press, 2013).

13. *Id.*, at 18.

14. *Id.*

15. *Id.*, at 17–23.

16. *Id.*, at 34

17. *Id.*

18. See James P. Hart, "John Hemphill—Chief Justice of Texas," *Southwestern Law Journal,* 3 (1949): 395.

19. See Michael Ariens, *Lone Star Law* (Lubbock: Texas Tech University Press, 2011), 15.

20. *Id.* at 38–39.

21. *Id.*, at 40–41.

22. *Id.*, at 32–33.

23. Ariens, *Lone Star Law*, 18–19.

24. *Id.*, at 20.

25. *Id.*

26. Hart, "John Hemphill," 403–404.

27. Ariens, *Lone Star Law,* 23.

28. *Id.*, at 54–55.

29. Haley, *The Texas Supreme Court*, 54–55.

30. *Id.*

31. *Id.*

32. http://www.statutes.legis.state.tx.us/?link=EL.

33. Robert McCormick, "Modernizing the Texas Judicial System," *Texas Law Review,* 21, no. 6 (June 1943), 11.

34. *Id.*

35. *Id.*

36. *Id.*, at 12–13.

37. Haley, *The Texas Supreme Court*, 179.

38. *Sweat v. Painter*, 339 U.S. 629 (1950).

39. *Brown v. Board of Education*, 347 U.S. 483 (1954).

40. Calvert served on the Court for over two decades—first as an associate justice from 1950 to 1961 and Chief Justice from 1961 to 1972.

41. Robert W. Calvert, "The next hundred years," *Houston Bar Journal,* June 1971.

42. Haley, *The Texas Supreme Court,* 205.

43. Greenhill served on the Court for twenty-four years –as an associate justice from 1957 to 1971 and Chief Justice from 1972 to 1982.

44. Haley, *The Texas Supreme Court,* 210

45. *Id.* at 210–212; and see generally, Champagne and Cheek, "Judicial Independence."

46. Champagne and Cheek, "Judicial Independence," 911–913.

47. *Id.*

48. Garth Jones (Associated Press Writer), The *Kerrville Times,* June 19, 1986.

49. Burka, "Heads, we win, tails, you lose," *Texas Monthly,* May 1987.

50. Thomas Petzinger, Jr. and Caleb Solomon, "Texaco Case spotlights questions on ingratiate of the Courts in Texas," *Wall Street Journal*, November 4, 1987, at 1

51. 60 Minutes: Is Justice for Sale? (CBS television broadcast, Dec. 6, 1987).

52. Kyle Cheek and Anthony Champagne, *Judicial Politics in Texas* (New York: Peter Lang, 2005), 41, 89–90, 96, 111.

53. *Manges v. Guerra*, 673 S.W.2d 180 (Tex. 1984).

54. Motion for Recusal of Justice C.L. Ray, *Manges v. Guerra* (Tex. 1983) (No. C-771); Motion for Recusal of Justices Ted Z. Robertson and William W. Kilgarlin, *Manges v. Guerra* (Tex. 1983) (no. C-771).

55. State Comm'n on Judicial Conduct, Findings, Conclusions and Public Reprimand Relating to Certain Activities of Justice C.L. Ray of the Supreme Court of Texas (1987).

56. State Comm'n on Judicial Conduct, Findings, Conclusions and Public Admonition Relating to Certain Activities of Justice William Kilgarlin of the Supreme Court of Texas (1987).

57. *Id.*; and see Robert Elder, Jr., "Sanctions spark more feuding," *Texas Lawyer*, June 15, 1987, at 17.

58. Elder, "Sanctions spark more feuding," 19.

59. Chapter 3 discusses Gammage's election to the supreme court in greater detail.

60. "Campbell resigns form Supreme Court," *Dallas Morning News*, January 7, 1988, at 1 A.

61. Anthony Champagne, "Judicial reform in Texas," *Judicature,* 72 (1988): 146, 151–157.

62. Franklin S. Spears, "Selection of Appellate Judges," *Baylor Law Review*, 40 (1988): 502, 520.

63. "No merit-election slam dunk, for sure," *Texas Weekly,* February 20, 1989.

64. "71% of respondents to Texas poll back election of judges," *Dallas Morning News*, February 19, 1990, at 21 A.

65. Donald W. Jackson and James W. Riddlesperger, Jr., "Money and politics in Judicial Elections: The 1988 Election of the Chief Justice of Texas Supreme Court," *Judicature,* 74, no. 4 (December–January 1991), at 185–186.

66. Timothy D. Howell documented that tort law rulings reached a liberal zenith in the 1970s and 1980s in "So long 'Sweetheart'—State farm fire & Casualty Co. v. Gandy Swings the pendulum to the right as the latest in a line of setbacks for Texas plaintiffs," *St. Mary's Law Journal,* 29 (1997): 47. The fact that courts in the state ruled more often in favor of plaintiffs in the 1980s was documented by Lee Shilofsky, "The changing face of first-party bad faith claims in Texas," *Southern Methodist University Law Review,* 50 (1997): 867.

67. See Anthony Champagne, "Tort reform and judicial selection," *Loyola of Los Angeles Law Review*, 38, no. 8 (2005):1483.

68. Robert Sherefkin, "Lee Iacocca's Pinto: A fiery failure," *Automotive News*, June 16, 2003, https://www.autonews.com/article/20030616/SUB/306160770/lee-iacocca-s-pinto-a-fiery-failure.

69. https://www.pbs.org/wgbh/pages/frontline/shows/justice/interviews/ross.html.

70. Frontline interview with Kim Ross, lobbyist for the Texas Medical Association. https://www.pbs.org/wgbh/pages/frontline/shows/architect/interviews/gwynne.html.

71. It is important not to lose sight of the fact that the Court during this time consisted not merely justices who were pawns of either the trial lawyers or the defense bar, but of individuals who held competing judicial philosophies and ideological positions on a range of legal and political issues including consumer protection, civil rights, freedom of expression, homosexual rights, privacy, and a range of other policy issues.

72. CNN.com inflation calculator. http://money.cnn.com/calculator/pf/inflation-adjustment/.

73. By comparison, eight years earlier, in 1980, the total amount of contributions to all Texas Supreme Court candidates running for election or reelection was a paltry $155,033 ($439, 712 in 2018 dollars).

74. This data was reported and examined by Anthony Champagne's study of the 1988 election in "Campaign contributions in Texas Supreme Court races," *Crime, Law & Societal Change,* 17 (1992): 91.

75. *Id.* at 95.

76. Donald W. Jackson and James W. Ribiddlesperger, Jr., "Money and politics in judicial elections: The 1988 election of the Chief Justice of the Texas Supreme Court," *Judicature,* 74, no. 4 (December–January, 1991): 184–189.

77. Bruce Hight, "Democratic judicial race pits 2 Austin attorneys," *Austin American-Statesman*, May 29, 1982.

78. See generally Melinda Gann Hall's *Attacking Judges: How Campaign Advertising Influences State Supreme Court Elections* (Stanford, CA: Stanford Law Books, 2015) for the most up-to-date and comprehensive account of campaign advertising research in state supreme court races.

79. Bert Brandenburg and Roy A. Schotland, "Justice in Peril: The endangered balance between impartial courts and Judicial Election campaigns," *Georgetown Journal of Legal Ethics,* 21, no. 4 (Fall 2008): 1229–1250.

80. Kyle Cheek and Anthony Champagne, *Judicial Politics in Texas: Partisanship, Money, and Politics in State Courts* (New York: Peter Lang, 2005). This brief text is an excellent overview of the various reform efforts, as well as one of the most useful accounts of Texas judicial politics.

81. Ben Wear, "Judicial Stalemate may affect Travis County," *Austin American Statesman*, November 28, 1994.

82. *Id.*

83. David Elliot, "The truth test: Texas Supreme Court." *Austin American-Statesman*, 1994, discusses the impact on the trial lawyers on the court. March 6, 1994.

84. Ben Wear, "Supreme Court races offer subtle choices," *Austin American-Statesman*, October 17, 1994.

85. See Texans for Public Justice report based on Texas Ethics Commission data, http://www.tpj.org.

86. *Id.*

87. *Id.*

88. See Champagne, *Crime, Law & Social Change,* 17 (1992):91.

89. See Kyle Cheek and Anthony Champagne, "Money in Texas Supreme Court Elections," *Judicature,* 84 (July–August 2000): 20–25.

90. *Id.*, 22.

91. *Id.*

92. The full report of the Texans for Public Justice study is found at http://www.tpj.org.

93. *Id.*

94. *Id.*

95. *Houston Chronicle*, July 23, 2001. Patty Reinert, Section A, p.1. Lexis-Nexis Judicial Election Search.

96. See "Checks and imbalances," Section B Tort Dodgers, www.tpj.org (2000).

97. See *Payola Justice*, www.tpj.org (1998).

98. The data for the report was collected by comparing campaign contribution data filed with the Texas Ethics Commission and Docket Data that covers "petitions for review" filed with the Supreme Court. The legal counsels contributions was determined by the aggregate of the attorney, attorneys law firm, a law firm's PAC, and other lawyers of the firm. The study screened total members of 1,766 petitioning parties, 5,060 petitioning attorneys affiliated with 1,717 law firms.

99. See Chris Griesel (Texas Supreme Court rules attorney), "TPJ 'Findings' just don't add up," *Texas Lawyer,* May 7, 2001, p. 46.

100. *Id.*

101. *Texas Lawyer*, April 30, 2001, p.6.

102. Jane Elliot, "'Dollar Docket' latest attempt to reform campaign money," *Texas Lawyer*, March 6, 2000.

103. Texas is one of 17 states that have carried out public trust and confidence studies in the courts. See Survey of Texans Regarding Trust and Confidence in the Courts and the Legal Profession in Texas, 1999. Hereafter known as Texas Public Trust and Confidence study.

104. Texas Office of Court Administration, "The courts and the legal profession in Texas—The Insider's perspective: A survey of Judges, Court Personnel, and Attorneys," (1998), http://www.courts.state.tx.us/publicinfo/publictrust/execsum.htm.

105. *Texas Senate News Release,* March 14, 1997.

106. *Id.*

107. *Ft Worth Star Telegram,* May 24, 1997.

108. *Ft Worth Star Telegram,* December 8, 2000, Friday Final Edition and *Austin American Statesman*, September 27, 2000.

109. *Texas Senate News Release,* March 14, 1997.

110. News Release from the Office of State Senator Rodney Ellis, March 14, 1997, http://www.senate.state.tx.us/75r/seante/members/dist13/pr97/p031497a.html.

111. V.T.C.A Election Code section 253.151-253.176.

112. See Daniel Becker and Malia Reddick, *Judicial Selection Reform: Examples from Six States* (Des Moines, IA: American Judicature Society, 2003), at 1–9.

113. House Research Organization: Judicial Selection: Options for Choosing Judges in Texas, March 10, 1997.

114. Senate Bill 621 and Senate Joint Resolution 25, 75th Legislative Session, 1997.

115. See *San Angelo Standard Times Online,* November 27, 1998 Editorial "Robert Duncan has it right on the issue of judicial selection."

116. House Bill 59, 76th Legislative Session, 1999.

117. Senate Bill 59, 76th Legislative Session, 1999.

118. Senate Joint Resolution 9, 76th Legislative Session, 1999 and Senate Joint Resolution 3, 77th Legislative Session, 2001. *The San Antonio Express,* March 30, 1999, "Adding the lower appellate courts to the plan may create more resistance, but the idea championed by Sen. Robert Duncan, R-Lubbock, is sound."

119. Shannon Davis, "The rise and fall of a Reform Bill," *Frontline,* 1999, http://www.pbs.org/wgbh/pages/frontline/shows/justice/howshould/risefall.html

120. Senate Bill 1570, 74th Legislative Session, 1995, Senate Bill 628, 75th Legislative Session, 1997, Senate Joint Resolution 26, 75th Legislative Session, 1997, Senate Bill 78, 76th Legislative Session, 1999, Senate Joint Resolution 11, 76th Legislative Session, 1999.

121. *Id.*

122. Senate Bill 720, 77th Legislative Session, 2001.

123. Senate Bill 720 Analysis, www.capitol.stae.tx.us/cgi/tlo/vietext.cmd?LEG=77&SESS=R&CHAMBER.2001.

124. Senate Bill 823, 77th Legislative Session, 2001.

125. SB 823 Bill Analysis, www.captiol.state.tx.us/cgi-bin/tlo/viewtext.cmd?LEG=77&SESS=R&CHAMBER. 2001.

126. Thomas R. Phillips, "Electoral accountability and judicial independence," *Ohio State Law Journal,* 64 (2003):137, 140.

127. Thomas R. Phillips, "Judicial independence and accountability," *Law & Contemporary Problems,* 61 (1998):127.

128. Wallace Jefferson, Op-Ed., "Making merit matter by adopting new system of Selecting Judges," *Houston Chronicle*, March 21, 2009, https://www.chron.com/opinion/outlook/article/Wallace-B-Jefferson-Make-merit-matter-by-1544078.php.

129. Andrew Cohen, "'A Broken System': Texas's Former Chief Justice condemns judicial elections," *The Atlantic*, October 18, 2013.

130. *Id.*

131. *Id.*

132. See generally Meryl Chertoff and Dustin F. Robinson, "Check one and the accountability is done: The harmful impact of straight-ticket voting on Judicial Elections," *Albany Law Review,* 75, no. 4 (2012): 1773–1797.

133. https://www.texastribune.org/2017/06/01/texas-gov-greg-abbott-signs-bill-eliminate-straight-ticket-voting/

134. Chertoff and Robinson, "Check one and the accountability is done," 1781–1782.

135. Approval of Amendments to the Texas Code of Judicial Conduct, Misc. Docket No. 02-9167 (Tex. Aug. 22, 2002) [hereinafter Texas Amendments] (amending Canons 3, 5 and 6 of the Texas Code).

136. 536 U.S. 765 (2002).

137. *Id.*

138. Canon 5 prohibits a judge from engaging in inappropriate political activity, such as making pledges or promises of conduct in office regarding pending or impending cases, specific classes of cases, specific classes of litigants, or specific propositions of law that would suggest to a reasonable person that the judge is predisposed to a probable decision in cases within the scope of the pledge. It also states that a judge or judicial candidate may attend political events and express his or her views on political matters in accord with this Canon and Canon 3B(10); however, "A statement made during a campaign for judicial office, whether or not prohibited by this canon, may cause a judge's impartiality to be reasonably questioned in the context of a particular case and may result in recusal." http://www.scjc.state.tx.us/.

139. Both cases cited *White.*

140. 213 S.W.3d 547 (2006).

141. 275 S.W. 3d 109 (2008).

142. David Saleh Rauf, "Settlement reached in ethics case involving Supreme Court chief justice," *San Antonio Express News*, October 28, 2015; and Molly McDonough, "Texas S.C. Justice Broke Ethics Law, Fined 29K," *ABA Journal*, December 2008, http://www.abajournal.com/news/article/texas_s.c._judge_broke_ethics_law_fined_29k/; Scott Gold and Richard A. Serrano, "A love that was benched by their careers," *Los Angeles Times*, October 8, 2005, http://articles.latimes.com/2005/oct/08/nation/na-couple8.

143. *Id.* at 554–555.

144. *Id.* at 551–552.

145. NPR.org. https://www.npr.org/series/4933926/harriet-miers-withdraws-as-high-court-nominee

146. *Id.*

147. Tex. Gov't Code Ann. Section 33.034(c) (Vernon 2004).

148. 213 S.W.3d 547, 580.

149. *Id.*, at 562–565.

150. *Public Admonition of Justice of the Peace Torres, No. 00-0689—JP (Comm'n Jud. Conduct*, Aug. 16, 2000).

151. *In re Hecht,* 213 S.W.3d 547, 560–563.

152. *Id.*, at 575–576.

153. Tex. Code Jud. Conduct, 2B.

154. 536 U.S. 765 (2002).

155. *In re Hecht,* 213 S.W.3d 547, 575–577.

156. https://www.ethics.state.tx.us/sworncomp/2007/2707161.pdf2

157. Chuck Lindell, "Greg Abbott's handling of Justice Nathan Hecht case raises questions," *Austin-American Statesman*, October 21, 2014.

158. *Id.*

159. *Ex parte James W. Ellis; Ex parte John D. Colyandro*, 275 S. W. 2d 109 (2009).

160. Travis County District Attorney Ronny Earle and Assistant District Attorney Holly Taylor filed the motions.

161. Third District, Austin.

162. Justice Waldrop was appointed by Governor Rick Perry in 2005, won election in 2006, and resigned in 2010, two years before his term ended.

163. *Ex parte James W. Ellis; Ex parte John D. Colyandro,* 275 S. W. 2d 109 (2009), 113.

164. The State cited Tex. R. Civ. P 18b(2)(a) which states that a "judge shall recuse himself in any proceeding in which . . . his impartiality might reasonably be questioned," and 18b(2)(b) which provides that a "judger shall recuse himself in any proceeding in which . . . he has a personal bias or prejudice concerning the subject matter."

165. *Id.*

166. *Id.* at 113.

167. *Id.*

168. *Id.* at 115 citing *Rodgers v. Bradley*, 909 S. W. 2d 872, 879 (Tex. 1995) (Enoch, J. concurring).

169. *Id.*

170. *Id.* at 119.

171. *Id.* at 136,137.

172. 129 S.Ct. 2252 (2009).

173. *Id.* at 2257.

174. *Id.* at 2265 (citing *FTC v. Comment Institute*, 333 U.S. 683, 702 (1948).

175. *Id.*

176. See Kate David and Jennifer S. Greenlief, "Juicy enough for Grisham, but does it have any bite? *Caperton v. A.T. Massey Coal Co.* and the Impact for Texas Courts," *Houston Lawyer,* 47 (September/October 2009): 38.

177. Texas Supreme Court Advisory Comm., Meeting of the Texas Supreme Court Advisory Comm. 20301, 20314-15, 20320, 20391 (2010), http:///www.supreme.courts.state.tx.us/rules/scac/2010/091710-trans.pdf. See also Seana Willing, "Post-Caperton recusal reform in Texas: Is it needed?" *South Texas Law Review,* 51 (2010): 1143.

178. (Westlaw and LexisNexis searches conducted by author, 2015).

179. 332 S.W.3d 448 (2011).

180. 348 S.W.3d 365 (2011).

181. No. 03-12-00014-CV, 2014 Tex. App. LEXIS 2641.

182. No. 07-12-00196-CV, 2014 WL 931260

183. No. 14-13-00518-CR, 2015 WL 1544790.

184. 332 S.W.3d 448, 453 n. 10 (2011).

185. No. 03-12-00014-CV; 2014 Tex. App. LEXIS 2641.

186. *Id.* at 15

187. 348 S.W.3d 365 (2011).

188. *Id.* at 372, 373.

189. No. 07-12-00196-CV, 2014 WL 931260.

190. No. 14-13-00518-CR, 2015 WL 1544790.

191. Tex. Elec. Code Ann. Section 253.15 (Vernon Supp. 2002). Specific limits are found on the Texas Ethics Commission's Campaign Finance Guide for Judicial Candidates and Officeholders, https://www.ethics.state.tx.us/guIbides/JCOH_guIbide.htm.

192. Debbie Graves, "Officials, lawyers demand reform of Judicial Elections," *Austin American-Statesman,* December 3, 1989, at BB8.

193. Bruce Hight, "Minorities criticize Judicial Merit Election Plan," *Austin American-Statesman,* December 4, 1989, at B1.

194. Lawrence E. Young, "Ruling likely to alter judges' campaigns," *The Dallas Morning News,* January 7, 1990, at 33A. T

195. *LULAC v. Clements,* 914 F.2d 620 (5th Cir. 1990).

196. *Houston Lawyer's Association v. Attorney General of Texas,* 501 U.S. 419 (1991).

197. *LULAC v. Clements,* 914 F.2d 831 (5th Cir. 1993).

198. See Russell Gold, "Lawsuit targets judges' election," *San Antonio Express-News,* April 3 2000; "Judicial elections well-deserved attack," *San Antonio Express-News*, April 7, 2000; Clay Robinson, "No easy way to change judicial selection," *Houston Chronicle*, April 9, 2000; and "Judging Texas," *Austin America-Statesman*, April 24, 2000.

199. Brief for appellants, Appeal from the U.S. District Court for the Western District of Texas, https://www.citizen.org/system/files/case_documents/bomerappellantsbrief.pdf

200. *Public Citizen, Inc. v. Bomer,* 115 F. Supp.2d 743, 746 (W.D. Tex. 2000).

201. Brief for appellants, Appeal from the U.S. District Court for the Western District of Texas, https://www.citizen.org/system/files/case_documents/bomerappellantsbrief.pdf

202. *Public Citizen, Inc. v. Bomer,* 274 F.3d 212 (2002).

203. *Id.* at 216.

204. *Id.* at 217.

205. *Id.*

206. See *Texas Lawyer*, July 10, 2000

207. *Lopez, et al. v. Gregg Abbott in his official capacity as Governor of Texas, Complaint for Declaratory and Injunctive Relief*, Civil Action No. 2:16-CV-00303 (2016). https://www.leagle.com/decision/infdco20170404e93.

208. *Id.*

209. 52 U.S.C. section 10301. The US Supreme Court ruled in *Chisom v. Roemer* in 1991 that Section 2 applies to the election of judges. Further, the suit alleged that under *Thornburg v. Gingles* in 1986 Texas meets the three preconditions for a voter dilution lawsuit.

210. Justice Alcala quoted in Alexa Ura, "Trial begins in Case Targeting Texas' Statewide Elections of Judges," *Texas Tribune,* February 12, 2018.

211. *Lopez, et al. v. Gregg Abbott.*

Chapter 5

Jurisprudence and Judicial Politics

A Final Assessment

> The majority opinion implies, by its reasoning, that the Texas Constitution places no limit whatsoever on the power of the legislature to establish school district boundaries. Such reasoning dangerously erodes that most precious of political rights—the right to be treated with respect and equality by the government, the right to full and participating citizenship in the state.[1]
>
> —Justice Bob Gammage dissenting
> in *Kirby v. Edgewood*

Bob Gammage's jurisprudence of civil rights and liberties encompasses a body of decisions addressing the right to privacy, freedom of speech and press, student rights, criminal due process, tort law, and equal protection of the laws. Gammage served on the Third Court of Appeals at Austin and on the Texas Supreme Court during a tumultuous period in Texas legal history that this book has named "Court Wars." This period witnessed numerous seismic shifts, including the manner in which judicial campaigns were conducted, a dramatic change in the partisan and ideological composition of the Texas Supreme Court (as well as Court of Criminal Appeals and most of the fourteen intermediate appellate courts), and the birth of the judicial reform movement in Texas. The purpose of this last chapter is twofold: first, to offer a final analysis of Gammage's jurisprudence based on his decisions examined in the preceding chapters; and second, to conclude the discussion of state and national trends in judicial politics in the second decade of the twenty-first century.

GAMMAGE'S JURISPRUDENCE OF CIVIL RIGHTS AND LIBERTIES

The term "jurisprudence" refers to a body of decisions that is attributed to an individual judge or collectively to a court. It can encompass a lifetime of decisions across a range of issues, or focus on one area of law, such as freedom of expression or the right to privacy. Its subject matter is broad, according to Professor Bodenheimer's classic work on the subject. Not merely a body of legal decisions, jurisprudence "encompass[es] the philosophical, sociological, historical, as well as analytical components of legal theory." It extends to basic legal ideas, "such as the concepts of rights, duty, liability, or corporate personality."[2] To this definition, I would add that jurisprudence includes normative questions of natural rights, morality, and justice. Furthermore, jurisprudence has two essential and interconnected elements: decisional and institutional. The decisional element of Gammage's jurisprudence encompasses the substantive legal doctrines or constitutional provisions that he adopted to reach an outcome in a dispute. To use one area of the law as an example, we must ask whether he supported an individual's privacy claim and, if so, which privacy doctrine or precedent did he apply and what was his justification for doing so. The institutional element of his jurisprudence refers to the philosophy of judging—his position on the proper role and function of the judiciary in the political system.

In his decisions, Gammage consistently argued for robust individual rights, whether those rights were implied in the Texas constitution, rooted in an evolving common law, or set out in state and federal judicial precedent. He believed that the state constitution protected a privacy right that exceeded the protections articulated by the federal constitution. The concept of "competing rights" intrigued and challenged him. In *Star-Telegram, Inc. v. Doe*, a landmark ruling in which the right to privacy was pitted against the freedom of the press, the Texas Supreme Court addressed the question of whether a newspaper may be held liable for disclosing private facts about a victim of sexual assault.[3] Gammage argued that even though highly personal information was revealed, he was not willing to rule that a privacy violation had occurred, since the private facts disclosed about a woman who was a crime victim were of legitimate public concern.[4]The data revealed in arrest records was highly personal but did not implicate privacy as autonomy, which extends to matters of marriage, procreation, or association. He *did* expressly recognize a type of privacy tort, the right to "freedom from public disclosure of embarrassing private facts," but *Star-Telegram* was a case without an easy solution: a chilling effect on the freedom of press would occur if newspapers were required by law to take measures to avoid the publication of facts that may or may not subject innocent persons to unwanted or unpleasant notoriety.[5]

Gammage often cited *Texas State Employees Union*,[6] in which the Texas Supreme Court ruled in 1987 that the right to privacy contained in the Texas constitution offered broader protections than the right to privacy under the US Constitution. Although the Texas constitution does not contain an express guarantee of an enumerated right to privacy, Gammage supported precedent that held that the right to privacy is derived from a constellation of five provisions of the state's constitution: section 19 of the Texas Bill of Rights protects against arbitrary deprivation of life and liberty.[7] Section 8 provides the freedom to speak, write, or publish.[8] Section 10 protects a person's privilege against self-incrimination.[9] Sections 9 and 25 guarantee the right to be free from intrusions into the sanctity of the home and person against intrusion.[10] Finally, section 6 protects an individual's right to freedom of conscience and religion.[11] Together, these five provisions create an implied right to privacy, much like that "found" by Justice Douglas in *Griswold v. Connecticut*. The constitutional right to privacy prevails except when it can be shown that an invasion is necessary in order to advance a compelling government objective, and that objective cannot be achieved by less intrusive means.

Notwithstanding his capacious definition of privacy, Gammage often demonstrated judicial restraint where no precedent provided the basis of a privacy claim. For example, in an unusual yet often-cited privacy case, *Colquette v. Forbes*,[12] he did not accept an argument positing that the terms of a consensual agreement made between two persons as a part of a divorce settlement, free from any government action, can violate a person's constitutional right to privacy. He reasoned that even though a family law judge approved the terms of a divorce settlement that intruded into the private life of an ex-spouse, the judicial recognition of the legality of the agreement is not the type of government involvement that is restrained by a right to privacy. The Texas Supreme Court had recognized as early as 1976 that the right to privacy prohibits "unwarranted government interference or intrusion into those areas deemed to be within the protected zone of privacy."[13] Therefore, Gammage could have plausibly argued that the judicial enforcement of the promissory note in the divorce settlement *was* an intrusion into Colquette's privacy as autonomy, recognized in *Griswold v. Connecticut*, because it violated a privacy interest that protects the decision to living with the lover or partner of one's choice.

Gammage was consistent in his application of the common law to grant legal relief to ordinary Texans. In doing so, he was often at odds with conservative justices who more often ruled in favor of the defendant, particularly if the person who caused the harm was acting on behalf of a large corporation or as an agent of the state; or if the ramifications of holding for the injured party might possibly have an economic impact. While on the court of appeals, Gammage argued in support of the recognition of a controversial tort doctrine called negligent infliction of emotional distress in the notorious sexual bondage case, *Twyman v. Twyman*.[14] He ruled that the tort had its foundations in the common law, which is constantly evolving to meet the needs of a changing society, a position that the conservative justices rejected. His decision was reversed a year later by a majority on the Texas Supreme Court, which refused to recognize the existence of that tort based largely on the supposition that by doing so would produce a cascade of litigation—hundreds of claims seeking the recovery of monetary damages in contested divorces, employment disputes, malpractice claims, and even in claims against lawyers by their clients. Support for this tort doctrine was divided along conservative versus liberal lines. At that time, forty-six other states recognized the tort of negligent infliction of emotional distress, but Texas was not one of them.[15] The majority could plausibly have argued for the adoption of this doctrine, without being viewed as judicial activists, but the idea of doing so seemed irresponsible to many of the justices. However, in *Twyman v. Twyman*, a majority of justices on the Texas Supreme Court *did* adopt the doctrine of *intentional* infliction of emotional distress, which requires a higher, more exacting standard when bringing a tort claim.[16]

Based on Gammage's reliance on the common law in so many of his decisions, including the issue of social host liability, it will come as no surprise that he often carried with him well-worn copies of Arthur R. Hogue's *Origins of the Common Law*[17] and Oliver Wendell Holmes's *The Common Law*.[18] Gammage often wrote that the common law was organic, continually evolving to help society understand the nature of obligations between persons. He believed that the majority sought to "stop the evolving common law dead in its tracks,"[19] in a case raising the question of whether the common law creates an obligation between a social host and a guest whom the host knows is intoxicated and will be driving. The foreseeable risk posed by the drunk driver justified imposing a common law duty on social hosts. Gammage rejected the majority's argument that the only the legislature can create a duty for social hosts, because, in his view, a duty already existed under the common law. The state's Dram Shop law addressed liability of commercial servers but stopped short of addressing social host liability, which is a real problem in modern society. The court's duty under the organic common law is to resolve this omission. Most conservatives on the court rejected what Gammage called the "evolving common law."

Gammage often explored the nature and scope of unenumerated rights in his opinions. In *Kirby v. Edgewood*[20] in 1988, he developed a cogent and comprehensive argument for unenumerated equal rights and fundamental freedoms. His understanding of unenumerated rights in the Texas constitution, in conjunction with the education clauses of the Texas constitution, played an important role in building the argument that ultimately persuaded a majority of judges and legislators to recognize the fact that the state's system of education funding discriminated against students living in poorer school districts. Years before the *Edgewood* cases, the US Supreme Court had held that education was not a fundamental right under the Fourteenth Amendment,[21] but Gammage pointed out in *Kirby* that the *Rodriguez* case was relying on the US Constitution, which *does not* include a specific provision for education, whereas the Texas constitution does. The right to an education is not found in the Texas Bill of Rights, but the Texas constitution recognizes education as indispensable to the exercise of fundamental rights and liberties. Even though a fundamental right may not be enumerated or have a specific textual basis in the state constitution, it does not mean that it does not exist, Gammage argued. Adopting an unenumerated rights argument that reflects the Ninth Amendment of the US Constitution, he argued that the Texas courts have historically protected implied fundamental interests such as the right to privacy, the rights of a parent to make autonomous decisions, and the right to pursue the occupation of one's choosing. Certain unarticulated rights are implicit in enumerated guarantees, and are often necessary for the protection and enjoyment of rights that are explicitly guaranteed. The majority in *Kirby* conceded the existence of unarticulated fundamental rights in theory, but argued that government has no obligation to provide the financial support necessary to exercise such rights or liberties.

Support for individual rights involves not only adopting substantive constitutional provisions and legal doctrines but also supporting the role of the judiciary to protect those rights. To that end, Gammage argued against a form of conservatism that he called judicial "non-interventionism" or judicial "abdication." He employed these two terms to describe what he believed to be a flawed form of judicial restraint. As conservative Republicans won more seats on the bench in the 1990s, the court became a textbook example judicial restraint, narrowly interpreting the rights found in the Texas constitution, highly suspicious of jury verdicts favorable to plaintiffs, and more willing to defer to the majoritarian process. Conservative jurists, such as Chief Justice Nathan Hecht, have bemoaned a shift away from reliance solely on precedent and the law to resolve legal disputes, to a willingness by many justices to use public policy arguments when deciding a case, as in the *Edgewood* litigation saga. Gammage understood the importance of the principle of judicial restraint but was critical of judicial deference to the political branches or majoritarian process; and strongly disagreed with those members of the court who demurred when asked to extend judicial review to statutes that violate individual rights.[22]

Gammage's jurisprudence defined liberty not simply as the absence of constraints on a person's autonomy but the freedom to express one's identity, as long as in exercising that liberty harm does not come to others. In *Valenzuela v. Aquino*,[23] for example, anti-abortion protestors were engaged in expressive conduct, but in doing inflicted pain and suffering on the physician and his family. Gammage agreed in principle with the conservative justices that the courts should be careful not impose a "chill" on speech by allowing plaintiffs to use the threat of winning monetary damages from a person or group engaged in protected speech. However, the individual who has been harmed should be free to recover damages that arise from conduct unrelated to protected expression.[24] This position is particularly relevant in light of the recent increase in the use of civil lawsuits as strategy to punish individuals and groups who advocate extreme and intimidating positions. It was doubtful that the radical anti-abortion group was interested in simply expressing their moral opposition to abortion, since the protestors targeted the Aquino family only at times when they knew Dr. Aquino would not be at home but his wife and children might be.[25] The protestors' intent was to intimidate and disrupt his family to the extent that he would ultimately succumb to the pressure and stop performing abortions.[26] For that reason, Gammage argued that it was constitutionally permissible to restrict the group's expression based on the family's privacy rights, a position reflected the US Supreme Court's ruling in *Frisby v. Schultz*.[27] The Texas constitution (Article I, section 8) states that "every person shall be at liberty to speak, write or publish his opinions on any subject, *being responsible for the abuse of that privilege*." Even when the speech component of a group's demonstrations is protected, the conduct components—if they are aimed at intimidation—are not constitutionally protected and may permit recovery of damages. One's liberty loses protection when the conduct associated with the exercise of the liberty is "so excessive and intrusive" that it does not deserve protection. The conservative justices who came down on the side of the pro-life protestors, downplayed the "abuse" clause of Article I, section 8 in order to circumvent the physician's privacy claim. It would have been interesting had there been a companion case involving radical environmental activists who caused harm by picketing the home of an oil company executive.

Gammage believed that rights protect liberty by legally defining the boundaries between persons and the coercive power of the state. Rights limit the degree to which the government can intrude into our lives. The role of the judiciary therefore is to protect the most basic fundamental freedoms: the freedom to speak one's mind or practice a belief system without fear of coercion or punishment, the right to move about freely, the freedom to associate with others, and the right to privacy in personal or intimate matters. Gammage adopted the position that in a system of ordered liberty, government does play a role in protecting us against those who abuse liberty and commit civil wrongs or criminal acts.

In the area of criminal due process, Gammage consistently voted to uphold due process rights of defendants. In deciding over 100 criminal due process cases while on Third Court of Appeals, a workhorse court which at that time had a liberal-leaning Democratic majority, Gammage voted to uphold convictions only in those instances when the procedural rights of defendants were strictly followed by the sentencing court. To ensure that defendants were afforded due process, he broadly interpreted the rules and doctrines of criminal procedure, including limiting the use of circumstantial evidence,[28] the right to have a jury instructed on a lesser charge,[29] the proper use of the state's unusual oral confessions law,[30] and a broad interpretation of state search and seizure law. In several cases on the court of appeals, Gammage objected to the trial court admitting incriminating evidence even though the defendant himself did not raise objections or file motions to suppress evidence.[31] His opinions in criminal due process cases do not reveal an ideological tilt but what was then a centrist interpretation of due process rights. However, if we compare his criminal due process decisions with those handed down by appellate courts after the state's judiciary grew more conservative in the late 1990s, Gammage's positions are strongly liberal by Texas standards. His decisions in criminal due process while serving on the Third Court of Appeals strengthened the due process rights of the accused relative to state authority. In many respects, his record as a judge in this area of the law reflected the progressive and compassionate penal code reforms that he sponsored or supported when he served in the sixty-third legislature in the 1970s.

Ideological labels, such as conservative and liberal, assigned to justices are limited in what they can tell us because these labels discount a host of factors that influence a judge's decision; the nature of the dispute, precedent, the role of *stare decisis*, the express and implied provisions of a constitution, and the group dynamics that take place on a court all have an impact on decision-making. Indeed, there is much scholarship on empirical measures of judicial preferences and assigning of ideological labels to judicial behavior.[32] Notwithstanding these limitations, based on the cases analyzed in this book, it is clear that Gammage had a solidly liberal-progressive record as a judge. In civil liberties cases, he was more likely to protect the rights of individuals, such as speech, equal protection, and due process, rather than allow the state to restrict these rights; he was also more willing to support the claims of individuals against corporations in civil suits. Conservative justices were more likely to vote in the opposite direction as Gammage in the cases before the court, thus upholding the government's restrictions on individual liberties and rights, as well as support corporations in civil suits. The characterization of Gammage, as well as bloc justices with whom he served (Doggett, Hightower, Mauzy and Spector) as liberal or progressive, is supported not only by the analysis of the cases in the preceding chapters but also by the comments of other judges, scholars, and journalists[33] who wrote about the court's decisions during his tenure. Interestingly, it is also supported by the

Table 5.1 Justices Serving with Gammage on the Texas Supreme Court: 1/1991–12/1995

Name	*Dates Served*	*Party*	*CF Score*	*Ideology*
Gonzales, Raul	1984–1998	Democrat	0.928	Strong Conservative
Mauzy, Oscar	1987–1993	Democrat	–0.534	Strong Liberal
Phillips, Thomas (CJ)	1988–2004	Republican	0.842	Strong Conservative
Cook, Eugene	1988–1992	Republican	0.985	Strong Conservative
Hightower, Jack	1988–1996	Democrat	0.593	Lean Conservative
Doggett, Lloyd	1989–1994	Democrat	–0.635	Strong Liberal
Hecht, Nathan	1989–present	Republican	0.971	Strong Conservative
Gammage, Bob	1991–1995	Democrat	–0.668	Strong Liberal
Cornyn, John	1991–1997	Republican	1.027	Very Conservative
Enoch, Craig	1993–2003	Republican	0.971	Strong Conservative
Spector, Rose	1993–1998	Democrat	–0.043	Lean Liberal

CF scores from Bonica and Woodruff.

only three published empirical studies of the voting patterns of Texas justices in the 1990s. Bonica and Woodruff calculated ideology scores of justices (CF scores) based on the type and political objectives of groups that contributed to each judicial candidate in a campaign.[34] Higher scores suggest a conservative ideology, while negative ones are indicative of liberal views. Table 5.1 shows the ideology, as well as partisan affiliation, of the justices during the years Gammage served.

For purposes of comparison, table 5.2 shows the partisan and ideological composition of the court after Gammage's last year on the bench at the end of 1995 up until 2013, which was the last year that CF scores were calculated by Bonica and Woodruff. After Justice Rose Spector's final year on the court in 1998, no Democrat or liberal has served on the Supreme Court.

A second empirical study of ideology conducted in 1999 by Rebe used amicus curiae support and dissenting votes in civil rights and liberties cases. It found that Gammage's ideology score to be liberal, a 32.35 on a scale of 0–100, with 0 being the most liberal and 100 the most conservative.[35] Analyzing the voting patterns of the justices once Republicans captured a majority of seats, Gammage dissented in 23 percent of all decisions while on the court, compared to Chief Justice Thomas Phillips who dissented in 0.05 percent of the cases. Lastly, a third empirical analysis of the Supreme Court of Texas from 1989 to 1998, published by Julie Segal in 1999, also confirmed that Gammage voted in a liberal direction 60 percent of the time in cases dealing with freedom of speech and press, 66 percent of the time in favor of privacy in cases where speech and privacy were competing rights, and 100 percent of the time in favor of equal protection claims.[36]

As stated earlier, the second element of jurisprudence is institutional, which refers to a judge's understanding of the role of the judiciary in the larger political system and the degree of willingness to apply judicial review

Table 5.2 Justices Serving after Gammage Resigned from the Court: 1/1991–12/1995

Name	*Dates Served*	*Party*	*CF Score*	*Ideology*
Hecht, Nathan	1989–present	Republican	0.971	Strong Conservative
Baker, James A.	1995–2002	Republican	0.967	Strong Conservative
Abbott, Greg	1996–2001	Republican	1.040	Very Conservative
Hankinson, Deborah	1997–2002	Republican	0.754	Strong Conservative
Gonzales, Alberto	1998–2000	Republican	0.895	Strong Conservative
O'Neill, Harriet	1999–2010	Republican	0.703	Strong Conservative
Rodriguez, Xavier	2001–2002	Republican	0.885	Strong Conservative
Jefferson, Wallace	2001–	Republican	0.911	Strong Conservative
Schneider, Michael	2002–2004	Republican	0.780	Strong Conservative
Smith, Steven	2002–2004	Republican	0.960	Strong Conservative
Brister, Scott	2003–2009	Republican	0.872	Strong Conservative
Wainwright, Dale	2003–present	Republican	0.931	Strong Conservative
Medina, David	2004–present	Republican	0.813	Strong Conservative
Johnson, Phil	2005–present	Republican	1.052	Very Conservative
Green, Paul	2005–present	Republican	0.815	Strong Conservative
Willett, Don	2005–2018	Republican	0.973	Strong Conservative
Guzman, Eva	2009–present	Republican	0.897	Strong Conservative
Lehrmann, Debra	2010–present	Republican	0.861	Strong Conservative

CF scores from Bonica and Woodruff.

to challenged laws and government action. As we saw in *Morales*, Gammage argued that judicial scrutiny should be appropriately applied to *all* "laws affecting the civil or personal rights of any number of citizens."[37] He believed that to hinder gays and lesbians from seeking remedies in a civil court, simply because there is no pending or anticipated criminal prosecution under the sodomy law, "disregard[s] the fundamental principle upon which such courts are established."[38] This gives us another glimpse of how Gammage understood the role of the judiciary. Recall that in *Barber*, Justice Gammage argued that the Texas Equal Rights Amendment of 1972 offered broader protection than the Fourteenth Amendment to the US Constitution.[39] Consequently, Gammage recognized in *Morales* that homosexuals constitute a class of people that face discrimination in housing, family law, and criminal justice matters because of the mere possibility of engaging in a particular sexual act. Even if the state's sodomy statute was never enforced, the mere existence of the law classified LGBT Texans as criminals, and, in doing so, sanctioned discrimination. Gammage raised the dystopic prospect that under the "unenforced law" concept that the majority of justices embraced, the state could pass a plethora of arbitrary criminal laws intended to stigmatize groups of people, and violate their constitutional rights, as long as the laws go unenforced. Of course, one of the weaknesses in Gammage's argument in *Morales* was that, in fact, the Supreme Court does not have jurisdiction in criminal sodomy cases. That responsibility rests solely with the Court of Criminal Appeals in

Texas. In addition, at the time of *Morales*, *Bowers v. Hardwick* was the law of the land. Yet, Chief Justice Phillips, by no means a liberal or a judicial activist, joined with Gammage in arguing the court should have heard the *Morales* case on its merits rather than dismissing it for lack of jurisdiction.

Gammage's position on judicial review can be summed up as follows: deference should never be given to the political branches when fundamental rights are at stake. For example, in applying this position in the *Barber* case, he rejected the established doctrine that held—and still holds in Texas—that school districts are autonomous entities that should be largely unfettered by judicial intrusion. While it is true that federal and state precedent holds that the rights of students must at times be subordinate to the legitimate interest of protecting children and safeguarding the educational process, schools, however, should not automatically be free from judicial scrutiny when students' constitutional rights are restricted.

Reiterating a point made throughout this book, as a Texas Supreme Court justice, Gammage had the discretion to analyze and resolve disputes from either the standpoint of the Texas constitution, the US Constitution, or a combination of the two. He took the view that when a state supreme court decides a case on independent state grounds alone, the higher federal court should show restraint when determining whether to apply judicial review.[40] This mode of judicial interpretation—where a state court looks primarily at the state constitution to resolve disputes—has been referred to as the primacy model of state judicial decision-making.[41] In cases where constitutional claims were raised, Gammage's opinions relied on the Texas constitution or state law whenever possible.[42] His judicial philosophy looked first to the state's constitution to resolve a dispute, and then to the federal constitution. Justice Doggett consistently embraced this position, as well.[43] Gammage also made certain that the ruling did not fall short of the "minimal rule for a diverse nation," established by US Supreme Court precedent.[44] This judicial philosophy reflects the position that "state courts no less than federal are and ought to be the guardians of our liberties."[45] Members of the conservative bloc at the time, such as Justices Hecht, Cook, and Cornyn, often disagreed with the primacy approach, when a federal constitutional right was allegedly violated.[46] This is not to suggest that other justices, either conservative or liberal, were necessarily in error in their approach to judicial review, but merely as a way to compare Gammage's judicial philosophy with that of his associates who relied more often on federal court precedent to resolve an issue, with little or no examination of the Texas constitution.[47]

On several occasions, Gammage's critics labeled him as a liberal judicial activist because of his broad interpretation of individual rights and liberties found in the Texas constitution. Activism is often used pejoratively by political commentators, but scholars also use the term to characterize the willingness of a justice to exercise judicial review. Much like the ideological labels liberal and conservative, the concepts of activism and restraint are limited in what they can explain about judicial behavior, but they too have become accepted intellectual shortcuts.[48]

An activist justice is more open to change and innovation, which suggests a greater willingness to break from precedent or interpret precedent in a manner that allows the law to meet the needs of an evolving society. For instance, the US Supreme Court's same-sex marriage ruling in 2015 was not only an adaptation of existing constitutional and legal precedent in order to protect the dignity of persons in same-sex relationships, but also a recognition by the court of the rapid changes in the attitudes of American toward gays and lesbians. In *Obergefell v. Hodges*, Justice Anthony Kennedy wrote that our society's views toward homosexuality have undergone change: no longer treating it as a disease or disorder but as a normal expression of human sexuality; ending the punishment of same-sex intimacy; and recognizing (by many states) same-sex unions and ultimately, marriage between members of the same sex. States began to allow gays and lesbians to adopt children individually and as same-sex couples. For this reason, argued Kennedy, attempts to deny same-sex couples the right to marry is a violation of the Due Process Clause and the Equal Protection Clause of the Fourteenth Amendment.[49] Without calling it activism *per se*, the dissenters in that case characterized the majority's ruling as a usurpation of the states' authority to define marriage and an articulation of rights that do not exist in the constitution.

When justice or fairness demands, the activist may rely on unenumerated, or implied, constitutional rights, or even the findings of social sciences. Furthermore, when faced with a dispute raising a constitutional challenge to a law, the activist judge may be more willing to challenge the legislative branch. Gammage proceeded from the presumption that the legislature acted constitutionally, but this presumption was never automatic. He placed the burden squarely on the legislature to prove that there is a compelling basis for the law. He would likely bristle at the thought of being classified as an activist, as might any judge, because the term suggests a disregard for precedent or established law, which Gammage was careful to follow.

Another characterization of judicial activism is when a judge decides a case based on his or her moral and political leanings instead of the law. Gammage often spoke of higher principles found in the constitution or the common law, but he strove to avoid moral questions, *per se*, preferring a legal solution over a moral one. Decisions cannot be made in a moral or political vacuum, in some instances, a ruling based on morality alone might be justifiable, particularly if a "higher law" has been implicated by an ordinary civil law.[50] Gammage was criticized on occasion for engaging in results-oriented judging, that is, for imposing his own policy preferences or sense of fairness. In three cases, *Valenzuela*, *Morales*, and *Boyles*, Gammage seemed outraged by the plight of the injured parties: the family of the gynecologist hounded by the protestors, the gays and lesbians unfairly classified by the sodomy law, and the young woman who was clandestinely videotaped while having sex with her boyfriend. He cited precedent and established doctrine to right these wrongs, but the morally offensive nature of the actions influenced his decisions, as well.

Turning to the mode of judging characterized as judicial restraint, we find that the judge embraces a more restrained application of judicial review. In a dispute raising a constitutional challenge to a law, the restraintist proceeds with the presumption that the legislature or governmental entity has acted constitutionally and is more likely to place the burden to prove unconstitutionality on the parties challenging the law. Many of the conservative justices with whom Gammage served were restraintists, very often resistant to adopting new common law doctrines, or expanding the court's jurisdiction, or challenging the prerogatives of local school districts. Some were also strict constructionists, interpreting the constitution narrowly (in some instances literally). A strict interpretation of the term "speech" would likely result in limits on the kinds of expression protected by the First Amendment. Therefore, governmental restrictions on symbolic forms of expression, such as flag burning or erotic dancing, would more likely be upheld.[51] Many judges would find "restraintist" to be an empty term in the modern era, preferring instead terms such as "strict constructionism" or, as in the tradition of the late Justice Antonin Scalia, "originalism" or "textualism."

In the end, the terms "activist" and "restraintist," "liberal," or "conservative" assist in the understanding of a judge's record, but they cannot fully explain the judicial philosophy that produces particular outcomes. Gammage intimated on many occasions that the term "judicial activism" does not necessarily have negative connotations. Rather than seeing it as a misuse of judicial authority, it ought to be seen as being independent and objective; not being swayed by majoritarian forces or stymied by the legal or constitutional status quo. In many of Gammage's dissenting opinions, he criticized his colleagues for turning a blind eye toward precedent. Clearly, ignoring, twisting, or overturning precedent runs counter to the judicial norm. A court that ignores precedent in order to reach a desired outcome might be considered an activist court. However, if the precedent is wrongly decided using a cramped, incorrect, or ideologically motivated construction of the constitution, it could be considered an activist decision. So the decision to overturn it would not be activism.

Judges themselves believe that the courts may go too far in interpreting or reinterpreting policy to the point of unnecessarily second-guessing lower court judges and legislatures. US Supreme Court justice John Paul Stevens once wrote in a dissenting opinion that although "it is a proper part of the judicial function to make laws as a necessary by-product of the process of deciding actual cases and controversies . . . to reach out so blatantly and unnecessarily to make new law in a case of this kind is unabashed judicial activism."[52] Objections to a court's incursion into the legislative realm are based on separation of powers arguments—that is, the court is "legislating from the bench."[53]

Another dimension of the institutional element of Gammage's jurisprudence was his commitment to the principle of judicial independence. He believed that judges must to be free from outside political pressure in order to make impartial and sound decisions. Beginning with his terms in the state legislature, including his role as a delegate in the 1974 constitutional convention, he worked to reform the method of judicial selection and restructure the judicial branch in order to strengthen the independence and impartiality of judges. Judicial candidates should not be under pressure to promise a particular kind of outcome in cases; nor should judges be forced to accede to the fact that they cannot win office without the support of a powerful cartel of professional interests. Gammage's recusal philosophy in *Rogers v. Bradley* in 1995 states that the focus should be not only on the judge's behavior or appearance of any conflict of interests but also on the activities of persons or entities that have a disproportionate influence on the outcome of judicial elections. His position would not change Texas recusal law in the short term, but his progressive position on recusal was later reflected in the US Supreme Court's 2009 groundbreaking ruling in *Caperton v. Massey Coal Company*-[54]that third party attack ads, coupled with weak judicial recusal laws, have the potential to undermine independence and thus threaten due process. Wealthy individuals, like the CEO of Massey Coal, or the slick Court Wars video bankrolled by the Texas Medical Association, create the appearance that justice is for sale.

Gammage did not believe that judicial independence meant rule by judicial fiat, or that the judicial branch was first among equals, but that decisions should be governed by precedent, the law, and by facts, not by elections or campaign contributions. This was the position he brought to the reform movement. It is unfortunate that the realities of fundraising and highly partisan campaigns drove Gammage, as well as other talented and committed judges, to resign or not seek reelection.

COURT WARS 2020: STATE AND NATIONAL TRENDS IN JUDICIAL POLITICS

Chapter 4 documented a long and complex history of judicial reform efforts in the Lone Star State. Texas has faced many problems, including ethical lapses of judges, runaway campaign contributions, weak recusal standards, a lack of gender and racial diversity on the bench, and low public confidence in the justice system, to name but a few. Reformers have had some success, such as the Judicial Campaign Finance Act of 1995, but a political culture resistant to change, competing vested interests, and the inability to reach a consensus, have precluded many problems from being resolved. There is widespread consensus, however, that the root cause of most of these intractable problems is the method by which judges are selected in the state: partisan election.

In 1995, the year Gammage announced his retirement from the bench, he was hopeful that the legislature would replace partisan election with the merit plan for all appellate judges.[55] Another bill that year called for the nonpartisan election of district (trial court) judges.[56] There was also a proposed constitutional amendment[57] that would have provided for the appointment of appellate justices and judges by the governor, with staggered retention elections on a nonpartisan ballot. A second proposed constitutional amendment called for the election of district court judges initially through nonpartisan election, but then employ retention election plan following a term of office.[58] These bills would have abolished all party labels and straight-ticket voting. None of these reforms passed. Professor Anthony Champagne, succinctly summed up the problem when he observed:

> On the surface, Texas seemed to have all the components that one might think necessary for change: Intensely partisan and expensive judicial elections; a major judicial scandal; widespread negative publicity about the state's judiciary; and an active reform movement led by a well-known major figure. Still the system did not change.[59]

During every legislative session since 1995, measures have been introduced to reform Texas' method of judicial selection. Texas continues to use partisan elections with straight-ticket voting, however, since straight-ticket voting will be phased out in 2020 by an act of the legislature, if Texas lawmakers decide to replace the partisan election of judges, they would likely choose from one of three viable options: (1) nonpartisan election of judges, (2) gubernatorial appointment of judges with the use of a nominating commission and Senate confirmation, and (3) gubernatorial appointment of judges with the use of a nominating commission and retention elections following a judge's term of office. Changing the method of selection from partisan to nonpartisan election would require legislation passed by a majority vote in both houses of the legislature, followed by the governor's approval. However, the adoption of options two and three would require a constitutional amendment, since the Texas charter requires the popular election of judges.[60] The constitution cannot be amended without the two-thirds vote of both houses of the legislature to propose the amendment and a majority of voters of the state to ratify it.

Table 5.3 shows the methods of selection used by the fifty states as of 2019, including the date that each state adopted its current method to illustrate possible trends.[61] Notwithstanding holdouts like Texas and the six other

Table 5.3 Methods of Selection: State Courts of Last Resort (Including Date of Adoption of Current Method)

Partisan Election	*Nonpartisan Election*	*Pure Gubernatorial (G) or Legislative (L) Appointment*	*Merit Selection (Assisted Appointment)**
Alabama—1850	Arkansas—2001	Maine (G/Senate)—1819	Alaska (nc/re)—1959
Illinois—1848	Georgia—1983	New Jersey (G/Senate)—1844	Arizona (nc/re)—1974
Louisiana—1852	Idaho—1934	South Carolina (L)—1778	California (nc/re)—1934
Ohio—1851	Kentucky—1975	Virginia (L)—1870	Colorado (nc/re)—1966
Pennsylvania—1850***	Michigan—1939		Connecticut (nc/both houses)—1986
Texas—1851	Minnesota—1912		Delaware (nc/Senate)—1977
West Virginia—1862	Mississippi—1994		Florida (nc/re)—1976
	Montana**—1935		Hawaii (nc/Senate)—1978
	Nevada—1864		Indiana (nc/re)—1970
	North Carolina—2002		Iowa (nc/re)—1962
	North Dakota—1909		Kansas (nc/re)—1958
	Oregon—1931		Maryland (nc/senate/re)—1976
	Washington—1907		Massachusetts (nc/lifetime term)—1780
	Wisconsin—1848		Missouri (nc/re)—1940
			Nebraska (nc/re)—1962
			New Hampshire (nc/executive council)—2000
			New Mexico (nc/re)—1965
			New York (nc/Senate)—1977
			Oklahoma (nc/re)—1987
			Rhode Island (nc/both houses)—1994
			South Dakota (nc/re)—1980
			Tennessee (nc/both houses)—1994
			Utah (nc/Senate)—1985
			Vermont (nc/senate/both houses)—1974
			Wyoming (nc/re)—1972
Total: 7 states	Total: 14 states	Total: 4 states	Total: 25 states

*Originally called Missouri Plan; later called merit selection; more recently referred to as assisted appointment. In most instances, the governor appoints using nominating commission. (nc) followed by retention election (re) at the end of judges' designated term.

**In 1973 a judicial nomination commission was created to recommend candidates to the governor to fill vacancies. In 1974 a law was passed requiring that when an incumbent judge is unopposed for reelection, the ballot asks voters whether the judge should be retained.

***All judges then run in retention elections after serving a term of office.

Source: Based on data provided by the National Center for State Courts, 2018.

states that use partisan election, the trends over time in the United States have steadily been in the direction of nonpartisan elections and merit selection. Reforms occurring in the twenty-first century included the decisions of Arkansas and North Carolina to move from partisan to nonpartisan elections in 2001 and 2002. New Hampshire, which adopted a nominating commission in 2002, employs an unusual selection method in which the governor appoints a candidate based on the recommendations of the state's judicial nominating commission. The candidate is then, in turn, confirmed by the popularly elected five-member New Hampshire Executive Council.[62]

The primary advantage of continuing to utilize an elective system in Texas is maintaining the accountability of judges to voters, thus offsetting the influence of the governor and legislature over the composition of the judiciary, as well as guaranteeing to the electorate the power to remove unethical or incompetent judges. Among the twenty-two states that use an elective system, some variation exists. Michigan, state supreme court candidates are nominated by political parties at state conventions but appear on the ballot in the general election without party affiliation. In New York's unusual election system, judicial candidates in the general election are chosen by party convention delegates who must first be chosen by voters. In North Dakota, the two candidates receiving the highest number of votes in a nonpartisan primary election run against each other in a nonpartisan general election. Ohio is another large state that uses nonpartisan general elections, although candidates run in party primaries.

Theoretically, the advantage of adopting nonpartisan elections in Texas would be that voters could continue to hold judges accountable at the ballot box, but no longer be able to rely solely on party labels alone; instead voters would need to educate themselves about the candidate's qualifications and record using bar poll results, candidate websites, or newspaper and social media endorsements. In partisan elections, party labels are often all that voters need to make a choice—even though most disputes before the courts have little to do partisanship or positions on the high visibility cultural issues, such as abortion or same-sex marriage, and more to do with property disputes, corporate law, criminal due process, contracts, and tort law. Efforts to adopt nonpartisan elections in Texas have been thwarted not only by political party organizations, and political action committees but by those who fear that without partisan cues, voters would either avoid voting for judicial candidates down ballot, or choose candidates based on surnames, thus placing those with Hispanic (or non-Anglo) names at a disadvantage. Of course, the major disadvantages of any form of elective method of selection include the politicization of the law and an increase in the role that money places in the judicial selection process.[63]

In addition to Texas, only three other states (Alabama, Indiana, and Pennsylvania) use straight-ticket party voting. Indiana elects only trial judges in partisan elections—intermediate and Supreme Court justices are appointed by the governor using the recommendations of nominating commissions. Pennsylvania holds partisan elections but then after judge serves a term of office, retention elections are subsequently held.[64] Thus, as of 2019, only Alabama and Texas use straight-ticket partisan elections for all judicial offices. The main problem associated with straight-ticket voting is that it results in partisan sweeps, in which a vast majority of voters are voting for down ballot judicial candidates only as a result of their straight-ticket partisan votes for candidates at the top of the ballot, with little or no consideration of the qualifications and record of judicial candidates. However, this problem will become moot in 2020, when straight-ticket voting for all candidates on the ballot will no longer exist in Texas.[65]

In the twenty-four states that use merit selection, in most instances, the governor makes the initial appointment using some form of nominating commission. Following the candidate's initial appointment (in the majority of states that use a merit plan), a retention election is held at the end of the judge's designated term. In 1934, California became the first state to adopt an appointive system that was coupled with retention elections. Then, nearly thirty years later, in 1960, the state's voters approved an initiative measure creating a commission on judicial performance that confirms the governor's appointments. The three-member commission consists of the chief justice, the attorney general, and the senior presiding justice of the state's court of appeals. California justices then go on to serve twelve-year terms (double the six-year terms of justices in Texas), after which they run unopposed in retention elections. New Jersey and Maine have relied solely on the governor and state Senate since the nineteenth century; justices in both states serve seven-year terms after which they must go through the same appointment and confirmation process again. Neither of the two states requires the governor to use a nominating commission to create a list of qualified candidates from which to choose, but governors have voluntarily adopted the practice of consulting a judicial selection committee.

Problems with merit selection include the fact that it can be a closed system, rife with insider politics, and lacking strong incentives to promote gender and racial diversity. Many nominating commission meetings are conducted behind closed doors and the records of potential nominees are kept secret. A newly elected governor comes into office with not only his or her ideological preferences, but also a preference for potential commission members who have their own ideas on how judges ought to rule on issues ranging from insurance regulation, medical malpractice, or civil rights. It is important to note that Texas and forty-eight other states give the governor power to appoint judges to fill midterm vacancies or unexpired terms of office.

Only two states, Illinois and Louisiana, legally prohibit the governor from making interim appointments. Interestingly, in Illinois, the role of making interim appointments falls to the state supreme court. The appointee then runs in the next general election. Louisiana uses special elections called by the governor to fill vacancies that occur on the bench. The advantages of gubernatorial appointment with a nominating commission include: maximizing judicial independence and eliminating the role of money in judicial campaigns. Disadvantages include the lack of accountability to voters and the possibility of political patronage or cronyism. The use of nonpartisan nominating commissions *and* retention elections, however, strikes a balance between judicial independence and accountability.

With New Hampshire being the last state to adopt merit selection (in 2000), twenty-four states require the governor to select nominees from a list of candidates selected by a nominating commission. Terms of office after the initial appointment is made varies widely, with some judges serving for life—as in Massachusetts and New Hampshire—and others running in retention elections after a six-year term—as in Alaska and Florida. Since 1780, Massachusetts has used a constitutionally created governor's council—not the legislature—to approve the governor's appointments. The benefit of what was first eponymously called the Missouri Plan, but later called merit selection, is that it enables the governor to appoint a qualified candidate to serve for a term of office while giving the voters the opportunity to hold the incumbent justice accountable through a nonpartisan retention election. Voters are asked to "retain" or "do not retain" a justice after he or she serves a term of office. As more states adopted merit selection, some began experimenting with nominating commissions consisting of various combinations of judges, attorneys general, lawyers, and lay experts (typically academics).

Appointment based on the recommendations of nominating commissions ideally promotes judicial independence and competency. However, retention systems do not always eliminate the myriad of problems associated with elections. For example, if retention elections become highly competitive (and perhaps are fueled by "dark money" contributions) or if special interests seek specific outcomes from the judicial branch that favor big business or advance a cultural agenda, we witness the corrupting influence campaign contributions and negative attack campaigning intended to unseat incumbents. Last minute "hit jobs" occur days before an election when opponents of the incumbent judge run slick television ads accusing the judge of everything from being soft on criminals to child abuse. Vermont addresses this problem by using a retention vote by the state legislature rather than popular vote.

Only two states—South Carolina and Virginia—rely solely on their state legislature to appoint justices. Although we tend to compare each of the methods of selection in the states with the federal model (president appoints, Senate confirms, and judge holds office for life), in many ways legislative appointment embodies the republican ideal of having the most representative body choose judges. Recall from the discussion in chapter 4, the Texas Republic's 1836 constitution delegated to the Texas Congress alone the power to elect judges, using a joint vote of both houses, and to create courts inferior to the Supreme Court. In South Carolina, both chambers of the state's legislature conduct a joint vote to select the state's justices, who then serve decade-long terms before they stand for reelection by the legislature. In Virginia, the two chambers of the general assembly hold separate votes. Justices then serve for twelve years before standing for reelection by the legislature. Very few states have even considered moving to adopt this method of selection. The method is not without flaws, including a lack of checks and balances and a tendency to appoint a disproportionate number of legislators to the judiciary. In addition, given the current reality of extreme political polarization, one-party domination, and dysfunctional legislatures, it is highly unlikely that Texas, or any other state, will adopt legislative appointment of judges.

It is important to note that for all of the arguments for and against election or appointment, at the end of Election Day, however, 70 percent of all judges on state appellate courts are elected by voters. It is just a question of at which point in the respective state's selection process that voters provide their input: a party primary, a special election, the general election, or retention elections.

The problem of money in judicial elections figured prominently in our discussion of "Court Wars" in Texas in the previous chapter. As we enter the second decade of the twenty-first century, a recent snapshot of campaign spending in judicial elections nationwide, published in 2017 by the Brennan Center for Justice, showed that campaign contributions in thirty-three state supreme court races approached $70 million. This amount includes the sum of all candidate fundraising, spending by outside groups, and spending by political parties. Pennsylvania led all other states with a total of $21,417,861 for three open seats, followed by North Carolina at $5,19,151 for one open seat, and West Virginia at $4,963,973 for one seat. Texas was a distant seventh with $4,205,358 for a total of three open seats.[66] Nationally, the largest contributors included the usual cohorts—led by business interest groups, lawyers, lobbyists, political parties, and, to a lesser extent, labor unions. Most of the money was spent for media ads, specifically the same type of negative media ads that we have seen in Texas: attacking candidates as weak on crime (regardless of whether their court has criminal jurisdiction), failing to protect women and children, being in the pockets of trial lawyers, or in thrall to big business.[67]

Nationally, the top three individual fundraisers for judicial races in the 2015–2016 election cycle were all from Pennsylvania. Kevin M. Dougherty raised $5,650,148, David N. Wecht $3,642, 568, and Christine L. Donohue $2,107, 886. Two candidates for the Texas Supreme Court were among the top ten individual candidate fundraisers according to the same study.[68] Incumbent justices Eva Guzman was ranked sixth nationally with total contributions raised at $1,126,348 and Debra Lehrmann ranked tenth, having raised $994,854.[69]

In one high-profile race in the 2018 election cycle in Arkansas, nearly two million dollars was spent in an attempt to unseat one justice on the Arkansas Supreme Court named Courtney Goodson because of her ruling on voter ID laws, which is one of the newest wedge or "dog-whistle" issues in national and state politics. Four years earlier, the Arkansas Supreme Court unanimously struck down a state voter ID law,[70] with Goodson concurring (the court then upheld a revised voter ID law in 2018). Defending herself against a blitz of televisions attacks from the political right, Goodson successfully deflected attacks by framing her reelection in terms of her opposition to "dark money" in the state's judicial races. Dark money is that which is spent by "outside groups" who conceal the identity of contributors.[71] Groups target a judicial election or confirmation fight and then funnel millions into that state. Although Arkansas has used nonpartisan elections, Goodson's critics ran ads calling her a "stooge" for then-president Obama, accusing her of inappropriate vacation trips, being in cahoots with Democratic trial attorneys, and encouraging illegal immigrants to vote. Judicial Watch, a right-wing organization that arose during President Bill Clinton's impeachment, spent over $600,000 in 2016 successfully thwarting Goodson's campaign for chief justice. Over $1 million was spent by another conservative group, the Judicial Fairness Initiative, to defeat Goodson in 2018. Despite last-minute attack ads, Goodson went on to win reelection.[72] Notwithstanding Goodson's successful reelection campaign, many incumbent judges are watching their backs as outside groups pour dark money into states.

In addition to the threat of "dark money," another recent attack strategy on judges—and entire courts, for that matter—are partisan-motivated impeachment threats by Republicans who have achieved supermajorities in state legislatures.[73] In 2018, there was an effort to impeach the entire West Virginia Supreme Court for a host of ethical violations. Recall, from chapter 4, that the behavior of several justices on that state's highest court led to the US Supreme Court's ruling in *Caperton* in 2009. In 2018, Republican legislators in Pennsylvania passed articles of impeachment against state supreme court justices who had the temerity to strike down as unconstitutional the state's gerrymandered congressional map.[74]

One of the major reform issues in 2020 is the representation of minorities and women on the bench in Texas and other states. Although some lingering debate remains over whether judges are in the true sense of the word "representatives," the argument for increasing minority and gender representation on state courts is, simply put, that our judges ought to look like the populations they serve; that the personal backgrounds of judges influence how decisions are made. As with any branch of government, representation of minorities and women in judicial positions adds to the perceived legitimacy of decisions.

There are currently 3,151 judges serving on courts in Texas. This number includes the state's 2 highest appellate courts, 14 intermediate courts of appeal, 477 district courts, 524 county-level courts, 18 probate courts, 802 justice courts, and 1,325 municipal courts. When looking at the racial and ethnic composition of the Texas courts, according to the *Gavel Gap* study undertaken in 2013 by the American Constitution Society, around 26 percent of all judges in Texas are considered to be judges of color (the study does not break this category down into specific races or ethnicities), even though people of color as percentage of state population in Texas is approximately 55 percent. This fact, according to *Gavel Gap*, makes Texas thirty-first in terms of its "representativeness rank."[75] Based on comparable demographic data made available by the Texas Office of Court Administration in 2018, the percentage of judges of color is 24 percent of all judges statewide, with approximately 5 percent African American, 17 percent Hispanic/Latino, 1 percent Asian, and less than a third of 1 percent Native American.[76] The state's population as a whole is 70.4 percent white, 32.8 percent Hispanic/Latino, 11.8 percent African-American, 0.7 percent Asian, and 0.1 percent Native American.

In terms of gender representativeness of Texas courts, women make up 50 percent of the total state population but 35 percent of all state judges according to the *Gavel Gap* study. This finding ranks Texas tenth in overall gender representativeness, following closely behind Massachusetts at ninth with women making up 37 percent of the state's judges. Oregon ranks first with women making up 44 percent of all state judges. No state has the same percentage of woman judges as women residents. Nationally, women make up more than 50 percent of the population of the United States but represent only around 30 percent of state judges. This finding is in light of the fact that women make up one-half of law students nationally but are only one-third of all judges.[77]

The authors of the Gavel Gap study also published the findings of a second project undertaken in 2014, focusing on all appellate courts and general jurisdiction trial courts in the nation. A breakdown of all state courts in the United States found that 80 percent of all state judges are white, 7 percent African American, and 5 percent Hispanic. In terms of gender representativeness, 70 percent of all state judges are male and 30 percent female.[78] Proposed solutions to the problem of underrepresentativeness include increasing law school graduation rates (and bar passage rates), greater diversity in major law firms, and the adoption of reforms in the methods by which judges are selected.

Concluding the discussion of Court Wars would not be complete without a brief discussion of some of the recent electoral trends in Texas judicial politics. Republicans have not only dominated the Texas judiciary since the mid-1990s but with each new election cycle, they become even more conservative than their predecessors. The presidency of Barack Obama (2008–2016) and candidacy of Hillary Clinton in 2016 motivated highly conservative Texans to vote in the Republican primaries that choose judicial candidates for the general election. This resulted in the necessity of many judicial candidates moving further to the right on the political spectrum. Many Republican incumbents and candidates fear being unseated not by Democrats in the general election but by far-right candidates in primary elections. This rightward push began during the tort reform movement and Reagan Revolution of the late 1980s and early 1990s. The Tea Party also played a role in this trend in the early 2000s, as did Trump anti-immigration populists in 2016. To a lesser extent, Democrats experienced this phenomenon in the 1970s and early 1980s, when progressive Democrats pushed judicial candidates to the left of center. Many conservative Democrats did not survive primary challenges that were mounted by younger more progressive candidates like Gammage.

Exit polls from the 2016 presidential election demonstrated that a large number of Republican voters were highly motivated by the fact that the next president would choose Justice Antonin Scalia's successor. Although to a lesser extent, Texans also followed statewide judicial politics carefully because of the same cultural issues. Since the days of Nixon's attacks on the Warren and Burger Courts as liberal judicial activists, Republicans (such as Karl Rove) have been more effective than Democrats in using "judicial activism" as a wedge issue or dog-whistle word to mobilize voter turnout. Another unfortunate trend is that state supreme court elections and confirmation hearings of federal judicial nominees have become increasingly and disturbingly similar. Both are centered less on competence and more on ideological purity on a number of hot-button cultural issues. Ideological advocacy groups spend millions of dollars on negative campaigns aimed at eroding support for candidates for state office, as well as undermining Senate support for federal judicial nominees through the use of scare tactics and personal attacks. Trump appointee Brett Kavanaugh's confirmation process in 2018 is the most recent illustration of this, although the lineage of the strategy can be traced back to the confirmation hearings of Clarence Thomas in 1991 and Robert Bork in 1987. A candidate or nominee who stands for any judicial office should reasonably expect to be attacked on the basis of sexual, moral, ideological and partisan purity.

Are there any indications that the political fortune of Democrats running for seats on the Texas judiciary will change? It is unlikely that Texas will have a Democratic governor in the near future, so Democrats will need to pick up judicial seats strictly through the electoral process.[79] Statewide demographic changes, including the growth of the Democratic strongholds in the major urban and suburban areas, such as Austin, Dallas, Houston, and San Antonio, suggested as early as 2008 that red Texas might turn purple as more Democrats win major offices. The 2018 midterm election may have begun an erosion of Republican-domination of the judiciary in Texas. The controversial and divisive presidency of Donald Trump mobilized Democratic voters, as did the candidacy of the young and charismatic Beto O'Rourke. A virtually unknown Democratic congressman from El Paso, Beto O'Rourke lost his bid to unseat incumbent US senator Ted Cruz, but in the process created a blue wave in Texas. The Beto-Effect increased voter turnout among first-time voters, college students, women, and Hispanic voters.[80] Beto voters, together with others reacting negatively to Trump, impacted many judicial races down ballot in the November 2018 election. Voting straight-ticket Democratic, Beto voters ousted two incumbent Republican members of Texas' congressional delegation, helped Democrats pick up seats in the Texas legislature, and unseated numerous incumbent Republican judges at the court of appeals and district court levels. Prior to 2018, Republicans successfully garnered majorities in the range of 55 percent to as high as 80 percent of the vote in state appellate court races. In the 2012, 2016, and 2018 general elections, Republicans won all seats up for election on the Texas Supreme Court and Court of Criminal Appeals. On the state's fourteen intermediate courts of appeal, of the thirty-seven seats up for election in 2012, Republicans won twenty-seven seats and Democrats ten seats. In 2016, of the twenty seats up for election on the state's fourteen courts of appeals, Republicans won seventeen and Democrats won three. However, a reversal of fortune occurred in the 2018 midterm general election. Of the forty-five seats up for election on the state's fourteen courts of appeal, Democrats won thirty-four seats and Republicans won only eleven. This blue wave flipped four of the fourteen state courts of appeal, including the three highly influential courts that sit in Austin, Dallas, and Houston.[81] On the Third Court of Appeals in Austin, on which Gammage served from 1982 to 1991, there were no Democrats serving on that court prior to 2018. However, in the November 2018 general election Democrats gained a 4-2 majority. All four Republicans incumbents on that court who were up for reelection lost to Democrats. The flip on the Third Court of Appeals is attributed to changing demographics in the counties that surround Austin and to Beto O'Rourke's coattails. College students at Texas State University in San Marcos who voted straight-ticket Democratic flipped Hays County into the Democratic column. Beto won twenty-three of the twenty-four counties in central Texas that fall into the judicial districts over which the Third Court of Appeals has jurisdiction and from which the justices on that court are elected. The Fifth Court of Appeals in Dallas, which hears close to 2,000 appeals a year, now has a Democratic majority.[82] Formerly very pro-business, the Dallas-based court will now have a more ideological diverse composition. The First and Fourteenth Courts of Appeals in Houston also have Democratic majorities after 2018. Democrats now have a majority of seats on seven of the state's fourteen courts appeals: the First, Third, Fourth, Fifth, Eighth, Thirteenth, and Fourteenth.[83]

What will be the immediate impact of the 2018 election? Most cases do not entail big constitutional or cultural questions but matters of law and order, divorce and family matters, property, and contracts. Ideological leanings, however, will have a major impact on cases that are on appeal to the intermediate appellate courts dealing with the rights of criminal defendants, the extent to which courts of appeal defer to jury verdicts in personal injury cases, and a myriad of lawsuits pitting consumer against businesses. State trial courts were affected, as well, most notably in those state district courts located in Harris County (Houston), where *all* Republican judges were voted out of office. Democrats controlled all seats on district courts as of January 2019. Further, of the newly elected judges in Harris County, seventeen are African American women.[84]

Democrats are aware of the fact that straight-ticket voting will be phased out in Texas in 2020, so many of the judicial candidates that benefited down ballot by Beto O'Rourke's candidacy cannot assume that they will be reelected. Yet, because of demographic changes in the state's population, a large number of seats on the state's bench will remain firmly in Democratic hands or will become competitive. As we have seen, as judicial elections become competitive, they also become more expensive. So, Texas may be faced with a new campaign contribution arms race.

Along with this blue wave in the 2018 midterm elections came renewed calls for reform, this time from many Republicans who are reexamining the wisdom of partisan elections. In 2019, in his State of the Judiciary Address to the eighty-sixth Texas legislature, Chief Justice Nathan Hecht compared the 2018 election to Hurricane Harvey and called on legislators to support merit selection and retention elections, as well as require new qualifications requirements for justices.[85] Hecht lamented:

> Of the 80 intermediate appellate judges, 28–35%—are new. A third of the 254 constitutional county judges are new. A fourth of trial judges—district, county, and justices of the peace—are new. In all, I am told, 443 Texas judges are new to their jobs. On the appellate and district courts alone, the Texas judiciary in the last election lost seven centuries of judicial experience at a single stroke.[86]

Also in 2019, longtime advocate of judicial reform, former chief justice Thomas R. Phillips reiterated that "the results of modern judicial elections are often almost random" and called on the legislature to pass a constitutional amendment that would provide for gubernatorial appointment of all judges using a bipartisan nominating commission, followed by retention elections after judges complete their terms.[87] The 2018 judicial blue wave will not only have an impact on the law, because of the election of many liberal and centrist judges, but may resuscitate a languishing reform movement that began over three decades ago.

NOTES

1. *Kirby v. Edgewood Independent School District,* 761 S.W.2d 859, 867–69 (Tex. App.—Austin 1988) (Gammage, J., dissenting), *rev'd,* 777 S.W.2d 391 (Tex. 1989).
2. Edgar Bodenheimer, *Jurisprudence: The Philosophy and Method of Law* (Cambridge: Harvard University Press, 1962), vii.
3. *Star-Telegram, Inc. v. Doe*, 915 S.W.2d. 471, 472 (Tex. 1995).
4. *Star-Telegram, Inc. v. Doe,* at 474–475. The Texas Supreme Court did not address the question of whether the information was or was not legally obtained.
5. *See Id.*, at 474–475.
6. 746 S.W.2d 203 (1987).
7. Texas Constitution, article 1, section 19.
8. Texas Constitution, article 1, section 8.
9. Texas Constitution, article 1, section 10.
10. Texas Constitution, article 1, sections 9 and 25.
11. Texas Constitution, article 6.
12. *Colquette v. Forbes*, 680 S.W.2d. 536 (Tex. App.—Austin 1984, no writ).
13. *Industrial Foundation of the South v. Texas Industrial Accident Board*, 540 S.W.2d 668 (Tex. 1976).
14. *Twyman v. Twyman*, 790 S.W. 2d 819 (1990).
15. David Crump, "Negligent infliction of emotional distress: An unlimited claim, but does it really exist?" *Texas Tech Law Review,* 49 (2017): 685.
16. *Twyman v. Twyman*, 855 S.W.2d 619, 622,623.
17. Arthur R. Hogue, *Origins of the Common Law* (Indianapolis, Liberty Press, 1966).
18. Oliver Wendell Holmes, *The Common Law* (Boston: Little, Brown and Company, 1963).
19. *Graff v. Beard*, 858 S.W.2d 918, 927 (Tex. 1993).
20. *Kirby v. Edgewood Independent School District.*
21. *San Antonio Independent School District v. Rodriguez*, 411 U.S. 1 (1973).
22. *See Barber v. Colorado Independent School District,* 901 S.W.2d 447, 453–55 (Tex. 1995) (Gammage, J., dissenting); *see also supra*, Part II.
23. *Valenzuela*, 853 S.W.2d at 512.

24. *Id.,* at 519–20 (Gammage, J., dissenting) ("[e]very person shall be at liberty to speak, write or publish his opinions on any subject, *being responsible for the abuse of that privilege . . ..*" (emphasis in original) (quoting Tex. Const. art. I, § 8)) (citing *Hustler Magazine, Inc. v. Falwell*, 485 U.S. 46, 56–57 (1988); *United States v. O'Brien*, 391 U.S. 367, 382 (1968)).

25. *Id.,* at 519.

26. *See Id.,* at 519.

27. *Frisby v. Schultz*, 487 U.S. 474 (1988).

28. *England v. Texas,* 727 S.W.2d 810 (Tex. App. – Austin 1984).

29. *Drew v. State,* 735 S.W.2d 655 (1987).

30. *Port v. State,* 736 S.W.2d 865 (Tex. App. 1987).

31. See *Jones v. Texas,* 680 S.W.2d 499 (1983).

32. The empirical research on judicial behavior by social scientists and legal scholars is too voluminous to recount here. A few excellent studies are: Vincent Martin Bonventre, "Court of Appeals: State Constitutional Review," *Pace Law Review,* 12 (1992): 1; Youngsik Lim, "An empirical analysis of Supreme Court Justices' decision making," *The Journal of Legal Studies,* 29, no. 2 (June 2000): 721–753; Jeffrey A. Segal, Lee Epstein, Charles M. Cameron, and Harold J. Spaeth, "Ideological values and the votes of justices revisited," *Journal of Politics,* 57 (August 1995): 812–823; Michael A. Bailey, "Is todays' Court the most conservative in sixty years? Challenges and opportunities in measuring judicial preferences," *Journal of Politics,* 75 (July 2013): 821–834; and Paul H. Edelman, David E. Klein, and Stefanie A. Lindquist, "Consensus, disorder, and ideology on the Supreme Court," *Journal of Empirical Legal Studies,* 9 (March 2012): 129–148.

33. See Janet Elliott and Richard Connelly, "Odd group crafts New Edgewood," *Texas Lawyer,* 6 (February 1995); and Ben Wear, "Texas Court tilts right, upends '80s decisions: Plaintiffs less likely to prevail in today's Supreme Court Statistics Show," *Austin American-Statesman*, September 13, 1995.

34. Adam Bonica and Michael J. Woodruff, "State Supreme Court ideology and 'New Style' judicial campaigns," October 31, 2012. https://ssrn.com/abstract=2169664. http://dx.doi.org/10.2139/ssrn.2169664. Ideology Scores are based at Stanford University's Social Science Data Collection: Database on Ideology, Money in Politics, and Elections; Public Version 2.0. https://data.stanford.edu/dime.

35. See Ryan Rebe, "Amicus Curiae and dissenting votes at the Texas Supreme Court," *Justice System Journal,* 34, no. 2 (2013).

36. See Julie F. Siegel, "The Supreme Court of Texas from 1989–1998: Independence determined by six-year terms," *Albany Law Review,* 62 (1999): 1649–1691. Segal's article is an excellent account of the Texas Supreme Court from 1989 to 1998—the only scholarly piece found that discusses the dynamics of the court during the time that Gammage served (as well as the only article that mentions Gammage).

37. *Morales*, 869 S.W.2d at 954 (Gammage, J., dissenting).

38. *Id.,* at 949 (citing *City of Austin v. Austin City Cemetery Association,* 28 S.W. 528, 530 (Tex. 1894)).

39. *Barber*, 901 S.W.2d at 452 (Gammage, J., dissenting).

40. *Michigan v. Long*, 463 U.S. 1032, 1035 (1983).

41. *See* Judith S. Kaye, "Dual constitutionalism in practice and principle," *St. John's Law Review,* 61 (1987): 399, 417 n. 67.

42. *See generally* Robert F. Utter, "Swimming in the jaws of the crocodile: State Court Comment of Federal Constitutional issues when disposing of cases on state constitutional grounds," *Texas Law Review,* 63 (1985): 1027–1030 (discussing the modes of state constitutional analysis).

43. Justice Doggett wrote in *R Communications v. Sharp*, 875 S.W.2d 314,315 (Tex. 1994) that "Where . . . violations of both the state and federal constitutions are alleged, we look first to the Texas Constitution."

44. Judith S. Kaye, "Contributions of State Constitutional Law to the third century of American Federalism," *Vermont Law Review,* 13 (1988): 49, 55 (noting that principles of federalism cannot be ignored).

45. William J. Brennan, Jr., "State constitutions and the protection of individual rights," *Harvard Law Review,* 90 (1977): 489, 491.

46. See, for example, *Davenport v. Garcia*, 834 S.W. 2d 4 (Tex. 1992), in which the supreme court unanimously ruled that a district court's "gag order" violated the free speech clause of the Texas constitution.

47. The approach is called lockstep. *See* Earl M. Maltz, "Lockstep analysis and the concept of federalism," *Annals of the American Academy of Political and Social Sciences,* 496 (1988): 98, 99.

48. The earliest reference to the term "judicial activism" found by this author is in a 1950 article by J. D. Hyman. He wrote in a piece on segregation that he lived in a "day that hears much talk about judicial activism." J. D. Hyman, "Segregation and the fourteenth amendment," *Vanderbilt Law Review,* 4 (1950): 555; Also see Keenan Kmiec, "The origins and meanings of 'Judicial Activism,'" *California Law Review,* 92 (2004): 1441; and Bradley C. Canon, "Defining the dimensions of judicial activism," *Judicature*, 66 (January 1983): 236.

49. *Obergefell v. Hodges*, 576 U.S. ___ (2015).

50. See Alpheus Thomas Mason, "Judicial activism: Old and new," *Virginia Law Review*, 55 (April 1969): 385.

51. See David W. Neubauer, *Judicial Process*, 2nd ed. (Fort Worth, Texas: Harcourt Brace Publishers, 1997), 502–505.

52. Justice Stevens dissenting in *Florida v. Wells*, 495 U.S. 1 (1990).

53. Some might argue that this term is so subjective ("I know it when I see it") that it ought to be excluded from serious research.

54. 129 S.Ct. 2252 (2009).

55. House Bill 810, 74th Legislative Session, 1995.

56. House Bill 811, 74th Legislative Session, 1995.

57. House Joint Resolution 60, 74th Legislative Session, 1995.

58. House Joint Resolution 61, 74th Legislative Session, 1995.

59. "Judicial reform in Texas: A look back after two decades," *Court Review,* 43, no. 2 (2006).

60. Mark P. Jones, "The selection of Judges in Texas: Analysis of the current system and of the principal reform options," *Rice University's Baker Institute for Public Policy* (January 2017), 17.

61. A massive corpus of research and commentary exists (beyond the scope of this chapter) on the methods of judicial selection in the states, chronicling the history, operation, benefits, and nuances of each method, not to mention the state-by-state variations of each of plans. In fact, many states employ a combination of methods depending on the level and jurisdiction of court and that the focus here is court of last resort. All information about the respective methods of selection discussed earlier is based on the most definitive and up-to-date source for information on judicial selection: the National Center for State Courts, "Methods of judicial selection," http://www.judicialselection.us/judicial_selection/methods/selection_of_judges.cfm?state=, accessed in 2018. Note that the adoption dates shown may not be representative of more recent attempts to modify the state's method of selection.

62. *Id.*

63. See generally Jones, "The selection of Judges in Texas".

64. *Id.*

65. https://www.texastribune.org/2017/06/01/texas-gov-greg-abbott-signs-bill-eliminate-straight-ticket-voting/; see also Chertoff and Robinson, "Check one and the accountability is done," 1781–1782.

66. Alicia Bannon, Cathleen Lisk, and Peter Hardin, "Who pays for judicial races?" *Brennan Center for Justice National Institute on Money and State Politics* (2017); and see Press Release, Brennan Center for Justice & Justice at Stake, "Spending in Pennsylvania Supreme Court race tops out over $16.5 million," November 6, 2015, http://www.brennancenter.org/press-release/spending-pennsylvania-supreme-court-race-tops-out-over-165-million.

67. *Id.*

68. *Id.*

69. *Id.*; and see chapter 5, that the Texas' Judicial Campaign Reform Act of 1995 limits contributions from individuals to $5,000 and from political action committees to $300,000. https://www.ethics.state.tx.us/guides/JCFA_Tips.pdf.

70. Andrew DeMillo, Associated Press, "Arkansas justice wins re-election despite outside spending," *U.S. News and World Report,* November 7, 2018, https://www.usnews.com/news/best-states/arkansas/articles/2018-11-06/arkansas-justice-hopes-to-survive-outside-groups-onslaught.

71. Bannon, Lisk, and Hardin, "Who pays for judicial races?" 22–25.

72. *Id.*, DeMillo, "Arkansas justice wins re-election despite outside spending."

73. Alan Greenblatt, "State Supreme Courts increasingly face Partisan impeachment threats," *Governing*, September 11, 2018, http://www.governing.com/topics/politics/gov-west-virginia-impeach-senate-trial-supreme-court-justices.html.

74. *Id.*

75. E. George Tracey and Albert H. Yoon, "The gavel gap: Who sits in judgment on State Courts?" *American Constitution Society for Law and Policy* (2013).

76. "Profile of trial and appellate judges," *Texas Judicial Branch*, http://www.txcourts.gov/media/1436283/judge-profile-sept-16.pdf.

77. Tracey and Yoon, "The gavel gap," 2.

78. E. George Tracey and Albert H. Yoon, "Measuring justice in State Courts," *Vanderbilt Law Review,* 70 (2017): 1887.

79. The current governor of Texas, Gregg Abbott, has appointed over thirty judges since taking office in 2014 (including one Supreme Court justice and five court of appeals judges). His predecessor, Rick Perry (2000–2015), appointed 118 judges (including eight Supreme Court justices and thirty-one court of appeals judges).

80. R. G. Ratcliffe, "Beto O'Rourke lost the battle but won the war," *Texas Monthly,* November 7, 2018, https://www.texasmonthly.com/politics/beto-orourke-lost-battle-won-war/.

81. *The Dallas Morning News*, "Other voices: Unsung blue wave puts Texas' most powerful courts in Democratic hands," November 13, 2018, https://www.news-journal.com/opinion/other-voices-unsung-blue-wave-puts-texas-most-powerful-courts/article_d4510ba2-e6d3-11e8-81e1-637c77b834b9.html.

82. John Council, "Three Dallas democratic Judges Announce bids for Fifth Court of appeals," *Texas Lawyer*, December 11, 2018, https://www.law.com/texaslawyer/2018/12/11/three-dallas-democratic-judges-announce-bids-for-fifth-court-of-appeals/?slreturn=20190015171944.

83. Emma Platoff, "Texas democrats' biggest win on election night may have been the courts," KUT-90.5.org, November 8, 2018, http://www.kut.org/post/texas-democrats-biggest-win-election-night-may-have-been-courts.

84. Mark Curriden, "Businesses face major changes in litigation appeals in Texas," *Houston Chronicle,* November 23, 2018, https://www.chron.com/news/article/Businesses-face-major-changes-in-litigation-13417538.php.

85. Emma Platoff and Julie McCullough, "Texas Supreme Court Chief Justice Nathan Hecht calls for nonpartisan judicial elections, bail reform," *Texas Tribune,* February 6, 2019, https://www.texastribune.org/2019/02/06/texas-supreme-court-judicial-elections-bail-reform-nathan-hecht/.

86. Chief Justice Nathan L. Hecht, *The State of the Judiciary in Texas. An Address to the 86th Texas Legislature*, February 6, 2019, https://www.txcourts.gov/media/1443500/soj2019.pdf.

87. Thomas R. Phillips, "Commentary: Judicial selection reforms are long overdue in Texas," *Statesman.com*, April 15, 2019, https://www.statesman.com/opinion/20190415/commentary-judicial-selection-reforms-are-long-overdue-in-texas.

Appendix

List of Cases

CHAPTER 1

Barber v. Colo. Independent School District, 901 S.W.2d 447, 455 (Tex. 1995).
Kirby v. Edgewood Independent School District, 761 S.W.2d 859 (Tex. App – Austin 1988).
San Antonino Independent School District v. Rodriquez, 411 U.S. 1 (1973).
Lawrence v. Texas, 539 U.S. 558 (2003).
State v. Morales, 869 S.W.2d 941 (Tex. 1994).
Michigan v. Long, 463 U.S. 1032 (1983).

CHAPTER 2

Kirby v. Edgewood Independent School District, 761 S.W.2d 859 (Tex. App.—Austin 1988).
Jones v. Texas, 680 S.W.2d 499 (1983).
Jacobson v. Texas, No. PD-1466-11 (2013).
England v. Texas, 727 S.W.2d 810 (Tex. App. – Austin 1984).
Schmuck v. United States, 489 U.S. 705 (1989).
Hall v. State, 225 S.W.3d 524 (Tex. Crim. App. 2007).
Drew v. State, 735 S.W.2d 655, 656 (1987).
Aguilar v. State, 682 S.W.2d 556 (Tex. Cr. App. 1985).
Royster v. State, 622 S.W.2d 442 (Tex. Cr. App. 1981).
Drew v. State, 735 S.W.2d 655 (1987).
Thompson v. State, 521 S.W.2d 230 (Tex. Cr. App. 1980).
Lugo v. State, 667 S.W.2d 144 (Tex. Cr. App. 1984).

Thomas v. State, 701 S.W. 2d 653, 656 (Tex. Cr. App. 1985).
Hall v. State, 225 S.W.3d 524 (Tex. Crim. App. 2007).
Port v. Texas, 736 S.W.2d 865 (1987).
Port v. State, 736 S.W.2d 865 (Tex. App. 1987).
Selman v. State, 663 S.W.2d 838 (Tex.Cr.App. 1984).
Dunn v. State, 721 S.W. 2d 325 (Tex.Cr.App. 1986).
Briddle v. State, 742 S.W.2d 379 (Tex. Cr. App. 1987).
Bryant v. Texas, 793 S.W.2d 59 (1990).
Walker v. Texas, 701 S.W.2d 316 (1985).
Brown v. State, 657 S.W.2d 797, 799 (Tex.Cr.App.1983).
Colquette v. Forbes, 680 S.W.2d. 536 (Tex. App.—Austin 1984).
Magallanez v. Magallanez, 911 S.W.2d 91 (1995).
Griswold v. Connecticut, 381 U.S. 479 (1965).
Billings v. Atkinson, 489 S.W. 2d 858, 859 (Tex. 1973).
City of Sherman v. Henry, 928 S.W.2d 464 (Tex. 1996).
Texas State Employees Union v. Texas Dept. of Mental Health and Mental Retardation, 746 S.W.2d 203 (Tex. 1987).
In re H.E.B. Grocery Co., L.P., 2014 WL 700749 (Tex. App. Corpus Christi 2014).
Industrial Foundation of the South v. Texas Industrial Accident Board, 540 S.W.2d 668 (Tex. 1976).
Texas Comptroller of Public Accounts v. Attorney General of Texas, 244 S.W.3d 629 (Tex. App. Austin 2008).
Roberts v. Houston Independent School District., 788 S.W.2d 107(1990).
Billings v. Atkinson, 489 S.W. 2d 858, 861 (Tex. 1973).
Milner v. Red River Publishing Company, 249 S.W. 2d 227 (Tex. Civ. App. – Dallas 1952, no writ).
Figure World v. Farley, 680 S.W.2d 33 (1984).
Rawlings v. Angelo State University, 648 S.W.2d 430 (1983).
City of Austin v. Davis, 693 S.W.2d 31 (1985).
Landreth v. Reed, 570 S.W.2d 486 (Tex.Civ.App.1978, writ dism'd).
City of Austin v. Davis, 693 S.W. 2d 31 (1985).
Hill v. Kimball, 76 Tex. 210, 13 S.W. 59 (1890).
Twyman v. Twyman, 855 S.W.2d 819 (Tex. 1993).
Underwriters Life Ins. Co. v. Cobb, 746 S.W.2d 810, 819 (Tex. App.—Corpus Christi 1988, no writ).
Bounds v. Caudle, 560 S.W.2d 925 (Tex. 1977).
Texas State Teacher's Association v. State, 711 S.W.2d 421 (1986).
Price v. City of San Marcos, 744 S.W.2d 349 (1988).
Twyman v. Twyman, 790 S.W.2d 819 (Tex. App. Austin 1990).
Twyman v. Twyman, 855 S.W.2d 619 (1993).
Boyles v. Kerr, 855 S.W.2d 593 (Tex. 1993).

Edgewood v. Kirby, Brown v. Board of Education, 347 U.S. 483 (1954).
Mendez v. Westminster School District, 161 F.2d 774 (9th Cir. 1947).
Swann v. Charlotte-Mecklenburg Board of Education, 402 U.S. 1 (1971).
Spring Branch Independent School District v. Stamos, 695 S.W.2d 556, 695 S.W.2d 556, 560 (Tex. 1985).
San Antonio Independent School District v. Rodriguez, 411 U.S. 1 (1973).
Stout v. Grand Prairie Independent School District., 733 S.W.2d 290 (Tex. App.—Dallas 1987).
Texas State Employees Union v. Texas Department of Mental Health & Mental Retardation, 746 S.W.2d 203, 205 (Tex. 1987).
Holick v. Smith, 685 S.W.2d 18, 20 (Tex. 1985).
Waller v. State, 68 S.W.2d 601, 604 (Tex. Civ. App.—Amarillo 1934).
Richmond Newspapers, Inc. v. Virginia, 448 U.S. 555, 579 (1980).
DeShaney v. Winnebago County Department of Social Services, 489 U.S. 189 (1989).
Poelker v. Doe, 432 U.S. 519, 521 (1977).
Edgewood Independent School District v. Kirby (*Edgewood I*), 777 S.W.2d 391, 399 (Tex. 1989).
Texas State Teacher's Association v. State, 711 S.W.2d 421 (1986).
City of Coleman v. Rhone, 222 S.W.2d 646 (Tex. Civ. App. 1949).
City of *Breckinridge v. Cozart*, 478 S.W.2d 162 (Tex. Civ.App. 1972).
Garcetti v. Ceballos, 547 U.S. 410 (2006).
Price v. City of San Marcos, 744 S.W.2d 349 (1988).
Tarrant County v. Ashmore, 635 S.W.2d 417 (Tex. 1982).
Massachusetts Indemnity and Life Insurance Co. v. Texas State Board of Insurance, 685 S.W.2d 104 (Tex. App.1985).
Pickering v. Board of Education, 391 U.S. 563 (1968).
Connick v. Myers 461 U.S. 138 (1983).

CHAPTER 3

Kirby v. Edgewood Independent School District, 761 S.W.2d 859 (Tex. App.—Austin 1988).
Edgewood Independent School District v. Kirby (Edgewood I), 777 S.W.2d 391, 399 (Tex. 1989)
Edgewood Independent School District v. Kirby (*Edgewood II*), 804 S.W.2d 491, 493, 495 (Tex. 1991).
Carrollton-Farmers Branch Independent School District v. Edgewood Independent School District. (*Edgewood III*), 826 S.W.2d 489, 492 (Tex. 1992).
Edgewood Independent School District v. Meno (*Edgewood IV*), 917 S.W.2d 717, 727 (Tex. 1995).

Texas Department of Mental Health v. Opal Petty, 848 S.W.2d 680 (1992).
Valenzuela v. Aquino, 853 S.W.2d 512 (Tex. 1993).
Frisby v. Schultz, 487 U.S. 474 (1988).
United States v. O'Brien, 391 U.S. 367 (1968).
Casso v. Brand, 776 S. W. 2d 551 (1989).
Billings v. Atkinson, 489 S.W. 2d 858 (1973).
Star Telegram, Inc. v. Doe, 915 S.W.2d 471 (Tex. 1995).
Florida Star v. B.J.F, 491 U.S. 524 (1989).
Griswold v. Connecticut, 381 U.S. 479 (1965).
Roe v. Wade, 410 U.S. 113 (1973).
Industrial Foundation of the South v. Texas Industrial Accident Board, 540 S.W.2d 668 (Tex. 1976).
Kimbrough v. Coca-Cola/USA, 521 S.W.2d 719.
Diamond Shamrock Refining v. Mendez, 844 S.W.2d 198 (1992).
Cain v. Hearst Corporation, 878 S.W.2d 577 (Tex. 1994).
Time, Inc. v. Hill, 385 U.S. 374 (1967).
Boyles v. Kerr, 855 S.W.2d 593 (Tex. 1993).
Twyman v. Twyman, 855 S.W.2d 619 (Tex. 1993).
St. Elizabeth's Hospital v. Garrand, 730 S.W.2d 649 (Tex. 1987).
Graff v. Beard, 858 S.W.2d 918 (Tex. 1993).
Smith v. Sewell, El Chico Corporation v. Poole, 732 S.W.2d 306 (Tex. 1987).
Otis Engineering Corp v. Clark, 668 S.W.2d 307 (Tex. 1983).
Smith v. Merrit, Reeder v. Daniel, State v. Morales, 869 S.W.2d 941 (Tex. 1994).
Lawrence v. Texas, 539 U.S. 558 (2003).
Passel v. Fort Worth Independent School District, 440 S.W.2d. 61 (Tex. 1969).
Bowers v. Hardwick, 478 U.S. 186 (1986).
SmithKline Beecham Corporation v. Doe, 903 S.W.2d 347 (Tex. 1995).
City of Sherman v. Henry, 928 S.W.2d (1996).
Barber v. Colorado Independent School District, 901 S.W.2d 477 (Tex. 1995).
Rogers, et al. v. Bradley, 909 S.W.2d 872 (1995).

CHAPTER 4

Republican Party of Minnesota v. White, 536 U.S. 765 (2002).
Chisom v. Roemer, 501 U.S. 380 (1991).
Manges v. Guerra, 673 S.W.2d 180 (Tex. 1984).
In re Hecht, 213 S.W.3d 547. *Ex parte Ellis*, 275 S.W.2d 109 (2009).
Caperton v. Massey Coal Company, 135 U.S. 868 (2009).

Gaal v. State, 332 S.W.3d 448 (2011).
Black v. 7-Eleven Convenience Stores, No. 03-12-00014-CV, 2014 Tex. App. LEXIS 2641.
McIntosh v. Texas State Board of Dental Examiners, No. 07-12-00196-CV 2014 WL 931260.
Barfield v. Texas, No. 14-13-00518-CR, 2015 WL 1544790.
Villareal v. State, 348 S.W.3d 365 (2011).
LULAC v. Clements, 914 F.2d 620 (5th Cir. 1990).
Public Citizen, Inc. et al. v. Elton Bomer, Secretary of State, http://laws.findlaw.com/5th/0051009cv0.html.
Rodgers v. Bradley, 909 S.W.2d 872, 879 (Tex. 1995).
Thornburg v. Gingles, 478 U.S. 30 (1986).
Lopez, et al. v. Gregg Abbott in his official capacity as Governor of Texas, Complaint for Declaratory and Injunctive Relief (2016).

CHAPTER 5

Kirby v. Edgewood Independent School District, 761 S.W.2d 859, 867–69 (Tex. App.—Austin 1988).
Star-Telegram, Inc. v. Doe, 915 S.W.2d. 471, 472 (Tex. 1995).
Colquette v. Forbes, 680 S.W.2d. 536 (Tex. App.—Austin 1984).
Industrial Foundation of the South v. Texas Industrial Accident Board, 540 S.W.2d 668 (Tex. 1976).
Twyman v. Twyman, 790 S.W. 2d 819 (1990).
Graff v. Beard, 858 S.W.2d 918, 927 (Tex. 1993).
San Antonio Independent School District v. Rodriguez, 411 U.S. 1 (1973).
Barber v. Colorado Independent School District, 901 S.W.2d 447, 453–55 (Tex. 1995).
Valenzuela, 853 S.W.2d at 512.
Frisby v. Schultz, 487 U.S. 474 (1988).
England v. Texas, 727 S.W.2d 810 (Tex. App. – Austin 1984).
Drew v. State, 735 S.W.2d 655 (1987).
Port v. State, 736 S.W.2d 865 (Tex. App. 1987).
See *Jones v. Texas*, 680 S.W.2d 499 (1983).
Michigan v. Long, 463 U.S. 1032, 1035 (1983).
Obergefell v. Hodges, 576 U.S. ___ (2015).

Bibliography

Adams, John. *Thoughts on Government (1776) in The Works of John Adams,* 10 vols. Boston, 1856, https://oll.libertyfund.org/titles/adams-the-works-of-john-adams-10-vols.

Ariens, Michael. *Lone Star Law: A Legal History of Texas*. Lubbock: Texas Tech University Press, 2011.

Baily, Michael A. "Is Today's Court the Most Conservative in Sixty Years? Challenges and Opportunities in Measuring Judicial Preferences." *Journal of Politics* 75 (July 2013): 821–834.

Bannon, Alicia, Cathleen Lisk, and Peter Hardin. "Who Pays for Judicial Races?" Brennan Center for Justice National Institute on Money and State Politics (2017), https://judicialpolitics.org/report/2015-16/.

Barton, Robert R. "The Code Means What it Says: Revisiting the Admissibility of Corroborated Unwritten Custodial Statements." *Texas Tech Law Review* 26 (1995): 779.

Blackstone, William. *Commentaries on the Law of England* (4 volumes 1765–69).

Bodenheimer, Edgar. *Jurisprudence: The Philosophy and Method of Law.* Cambridge: Harvard University Press, 1962.

Bonventre, Vincent Martin. "Court of Appeals: State Constitutional Review." *Pace Law Review* 12 (1992): 1–61.

Brace, Paul, Laura Langer, and Melinda Gann Hall. "Measuring Preferences of Supreme Court Judges." *The Journal of Politics* 62, no. 2 (May 2000): 387–413.

Brandenburg, Bert and Roy A. Schotland. "Justice in Peril: The Endangered Balance Between Impartial Courts and Judicial Election Campaigns." *Georgetown Journal of Legal Ethics* 21 (Fall 2008): 1229–1258.

Brennan, William J., Jr. "State Constitutions and the Protection of Individual Rights." *Harvard Law Review* 90 (1977): 489–504.

Callahan, Scott P. "Liability in Employer-Mandated Drug Testing – Drug Laboratories Have No Duty to Warn Employees That Ingestion of Certain Substances Could Cause False Positive Test Results." *South Texas Law Review* 38 (May 1997): 823.

Cannon, Bradley C. "Defining the Dimensions of Judicial Activism." *Judicature* 66 (1983): 236–247.

Champagne, Anthony. "Campaign Contributions in Texas Supreme Court Races." *Crime, Law & Societal Change* 17 (1992): 91–106.

Champagne, Anthony. "Judicial Reform in Texas." *Judicature* 72 (1988): 146–159.

Champagne, Anthony. "Tort Reform and Judicial Selection." *Loyola of Los Angeles Law Review* 38 (2005): 1483–1516.

Champagne, Anthony and Kyle Cheek. "Judicial Independence: The Cycle of Judicial Elections: Texas as a Case Study." *Fordham Urban Law Journal* 29 (2002): 907–939.

Cheek, Kyle and Anthony Champagne. *Judicial Politics in Texas: Partisanship, Money and Politics in State Courts.* New York: Peter Lang, 2005.

Cheek, Kyle and Anthony Champagne. "Money in Texas Supreme Court Elections." *Judicature* 84 (July–August 2000): 907–940.

Chertoff, Meryl and Dustin F. Robinson. "Check One and the Accountability Is Done: The Harmful Impact of Straight-Ticket Voting on Judicial Elections." *Albany Law Review* 75 (2012): 1773–1797.

Couch, Angela Christina. "*Wanted:* Privacy Protection for Doctors Who Perform Abortions." *American University Journal of Gender and Law* 4 (1996): 361–414.

Crump, David. "Negligent Infliction of Emotional Distress: An Unlimited Claim, But Does it Really Exist?" *Texas Tech Law Review* 49 (2017): 685.

David, Kate and Jennifer S. Greenlief. "Juicy Enough for Grisham, But Does it Have Any Bite? Caperton v. A.T. Massey Coal Co. and the Impact for Texas Courts." *Houston Lawyer* 47 (September/October 2009): 38.

Denton, Charles. *The Year They Threw the Rascals Out.* Austin: Shoal Creek Press, 1973.

Dix, George E. "Texas 'Confession' Law and Oral Self-Incriminating Statements." *Baylor Law Review* 41 (Winter 1989): 1.

Domino, John C. *Civil Rights and Liberties in the 21st Century,* 4th ed. New York: Routledge, 2018.

Domino, John C. "The Jurisprudence of Texas Supreme Court Justice Robert 'Bob' Gammage: A Legacy in Civil Rights & Liberties." *South Texas Law Review* 55 (Fall 2013): 27–69.

Dworkin, Ronald. *Taking Rights Seriously.* Cambridge: Harvard University Press, 1977.

Edelman, Paul H., David E. Klein, and Stefanie A. Lindquist. "Consensus, Disorder, and Ideology on the Supreme Court." *Journal of Empirical Legal Studies* 9 (March 2012): 129–148.

Enoch, Craig. "1995 Annual Survey of Texas Law: Forward." *Southern Methodist University Law Review* 48 (1995): 723–735.

Gamez, Higinio. "Comment: Son, Get a Haircut or Leave My School? Hair Length Restriction for Male Students Upheld by Texas Supreme Court in *Barber v. Colorado Independent School District.*" *Thurgood Marshall Law Review* 21 (1996): 185–209.

Gann Hall, Melinda. *Attacking Judges: How Campaign Advertising Influences State Supreme Court Elections.* Stanford, CA: Stanford Law Books, 2015.

Garbarino, Michael H. "Homosexuality and Texas Law: An Analysis of *Texas v. Morales* and Its Implications." *Texas Law Journal on Civil Liberties & Civil Rights* 1 (Spring 1994): 50.

Gerber, Scott Douglas. *A Distinct Judicial Power: The Origins of an Independent Judiciary, 1606–1787.* New York: Oxford University Press, 2011.

Ginsburg, Richard A. "The Supreme Court Giveth, and the Supreme Court Taketh Away: Negligent Infliction of Emotional Distress Is Not an Independent Cause of Action in Texas." *Texas Tech Law Review* 24 (1993): 1247.

Grimes, David A. Grimes. "Clinicians Who Provide Abortions: The Thinning Ranks." *Obstetrics & Gynecology* 80 (1992): 719.

Gunther, Gerald Gunther. *Learned Hand: The Man and the Judge.* Oxford: Oxford University Press, 1998.

Haley, James L. *The Texas Supreme Court: A Narrative History, 1836–1986.* Austin: University of Texas Press, 2013.

Hall, Elizabeth J. "Protecting California's Abortion Clinic Workers from Harassment and Violence." *McGeorge Law Review* 36 (2005): 797.

Hamilton, Alexander, James Madison, and John Jay. *The Federalist Papers.* New York: Bantam Books, 1982.

Hart, James P. "John Hemphill – Chief Justice of Texas." *Southwestern Law Journal* 3 (1949): 395–415.

Hoffheimer, Michael H. "The Rise and Fall of Lesser Included Offenses." *Rutgers Law Journal* 36 (2005): 351–439.

Howell, Timothy D. "So Long 'Sweetheart' – *State Farm Fire & Casualty Co. v. Gandy* Swings the Pendulum to the Right As the latest in a Line of Setbacks for Texas Plaintiffs." *St. Mary's Law Journal* 29 (1997): 823–883.

Hyman, J.D. "Segregation and the Fourteenth Amendment." *Vanderbilt Law Review* 4 (1950): 1464–1477.

Jackson, Donald W. and James W. Riddlesperger, Jr. "Money and Politics in Judicial Elections: the 1988 Election of the Chief Justice of Texas Supreme Court." *Judicature* 74, no. 4 (December–January, 1991): 185–189.

Kauffman, Albert H. "The Texas School Finance Litigation Saga: Great Progress, Then Near Death by a Thousand Cuts." *St. Mary's Law Journal* 40 (2008): 511–579.

Kaye, Judith S. "Contributions of State Constitutional Law to the Third Century of American Federalism." *Vermont Law Review* 13 (1988): 49–55.

Kaye, Judith S. "Dual Constitutionalism in Practice and Principle." *St. John's Law Review* 61 (1987): 399–417.

Kemerer, Frank R. *William Wayne Justice: A Judicial Biography.* Austin: University of Texas Press, 1991.

Kluger, J. *Simple Justice: The History of Brown v. Board of Education and Black America's Struggle for Equality.* New York: Knopf, 1975.

Kmiec, Keenan. "The Origins and Meanings of 'Judicial Activism.'" *California Law Review* 92 (2004): 1441–1476.

Leslie, Christopher R. "Procedural Rules or Procedural Pretexts?: A Case Study of Procedural Hurdles in Constitutional Challenges to the Texas Sodomy Law." *Kentucky Law Journal* 89 (2001): 1109–1157.

Lim, Youngsik. "An Empirical Analysis of Supreme Court Justices' Decision Making." *The Journal of Legal Studies* 29 (June 2000): 721–754.

Long, Joseph R. "Equitable Jurisdiction to Protect Personal Rights." *Yale Law Journal* 33 (1921): 115–132.

Maltz, Carl M. "Lockstep Analysis and the Concept of Federalism." *Annals of the American Academy of Political and Social Sciences* 496 (1988): 98–106.

Mason, Alpheus Thomas. "Judicial Activism: Old and New." *Virginia Law Review* 55 (April 1969): 385–426.

McCormick, Robert. "Modernizing the Texas Judicial System." *Texas Law Review* 6 (June 1943): 673–701.

McLeod, Jacqueline A. *The Life of Judge Jane Bolin: Daughter of the Empire State.* Champaign, IL: University of Illinois Press, 2011.

Neubauer, David W. *Judicial Process*, 2nd ed. Fort Worth, TX: Harcourt Brace Publishers, 1997.

Orsinger, Richard R. "Asserting Claims for Intentionally or Recklessly Causing Severe Emotional Distress in Connection With Divorce." *St. Mary's Law Journal* 25 (1994): 1253–1301.

Peters, Amanda. "Thirty-One Years in the Making: Why the Texas Court of Criminal Appeals' New Single-Method Approach to Lessor-Included Offense Analysis is a Step in the Right Direction." *Baylor Law Review* 60 (Winter 2008): 231–265.

Phillips, Thomas R. "Electoral Accountability and Judicial Independence." *Ohio State Law Journal* 64 (2003): 137–147.

Powe, Lucas A., Jr. *America's Lone Star Constitution.* Oakland, CA: University of California Press, 2018.

Powers, Deborah D. *The Court of Appeals at Austin: 1892–1992.* Austin: State House Press, 1992.

Quinn, Mae C. "The Garden Path of *Boyles v. Kerr* and *Twyman v. Twyman:* An Outrageous response to Victims of Sexual Misconduct." *Texas Journal of Women and the Law* 4 (1995): 247– 264.

Rebe, Ryan. "Amicus Curiae and Dissenting Votes at the Texas Supreme Court." *Justice System Journal* 34, no. 2 (2013).

Ross, M.W.C. "'Good Behavior' of Federal Judges." *University of Kansas City Law Review* 12 (1944): 119–136.

Schwartz, Bernard. *Super Chief: Earl Warren and His Supreme Court – A Judicial Biography.* New York: New York University Press, 1983.

Schwartz, Gary T. "Explaining and Justifying a Limited Tort of False Light Invasion of Privacy." *Case Western Law Review* 41 (1991): 885–920.

Segal, Jeffrey A., Lee Epstein, Charles M. Cameron, and Harold J. Spaeth. "Ideological Values and the Votes of Justices Revisited." *Journal of Politics* 57, no. 3 (August 1995): 812–823.

Shilofsky, Lee. "The Changing Face of First-Party Bad Faith Claims in Texas." *Southern Methodist University Law Review* 50 (1997): 867–896.

Siegel, Julie F. "The Supreme Court of Texas from 1989–1998: Independence Determined by Six-Year Terms." *Albany Law Review* 62 (1999): 1649–1656.

Skeen, Shelly L. "City of Sherman v. Henry: Is the Texas Constitutional Right of Privacy Still A Source of Protection for Texas Citizens?" *Texas Wesleyan Law Review* 4 (Fall 1999): 99–113.

Spears, Franklin S. "Selection of Appellate Judges." *Baylor Law Review* 40 (1988): 502–520.

Strum, Phillipa. *Louis D. Brandeis: Justice for the People.* Cambridge: Harvard University Press, 1984.

Tracey, E. George and Albert H. Yoon. "The Gavel Gap: Who Sits in Judgment on State Courts?" *American Constitution Society for Law and Policy* (2013): 1–30.

Utter, Robert F. "Swimming in the Jaws of the Crocodile: State Court Comment of Federal Constitutional Issues when Disposing of Cases on State Constitutional Grounds." *Texas Law Review* 63 (1985): 1025–1030.

Warren, Samuel D. and Louis D. Brandeis. "The Right to Privacy." *Harvard Law Review* 4 (1890): 193–220.

Wharton, Linda J. "State Equal Rights Amendments Revisited: Evaluating their Effectiveness in Advancing Protection Against Sex Discrimination." *Rutgers Law Journal* 36 (2005): 1201–1237.

White, G. Edward. *Justice Oliver Wendell Homes: Law and the Inner Self.* Oxford: Oxford University Press, 1993.

Zimmerman, Diane Leenheer. "False Light Invasion of Privacy: The Light that Failed." *New York University Law Review* 64 (1989): 364–387.

Index

About the Author

John C. Domino is Professor of Political Science at Sam Houston State University, where he teaches and writes in the areas of constitutional law, civil rights and liberties, judicial politics, legal studies, and Texas politics. He is the author of the book *Civil Rights & Liberties in the 21st Century*, and his articles have appeared in such journals as *Justice Systems Journal*, *South Texas Law Review*, the *British Journal of American Legal Studies,* and the *Journal of the Texas Supreme Court Historical Society*. Domino received his PhD from Miami University.

www.ingramcontent.com/pod-product-compliance
Ingram Content Group UK Ltd.
Pitfield, Milton Keynes, MK11 3LW, UK
UKHW020217290926
15470UKWH00001B/247

9 781498 578585